Research Methods
in Early Childhood

Sara Miller McCune founded SAGE Publishing in 1965 to support the dissemination of usable knowledge and educate a global community. SAGE publishes more than 1000 journals and over 800 new books each year, spanning a wide range of subject areas. Our growing selection of library products includes archives, data, case studies and video. SAGE remains majority owned by our founder and after her lifetime will become owned by a charitable trust that secures the company's continued independence.

Los Angeles | London | New Delhi | Singapore | Washington DC | Melbourne

Penny Mukherji & Deborah Albon

3rd Edition

Research Methods
in Early Childhood

An Introductory Guide

SAGE

Los Angeles | London | New Delhi
Singapore | Washington DC | Melbourne

Los Angeles | London | New Delhi
Singapore | Washington DC | Melbourne

SAGE Publications Ltd
1 Oliver's Yard
55 City Road
London EC1Y 1SP

SAGE Publications Inc.
2455 Teller Road
Thousand Oaks, California 91320

SAGE Publications India Pvt Ltd
B 1/I 1 Mohan Cooperative Industrial Area
Mathura Road
New Delhi 110 044

SAGE Publications Asia-Pacific Pte Ltd
3 Church Street
#10-04 Samsung Hub
Singapore 049483

Editor: Jude Bowen
Associate editor: George Knowles
Production editor: Tom Bedford
Assistant editor, digital: Chloe Statham
Copyeditor: Andy Baxter
Proofreader: Thea Watson
Indexer: Cathy Heath
Marketing manager: Lorna Patkai
Cover design: Wendy Scott
Typeset by: C&M Digitals (P) Ltd, Chennai, India
Printed in the UK

Library of Congress Control Number: 2017960432

British Library Cataloguing in Publication data

A catalogue record for this book is available from
the British Library

ISBN 978-1-5264-2370-2
ISBN 978-1-5264-2371-9 (pbk)

At SAGE we take sustainability seriously. Most of our products are printed in the UK using FSC papers and boards.
When we print overseas we ensure sustainable papers are used as measured by the PREPS grading system.
We undertake an annual audit to monitor our sustainability.

CONTENTS

ABOUT THE AUTHORS

Penny Mukherji has been involved in educating students in the field of early childhood for 30 years and during this time has developed a deep understanding of how to support students on their learning journeys. Before her retirement Penny was a Senior Lecturer in Early Childhood Studies at London Metropolitan University, where an important part of her teaching involved supporting both undergraduate and postgraduate students completing their research projects. Penny continues to be actively involved in the university, both as a tutor for students who are distance learners and as a supervisor for students completing their dissertations. With a background in health and psychology, Penny is an established author, with a special interest in the health and well-being of young children.

Deborah Albon is a Senior Lecturer in Early Childhood Studies at the University of Roehampton and formerly worked with Penny Mukherji at London Metropolitan University for many years. She has considerable experience teaching research methods to both undergraduate and postgraduate students as well as supporting them with their dissertations. Deborah's research interests are primarily focused around food and drink provisioning and play in early childhood settings. Deborah is widely published in this area and has also co-written *Negotiating Adult–Child Relationships in Early Childhood Research* with Rachel Rosen, which examines the 'messiness' of navigating research relationships in the context of early childhood settings.

ACKNOWLEDGEMENTS

First and foremost, we wish to acknowledge the *constant* support of our partners Dave and Ashu. They continue to make a huge contribution to this project, now in its third edition – without which it would not have been possible.

We wish to thank all the students who have inspired us and continue to inspire us with their research projects. It is because of their input that we know where the emphasis should go in our teaching and writing. Particular thanks go to former London Metropolitan University students: Abby Gumbrell and Yolande Bruzon for permission to refer to their work in this book.

In addition to this, we would like to thank Panayiotis Angelides and Antonia Michaelidou and the children in their research for their permission to use drawings published in their paper: Angelides, P. and Michaelidou, A. (2009) 'The deafening silence: discussing children's drawings for understanding and addressing marginalisation', *Journal of Early Childhood Research*, 7(1): 27–45.

Also, many thanks to Stephen Kemmis and Robin McTaggart for their permission to use a diagram of the action research spiral, published in their chapter: Kemmis, S. and McTaggart, R. (2005) 'Participatory action research: communicative action and the public sphere', in N.K. Denzin and Y.S. Lincoln (eds), *The Sage Handbook of Qualitative Research*, 3rd edition. London: Sage.

Finally, we would like to acknowledge the huge support we have had from Jude and the team at Sage – especially George – and the reviewers for their helpful suggestions.

ONLINE RESOURCES

This book is supported by a wide range of further resources which you can access at **https://study.sagepub.com/mukherjiandalbon3e**

For students…

- **Exclusive videos** with the authors and other experts in field. These include tips and advice on conducting your research, and critical questions to get the most out of your learning
- **Multiple choice quizzes** to test your methods knowledge
- **Free journal articles** to further your reading and achieve better grades
- **Activities** to help you think more critically about early childhood research
- **An interactive flashcard glossary** to understand difficult research jargon and use as a handy revision tool!

For instructors…

- **PowerPoint slides** featuring key concepts, figures and tables from the book, which are an ideal tool for supporting lectures.
- A **Testbank** containing multiple choice questions which can be used to assess student understanding.

A **Course Cartridge** contains all the student and instructor resources in one place. The **Course Cartridge** allows you to easily upload these resources into your institution's learning management system (e.g. your Blackboard or Moodle), and customise course content to suit your teaching needs. Visit the online resources or contact your local sales rep to find out more.

INTRODUCTION

WHAT DO WE MEAN BY 'RESEARCH'?

Research can sometimes appear daunting to a new researcher. We can recall a student telling us that the key difference between writing an essay and carrying out a piece of research is the 'venture into the unknown' or onus on the *student* to conduct the inquiry as opposed to having to write about the work of others. This, she suggested, was scary.

Yet we carry out research all the time. You will have made the decision to read this book based on a range of information: the recommendation of a tutor or student; a whim based on the cover of the book; or by thoroughly examining a range of research methods texts in person. Similarly, when deciding what school to send their child to, parents might ask for the opinions of other families that use the school, they might visit the school themselves and talk to the staff and observe what happens on a typical day. Alternatively, they might prefer to examine what they view as more 'objective' evidence such as school league tables. These examples could be regarded as 'research' and demonstrate that we are being 'researchers' a lot of the time. Young children and babies are also carrying out 'research', it could be argued, when they explore the possibilities of a particular object using all of their senses. It would seem, then, that to answer the questions that we pose for ourselves it is necessary to collect information, analyse it and interpret it in some way (Kumar, 2014) and this is a process we engage in at different points and for a variety of reasons throughout our lives.

But there is a clear distinction between this kind of 'kitchen sink' research and academic research. To qualify as *academic* research, there needs to be an understanding of the paradigm and methodological approach that underpins the research. The terms 'paradigm' and 'methodology' are ones that you will come across throughout the book, but especially in Chapters 4 and 5, and relate to the philosophy that underpins the research and the rules associated with producing knowledge, respectively, within that paradigm. The researcher needs to be able to argue the position they take with regard to this as well as the methods chosen in order to undertake their research. This is because *academic* research is open to greater scrutiny. An example would be the need to subject research that is put forward for publication to a rigorous process of peer review (Kumar, 2014). 'Kitchen sink' research is not subject to such scrutiny. Decisions made in relation to academic research need to be justified carefully in the same way as one would draw upon published work to support the points made in an academic essay. This would not be required in less formal writing, such as a text sent to a friend, for instance. But we should remember that knowledge and skills in relation to *research*, like essay writing, are something that can be developed and improved upon.

At this point it is imperative that we point out that individual universities and colleges are likely to differ in the extent to which they expect you to demonstrate understanding of research paradigms and methodology. This will depend on the kind of course you are undertaking. A Foundation degree course is less likely to expect detail in this area than a postgraduate course, for instance, so be guided by your lecturers in this. Most likely, you will *all* need to demonstrate an understanding of *methodology* – whether a piece of research is quantitative or qualitative in terms of its research design. Perhaps some of you will not need to discuss the paradigm within which a piece of research is located in your assignments. So we strongly suggest you are guided by your tutors on matters such as this as they are best placed to know your institution's requirements for particular courses and modules.

The exact purpose of the research will determine the type of research study that is undertaken. Johnson and Christensen (2012) identify five different kinds of research undertaken with or about children: basic research, applied research, evaluation research, action research and orientational research. We will look at these briefly in turn:

1. *Basic research.* This is research that is aimed at finding out the fundamentals of scientific and human processes. In the sphere of early childhood there is much fundamental research being undertaken to discover underlying brain mechanisms. For example, in 2007 it was reported that Gallo et al. had discovered new information about processes involved in the repair of white matter in the brain. Gallo commented that 'By understanding the fundamental mechanisms of brain development, we get closer to finding clear instructions to repairing developmental brain disorders and injuries' (quoted in Darte, 2007: 1). Often it is not immediately apparent how the information discovered in basic research will help us in everyday life, but it is upon these fundamental discoveries that applied research is based, which can lead to advances in practical applications of basic knowledge.

2. *Applied research.* This is research that is focused on answering or finding solutions to 'real-life' questions. Applied research may draw upon the findings of basic research to point the way to solutions. This is the type of research that early childhood practitioners and students of early childhood studies are most likely to be involved with.

Basic research and applied research can be considered to be two ends of a continuum, as often research projects have elements of both, in varying proportions.

3. *Evaluation research.* This type of research, a form of applied research, is undertaken when a new intervention or project has been implemented and is designed to evaluate the effectiveness of the initiative. Evaluation research projects are often undertaken to see if the new programme should be rolled out for wider participation.
4. *Action research.* This is research based in the workplace, and is another example of applied research. It arises out of the identification of a problem or need within the workplace, and the practitioners within the setting design and implement the research study. The objective is to arrive at a solution or intervention that can be implemented and evaluated by the staff team. Action research is looked at in more detail in Chapter 11 of this book.
5. *Orientational research (critical theory research).* This is research that aims to collect information to help strengthen the argument of those who wish to promote a particular ideology or political position, with the intention of improving society (Johnson and Christensen, 2012). Orientational researchers aim to promote the most disadvantaged sections of society and focus on social inequalities, and, therefore, make their ideology (orientation) explicit. You will find out more about this in Chapter 5.

AIMS AND SCOPE OF THIS BOOK

Our aims in writing this book are many. We hope that students who are new to early childhood research will learn about some of the major paradigms, methodologies and methods that are used in early childhood research. Of course many of these might relate to research in general, but our aim throughout is to write a research methods text with *early childhood studies* at its heart.

Therefore, in recognition of the multidisciplinary nature of early childhood studies, we draw upon research from a variety of theoretical and professional fields. We will be looking at research from health studies, psychology, anthropological studies and education, for example. In doing this, we will be reflecting upon small-scale and large-scale studies as well as studies that are longitudinal or provide a snapshot of an issue. Some of the research we will be referring to may already be known to you, some is likely to be new to you. As previously noted, the guiding principle has been to include reference to research in the field of 'early childhood' or that has clear relevance to this area.

In addressing an international audience, we have aimed to include studies from a wide range of countries and regions but recognise that we can never do justice to the wealth of research that is being carried out across the world. We also acknowledge that – at times – the language we use may seem less familiar in different contexts.

By way of example, our preference for using the terms 'early years setting' or 'nursery' to include settings offering education and care of children until they start formal schooling at around 4 or 5 years of age may be unfamiliar to those of you who are more used to the terms 'day care', 'pre-school' or 'pre-kindergarten'. We try to tease out what we are meaning in terms of terminology where pertinent throughout the book but wish to highlight here that 'nursery' and 'early years setting' are terms you will encounter throughout the book.

By 'early childhood research' we are referring to research that has been carried out with or about children from birth to 8 years and associated issues, such as those relating to practitioners who work with this age group or parents of children in this age group. As many of you are probably aware, some of the research that falls under the 'early childhood' umbrella might actually be carried out with adults, especially parents and practitioners, rather than *directly* involving young children. In addition, as you will see in Part 4 of the book, early childhood research might involve looking at documents that are pertinent to the field, such as diaries and other forms of 'text'.

We hope that reading this book will equip you with some of the knowledge that will enable you to critique the research of others. In doing this, though, we wish to stress that no research lies outside the possibility of criticism. There are always possibilities and limitations with *any* research design and, as new researchers in particular, you should aim at being tentative and considered when critiquing the work of others as opposed to merely declaring it to be 'wrong' or 'flawed' in some way. This is another skill to develop in becoming an early childhood researcher. You will notice that in this book each chapter will outline the possibilities and limitations of the paradigm, methodology, approach or method discussed in the chapter. Sometimes this is in the form of a distinct section towards the end of the chapter, and on other occasions this discussion is threaded throughout the chapter.

Greig et al. (2013) point out that a key difference between training to be a professional, such as a teacher or nursery nurse, and learning how to be a researcher is that the trainee professional usually has an opportunity to observe the skills of other, more experienced practitioners. They also have an opportunity to reflect on their professional training experiences with other student practitioners and their lecturers at college. Such opportunities are often not replicated for the novice researcher. We hope that in this book, by reflecting upon early childhood research in our Research in Focus sections and by reading about the experiences of people who have embarked upon their own research projects in the Case Study sections, you will be afforded such opportunities. Certainly the development of the 'Research Methods in Early Childhood' module on the degree course that we were both involved in came about as a result of the need to support students in developing knowledge and skills in relation to research on the course, especially as they prepare for their final dissertations or projects.

HOW THE BOOK IS ORGANISED

This is the third edition of *Research Methods in Early Childhood*, and we have taken the opportunity that this revision provides to make modifications to the way that the book is organised. Students rarely read a textbook, such as this, straight through from page one to the end, and with this in mind we have tried to arrange chapters in a way that seems logical and meets the learning needs of students. We are thankful for the support of a range of reviewers from across the world for their support and suggestions with this. Inevitably, when writing a text such as this, decisions as to where to place different topics have sometimes been difficult to make. In previous editions of this book the chapters were sequenced to provide students with information about paradigms and methodology, ethics, and data-collection methods before the chapters on planning and writing up a research study. This suits students who undertake a module on research methods, prior to planning and conducting their own research project. However, some students are required to produce proposals for their research projects in advance or as part of a module on research methods. To accommodate the needs of these students we have put information about planning a research study or project at the beginning of the book. We are sure you can make your own decisions as to the order in which you read this.

The book is divided into five parts. As mentioned previously, at the beginning of the book we have included information on how to plan a research study and we have deliberately kept this fairly simple as later chapters in the book take up some of the issues raised in far greater depth. Chapter 1 looks at research design and this leads on to Chapter 2, where you will learn how to write a research proposal. This section of the book concludes with Chapter 3, where we think about the role that previous research and theoretical ideas play in contextualising our own research. We will look at how to conduct and write a literature review. These chapters do not stand in isolation from each other; you will find that conducting a literature review will help you decide upon your research question which in turn will guide your research design. Nor does Part 1 stand in isolation from the other sections of the book. As you read through the chapter on research design you will find that you will need to look ahead at chapters further on in the book, which will give you information on methodology, approaches and data-collection methods.

Part 2 of the book looks at some of the fundamental ideas (paradigms and principles) that underpin early childhood research. We think about positivism in Chapter 4, and in Chapter 5 we explore theories such as interpretivism and 'critical' theories, as well as post-structuralism. As noted earlier, the extent to which you need to demonstrate understanding of these areas is linked to the kind of course you are undertaking. Within these two chapters we also discuss methodological approaches. We will show how the positivist paradigm has a tendency to employ a quantitative methodological approach, whereas the paradigms discussed in Chapter 5 tend to embrace a qualitative methodological approach. You will also find that we thread discussion about research paradigms and methodology throughout this book.

Chapter 6 focuses upon ethics and in Chapter 7 we look at listening to young children in research. Although these appear in the second part of the book we believe that ethical principles should underpin any piece of research and should be key considerations when designing a research project and writing a research proposal. We draw upon Lahman's (2008: 285) notion of the *'competent* yet *vulnerable* child'* in Chapters 6 and 7 to highlight the way that one's view of the 'child' underpins a research project. By emphasising the child as *competent*, we wish to highlight the potential of seeing the child as a participant in research – as opposed to the object of research. By recognising the child as *vulnerable* we are highlighting the necessity of keeping the needs of young children firmly in mind when carrying out research. This is in recognition of the fact that research that directly involves very young children and babies, in particular, is likely to be different to research carried out with children of secondary school age, for instance. However, in saying this, we believe that in research *everyone* is vulnerable in some sense and it is important that researchers keep this in mind. Ethical issues are woven into other chapters where there is a specific point we wish to raise in relation to the topic under discussion, but you should note that the more substantive discussion will be held in Chapters 6 and 7.

Part 3 of the book looks at some approaches that are used in early childhood research. We look at surveys, ethnography, case studies and action research. These approaches might draw upon a range of different methods and it is these 'tools' or methods of research that we discuss in Part 4 of the book. Here, we look at observation, interviewing, questionnaires, using documents and other visual 'texts', journaling, and creative methods for involving children in research.

The final part of the book, Part 5, looks at what happens once you have collected your data. We look at how to discern what all the data means and how to share your findings, both by writing a coherent research report and using other ways to disseminate your results. Chapter 18, which looks at analysing and presenting data, is a lengthy chapter in comparison with others, owing to the volume of information we wish to cover.

We hope that as you read through the book you will have developed some understanding of paradigms, methodologies, principles and approaches to research, as well as methods themselves that will help you in planning your own research project. The boxed Research in Focus sections, Case Studies, Reflection Points and Activities aim to encourage you to think further about a point that has been raised or provide an exemplar from a piece of published research or student project. Some of the Activities will involve you in accessing particular websites. If these prove difficult to open, try shortening the web address to its main page. For example, if the British Psychological Society's code of human research ethics is difficult to access on the following website – www.bps.org.uk/system/files/

Public%20files/inf180_web.pdf – you could shorten the web address to www.bps. org.uk and carry out a search within their particular website.

Linked to this edition of the book is a new online Sage resource which is far more comprehensive than the website developed alongside the second edition. At the end of chapters you will find links to the online resources in which we have devised activities to extend your understanding of a particular topic and there is also direct access to some key readings associated with the chapter. This, we hope, will be a useful resource for students and lecturers alike.

Finally, in reading this book, we hope that you will develop knowledge and skills in relation to *early childhood* research. We especially hope that you will have the confidence and enthusiasm to undertake your own piece of research, in an area that you feel *passionate* about. In doing this, whether you are carrying out research aiming at instigating a change in practice or developing a greater understanding of an issue, you will be contributing to a body of knowledge that enriches our understandings of young children and the many factors that impact upon their lives.

PART 1
PLANNING YOUR RESEARCH STUDY

Chapter 1 'Research Design', takes you through all the stages that you will undertake to complete a research project. We take you from the beginning, when you are trying to decide on a suitable topic, through to choosing an appropriate research design and choice of methods, to issues that need to be considered when choosing your participants. Throughout this chapter we will be looking at the decisions that have to be taken at the design stage to ensure that your research is *reliable* and your findings *valid*. Each project is different and the decisions that you make in the planning stage will depend on the context of your research, your underpinning attitudes and beliefs about early childhood, and the research paradigm within which your research is located. Each step in the decision process should be taken logically and in such a way that you can fully justify your decisions. This chapter will use terms and concepts that some of you, who are new to research, may find challenging. With this in mind we have provided signposts to where the information you need can be found in the book.

Once you have refined your research question (aided by a survey of the relevant literature – Chapter 3) and have decided upon the design of your research, the next step will be to write a research proposal. As a student this proposal is often an assessed piece of work, or something that your teachers will need to see, and approve, before you are given 'permission' to proceed with your research study. Chapter 2 looks in some detail at how to write your research proposal.

Reviewing the literature is an essential part of the research process because it locates your study in the context of what is already known in that area. By reviewing the literature you will gain an understanding of what is known already about your chosen research topic. Chapter 3 will guide you through the process of structuring and writing your literature review and contains practical advice about finding sources of information, so that you can avoid common pitfalls.

──── **ACTIVITY** ────────────────────

Kerry, a student about to embark on her undergraduate project, has decided that she is interested in partnership with parents. Draw a topic web of all the different areas that this might include.

- Discuss your area of interest with colleagues in your setting, if you are a practitioner, to see if there is an aspect of this that needs investigating or developing.
- Talk to your project supervisor.

 ──── **REFLECTION POINT** ────────────

Kerry works with children aged 3 to 5 in a private day nursery. Her colleagues have suggested that she could look at developing ways to improve the way that the nursery works in partnership with parents.

Kerry has two terms to complete her research. What factors does Kerry have to take into consideration before finally deciding what she will do?

Other factors to think about when narrowing down the focus of interest include the length of time available to complete the study and the resources that might be needed:

- *Time*. It always takes more time than you think to get a research project under way. You will need to consider how long it will take to get your proposal approved and the length of time it may take to gather the necessary permissions and approvals if you intend to use an early years setting. In some settings, such as hospitals, your proposal may have to be approved by an ethics committee. You will need to estimate the length of time needed to collect your data and how long it will take to write up the research.
- *Resources*. The questions you need to think about here include:
  - Will your study involve a financial outlay? Do you need a camera or a tape recorder? Will you need to pay for postage if sending out a questionnaire? If you are in employment, will you need to request unpaid leave to visit settings? Will you have to buy specialist books and materials?

o Have you access to appropriate sources of information?
o Where will you collect your data and with whom? Will you be able to gain access?

Clough and Nutbrown (2012) describe two tools that can be used to narrow down the focus of an investigation; the Russian doll principle and the Goldilocks test.

> Applying the Russian doll principle means breaking down the research question from the original statement to something which strips away the complication of layers and obscurities until the very essence - the heart - of the question can be expressed. This may well mean phrasing and rephrasing the question so that each time its focus becomes sharpened and more defined - just as a Russian doll is taken apart to reveal a tiny doll at the centre. (Clough and Nutbrown, 2012:41)

Once this process has been undertaken the Goldilocks test is applied. This is done by asking a series of questions.

- Is the question too big (in terms of time/resources, etc.)?
- Is the question too small (of too little substance to form the basis of your dissertation)?
- Is the question too hot? (A topic that is very sensitive, could lead to bad feelings or destroy relationships.)

DECIDING ON THE GENERAL AIM OF YOUR RESEARCH

Kerry has decided upon an area of interest: something relating to parental partnership in the setting in which she is working. However, this topic can be viewed from a variety of different standpoints and Kerry needs to decide exactly what aspect of parental partnership she is interested in and the outcome she is aiming for. Her colleagues may already have pointed her towards a particular direction and Kerry may already have a precise aim. For example, her colleagues may feel that it is difficult to establish effective communication with busy working parents and have suggested that she undertakes an exploratory study of both parental and practitioners' suggestions on ways that communication could be improved. It is more likely that Kerry, at this stage, has not developed her thinking to the extent that she can articulate exactly what she wants to find out and why. To help her she needs to undertake an initial review of the literature so that she can identify the different approaches previously taken by researchers and experts in the area. A good, general understanding of the literature will help her decide exactly what she wants to do and will help her develop an appropriate research question. Although it is recognised that reading around the subject area will be ongoing, at this stage students need to have read in sufficient depth to have identified the different debates or topics within the subject area and to have a good knowledge of important research studies that underpin our understanding. Chapter 2 looks at the requirements of the literature review for the final research proposal and Chapter 3 looks at what is needed to write the literature review for a research report.

Our student Kerry decides to undertake an exploratory study to find out the ways both practitioners and parents suggest their partnership with the nursery could be improved. From this you can see that Kerry has a general aim for her research; that is, in general terms she knows what she wants to find out and why, although at this stage she may not have a clear idea of the methods she will be using.

Once you have an overall aim this can be set out in formal terms. Kerry's aim might look like this: 'The aim of this piece of research is to investigate ways in which partnership with parents can be improved in a private nursery'.

FORMULATING THE AREA OF INVESTIGATION, RESEARCH QUESTION OR HYPOTHESIS

Whether or not you will have an area of investigation, research question or hypothesis depends, to some extent, on your underlying research paradigm which is discussed in detail in Chapters 4 and 5. A paradigm is a theoretical framework that underpins how one sees the world. Researchers who hold the underlying assumption that there are specific 'truths' which can be uncovered by the strict application of scientific principles tend to locate their work within a 'positivist paradigm' (Crotty, 1998). In contrast, much early childhood research is influenced by paradigms such as interpretivism. Interpretivists are influenced by the view that what is accepted as the 'truth' varies according to individuals' viewpoints, which are strongly influenced by their social and cultural context (Hughes, 2010). The paradigm which influences your thinking will have an effect on the methodological approach within which you choose to frame your research. For example, if you are operating within a positivist paradigm, you are likely to use quantitative methodology which uses methods designed to collect data in numerical form from a large sample, with the aim of uncovering a truth which can be applied to a much larger 'population'. If your research is framed within an interpretivist paradigm, you are likely to choose a qualitative methodological approach which emphasises trying to get an in-depth understanding of a topic by using a small sample or case and by using methods designed to uncover people's beliefs and ideas (Roberts-Holmes, 2011). The requirement to demonstrate an understanding of paradigms depends upon the specifications of your course; however, most of you will be asked to demonstrate an understanding of methodology as this will influence the decisions you make about your research questions.

— 💡 —— REFLECTION POINT ————————————————

After reading Chapters 4, 5 and 6 of this book try to answer the following questions about Kerry's proposed research.

1.   What paradigm is likely to underpin this research?
2.   What methodological approach will be most appropriate for this study?
3.   What ethical issues need to be considered?

It is likely that Kerry will be using a design which is guided by an interpretivist paradigm. Research conducted within an interpretivist paradigm is likely to use a qualitative research design, which focuses on words and meanings, rather than aiming to produce data in numerical form. In any piece of research there are ethical issues to be considered. Here are a few issues that Kerry would need to think about (but it is not an exhaustive list): confidentiality and anonymity of the setting and participants as well as the notion of informed consent. Kerry would need to reflect on the powerful position of the practitioners in relation to the parents – parents may tell her what they think she wants to hear as their own children attend the setting and they may fear repercussions if they express negative views. In addition, Kerry may find herself in a difficult position if parents tell her negative things about other members of staff.

With an understanding of the methodological approach which will frame your research you will now be in a position to refine your research question. Denscombe (2012: 72) considers that research questions have three things in common:

1.   They ask questions that are vital for the topic to be researched. They ask the most pertinent, revealing, and incisive questions about the topic. In other words the questions are not trivial and are worth answering.
2.   In empirical research the questions are precise and specific. They are not just abstract ideas, but questions that can be answered by the collection of data.
3.   The question gives an indication as to the kind of data that will be collected.

Quantitative methodology generates research questions which can be answered by the collection of numerical data and can be posed in a variety of ways. One way is by formulating a hypothesis; a statement that can be tested using quantitative scientific methods, derived from a theory. If the findings from your research do not support your hypothesis then the conclusion is that the theory is either untrue or needs modifying.

Hypotheses should be written in such a way that there is no ambiguity (Cardwell et al., 2000), the variables are stated clearly, and how the hypothesis is to be tested is clear. For example, in Chapter 4, we look at an imaginary scenario where a teacher has a theory that children learn better in the morning than the afternoon.

— 💡 —— REFLECTION POINT ————————————————

Read Chapter 4 and familiarise yourself with the Case Study about a teacher planning a research study on children's learning. Her first attempt at writing a hypothesis is, 'Children will learn spellings more efficiently in the morning than the afternoon'. Later on she changes it to: 'Children learning a list of five spellings in the morning will remember more spellings 24 hours later than children who learn a list of five spellings in the afternoon'.

What changes have been made and why?

The hypothesis stated in the Reflection Point is a *prediction* that there will be an effect present; that is, that there will be a change in the dependent, or outcome, variable (the number of spellings learned) because of a manipulation of the independent variable (the time of day). This is called the alternative hypothesis. It is convention, in positivist research, for the hypothesis to also be given in terms that suggest that no effect will be present. This is the null hypothesis (or status quo). In our example the null hypothesis will look like this: *'There will be no significant difference in the number of words recalled 24 hours later between children learning a list of five spellings in the morning and children who learn a list of five spellings in the afternoon'*.

— ✈ —— ACTIVITY ————————————————————

There are many good online tutorials on formulating null and alternative hypotheses; YouTube has a variety of free resources that you can use. You may also find the following book (available as an e-book) useful: Coolican, H. (2014) *Research Methods and Statistics in Psychology*, 6th edition. Abingdon: Taylor and Francis.

In the example we are looking at we may find that 100 per cent of the children who learn the spellings in the morning remember all of them 24 hours later, but only 75 per cent of the children who learn the spellings in the afternoon remember all of them. If this is the case, can we reject the null hypothesis and accept that the alternative hypothesis is true? Do the results *prove* that learning spellings in the morning results in more spellings being remembered? Could the results just be due to chance alone? If you repeated the experiment over and over again and averaged out the results, would no effect be seen? To answer these questions we can subject the results to statistical analyses, known as *tests of significance*, which tell researchers if any effect is likely to be due to chance or not. The tests tell us what the probability is that a particular result will occur.

Probability is measured on a scale, with something that is not possible being given a probability level of 0, and something that must happen or always happens being given a probability of 1 (Coolican, 2014). Generally, if the probability that our results would occur by chance alone is less than 0.05, the null hypothesis can be rejected and the alternative hypothesis accepted.

Our experience of working with students on early childhood studies courses is that it is *very rare* for them to do research that involves the testing of hypotheses and the use of tests of significance. This is due to the difficulties that are encountered in conducting worthwhile research involving the rigorous control of variables outside of a laboratory situation. Furthermore, a high level of statistical analysis is involved. For students who want to research in this way we recommend that they look at Field, *Discovering Statistics Using SPSS* (2013).

Sometimes, still within the positivist paradigm, it is not appropriate to use a hypothesis because a prediction is not being made, or there is no underlying theoretical model that is being tested. The aim of the research may be to investigate or explore a phenomenon in a way that generates numerical information. In this case a quantitative research question is used instead. *'How often do 3-year-old children show acts of empathy?'* is an example of a quantitative research question.

Most students undertaking a small-scale research project will not be operating within a positivist paradigm; it is more likely that they will be taking an interpretivist approach, for example, which is less concerned with confirming or refuting theory in a way that allows findings to be generalised out to a wider population, and more concerned with looking at making sense of the researcher's immediate world. In these situations the use of a hypothesis or a quantitative research question would be inappropriate, and a more general, qualitative research question is likely to be used.

Qualitative questions are generally more open ended; often they are more like the aims discussed earlier on in the chapter. They tend to ask questions about a process, issue or phenomenon to be explored (Johnson and Christensen, 2012: 63). Green (2008: 47) suggests that qualitative research questions or 'problem statements' should have at least six properties. They should be:

1. Interesting.
2. Relevant.
3. Feasible.

4. Ethical.
5. Concise.
6. Answerable.

Previously, we looked at Kerry's research into parental partnership. She formulated her aim as follows: 'The aim of this piece of research is to investigate ways in which partnership with parents can be improved in a private nursery'.

─ 🔆 ──── REFLECTION POINT ───────────────────

Kerry's first attempts at writing her research question were as follows:

1.   What can the nursery do to make parents attend parent consultation sessions?
2.   Why do parents not communicate well with the nursery staff?

On reflection Kerry decided that neither of these questions was appropriate. What do you consider to be the problem with these questions?

In the Reflection Point activity you may have realised that, in both cases, the *parents* were seen to be the 'barrier' to effective partnership, perhaps reflecting a deficit model of parental partnership being held by Kerry and her colleagues. This would be a 'conforming' model of parental partnership (MacNaughton and Hughes, 2003). Beginning the research with such a negative viewpoint raises ethical issues (see Chapter 6) and would probably be too 'hot' according to the 'Goldilocks test'. In addition, the questions are very narrow in focus and may limit the amount of valuable data that could be obtained.

After consulting her project supervisor Kerry amended her research question. Her final version was: 'What do parents and early years practitioners at a private day nursery in London perceive to be the benefits and barriers to an effective partnership between parents and practitioners? What suggestions do they have for improving the partnership?'

CHOOSING A RESEARCH DESIGN

Once a concise hypothesis, area of investigation or research question has been reached, decisions need to be made as to the strategy that will be used to investigate the issue. When we were discussing how to formulate your research question, we emphasised that your decisions should be guided by the paradigm or methodological approach underpinning your research. In the same way, depending upon the requirements of your course, you will be expected to demonstrate that your understanding of research paradigms or methodology has guided your choice of research design.

Traditionally, the concept of a research design belongs within the positivist-tradition and in Chapter 4 we look at one of the main positivist research designs, the experiment. However, if it is considered that a research design 'is the process by which the topic is turned into a researchable project' (Hayes, 2010: 105), then qualitative or mixed modes of research will also have a 'design'.

Kumar (2014: 133) suggests that it is useful to classify research design according to three perspectives:

1.   The number of contacts with the study population.
2.   The reference period of the study.
3.   The nature of the investigation.

We will look at each of these in turn.

STUDY DESIGN BASED ON THE NUMBER OF CONTACTS

This classification looks at how many times the participants are involved in the research:

- *Cross-sectional study*. This is probably the most common form of research whereby the participants are investigated at a single point in time or during a brief time period. An example of this would be if you wanted to investigate parents' perspectives on healthy eating. This could involve you interviewing a group of parents in a setting over a period of a couple of weeks. Sometimes, data are collected from more than one group of participants. For example, if you wanted to investigate language development in children you could observe the language development of a sample of children of different ages. This would give you a reasonable idea about how language develops as children age. The main advantage of the cross-sectional study is that it is possible to conduct research in a short space of time, and participants are not likely to drop out of the study (Coolican, 2014). Most undergraduate students will be conducting cross-sectional studies primarily because of the time factor involved in doing something that takes longer to complete. The disadvantage of this design is that it is not possible to follow individual participants to see if there are any changes over time.
- *The before and after study design* (pre-test/post-test). The before and after study design can be used in both quantitative and qualitative research and is typically used to assess the effect of an intervention on a group of participants. For example, two groups of reception-aged children could be weighed and measured at the beginning of the school year to find out their body mass index (BMI). During the course of the year, one group would be given an intervention aimed

to increase their levels of physical activity during school hours. At the end of the school year both groups of children would be weighed and measured again.

The disadvantage of this design is that it takes longer to collect data and, between the first contact point and the second contact point, participants may have dropped out. Another problem with the design is that, unless a control group is used, as in the example discussed above, it is difficult to work out if any observed change at post-test is due to the intervention or to other variables. For instance, if no control group was used in the example discussed, any reduction in BMI could be due to a reduction in the calorific value of school meals. If investigating children, the interval between pre- and post-test may itself introduce a source of variance, as young children can change dramatically in a few months. Of course, in using a 'control' group, the researcher would also have to be mindful of Robson's (2011a) concern about withholding the possible benefits of research to a group of participants.

- *The longitudinal study design.* This is the design of choice for looking at patterns of change over time, and as such is not a design that students are likely to use. In the longitudinal design a group of participants are investigated at several points, over an extended period. The disadvantages of longitudinal studies are similar to those of the before and after design, but more exaggerated as the likelihood that participants will be 'lost' to a study is far greater if the study is undertaken over decades (Kumar, 2014).

 CASE STUDY

Ashley is an early childhood student on placement in a private day care facility in the USA, caring for children from the ages of 9 months to 4 years. She has read about a study undertaken in Scandinavia (reported in Halsan, 2014) that indicated that girls have better motor skills than boys in the early years and wondered if this was true for the children in her setting. She decides to observe children of different ages, two boys and two girls aged 1 year, 2 years, 3 years and 4 years. She aims to observe their:

- fine motor skills; holding a crayon and mark making
- gross motor skills; walking, running, riding tricycles and throwing a ball
- selfhelp skills such as feeding themselves and dressing.

Because Ashley will be observing the children over a short period of time this is a cross-sectional study. The Scandinavian study was a longitudinal study. What are the advantages and disadvantages for Ashley in choosing a cross-sectional design? Here is the link to the study and do note that the original study looked at 1,000 children: http://sciencenordic.com/girls-have-better-motor-skills-boys-do (accessed 17 December 2016).

The main advantage for Ashley is that she will be able to undertake a cross-sectional study in the time available for her to complete her research project. The main disadvantage is that she is looking at *different* children at different ages. A longitudinal study conducted on the *same* children as they grow older may give a truer picture of the children's development. We would want to add at this point that it would be difficult to say something general pertaining to gender from Ashley's very small sample and this would need acknowledgement when writing up her research.

STUDY DESIGNS BASED ON THE REFERENCE PERIOD

Some studies look back at past events and some look forward to what might happen in the future:

- *Retrospective designs* investigate issues that have happened in the past, using data available from the time, or relying on the memory of participants.
- *The prospective study design* is one that is designed to wait until the future to find out, for instance, the outcome of an event/intervention or the effect of a variable.

STUDY DESIGNS BASED ON THE NATURE OF THE INVESTIGATION

The paradigm and methodological approach within which you are working will affect your choice of research design.

Quantitative designs include:

- *Experiments.* Here the researcher tries to control as many variables as possible while only altering the independent variable. There are a variety of ways that experiments can be designed and some of these are discussed in Chapter 4.
- *Quasi-experiments.* Often it is not possible or ethical to conduct experiments on children. For example, it would not be ethical to conduct a true experiment about the effects of passive smoking on children, as it would be wrong to deliberately expose children to smoke in order to investigate the outcome. However, it is possible to investigate the effects on children who are born into households where the parents smoke.
- *Non-experimental designs.* These would include correlations, as discussed in Chapter 4.

Qualitative designs include:

- *Case studies.* Greig et al. (2013: 187) define a case study as 'an investigation of an individual, a family, a group, an institution, a community, or even a resource, programme or intervention'. Case studies are looked at in depth in Chapter 10.

STRATIFIED SAMPLING

In this method of sampling the researcher decides beforehand what variables are likely to affect the outcome of the study, finds out the proportions of these variables within the population and then chooses a sample that reflects these proportions. For example, if you wanted to conduct a study looking at the extent to which parents support their children's education at home, it may be considered that social class of the family is important. The researcher would separate out the population according to social class and then draw a sample, at random, that reflected social class *in the same proportions* as the population.

NON-PROBABILITY SAMPLING

OPPORTUNITY SAMPLING

This involves the researcher choosing anyone who is available to take part in their research from a particular population. This is a common form of sampling used by students. For example, in Kerry's study on parental partnership, her sample of parents to be interviewed may consist of the parents she sees every day, with whom she has a good rapport, and who have the time to help her (although we revisit this issue later on in the book as potentially problematic in terms of whose voices are potentially silent in the research if one approaches research in this manner). Opportunity sampling is also known as convenience sampling 'in which individuals who fit the criteria of a study are identified in any way possible (Emerson, 2015: 165).

SNOWBALL SAMPLING

In snowball sampling, every participant recruited into a study is asked to identify others who may be appropriate or willing to be a participant. For instance, if Kerry had wanted to know about parents' views on parental partnership in general, rather than being specific to her workplace, she could have asked the parents from her nursery to ask their friends if they would be willing to be interviewed. This can be useful in gaining access to groups that might be deemed 'difficult to reach' (see, for instance, Standing's work [1998] on lone mothers).

We would suggest that, for the purposes of a small-scale student research project, opportunity/convenience sampling and snowball sampling may be the most realistic option. If you find yourself in the position of having to use these methods then you should acknowledge the weaknesses inherent in your sampling and evaluate how your sampling method may have affected your findings when you write your discussion in your final report.

SELF-SELECTED SAMPLING

In this type of sampling, participants volunteer to take part in research. It is a method often used to test drugs or medical procedures and you may have seen advertisements for volunteers in newspapers. Students sometimes use this as a sampling method – for example, if they wanted to find out about early childhood studies students' opinions on play, they could ask for volunteers in their class. The disadvantage of this is that the sample may be very unrepresentative of the population as a whole. For example, if the population (here this means the early childhood studies students as whole) consists primarily of people who are already qualified early years practitioners and your sample consists of younger students who are yet to work professionally with young children, then your sample will not represent the population as a whole. Students who are also practitioners may have very different views on play, which are based on professional experience.

THEORETICAL SAMPLING

This is a method of sampling used in some qualitative studies, where participants are chosen *as the study evolves*. Qualitative studies often take a cyclic approach to research, with data being analysed and additional participants chosen according to the researcher's understanding of the theoretical strands that emerge (Robson, 2011a).

PURPOSIVE SAMPLING

Theoretical sampling is similar to what Johnson and Christensen (2012) describe as *purposive* or *criterion-based* selection, where cases are chosen that provide the information needed for the purpose of the research. Setia (2016) notes that purposive sampling is often used in qualitative studies involving focus groups where participants are chosen on the basis of who can give information on specific subjects. For example, if a student wanted to find out parental views on how children with special needs are supported in a setting, then it is justifiable to ask parents who have children with special needs. Purposive sampling can also be called selective, subjective or judgement sampling, as the researcher relies on his or her judgement as to who to include in the study (Black, 2010). As with opportunity or convenience sampling, purposive sampling has the disadvantage of not selecting participants at random; but, in qualitative studies, where the results are not meant to be universally applied, purposive sampling can be a very useful tool.

—— ACTIVITY —————————————————————

Look at the following research articles and identify how the sample used in the research was chosen. In each case reflect upon how the method of choosing the sample could have affected the findings:

Townsend, E. and Pitchford, N. (2012) 'Baby knows best? The impact of weaning style on food preferences and body mass index in early childhood in a case controlled sample', *BMJ Open*, 2(1): 1–6. (A UK study.) http://bmjopen.bmj.com/content/2/1/e000298.full.pdf+html (accessed 18 December 2016).

Walker, S., Chang, S., Vera-Hernández, M. and Grantham-McGregor, S. (2011) 'Early childhood stimulation benefits adult competence and reduces violent behaviour', *Pediatrics*, 127(5): 849–57. (A Jamaican study.) http://pediatrics.aappublications.org/content/127/5/849.full.pdf+html (accessed 18 December 2016).

Isong, A., Luff, D., Perrin, J., Winickoff, P. and Ng, M. (2012) 'Parental perspectives of early childhood caries', *Clinical Pediatrics*, 51(1): 77–85. (A US study.) http://cpj.sagepub.com/content/51/1/77.full.pdf+html (accessed 18 December 2016).

RELIABILITY AND VALIDITY

When undertaking research, the overall aim is to collect information (data) about an issue and to draw conclusions using this information. It is, therefore, important that you can trust that these data will actually allow you to make appropriate conclusions, and for this to happen your methods must be both reliable and valid. The concepts of reliability and validity have different meanings depending on whether a quantitative or qualitative approach is being taken (Greig et al., 2007) and on the paradigm within which the research is located.

RELIABILITY

When using quantitative methodology, reliability is concerned with the stability of the measurements you are collecting. If a method of obtaining information, such as a test, rating scale, observation or questionnaire is to be reliable it must give the same results when administered on different occasions or administered by different people.

Atkinson et al. (1996) identify two sorts of reliability: temporal stability and internal consistency. A method of obtaining information is said to have temporal stability if the results obtained from a group of participants on one occasion are replicated when the procedure is repeated under similar circumstances on another occasion. For example, in Chapter 4, we look at an experiment on memory conducted by a teacher. Her way of assessing memory was the number of words correctly spelled from a five-word list recalled after 24 hours. To be reliable, the scores obtained from the group would need to be similar if the experiment was repeated on a second occasion.

 — **REFLECTION POINT** ————————————————

Can you think of a problem about establishing temporal stability in a test of memory, if the outcome is number of words correctly spelled?

Your reflections upon the memory experiment may have led you to conclude that if the same list of words was used for the second test, then the children's scores should be better as they will have had another chance to learn them. To get around this problem, researchers, wishing to check the reliability of a test, will often produce two tests that are of comparable difficulty and use a different test the second time around.

Internal consistency is the degree to which items in a test measure the same thing. For example, one can use personality tests to assess an individual's level of extraversion or introversion. One way to test this is to give the test to a group of individuals and to score the first half and second half of the test separately. If the test is reliable then the scores for the first half should be very similar to the scores for the second half. Devising reliable tests is a skilled business and demands knowledge of statistics. Because of this, researchers often do not make up their own tests, but use pre-prepared tests (Field, 2013). Any student considering the use of a test in this way should seek the help of their supervisor as this is not an approach we would advise many students to take.

When using qualitative methodology the issue of reliability is slightly different as this type of research does not involve statistically devised tests, but may use methods such as in-depth interviews to elicit the participants' underlying attitudes and beliefs. Siraj-Blatchford and Siraj-Blatchford (2001) suggest that reliability in these situations is the degree to which the researcher's theoretical analysis and conclusions 'fit' or correspond to the actual data that were obtained.

Cohen et al. (2011: 203) reiterate this viewpoint, suggesting that the criteria for reliability for quantitative and qualitative research differ and that in qualitative methodologies, 'Reliability includes fidelity to real life, context and situation specificity, authenticity, comprehensiveness, detail, honesty, depth of response and meaningfulness to the respondents'.

VALIDITY

A valid data-gathering instrument is one that measures what it sets out to measure. For example, Eysenck (2004) describes historical attempts to measure intelligence in terms of an individual's intelligence quotient or IQ. Although popular at one time, the idea that a person's intelligence could be measured and reduced to one number has been discredited. There have been great concerns about the validity of such tests, as not all areas of intelligence were measured and the amount of education and the cultural background of the participant impacted upon the test results.

In qualitative research, validity is viewed differently but is nonetheless important. Authenticity is of paramount importance. As Edwards (2010: 162) notes, 'Validity in qualitative research is a matter of being able to offer as sound a representation of the field of study as the research methods allow'.

The researcher needs to be able to say that their research is as truthful an account of the area of study as is possible. For some researchers, this is reached through careful triangulation. This might be done through using a variety of sources of data; multiple methods; different theoretical perspectives; or more than one researcher looking at the issue under study (Denzin, cited in Edwards, 2010: 163).

RESEARCH IN FOCUS

USA

The Hawthorne effect (the value of triangulation)

Denscombe (2014) describes a series of studies undertaken at the Hawthorne factory in Chicago in the 1920s and 1930s. The aim of the research was to find out what factors increased or decreased the productivity of the workers. The researchers manipulated all kinds of variables such as light levels and temperature and moved on to look at things such as levels of tiredness and the monotony of tasks. They used a quantitative approach which endeavoured to measure the effect of these variables. The results were confusing and it wasn't until interviews of the employees were undertaken (a qualitative approach) that the findings became clearer. The findings from the interviews indicated that personal and social factors were powerful motivators as well. Later a third data-collection method was added, where the informal group behaviour of the workers was observed, adding further clarification.

For researchers working within a post-structuralist paradigm, the idea of triangulation implies the identification of a fixed point that can be reached with certainty and is in opposition to their position of multiple and ever-changing realities. Richardson and Adams St Pierre (2005), for instance, employ the metaphor of a crystal as it helps them to highlight the way that how we see depends on the position from which we are viewing. Moreover, as a crystal grows, it represents the changing nature of reality. Guba and Lincoln (2005) note how the notion of arriving at a position of 'truth' itself is seen as questionable for researchers working within this paradigm, especially as they often aim at problematising commonly held 'truths'. They maintain that for some post-structuralist researchers, being 'transgressive' in this way is how validity is reached. For others, validity is seen as occurring through the ethical relationships developed in the course of the research and the degree to which the researcher supplies a reflexive account of their study (Guba and Lincoln, 2005). These ideas are complex, but are included here to show how validity is viewed differently according to the paradigm within which the researcher has positioned their research. We will examine paradigms in more detail in Chapters 4 and 5 so do not worry at this point if this is a little confusing.

 —— **KEY POINTS FROM THE CHAPTER** ——

- Planning the research process is key to the success of your project and starts with finding and refining the topic you are interested in.
- Once the overall aims of your research have been decided upon, you are in a position to choose an area to investigate, formulate a hypothesis or develop a research question.
- Research design depends upon:

  o   the number of contacts with the study population
  o   the reference period of the study
  o   the nature of the investigation.

- The methods chosen must be reliable and valid.
- Choosing participants for your research has to be undertaken with care. This is known as sampling.

—— **FURTHER READING** ——

Blaxter, L., Hughes, C. and Tight, M. (2010) *How to Research*, 4th edition. Maidenhead: Open University Press. Chapters 1 and 2 are helpful for students who are considering what they want to do for a research project.

Edwards, A. (2010) 'Qualitative research designs and analysis', in G. MacNaughton, S. Rolfe and I. Siraj-Blatchford (eds) *Doing Early Childhood Research: International Perspectives on Theory and Practice*, 2nd edition. Maidenhead: Open University Press. The beginning of this chapter looks at some key issues in designing a qualitative study.

Don't forget to visit the online resources at https://study.sagepub.com/mukherjiandalbon3e for access to free SAGE journal articles, weblinks, videos, exercises, mini quizzes and an interactive glossary.

2. An extended piece of work which critically analyses previous research and theory presented as a chapter in an academic dissertation (undergraduate, Masters or PhD). This is what you will produce as part of your final written report and is discussed in Chapter 3.

3. A summary of previous research and theory written as part of a journal article reporting on the findings of a research study. Journal articles are usually only a few pages long so the literature review is usually only two or three pages and acts to place the study within a theoretical and research context.

4. An academic piece of work looking at research findings and theory, from books and journal articles, proceedings from conferences, etc., to inform others about what is currently understood about a topic. These are 'stand-alone' articles or longer documents that are not, in themselves, a basis for future research (although the authors may suggest areas for future research). An example of this type of literature review may be an article reviewing all the research evidence for the efficacy of certain medical procedures. The audience for this type of review would be medical practitioners needing to keep up to date. Longer literature reviews may form the basis of Government policy such as the *Early Years Learning and Development Literature Review* (Evangelou et al., 2009) which informed the 2011 Tickell review of the Early Years Foundation Stage in England.

As Heath and Tynan have argued (2010: 151): 'A good proposal should persuade its readers both that there is an issue worthy of research and that the researcher is sufficiently familiar with the key existing literature to do so in a meaningful way'. It is therefore a significant element in a research proposal whether delivered orally or in writing.

The literature review should contain a discussion of the most relevant ideas, issues and research findings relating to your topic with the aim of demonstrating that you have a good understanding of the subject. The review should act as a guide to your decision as to the specific aspect of the subject that you wish to investigate, and how your research will contribute to the existing body of knowledge (Kamler and Thompson, 2014).

When discussing the literature for your research proposal it is essential that you do not just describe what you have read. The literature review should:

- Be authentic and credible, referring to sources such as peer-reviewed journals, textbooks and proceedings from conferences as much as possible. It is not appropriate to include information from popular media such as TV and newspapers unless you are critiquing such sources. If your research relates to a topic that is currently receiving media attention then this can be discussed in your introduction.
- Be analytical. You should be looking to identify the main themes, theories and perspectives in the literature and identify ongoing debates.

- Be critical. This does not mean that you look at previous research studies and are critical of the methods used, etc. (although there may be an element of this if you think that your research will be designed in such a way as to counteract a methodological flaw). Criticality when writing a literature review relates to how ideas are threaded together and juxtaposed to create a sense of flow and argument. The next chapter provides more detail on this crucial aspect of writing a literature review.
- Be well structured with an introduction, a middle section where you outline your argument and a conclusion. Additionally, it should be well-written.
- Be logical. There must be a logical flow of ideas *within* your literature review as well as *between* the various sections of your proposal. So, for example, if the title of your proposal is about a particular aspect of parental partnership, the introduction must clearly indicate why you have decided to investigate this particular issue and the literature review should be structured in such a way that it is clear where your research question 'fits in' to the various ways of looking at parental partnership.
- Be accurately referenced.

THE METHODOLOGY/METHODS SECTION OF THE RESEARCH PROPOSAL

In Chapter 1, we looked in some detail at designing research projects; it is in this section of the proposal that you outline the methodology you will be using and give details of your proposed data-collection methods and how you propose to obtain your sample of participants, explaining your thinking behind your choices. Depending upon the requirements of your institution you may be expected to demonstrate the relationship between the paradigm within which the proposed research is located, the proposed methodological approach and the proposed data-collection methods. There needs to be logical consistency between this and the aims of your research and the actual research question (Robson, 2011a). For example, if you are interested in finding out how musical activity is embedded in the everyday 'life' of a nursery class then one would expect to see a qualitative approach being taken, possibly an ethnographic approach. Following on from this, one would expect to see discussion of qualitative methods such as narrative observation and semi-structured interviewing. It would not 'fit' to see a structured questionnaire as the method employed here would not provide insight into the everyday activity of the nursery class to anywhere near the extent that immersion in the field (ethnography) and detailed observation would facilitate.

Either within this section, or in a separate section, there should be a discussion about how you propose to ensure that your study is ethical, remembering that your ethical stance should reflect the paradigm in which your research is located. Research ethics are considered in detail in Chapter 6 of this book.

DATA ANALYSIS

Within your proposal there should be a discussion about how you intend to analyse your data. Details about how to analyse data can be found in Chapter 18 and it is suggested that you read that chapter before writing this section of your research proposal. Describing the way you intend to analyse your data is especially important if you propose to conduct a highly quantitative study that involves the statistical testing of a hypothesis. If you have previously studied a subject such as psychology and are confident with statistical analysis this may be a realistic option. You will already be aware that your research needs to be designed with specific statistical operations in mind. In the proposal you will specify the particular statistical tests you propose to use and whether or not you will be using a computer program such as SPSS. However, it is our experience that the majority of students will be using a qualitative methodological approach or mixed methodology. If any of your data-collection methods involve the collection of numerical data, then you will need to explain how you intend to analyse these data. The most common way for students to analyse their data is by using descriptive statistics, which involves analysing data by using frequencies, averages and ranges, details of which are given in Chapter 18.

Qualitative studies, which use data-collection methods such as informal interviews or focus groups, will use techniques such as thematic analysis where themes and patterns in data are analysed (Braun and Clarke, 2006). In your research proposal it is sufficient to say that the interviews will be analysed using qualitative methods of analysis such as thematic analysis.

 ——— ACTIVITY ————————————————————

Investigate this journal article: Heath, M. and Tynan, C. (2010) 'Crafting a research proposal', *The Marketing Review*, 10(2): 147–68. www.nottingham.ac.uk/business/nexus/Documents/MaMSc/Dissertation/PereiraTynan-CraftingaResearchProposalTMR_2010.pdf (accessed 26 December 2016).

This is a very 'readable' article written by authors with many years' experience of supervising students as they start on their research journeys.

TIMELINES

It is useful at the proposal stage to indicate a timeline of activity for the research to include the planning stage, the fieldwork stage and the writing up. Some institutions may even require that you do this as part of your proposal. A grid can be useful here as it highlights the jobs to do and can keep you on track.

CASE STUDY

Dilveen is a student who plans to interview six early childhood practitioners about their previous training as well as training they would like to have in supporting young children with additional needs. She plans to use semi-structured interviewing to undertake this research project. Her course is structured in such a way that she has been allocated her supervisor in early December and hands in her assignment at the beginning of May. Table 2.1 shows what her timeline might look like.

Table 2.1 Dilveen's project timeline

December	January	February	March	April
Read around the topic. Plan the research in detail, identifying ethical issues. Read relevant material on chosen research methods.	Design letters of access and contact participants. Design data-collecting instrument, i.e. the interview schedule. Continue to read on the topic. Work on literature review.	Carry out data collection (the six interviews) and transcribe. Continue to read on the topic (making note of any links with data from the interviews). Write up literature review.	Analyse data from the interviews and note areas for deeper discussion. Write up methodology chapter. Write up introduction chapter.	Write up the data analysis and discussion chapter(s). Write the conclusion chapter with any recommendations, etc. Finalise the report, e.g. contents page, abstract, any acknowledgements, appendices in order, etc., ready for submission in early May.

Timelines are affected by the other modules you are doing as well as other possible commitments outside of your studies. Dilveen, for instance, is not planning a holiday in this time period and only has one other module in the spring semester. Illness or unforeseen circumstances can also affect a timeline as can difficulties with gaining access to participants (it is not always easy) so it is vital to keep in contact with your supervisor.

KEEPING A RESEARCH DIARY OR JOURNAL

There are important reasons why keeping a journal is recommended:

- A journal can act as a record of what you have done, together with notes you make as you go along about what has to be done.
- A journal can be used to *record your ideas and feelings* about how the research is going, an approach particularly valuable in qualitative studies.

There are many ways to organise a research diary or journal. Some journals may look like a personal diary, some may be more structured. However you organise your diary or journal, it will be invaluable when preparing for meetings with your supervisor and when you are writing up your project. If you wish to read more about this, please refer to Chapter 16, which looks at journaling in more detail and also includes discussion of using journaling as a research method in itself.

WORKING WITH A RESEARCH SUPERVISOR

A research 'supervisor' is usually a member of the academic team in an institution such as a university, who has the responsibility of overseeing your project. Usually you will be allocated a supervisor because they have specialist knowledge in the area you have chosen. In addition, perhaps more importantly, your project supervisor will have a good understanding of the research process and the requirements of *your particular course.*

Academic institutions will all have different ways of organising supervision. It may be that it is your responsibility to make the first contact, or it may be the supervisor who contacts you to arrange a first meeting. Most meetings will be face to face, but if you are a distance learner you may have primarily telephone tutorials or email contact. Whatever the mode of contact, the first meeting is important. Ideally you will have some ideas about the topic you are interested in and have begun to think about your research question and methodology before you meet your supervisor. The first meeting will be concerned with setting parameters for the research process and may include:

- clarification of how many hours are available for supervision/how often the sessions will occur
- an exploration of the best ways to keep in contact (email/telephone?)
- confirmation about the expectations in terms of hand-in date, word length and such like
- discussion about the topic, suitability of the research question, methodology and ethics
- action planning, such as thinking about timescale.

The success of supervision relies both on the skill of the supervisor and the motivation and openness of the student. It works best when students:

- Are independent.
- Keep appointments.
- Send draft sections/chapters to be looked at with plenty of time for their supervisor to review them before planned meetings, so that this time is used in discussion rather than reading.
- Tell the supervisor when there are problems, so there can be a discussion about how to deal with them.

Most institutions will insist that no data collection takes place until students have discussed their proposed research with their tutor and have had ethical clearance.

KEY POINTS FROM THE CHAPTER

- A research proposal is a highly structured, written document that outlines the plan of your research study and forms the basis of discussions with your research supervisor and other gatekeepers.
- The introduction should present a clear rationale for the study, perhaps drawing on your personal and/or professional motivations to explore the topic alongside justification that it is a topic of significance to the field of early childhood studies.
- A literature review is an important component of a research proposal, containing a discussion of the most relevant ideas, issues and research findings relating to your research. The review acts as a guide to your decision as to the specific aspect of the subject that you wish to investigate, and how your research will contribute to the existing body of knowledge.
- The methodology section is designed to explain the methodological approach you will take to data collection and outlines the data-collection methods you will use.
- One important aspect of a research proposal is a discussion as to how you plan to analyse the data you will collect.
- Developing a timeline and keeping a research journal or diary helps you to keep track of your research and will allow you to record ideas and reflections that will help you when writing up your research.
- Research supervisors are there to support you through the research process. Supervision works well if the student is motivated and proactive in keeping in contact with their supervisor.

FURTHER READING

Dawson, C. (2009) *Introduction to Research Methods*. Oxford: How To Books. Chapter 6 is a very easy to understand, basic outline of how to write a research proposal.

Denscombe, M. (2012) *Research Proposals: A Practical Guide*. Maidenhead: Open University Press. This is an excellent text which takes you stage by stage through writing a research proposal and which contains examples for you to look at.

Don't forget to visit the online resources at https://study.sagepub.com/mukherjiandalbon3e for access to free SAGE journal articles, weblinks, videos, exercises, mini quizzes and an interactive glossary.

This can be contrasted with journalism. An article in a newspaper or magazine is unlikely to have gone through such thorough reviewing and is unlikely to draw upon the range of reading or expertise. This is not to say that journalism has no place in a literature review but, rather, that it needs to be recognised for its limitations. Journalism is useful, for instance, in gaining a sense of the media issues that are prominent at a given time. Debbie Albon's research into young children's food and eating (Albon, 2007, 2009), for instance, was carried out at a time when there was a huge amount of media reporting and policy initiatives relating to the issue. Thus, her research needs to be seen as part of a bigger picture; a picture in which food and eating are the subject of much policy and media interest.

There may also be occasions when you might draw upon literature that is 'outside the box'. By this, we mean outside the early childhood studies canon. As early childhood studies has always drawn upon a range of disciplines, owing to the multi-disciplinary nature of the field, it may well be appropriate to draw upon an eclectic range of literature. The key deciding feature is its *relevance* to the topic under study.

— 🔍 — CASE STUDY

Here are some examples of ways in which some students have incorporated literature beyond the 'usual' early childhood studies readings:

- A student researching using a local allotment as a stimulus to her reception class children's learning incorporated a small amount of reading about the history of allotments and their place in communities into her study. This was justifiable because she was highlighting the importance of using the allotment to enhance children's developing sense of citizenship.
- A student looking at the views of West African parents about nursery education in her local area incorporated some reading in relation to West African history to help her to contextualise her study. This was important in highlighting the legacy of colonialism in West Africa, as well as the type of early childhood provision that developed. This, in turn, she argued, may have impacted on the views West African families have of nursery education on entry to the UK.

In this sense, a whole range of literature may be relevant – we say *may be*, because it is up to the researcher to demonstrate the relevance of any literature used to the study undertaken. When writing a literature review, it is very easy to drift away from the point, so when deciding what to include and what to exclude, try to think about the following:

- What type of writing is this? Is it a reliable source?
- Is it relevant to my study; that is, does it link to my research question or research aims?
- Does it help to contextualise my study; that is, does it help me in telling the story of my research?

Campbell et al. (2004) suggest four types of literature that the researcher might use in a study:

1. Previous research in the chosen area.
2. Methodological texts (but these will mostly be employed in the methodology chapter).
3. Literature about theory and practice in the area of study. Here, the researcher might be drawing upon work that locates their study within a broader body of sociological or psychological writing, for instance, that helps to inform their understanding of some of the underpinning issues relevant to their own study.
4. Finally, there are many other sources that could be of use. As noted earlier, these may be eclectic, such as from historical and philosophical writings, literature, and possibly film or television. Campbell et al. (2004: 67) maintain that this area is unlikely to be the first or major source of information that will be drawn upon. However, they argue that sources such as these, alongside discussions with other interested parties in the research, might 'add to the theoretical argument, provide insight to the analytical process, illuminate the analytical frame or simply enliven the writing'.

DISCUSSION OF KEY TERMINOLOGY

In many research projects, there is likely to be key terminology which, on the face of it, seems unproblematic, but on deeper reading may well prove to be more complex. In order to exemplify this further, consider the following terms:

- disability
- poverty.

In the first example there are different perspectives as to how disability might be viewed. A medical model of disability focuses on the child as an individual and the problems their condition might present, whereas a social model of disability is a perspective that looks at the structural conditions that impact on the experience of people with disabilities, such as people's attitudes towards disability and the environment. Thus, the second model sees *society* as crucial in *disabling* the person with a disability (Olsen and Clarke, 2003).

In the second example, you would need to consider whether you are thinking about the issue of poverty as absolute or relative. Absolute poverty refers to the kind of poverty where people have little or no access to running water, food and shelter, whereas relative definitions of poverty see poverty in relation to other people in society (Townsend, 1979). Therefore, you could be considered as living in relative poverty if you cannot afford a television or a telephone if most people living near to you, who want these things, have them.

In these examples, a critical discussion of the terminology you will be using is significant in positioning your research. This is because, if written well and drawing upon a range of reading, you will be arguing *why* you are adopting a particular definition. You will notice that we are not suggesting that you obtain dictionary definitions here; a literature review needs to explore definitions from relevant literature in order to highlight the complexity of trying to form a definition of the terminology used.

CRITICAL ANALYSIS OF THE TOPIC UNDER DISCUSSION

It would be very easy, when carrying out a literature review, to *describe* an aspect of an author's or a group of authors' work. However, description on its own is unlikely to make for a successful review of the literature. Silverman (2013: 343) argues for seeing a literature review as 'dialogic rather than a mere replication of people's writing'. In doing this, the researchers should view the review as helping them to answer a series of relevant questions to their research.

Clough and Nutbrown (2007: 101–2) argue for a 'radical reading', interactive approach to the literature. They advocate that you ask yourself questions such as the following as you read:

- What is the author trying to say?
- To whom is the author speaking?
- What is the author trying to achieve?
- What evidence does the author offer to support their claim(s)?
- Do I accept this evidence – does it relate to what I know of the world? What reasons do I have for this?

We would also like to add that you should try to gain a sense of the particular contribution a writer has made to the field. In addition, when reviewing the literature, you may find that different writers appear to be saying something similar about a given issue. Try to ask yourself what it is about their work that leads you to think they hold a similar position. Are they writing within a similar theoretical frame, such as drawing upon psychoanalytical perspectives to support their arguments? Conversely, there may be authors whose thinking on a given issue differs. Try to think about where their ideas differ, and why they might differ. Sometimes, these differences will be very subtle.

Wherever possible, we would recommend that you try to read people's work in the original, rather than relying purely on other people's understandings of that work (although you need to refer to this too). Different writers hold different views of key theorists, for instance. If we take Piaget as an example, look at the following two quotations about his work: 'Although Piaget's theory has been criticized and found wanting in some respects, there is no theory that has been so supportive to practice in this respect because it is the most over-arching so far in relation to motor play' (Manning-Morton and Thorp, 2003: 52) or 'The net effect of Piagetian frameworks has been to devalue what children know, and hence their knowledge' (Mayall, 1996: 45). As you can see, there are a range of viewpoints in relation to key theorists such as Piaget, and, if relevant to your study, you might need to argue why you are adopting a particular position, with references to the authors who think that way.

Silverman (2013) argues that some readings will be more important to your study than others and this should be a guiding principle in the amount of attention that is paid to the text in the literature review. While a sentence may be sufficient in describing a text that acts as background information, key texts need greater critical analysis, such as a critique of the theoretical frame used by the writer or the research methods employed by the writer in their research. In doing this, Silverman argues for an approach that is both respectful of the writer as well as advancing the reader's thinking about that literature.

Finally here, the way that you organise the review will also provide evidence of analysis, because although you will be collecting lots of information from a range of sources, these need to be organised and classified into a 'coherent pattern' (Bell, 2010: 112). If this is not done, Bell (2010) argues that a literature review can read like a catalogue or list of items. Thus, structure is an important component in demonstrating critical analysis too.

CLEAR STRUCTURE

Another important way that a literature review can show evidence of critical analysis is in the way that themes or issues are developed as an organising feature of the chapter (MacNaughton and Rolfe, 2010). In reading about the topic related to your research, you are likely to notice similar points being raised by different authors. You might try to assign a title to these different themes or issues.

 — ⏻ —— REFLECTION POINT ——————————————

It might be helpful to see how other people have structured their reviews.

In Albon's (2005) review of approaches used in the study of children, food and sweet-eating, she organises her paper around the following themes:

- biomedical approaches
- structuralist approaches

(Continued)

- materialist approaches
- post-structuralist approaches
- children's culture.

In doing this, Albon summarises the contribution each theoretical perspective has made to the study of children, food and sweet-eating, arguing – among other things – that sweet-eating should be positioned as a popular cultural artefact as opposed to a food.

Alternatively, in reviewing the literature around playtimes, Towers (1997) uses the following themes:

- the neglect of playtime
- playtime's recognition
- the 'romantic' view
- the 'problematic' view
- the value of the playtime experience
- the future direction of playground research.

In doing this, Towers is able to outline a range of perspectives on the issue of playtimes. In writing this review, Towers makes clear that she believes playtimes are an important area for consideration.

While you need to develop a range of themes around which to organise the review, it is also important to think about introducing and concluding the chapter. One of the differences many students find when writing up a research project is that it is organised into chapters. Book chapters will usually begin by outlining what the reader will expect in the chapter and will conclude by reiterating some of the key themes from the chapter. This is no different to a literature review (and, indeed, the other chapters in a student research project). We discuss the importance of structure further in the final chapter.

WELL-WRITTEN

Communicating ideas clearly is an important part of any research project in the same way as it is in an essay. For many of you, writing up a project will be one of the longest pieces of writing you will have undertaken thus far. For BA students it is likely to be approximately 10,000 words, and for MA students around 20,000 words, although this varies between institutions. Good writing will keep your audience, that is the readers of your research, interested. While one aspect of this is ensuring there is a clear structure, spending time on the grammar and spelling is very important.

Another, sometimes less discussed, area of writing that can improve clarity of communication is signposting. By 'signposting' we are talking about the words and phrases that serve to guide the reader through your work, sometimes reminding them of what has been written previously, sometimes foregrounding points that are going to be made (Northedge, 1990). In a long piece of work, such as a research project, signposting assumes greater importance.

 ACTIVITY

Try to access a published literature review such as those discussed earlier. Use a highlighter pen and mark the words and phrases that link points together, introduce new topics or tell the reader that the next section of writing contrasts with what has just been written.

CORRECT REFERENCING

While individual colleges and universities are likely to have their own student guidance about referencing, they will all share the view that this is an important aspect of a student's work. Not only this, but referencing is part of the process by which academic knowledge is disseminated as well as acting as respectful acknowledgement of the origin of the ideas you are discussing.

The literature review will not have a separate reference section. All the references used throughout the research project as a whole will be incorporated in alphabetical order in one reference section at the end of the project report. Some key things to ensure are as follows:

- Ensure that all the references you use in the text have a corresponding reference in full in the final reference section.
- Ensure that the reference section is in alphabetical order by the first author's last name. (It is likely that the referencing system used in your college will require this. In this book, we are using a system called 'Harvard referencing'. It is commonly used in early childhood books and journals.)
- Ensure that Internet references have the date of retrieval clearly referenced in the reference section.
- Ensure that you include the publisher and place of publication as part of the full reference in the reference section.

When referencing a chapter in an edited book, it might look like this:

Allen, G. (2005) 'Research ethics in a culture of risk', in A. Farrell (ed.) *Ethical Research with Children*. Maidenhead: Open University Press.

When referencing a journal article, it might look like this:

Angelides, P. and Michaelidou, A. (2009) 'The deafening silence: discussing children's drawings for understanding and addressing marginalisation', *Journal of Early Childhood Research*, 7(1): 27–45.

When referencing a book, it might look like this:

Arnold, C. (2003) *Observing Harry: Child Development and Learning 0–5*. Maidenhead: Open University Press.

When referencing from the Internet, it might look like this:

Office for National Statistics. www.ons.gov.uk/ons/guide-method/census/2011/index.html (accessed 28 July 2013).

You are likely to have student guidelines that help you with referencing in your college or university. Follow this guidance carefully as it is very frustrating to lose marks for poor referencing.

LITERATURE REVIEWS IN QUANTITATIVE AND QUALITATIVE RESEARCH

As we have previously discussed in Chapter 1 (and elaborated on in the following two chapters), the paradigm that underpins your research study will influence decisions such as how the research question is posed and the overall research design. In the same way, the underpinning paradigm and resultant methodology may influence the way that the literature review is structured.

Researchers guided by a positivist paradigm, using a quantitative methodological approach will, very likely, formulate a hypothesis. The literature review will be organised in such a way that past research findings in the area are examined and there is a clear and logical link between previous findings and the hypothesis that is to be tested in the current study. In addition there is likely to be an examination of research methods used in previous studies which will act as a guide to the choice of methods to be used in this study (Mertens, 2015).

Although it is important for researchers conducting qualitative research to demonstrate a good understanding of the literature, there is no expectation that there will be a fixed hypothesis, indeed this would be inappropriate. The very nature of such research often throws up new and novel lines of enquiry that may require the researcher to look at additional research in this new area so there is a process of working back and forth between one's data and the literature throughout the research. However, with this in mind, Mertens (2015: 93) cautions that researchers should 'be careful so that their perceptions of their findings emanate from their own data and not on expectations generated by reading extant literature'.

HOW TO GO ABOUT REVIEWING THE LITERATURE

Undertaking a search for literature can be a daunting process for the novice researcher. This section aims to give you some ideas in order to make this more manageable.

WHERE TO FIND RELEVANT LITERATURE

The previous section argued that it is important to refer to key readings relating to your chosen topic. Sometimes, as a new researcher, it might be difficult to decide who the key writers are in the field of study under exploration. Some helpful ideas in this area might include:

- *Look at relevant module reading lists.* Bell (2010) notes that books and articles considered to be 'required reading' for modules may well be useful as a starting point. It may be that some of the reading you did for a particular module motivated you to carry out your own research.
- *Ask your allocated research project tutor.* Usually you will be allocated a tutor, who will support you with your project. This person may have specialist knowledge of your chosen research area, and is certainly likely to have a wide knowledge of early childhood studies. This person may be able to steer you towards the most important sources. However, it is important to note that as a student-researcher, one of the key things your college or university will be hoping is that you develop the independent study skills necessary to carry out a research project. One way of demonstrating this is in a thorough literature search and a well-written review.
- *Look at the reference sections of recently published material.* If you look at recently published material in your chosen area, you will often find that the writer has drawn on a range of sources that you might like to explore. Look at the reference section and note the full reference and try and get hold of the source yourself.
- *Use your college or university library.* Most university libraries will have an online catalogue enabling you to search according to author/title/key word. This type of system is useful not only in locating relevant books and journals, it will also usually show you whether these books are available in the library at the present time as well as whether you can reserve them. You may even be able to do this from home online. Journals are likely to be catalogued in terms of the journal title, so you will probably have to search within these. In some instances, the journal title will clearly have relevance to your study; for example, if you are searching for information about promoting healthy eating, the journal *Health Education* is likely to have relevant articles within it in some or many of the editions. However, there may well be articles that are relevant in

PART 2
PARADIGMS AND PRINCIPLES

This second part of the book, entitled 'Paradigms and Principles', contains information that will underpin the decisions you will be making if you are planning to carry out early childhood research and will look in more depth at some of the issues that were briefly raised in Part 1. We strongly believe that the chapters in this section are key to being able to understand and conduct early childhood research and, although we recognise that some universities and colleges may not require you to demonstrate a detailed understanding of paradigms in your assignments, we would recommend that you read these chapters *before* embarking upon your research journey.

Chapters 4 and 5 look at paradigms that guide early childhood research; positivism and, as a reaction to this way of conceptualising the world, interpretivism, 'critical' theories and post-structuralism. These paradigms reflect our underpinning assumptions about the nature of knowledge and the best ways of understanding the world around us. Positivism is an approach to research that is founded on the underlying assumption that there are 'truths' to be uncovered, and that the best way to uncover these 'truths' is to use scientific methods. This approach guides research in subjects such as physics, chemistry and biology. Any paradigm that we hold not only frames what we believe to be the nature of knowledge, but also underpins the methodology we will use to investigate this knowledge. Hughes (2010: 36) defines methodology as 'what to investigate, how to investigate it, what to measure or assess and how to do so'. Positivism tends to use *quantitative* methodology that aims to produce information, or data, in numerical form that can be analysed by using statistics. In Chapter 4, we will look at how this approach has been applied to early childhood research. We will, however, discover that there are limitations to this approach, which have led to the increasing prominence of other paradigms such as interpretivism. Interpretivism is an approach that, far from assuming that it is possible to reveal 'the truth' by the strict application of scientific methodology, accepts that 'the truth' varies according to the perspectives of those involved and the context within which research is located. Interpretivism uses *qualitative* methodology, which focuses more on words and meanings than quantitative methodology.

Whatever the paradigm that is guiding researchers' thinking, researchers have to ensure that their research conforms to the highest ethical standards. In the same way that the paradigm we hold will steer decisions about the research we undertake, our 'moral philosophy or set of moral principles' define our ethical stance, which in turn will decide how we conduct our research (Aubrey et al., 2000: 156). It could be considered that the paradigm we hold has a direct influence on the ethical stance that we take, as, within a positivist paradigm, children may be seen as *objects* to be studied, as opposed to being seen as *active participants* in the research process (Woodhead and Faulkner, 2008). Chapter 6 looks broadly at ethics in relation to early childhood research and Chapter 7 examines issues relating to listening to children. We include these chapters in this part of the book because of our belief that they are important principles in research.

In Chapter 7, we discuss how the way we 'see' children influences the degree to which we consider children's voices should be heard. We will argue that there has been a shift away from researchers thinking that children are not competent enough to join in the research process, that they are passive and powerless, to an increasing emphasis on children's abilities to be active participants in research. This, as we will see, has ethical implications.

— 🔍 —— **CASE STUDY** ————————————————————

Indrani is studying for an early childhood degree and is in the initial planning stages of her research project. She has observed that the early childhood practitioners, where she is on placement, seem to be a very ebullient, extravert team. She has read that the ratio of extraverts to introverts in the adult population is roughly 1:1, and thinks that there may be a higher ratio of extraverts to introverts than this amongst her colleagues. She has an idea that early childhood attracts people who are naturally extravert and to test this idea she plans to ask permission to administer personality tests to the staff at four early childhood settings to see whether the ratio of extraverts to introverts is higher than in the general population in all four settings.

What does this tell us about Indrani's assumptions about knowledge and the nature of enquiry? Firstly, Indrani's ontological stance is that the personality dimensions *extraversion* and *introversion* exist and that it is possible to measure these personality traits. Secondly, Indrani's epistemological assumption is that the way to measure the extent to which an individual is either extravert or introvert is by using a psychological test. (These tests are readily available on the Internet and usually consist of a series of questions designed to find out the personality traits of the participant, with the data being presented in a numerical form.) Later on in this chapter you will see that Indrani's ontological and epistemological approach is consistent with positivism.

We have seen that epistemology relates to the way that we find out about things, how we acquire knowledge. Johnson and Christensen (2012) identify three sources of knowledge: experience, expert opinion and reasoning.

EXPERIENCE

This is the first way that babies begin to learn about the world around them, as they explore the world via their senses. The idea that knowledge comes from experience is known as empiricism (Nolen-Hoeksema et al., 2014) and, according to this way of thinking, only the knowledge that we obtain through our senses can be said to be true. From this concept is derived the word 'empirical', the idea that a statement can be proved or disproved by observation, experiment or experience (Johnson and Christensen, 2012). Later on in the chapter we will see that positivist methodology relies on the collection of empirical data – facts or information that have been derived by observation or experiment.

EXPERT OPINION

The sum total of human knowledge would not grow very fast if we had to formulate our knowledge and understanding of the world by 'first principles' all the time. Much of our knowledge has been passed down to us from others. Among the sources of information are our parents, other family members, friends, educators and 'experts'. It is difficult to turn on the television or read a newspaper without encountering the ideas of experts. As we grow older we come to realise that not everything that we are told by experts is true or helpful. We learn to practise discernment and realise that sometimes expert advice can be contradictory. Nevertheless, learning from others remains an important source of information about the world around us.

REASONING

Whereas empiricists argue that the only valid way to find out about the world around us is by observation, experiment and experience, adherents of rationalism consider that *reason* is the primary source of knowledge (Johnson and Christensen, 2012). Through the processes of thinking and reasoning, rationalists believe that it is possible to develop an understanding of a subject, without actually directly observing a phenomenon.

Nolen-Hoeksema et al. (2014) identify two main types of reasoning: deductive reasoning and inductive reasoning.

- *Deductive reasoning* is the process of drawing conclusions about something on the basis of prior knowledge known to be true. For example, one may agree that the following statement (premise) is true: 'Newborn babies cannot talk'. Then, given another statement, 'Baby John can say "DaDa"', it is possible to deduce that John cannot be a newborn baby. Deductive reasoning is only successful if the first premise is true.
- *Inductive reasoning* is when one draws conclusions about something on the balance of probability that a statement is true, based on what has previously occurred. For example, you may have noticed that every cat you have seen has a furry coat and from this you reason that it is probably true that all cats have furry coats. However, when using inductive reasoning it is always possible that the exception to the rule may come along, which will disprove the theory.

WHAT DO WE MEAN BY A 'PARADIGM'?

Research is about asking questions and seeking information to answer the questions that we pose. Influencing the questions that we ask and underpinning the research approach we eventually take are our ontological ideas and conceptions about childhood and children. This understanding of children and childhood ultimately influences the paradigm in which our research is positioned.

It is worth taking some time to discuss what a paradigm is as it is a term that will be used frequently in this book. In common usage, a paradigm is an exemplar or a model. However, the term has come to mean something more specific when used in relation to research, mainly because of the work of Thomas Kuhn in the 1960s and 1970s (Hammersley, 2007). According to Mackenzie and Knipe (2006) a paradigm is a theoretical framework. They cite Bogdan and Biklen (1998: 22) as defining a paradigm as 'a loose collection of logically related assumptions, concepts and propositions that orient thinking and research'. Hughes (2010: 35) describes a paradigm as a way of seeing the world that 'frames a research topic' and which influences the way that we think about the topic. Similarly, Fraser and Robinson (2004: 59) describe it as a 'set of beliefs about the way in which particular problems exist and a set of agreements on how such problems can be investigated'. From this it is clear that our choice of paradigm is important in influencing the methodology we choose, but it also shapes our perceptions of children and childhood, as we will see.

Hughes (2001) illustrated the connection between underlying beliefs and research methodology when he looked at a number of research studies into the influence and significance of the media in children's lives. He concluded that the way that the various research studies were conducted reflects the *model of childhood* held by the researchers, and that this underlying model influenced the research that was conducted. For example, researchers who held the underlying belief that children are like 'little sponges', uncritically absorbing messages from the media, asked the question 'What does the media do to children?' Researchers who saw children as more active, discriminating consumers tended to ask the question 'What do children do with the media?' (Hughes, 2001: 356).

Although various authors (Hughes, 2001, 2010; Mackenzie and Knipe, 2006) have identified a number of paradigms that underpin research into children, Kumar (2014) suggests that the two main paradigms that form the basis of research in the social sciences are the *positivist approach* and the *'naturalistic' approach* (also known as the interpretivist approach), and it is these two main approaches to research that we will be looking at in more detail in both this chapter and the next.

THE MEANING AND ORIGINS OF POSITIVISM

The positivist paradigm is one that has its roots in physical science. It uses a systematic, scientific approach to research. Hughes (2010) explains that the positivist paradigm sees the world as being based on unchanging, universal laws and the view that everything that occurs around us can be explained by knowledge of these universal laws. To understand these universal laws we need to observe and record events and phenomena around us in a systematic way and then work out the underlying principle that has 'caused' the event to occur. An example of this process in action is the story of Sir Isaac Newton and the apple. It is said that Isaac Newton was walking in an apple orchard and saw an apple fall straight down to the ground. He started wondering about how far above the Earth the force of gravity had an effect and began to develop his theory of gravity. In this example the observed event was the falling apple and the underlying universal law was that of gravity (Keesing, 2008).

Scientific discoveries have been made since ancient times – for example, as early as 4800 BC there is evidence that standing stones were being used for astronomical calculations in an area of Africa near the Sudanese border with Egypt (Lee, 2008). The positivist paradigm, however, is not just associated with scientific discovery, it involves the application of scientific methodology. The development of the scientific method as a means of exploring the world around us probably emerged around the time of the European Renaissance (the fifteenth and sixteenth centuries) and the Enlightenment (the eighteenth century) (Fraser and Robinson, 2004).

THE SCIENTIFIC METHOD

In the section above we outlined that positivist researchers in the field of early childhood, and indeed other subject areas, have to make a basic assumption that what is being studied is subject to underlying, unchanging, universal laws. Johnson and Christensen (2012) point out that positivist researchers also have to make other assumptions, including that they should operate within agreed norms and practices, as well as the idea that it is possible to distinguish between more and less plausible claims and that science cannot provide all the answers, for example, for questions to do with morality.

The key features of the scientific method include:

1. Observation and collecting data.
2. Looking for patterns and developing a theory.
3. Forming a hypothesis to test the theory.
4. Conducting research to test the hypothesis.
5. Support or adjustment of the theory (Coolican, 2014).

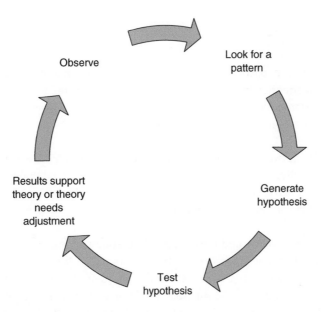

Figure 4.1 The research wheel

These steps are often represented as a cycle or wheel (see Figure 4.1).

Within this framework Johnson and Christensen (2012) identify two different approaches: an *exploratory* approach and a *confirmatory* approach.

- *The exploratory approach* starts with the researcher making observations and searching for a pattern. If a pattern is found then the researcher puts forward a theory or idea about why this pattern occurs. This approach is sometimes known as the inductive method.
- *The confirmatory approach* is where a researcher starts with a theory about why a particular phenomenon is occurring and develops a hypothesis (a prediction) based on the theory. The next stage of this approach is when the researcher conducts an empirical investigation to test the hypothesis. If the data uphold the hypothesis then this supports the underlying theory. This approach is sometimes known as the deductive method.

You may find it helpful to look at the section on 'Reasoning' earlier on in this chapter to remind yourself about inductive and deductive reasoning.

In reality these two approaches often work hand in hand with each other, as the following Research in Focus will show.

RESEARCH IN FOCUS

In an Australian study, published in 2013, Farrant and Zubrick wanted to see if low levels of parental/child joint attention in infancy and low levels of parents reading to young children are associated with children having poor vocabulary skills on school entry. The study is based on observations and previous research findings showing that:

1. Joint attention between parents and infants/young children increases the vocabulary of children. (Joint attention is where an adult talks about something that has caught a child's attention or draws the child's attention to something that they have heard or seen.)
2. Children's vocabulary increases if parents read to them.

From these research findings and observations the authors formed a hypothesis that low levels of joint attention and book reading by parents would lead to children having poor vocabulary skills on school entry. The research was based on the findings of a large prospective longitudinal study of over 2,300 Australian children who were investigated from the ages of about 9 months to 5 years. Findings upheld the hypothesis. Children who received poor joint attention as infants and whose parents did not read to them very much had significantly poorer vocabulary skills at age 5 years.

In this research the research cycle is clearly demonstrated. In the deductive phase, observations and research findings by others led Farrant and Zubrick to generate a hypothesis that they tested in the confirmatory phase, using data from the longitudinal study. The results supported their hypothesis. You will find information on surveys and longitudinal studies in Chapter 8.

CAN WE USE SCIENCE TO STUDY CHILDREN?

Before concluding this discussion on the scientific method, it is important to consider whether it is possible or desirable to use science to study children in the same way that science is used to study the physical world.

Up until the eighteenth century, children and childhood were not considered to be topics for scientific study, but from the time of Rousseau there is evidence that children were subject to observation, although it was not until the late nineteenth and twentieth centuries that systematic, scientific observation of children took place. Chapter 12 of this book looks at the historical origins of child observation in more detail. The application of scientific methodology to social and psychological phenomena has been, and continues to be, passionately debated. Whereas it is possible to use scientific methods to research the *biology* and *physiology* of children, it is harder to see how these methods can be employed to investigate attitudes and feelings and the social world in general. This is a key criticism of positivist research.

Greig et al. (2013) consider the question as to whether we can legitimately use scientific methods to study children to be a pseudo debate. They point out that children are complex individuals in whom there is a highly sophisticated interplay between physical, biological and chemical characteristics and 'psychological' characteristics. In addition the environment does not act passively upon children; they are active agents able both to adapt to and alter their environment. The complexity of children and childhood is such that no single approach will be wholly satisfactory, and scientific methodology should be viewed as part of an eclectic approach to research about and with children (Greig et al., 2013). The scientific method is an especially important approach in research into children's physiology – after all, in testing a new medical treatment to be used on young children, it is vital that it has gone through a rigorous scientific process.

POSITIVISM AND THE QUANTITATIVE METHODOLOGICAL APPROACH

As we have seen previously, the positivist paradigm leads to a scientific, systematic approach to research and as such lends itself to the use of quantitative methodology. Researchers using a quantitative methodological approach usually (but not always) concentrate on the *confirmatory* stages of the research cycle; that is, the formulation of a hypothesis and the collection of numerical data to test this hypothesis. Farrant and Zubrick's (2013) study is an example of this. Thus, quantitative methodology aims to measure, quantify or find the extent of a phenomenon, as opposed to qualitative methodology, which is usually more concerned with describing experiences, emphasising meaning and exploring the nature of an issue (Coolican, 2014). Kumar (2014) describes the quantitative methodological approach as being a *structured* approach, in which all aspects of the research process are decided upon before data collection begins. The qualitative methodological approach is seen to be more *unstructured*, with aspects of the research process subject to change in response to events as they occur. Qualitative methodology will be looked at in more detail in Chapter 5.

CHARACTERISTICS OF QUANTITATIVE RESEARCH

Johnson and Christensen (2012: 34) outline the characteristics of quantitative research as follows:

- The confirmatory part of the research cycle is emphasised.
- Behaviour is seen to be predictable and regular.
- Common aims of research are to explain and predict.

- The researcher is interested in understanding general laws that apply to whole populations rather than particular groups in particular contexts.
- There is an attempt to study behaviour under controlled conditions with an attempt to isolate the effect of single variables.
- An objective approach is taken; that is, different observers should be able to agree about what is being observed.
- Data are based upon precise measurement using structured and validated data-collection instruments.
- Data analysis aims to look at statistical relationships.

THE DIFFERENCE BETWEEN METHODOLOGY AND METHOD

Hughes (2010: 36) defines methodology as 'what to investigate, how to investigate it, what to measure or assess and how to do so', and we can see, from the previous discussion about quantitative methodology that it is not just a description of data-collection methods and techniques used in research. It is our experience that students often use the term 'methodology' and 'method' interchangeably, which is a common mistake. *Methodology* explains the principles behind the reasons why we use particular data-collection methods in our research. *Methods* are the research techniques that we use, such as questionnaires or interviews, to obtain the information we are seeking.

Although positivism is strongly associated with quantitative methodology that is not to say that qualitative *methods* are never used. For example, it is possible to conduct a very large, quantitative longitudinal study that has thousands of participants, which includes interviews of hundreds of these participants. Interviews are generally considered a qualitative method, but in this scenario the interviews are likely to be used in a quantitative way; that is the information obtained is likely to be reduced to numerical data. There is an ongoing debate as to the appropriateness of combining quantitative and qualitative methodologies, which is discussed in Chapter 5; however, in the scenario just described one could argue that, because the data from interviews is presented in numerical form, the method is underpinned solely by quantitative methodology.

EXPERIMENTAL METHOD

We have seen that the confirmatory stage of the research cycle involves the testing of a hypothesis, an investigation of cause and effect. One way of doing this is by conducting an experiment. An experiment is a way of testing a hypothesis by precisely controlling the variables involved. It is very unlikely that students of early childhood will use an experiment in their research, but we describe this method here as it will help you interpret the research findings of others.

VARIABLES

Consider this imaginary piece of research. Members of staff in a local reception class have noted that children who come to them from one particular children's centre (centre A) appear to have attained a higher level of language development than children from another children's centre (centre B). Observations and records of children's language skills over a period of several years seem to support this view. The staff conclude that the difference is attributable to the higher quality of language interaction between the staff and children in centre A.

 — **REFLECTION POINT**

Thinking about the conclusion made about the two children's centres in the above scenario, do you consider that the conclusion is appropriate? What other factors might be involved?

There has been a flaw in the reasoning behind the conclusion made, because the findings may have nothing to do with the quality of language interaction at all. It may be that one centre drew children who come from an area of higher social disadvantage than the other. The children may have entered centre B with very poor language development compared with the children entering centre A. In fact, the quality of interaction in centre B may be better than centre A as the gap in language skills between the two groups of children may have actually closed while they were attending centre B. Factors that may affect the outcome of research in this way are called variables, and for appropriate conclusions to be drawn the variables have to be controlled. In this case, one would have had to look at the language development of the children on entry to the two children's centres as well as when they arrived in the reception class to have any chance of reaching a sensible conclusion. Even then, controlling for variables in 'real-life' situations such as this is near to impossible.

Nolen-Hoeksema et al. (2014) consider that anything that can occur with a different value is a variable, so time, age, social class, gender, for instance, are all examples of variables. In an experiment, the researcher takes control over the variables that may affect the outcome of the research, and it is the *precise control* of variables that distinguishes an experiment from other scientific methods of enquiry.

For example, a teacher has a theory that children learn better in the morning when they are 'fresh'. She decides to conduct an experiment to find out if this is true. Before she starts her experiment she needs to make several decisions.

- *How will she measure 'learning'?* In this case the teacher decides that her measure will be the number of spellings remembered after 24 hours from a list of five spellings.
- *What will her hypothesis be?* In this case she decides that her hypothesis will be 'Children learning a list of five spellings in the morning will remember more spellings 24 hours later than children who learn a list of five spellings in the afternoon'. The number of spellings remembered is called the dependent variable because this is what is being measured and the hypothesis is that the number of spellings learned is dependent on the time of day. The time of day is known as the independent variable as it is not under the control of (independent of) the participant; it is manipulated by the experimenter.
- What other variables need to be taken into account and how will they be controlled? The teacher comes up with the ideas in Table 4.1.

Table 4.1 Possible sources of variation and how these will be controlled

Variable	How it can be controlled
Age of child	Children will be chosen between the ages of 6 years and 6 years, 3 months
Gender of child	Half the children will be boys, half will be girls
Health of child	Only children who are fit and well will be tested
Language	Children whose first language is not English and who are not yet fluent will be excluded
Hunger	Efforts will be made to test the children approximately two hours after they have had either breakfast or lunch
Environment	The children will be tested in the same room, with noise levels kept to a minimum
The spelling list	The list will be the same for all children

 —— REFLECTION POINT ——————

Do you think the ability to remember spellings is the best way to measure *learning*? Are there *other* ways that you can think of that would enable this teacher to test her theory that children learn best in the mornings?

The key feature of an *experiment* is that the researcher tries to control as many variables as possible while only altering the independent variable.

EXPERIMENTAL DESIGN

The design of an experiment is the actual way that the experiment is put together. The simplest designs are similar to the one that we have just outlined; that is, there is one independent variable and one dependent variable (Nolen-Hoeksema et al., 2009).

In the hypothetical experiment outlined previously, the teacher decides that she will choose two groups of eight children, four girls and four boys, who fit in with the criteria outlined above. She gives one group the spellings in the morning, giving them 15 minutes to learn them. She tests them 24 hours later. She gives the spellings to the other group in the afternoon, again with 15 minutes to learn them, and tests them 24 hours later. She makes sure that she gives both groups exactly the same instructions. This is known as an *independent sample design*; that is, that there are two different groups being tested under similar conditions (Coolican, 2014). The advantage of an independent sample design is that you can use the same 'test'. In this case, the same list of spellings was used, reducing the variance that could occur with different words. The disadvantage is that having two groups introduces other sources of variance, because individuals can differ according to a variety of dimensions such as personality, learning style, class and culture. These variables, for which the researcher has not controlled, are sometimes called confounding variables (Johnson and Christensen, 2012).

The alternative to the independent sample design, which controls for individual differences, is the *repeated measure design*, where the same group is tested under different conditions (Field, 2013). In our example this would involve using a different set of spellings, which would introduce another source of variance.

One solution to the disadvantages of both of these designs is the *matched pair design* (Cardwell et al., 2000). In this design two groups of participants are used, but each participant in one group is matched as far as possible with someone from the other group, according to relevant variables. So in the hypothetical example we are discussing, each child would be partnered with another and matched according to variables such as level of mother's education, social class of the family and cultural background. Identical twins are often used as participants in this sort of design because they are usually natural matched pairs.

TYPES OF EXPERIMENT

When we think of scientific experiments, we often think about laboratories and, indeed, many experiments in the field of child development have been undertaken in a laboratory situation, but experiments can be conducted in other ways. Coolican (2014) outlines the following experimental situations.

- *Laboratory experiments.* It is easier to control variables in a laboratory and some notable examples of research with children, such as Bandura et al.'s (1963) research on aggression, have been undertaken in laboratories. Laboratory experiments have, however, been criticised because of the narrowness of the situations being investigated and the artificiality of the situation. Children, in particular, are unlikely to react the same way in 'real life' as they do in controlled laboratory situations.

RESEARCH IN FOCUS

Piaget (1896-1980) famously conducted a series of laboratory-based experiments designed to show that the way children think and reason is different from adults. Robson (2012) describes an experiment conducted by Piaget to demonstrate that young children under about the age of 7 find it very difficult to see things from another's point of view. The experiment involved a model of three mountains that was placed on a table top. The three mountains were different in colour and were easy to tell apart because one had a house on its summit, one had a cross and another was covered by snow. A toy doll was placed looking towards the mountains, with the child being 'tested' being placed looking at the model, but at an angle to the doll. The child was asked 'What can the doll see?' and given photographs of the three mountains taken from a variety of positions. Children of different ages were tested under the same conditions and it was found that children under 7 typically chose the photograph that represented the view that they could see. This was taken as confirmation that young children were egocentric and cannot 'decentre' (Cardwell et al., 2000).

- *Field experiments.* These are carried out in 'naturalistic' surroundings. In the memory experiment that we were discussing previously, the experiment would have been carried out in the children's school. Obviously, children react more naturally in a field situation, but it is more difficult to control sources of variance.
- *Natural experiments.* Sometimes it is possible to exploit a naturally occurring event for research purposes. For example, a nursery may introduce a key person approach and it may be possible to compare the time taken for new children to settle before and after the change. Coolican (2014) points out that this is a 'quasi' experiment as the researcher has no control over the independent variable (the change in policy).

CORRELATIONAL METHOD

Experiments are not the only way to conduct scientific research. Other non-experimental approaches that can be included within the positivist paradigm include correlational studies (Field, 2013). Correlational studies are used in situations when it is difficult or impossible to use experiments, but the researcher wants to see if there is a relationship between two variables.

Consider this imaginary scenario. A researcher has a theory that childhood obesity is related to the amount of 'fast food' that a child consumes. It would be unethical to conduct an experiment where one group of children was fed a diet consisting only of 'fast food', and another group of children was not allowed to eat any 'fast food' at all. More indirect ways of looking at this issue need to be used so the researcher formulates a hypothesis that the more fast-food outlets there are in a town or city, per head of population, the higher will be the levels of childhood obesity.

In this study the independent variable is the number of fast-food outlets and the dependent variable is the percentage of overweight children (as recorded on school entry as part of the National Child Measurement Programme [DoH, 2014], for instance). An important difference between a correlational study and an experiment is that the researcher does not manipulate the independent variable, but just measures it. In this example, the hypothesis is that there will be a positive correlation between the two variables; that is, the more fast-food outlets there are per head of population, the higher will be the percentage of childhood obesity. A negative correlation would involve one variable increasing as the other decreases. In this case there would be a negative correlation if the levels of obesity reduced as the number of 'fast-food' outlets increased. To conduct a correlational study, one needs to have variables that can be measured on a scale or counted – interval data, rather than data that describe categories such as male/female and hair colour (Coolican, 2014).

It is important to note that, even if a positive correlation is found, this does not *prove* cause and effect. In the example we are using a positive correlation suggests an association between the number of 'fast-food' outlets and obesity, but does not prove that 'fast food' causes obesity. It may be that there is an intervening variable; for instance, there may be more 'fast-food' outlets in poorer areas, and higher levels of obesity in areas of disadvantage.

VALIDITY AND RELIABILITY

Scientific method, with its rigorous control of variables, aims to produce findings that are valid and reliable. Validity, according to Blaxter et al. (2010: 245), 'has to do with whether your methods, approaches and techniques actually relate to, or measure, the issues you have been exploring'. Reliability relates to how well research has been carried out. Findings are said to be reliable if other researchers can replicate the findings of a study by using the same methods (Blaxter et al., 2010: 199).

The positivist paradigm starts with an assumption that 'the truth is out there'. Quantitative methodology, which derives from this, aims to improve *validity* by 'careful sampling, appropriate instrumentation and appropriate statistical treatments of data' (Cohen et al., 2011: 197). Reliability, using quantitative methods, involves choosing measures that demonstrate 'consistency and replicability over time, over instruments and over groups of respondents' (Cohen et al., 2011: 119).

However, not everyone agrees that there is a universal truth, waiting to be discovered. An alternative viewpoint is that each individual interprets and understands the world around them differently, influenced by their social and cultural context and that there may be multiple explanations for actions (Hughes, 2010). This point of view belongs to the interpretivist paradigm that is outlined in Chapter 5. Cohen et al. (2011) point out that discussions about reliability and validity should be framed by the paradigm and methodological approach taken. Thus, reliability, when using a qualitative methodological approach may involve trying to ensure that different researchers are consistent in the way that they interpret or categorise observations or interviews, or that the same researcher will show consistency over time (Silverman, 2013). Validity in qualitative research tends to relate to the extent that the research provides an authentic account of the participants' voices – notably in interpretivist research (Hughes, 2010) – as well as a reflexive account of the researcher's own role in the production of the data (Coffey, 1999). Validity and reliability are key concepts in research and are revisited throughout this book.

POSSIBILITIES AND LIMITATIONS OF POSITIVIST RESEARCH

In reading this chapter, we can see that positivism is an important paradigm in research. The positivist approach has led to advances in our understanding about children and childhood, particularly in the area of biology. We conclude this chapter by summarising the key possibilities and limitations of positivist research and the quantitative methodological approach that is informed by this paradigm.

POSSIBILITIES

- There is recognition that children and childhood are legitimate subjects for scientific study and this has led to real advances in our understanding, especially in the field of physiology and medicine.
- By applying highly controlled procedures and quantifying variables it is possible to obtain results that can help to refine theory.

- Because of the rigid control of variables, findings are generalisable; that is, the findings from the participants under study can be applied to a wider population (Robson and McCarten, 2015).
- The emphasis on the strict application of scientific method and the control of variables means that the findings are seen as valid and able to be replicated by others.
- Positivism gives rise to quantitative methodology and the use of statistical analysis. In early childhood this approach has been valuable as the basis for the large cohort studies of children (see Chapter 8).

LIMITATIONS

- Because of the need to control variables, research on children is often undertaken out of context, so the holistic nature of children's childhoods is lost (James, 2007). This is especially true if children are investigated under laboratory conditions, as their behaviour may be very different than in everyday, 'naturalistic' situations.
- The need to control variables often leads to very small units of human behaviour being studied, for example, memory, attention and attachment, without regard for how all these aspects work together in an individual.
- Scientific methods, such as the use of highly structured questionnaires, may produce superficial information. If you *really* want to find out about the complexity of children and childhood(s) you need to use methods that delve deeper.
- Strict scientific method requires the researcher to be objective, but in 'real life' one does not find out about other individuals by remaining distant (Coffey, 1999).
- Objectivity may be an illusion anyway. As we will see in the next chapter, it is impossible to remove the influence of the researcher in the data-gathering process (Coffey, 1999).
- Some scientific research entails a degree of deception, with the participant not being told the real reason for the research. This raises ethical concerns, which will be discussed in Chapter 6.
- Scientific methods often put the researcher in a more dominant, powerful position than the participant. Coolican (2014) comments that the participants' behaviour may mirror this and adversely influence findings.

The next chapter will pick up further on some of these criticisms as we will be discussing paradigms that have developed as a response to positivism.

CASE STUDY

Noleen is studying for an early childhood degree. She is funding her way through college by working part time in a private nursery in an ethnically mixed, inner city area in London. About two thirds of the children are from BAME families (Black and minority ethnic). She has observed that although there are plenty of books available which portray BAME children in positive and empowering roles, the practitioners rarely read these books to the children. The manager of the setting has arranged an in-service training day on promoting equality for the staff and this is scheduled for one month's time. Noleen has decided that for her research project she will record the titles of the books read to the children for a two-week period before the training (on the days that she attends the setting) and for two weeks after the training. She will analyse the titles and record what percentage of the books contain positive images of BAME children.

Her hypothesis is: 'There will be a higher percentage of books chosen to be read to children by practitioners, which reflect positive images of BAME children, after practitioners have received training on promoting equality than before the training'.

1. Identify the paradigm in which this research is located.
2. What methodological stance has been taken?
3. This is known as a quasi-experimental design. Why would you not describe it as an experiment? (Chapter 1 will help you.)
4. What variables have been controlled for in this design?
5. What sources of variance have not been controlled?
6. Is the research likely to produce worthwhile results? Can you think of other approaches that could be taken that may uncover the reasons behind the practitioners' choices?

✔ KEY POINTS FROM THE CHAPTER

- The decisions we make about the research process depend upon the paradigm we hold. A paradigm is a set of beliefs about the way in which particular problems exist and a set of agreements on how such problems can be investigated.
- A positivist paradigm is one that assumes that early childhood can be studied using the same scientific method as one would use when studying the physical world, and that the subject being studied is subject to the same universal laws that govern the universe.

(Continued)

- Scientific method involves a cycle of investigation including the following stages: observation, identification of underlying patterns and generating a theory, forming a hypothesis, conducting research to test the hypothesis, and accepting or rejecting the theory.
- Positivism gives rise to quantitative methodology. This is methodology that involves the collection of 'scientific' data that are precise and based on measurement and are often analysed using statistics with the intention that the findings be generalisable.
- One approach used in positivist research is the experiment. The key feature of an experiment is that the researcher tries to control as many variables as possible while only altering the independent variable.
- Correlational studies are another scientific approach where the researcher looks for an association between two variables, but the independent variable is not manipulated.
- However, positivist research is not without criticism. It could be regarded as being very narrow and unable to demonstrate the holistic nature of children and childhood. The findings from positivist studies are often superficial and fail to contribute to a deep understanding of an issue. Finally, by applying research principles about the natural world to the social world of human beings, positivist research seems to ignore the complexity of human life and the difficulty of the researcher remaining objective and detached from the people with whom s/he is carrying out research.

————— FURTHER READING —————

Coolican, H. (2014) *Research Methods and Statistics in Psychology*, 6th edition. Abingdon: Routledge. This book contains a clear introduction to positivist research and quantitative research designs.

Hughes, P. (2010) 'Paradigms, methods and knowledge', in G. MacNaughton, S. Rolfe and I. Siraj-Blatchford (eds) *Doing Early Childhood Research: International Perspectives on Theory and Practice*, 2nd edition. Maidenhead: Open University Press. Although written a few years ago this is still a very useful chapter as it outlines some of the major research paradigms and provides illustrative examples from early childhood research.

Don't forget to visit the online resources at https://study.sagepub.com/mukherjiandalbon3e for access to free SAGE journal articles, weblinks, videos, exercises, mini quizzes and an interactive glossary.

5

BEYOND POSITIVISM

INTERPRETIVISM, 'CRITICAL' THEORIES AND POST-STRUCTURALISM

---------------------- CHAPTER OBJECTIVES ----------------------

- To develop an understanding of interpretivism, 'critical' theories and post-structuralism in research.
- To consider the significance of such paradigms for *early childhood* research.
- To develop an understanding of qualitative methodological approaches to research.
- To reflect on the possibilities and limitations of qualitative research.
- To consider how quantitative and qualitative research methods can be combined.

This chapter describes paradigms which have arisen out of criticisms of positivist research. It will discuss interpretivism, 'critical' theories in research such as feminism and Critical Race Theory, and will introduce you to post-structuralism. As noted in the first chapter, all research falls within a particular paradigm – in other words, all research is underpinned by a particular philosophy or way of seeing the world and making sense of it (Hughes, 2010). In reading the chapter you will see that the theories discussed tend to favour a qualitative methodological approach. Thus, we also include a discussion of what is meant by qualitative research and the kinds of methods that fall within this methodological approach.

WHAT DO WE MEAN BY INTERPRETIVISM?

As noted previously, any piece of research has a philosophical basis, which links to the way knowledge is viewed and appropriate methodologies to use in research (Crotty, 1998). The previous chapter discussed positivism, which has a longer history when compared with interpretivism. Positivism, you may recall, tends to be characterised by the use of the quantitative methodological approach, which emphasises the need to make generalisations about the world and the need for accurate measurement. It is underpinned by a belief that the 'truth' is possible to discover and often involves the setting out of a hypothesis with the aim of proving or disproving it. In addition, positivist research is concerned with maximising objectivity – in other words, minimising the effect of the researcher on the research subjects and/or research context.

Aubrey et al. (2000: 33) trace the development of qualitative research as arising from a 'fundamental disquiet at the logico-positivist position which claimed a single, objective and value-free reality that could be deduced through experimental methods'. Similarly, Scheurich (1997) locates positivist research within the modernist tradition, which believes it is possible to construct universal generalisations about the world. He argues that uncertainty and ambiguity as well as the complexity of the real world are seen as needing to be *erased* from such an approach, something he sees as impossible and undesirable. Crucially, positivist research is criticised for its belief that the social world can be interpreted and categorised in a similar way to the natural world through the application of scientific theories and principles in the hands of the researcher (Hughes, 2010).

It should be noted here that research that falls within the interpretivist paradigm tends to be qualitative as opposed to quantitative in nature. This, as we will see, means the research tends to focus more on words than numbers and is smaller scale in focus. However, interpretivist researchers and positivist researchers may employ both qualitative and quantitative methods (Roberts-Holmes, 2011). As you read on, you will find out more about the qualitative methodological approach.

By way of contrast to positivist approaches to research, interpretivism is a position that emphasises gaining a detailed insight into an issue as opposed to being concerned with being able to make generalisations about the world. Furthermore, interpretivist research acknowledges that there may be multiple explanations for actions and is interested in the *meanings* people ascribe to their actions – the reasons why particular people do what they do. Hughes (2010: 41) states:

> Interpretivists argue that rather than simply *perceiving* our particular social and material circumstances, each person continually makes sense of them within a cultural framework of socially constructed and shared meanings, and that our interpretations of the world influence our behaviour in it.

 —— **REFLECTION POINT** ————————————

Let us look closely at what is being said in the quotation taken from Hughes (2010). There are some complex ideas being expressed here:

- the idea that culture impacts on the way we view the world
- the idea that within this cultural framework we develop understandings of the world *with other people*
- the idea that these understandings that we have developed about the world actually impact upon the world.

Therefore, a key idea that is being expressed is that there is not one way of understanding the world; there may be multiple interpretations of a given thing. This can be further exemplified if you think about the following questions:

- How should practitioners assess learning in the early years?
- Should young children be encouraged to play with their food?
- How should practitioners support war and weapon play in the early years (if at all)?
- Should babies and young children be given dummies (pacifiers)? Is there a 'right age' when they should stop using them?

We are sure that you are familiar with at least one of these questions either from your professional work or from your own personal background. People come to a view on questions such as these based on cultural, political and socio-economic context, personal background, historical moment, professional training and suchlike. Furthermore, how they might answer these questions may well change - we are sure your own views on some of these questions are likely to change, as do the ideas of the early childhood community itself, over time in the light of new knowledge and experience.

As you can see, this is far removed from the idea that there is one truth waiting to be discovered that remains the same for all time, as in the positivist paradigm.

WHAT DO WE MEAN BY 'CRITICAL' THEORIES IN RESEARCH?

'Critical' theories in research are – in reality – a number of related theories, which are framed around the idea that our experiences and ways of viewing the world are shaped by structures of inequality, power and domination in society. These might include anti-disablist research, queer theory, Critical Race Theory (CRT) (see Gillborn, 2006) and feminism. Researchers who frame their work in this way are looking for more than how different people interpret phenomena in their different ways, which is the key intention of interpretivists. Rather, they seek to understand, and also challenge, the social, political and economic circumstances which underpin people's experience of inequality and oppression. Thus, there will be more emphasis on people as belonging to particular social categories (such as those relating to gender, age, sexuality, 'race', social class, etc.) as opposed to people as individuals. You will notice that there is far more emphasis on social justice in this kind of research and this might also be extended to the kinds of methods the researcher employs, such as using methods which are empowering or emancipating for the participants. In this respect, we can see another example of a difference in thinking about research design from positivist researchers, whose concern is with objectivity, predictability and measurement. Far from the notion of objectivity and value-free research associated with positivism, researchers working within 'critical' theories are looking to both understand and change positions of inequality for research participants and/or social groups. Thus, we can see a different emphasis when compared with interpretivists too, as here the driver is towards enacting social change.

RESEARCH IN FOCUS

GERMANY

Kurban and Tobin (2009) examine multiple readings of a transcript of a group interview undertaken with two Turkish-German girls (aged 5 years) who attended a kindergarten in Berlin, Germany. The researchers employed a combination of theories to help them interpret the data – including Critical Race Theory and post-structuralism. The paper outlined here forms part of a wider project involving researchers from Germany, France, the UK, the USA and Italy, who worked together on a project entitled 'Children Crossing Borders'. As the title of the project suggests, the researchers' aim was to examine the experiences of immigrant families coming into early childhood settings and to explore how such settings approach working with children of recent immigrants. The aim was to enhance dialogue between immigrant families and early childhood settings and to improve ways of working with immigrant families.

The method used in the research was the 'video-cued multivocal ethnographic method' used in the 'Preschool in Three Cultures' studies (Kurban and Tobin, 2009; Tobin et al., 2009). In essence, this involves showing a piece of video of a typical session in an early childhood setting to children, parents, practitioners and the manager of a setting.

(Continued)

Here is an extract of talk from the girls' interview with Fikriye Kurban (Kurban and Tobin, 2009: 26):

Fikriye: Do you play with the German kids?

Ayla: No, we don't like them.

Fikriye: Why don't you like the German kids?

Ayla: Once I asked Lelesa if I could play with her and she did not want me. So we don't want to play with them.

Fikriye: What if they want to play with you?

Ayla: We speak Turkish. We speak Turkish so they won't understand and they will go away.

Fikriye: Do the teachers let you speak Turkish?

Selda: Yes, but not at lunchtime.

Fikriye: Why?

Selda: Because they are big. They don't understand. They don't know Turkish.

When shown the video, the girls' parents were surprised how much Turkish the girls were speaking as well as the girls' expressions of their Muslim identities in the kindergarten, such as praying - something the parents had not observed at home. One interpretation suggested by Kurban and Tobin (2009) is that perhaps this 'performance' of cultural identity in the kindergarten is a reaction to assimilationist and discriminatory discourses in wider society, which are mirrored in early childhood settings. By 'assimilationist', they are referring to the idea that the 'host country' often expects *immigrants* to change - so as to merge into the cultural and linguistic 'norms' of the majority - whereas the 'host country' itself does not change.

Kurban and Tobin (2009: 33) conclude that immigrant children are acutely aware of the struggles their cultural group is experiencing in wider society. In early childhood practice, they suggest that many white practitioners are unaware of the extent of difficulty such children and their families face and are often overwhelmed as to what their responses should be to such alienation. They state: 'the preschool is not and cannot be a site which is immune from the tensions and discourses that circulate in the larger society, and none of us are immune from reflecting and reproducing our society's discriminatory thoughts, words and actions'.

Their intention in the next phase of the research was to return to the kindergarten in which this part of the research was undertaken, to share their findings and work to support an exchange of views between staff, immigrant and non-immigrant families. Kurban and Tobin end their paper by noting the tentativeness of their interpretations of the data, but argue that it is important to attempt interpretation - to really try to listen to children's experience of religious, linguistic and cultural difference no matter how difficult this might be. The research, as you can see, is not content with merely understanding an issue: it aims at promoting social change and hence fits into the 'critical' theories discussed in this part of the chapter.

WHAT DO WE MEAN BY POST-STRUCTURALISM?

Very simply – and it is not a simple theory – post-structuralism problematises the idea that 'truth' is knowable; indeed, it often seeks to disrupt commonly held understandings of what is 'normal' and 'true' (Albon, 2011). In terms of research, the idea that the researcher can 'capture' data and arrive at the truth in some way is viewed as impossible as ideas are seen as ever changing and knowledge is regarded as uncertain. Richardson and Adams St Pierre (2005), for instance, employ the metaphor of a crystal as crystals have many facets; they are changeable and light refracts as it shines through them. Applied to a research context, this means that there are multiple ways of viewing reality and these depend on the position from which we look – a position which is ever changing. The position of the researcher is therefore very important and post-structuralist researchers will often position themselves clearly within the text so that the reader gets a sense of 'where they are coming from' and how this might have impacted on the study.

Post-structuralist research further seeks to deconstruct or 'unpick' dominant discourses and is interested in the shifting nature of power in relation to knowledge. So it might ask questions about how particular ideas gain prominence at particular times, for example that play in early childhood is related to learning or that there is a universally agreed understanding of 'normal' development which can be assessed objectively (Albon, 2011).

AUSTRALIA

RESEARCH IN FOCUS

Davies and Robinson (2010) examine issues of risk and regulation in relation to furnishing children with accurate knowledge in relation to sexuality. Their research was carried out in New South Wales, Australia and looked at sex education curricula in the region over a period of time. Part of the research involved two day care centres, with the researchers interviewing children aged 3-5 years and their parents in focus groups. The abstract to their paper follows and you will see that we have underlined some key phrases that help alert the reader to the theoretical positioning of the researchers:

ABSTRACT Children's access to sexual knowledge has always been <u>considered 'risky'</u> and <u>controversial</u> due to the fraught relationship between childhood and sexuality. Based on focus groups with children and their parents, the authors explore the relationship between risk and regulation associated with providing children with accurate knowledge about sexuality. Two main issues are examined: parents' anxieties associated with educating their children about sexuality; and how children actively build narratives around relationships and sexual knowledge based on the fragments of information available to them. The authors argue that <u>dominant constructions of childhood</u>

(Continued)

and childhood innocence negate the effective education of children around sexuality, gender and ethical relationships. Additionally, they examine the tensions that exist for many parents around the *discourse of child protection* and the ways in which this impacts on their education of young children about sexual matters.

Let us examine the phrases underlined:

- To say something is 'considered "risky" and controversial' should alert the reader as to the positioning of the researchers as 'risky' is put into inverted commas to denote that it is problematic to suggest that giving children access to sexual knowledge is risky. It is a view that can be contested.
- The idea that there are 'dominant constructions of childhood and childhood innocence' implies that childhood is not a given, but is open to interpretation and that some interpretations are more pervasive at a given time than others.
- The use of the phrase 'discourse of child protection', used as it is, alerts the reader that the researchers maintain that educating children about sexuality can be seen in *one of many* ways. One of these is that parents should protect their children from sexual knowledge and that this is a pervasive view held by many parents at the current time.

Davies and Robinson (2010) put forward compelling arguments that for children to have 'confidence, competence and resilience' (p. 259) in relation to sexual matters, parents and practitioners need to be able to have open and frank discussions about the topic. Furthermore, parents need support in how to communicate about sexuality with their children.

They conclude: 'Building a society that is more critically reflective about gendered and sexual ethical relationships, in order to contribute to new cultural norms of nonviolence and ethical relationships, needs to begin in early childhood' (p. 259). In this statement we can see that the researchers express a strong commitment to issues of social justice. Therefore, their research can also be regarded as positioned within 'critical' theories as the researchers aim at challenging inequalities and oppression – here in relation to gender and sexuality – in their research. This blurring across 'critical' and post-structuralist paradigms is important to acknowledge as it is sometimes difficult to 'fit' research neatly within one particular paradigm. Some researchers (see also Osgood [2010] who examines professionalism in early childhood) regard themselves as, for example, 'feminist post-structuralists'. This demonstrates how some ideas might be brought together and how there are constellations of ideas. By this we mean some ideas work together (as in Davies and Robinson's research featured here) and others do not sit so easily together. It would be difficult (nigh on impossible!) to argue for a piece of research to be positioned as both post-structuralist *and* positivist because the former suggests 'truth' is in permanent flux and the latter regards the truth as out there waiting to be discovered. Whilst this is quite a difficult idea to grasp for a new researcher or someone new to such thinking, these kinds of ideas gain increased prominence for students studying at MA and Doctoral levels.

QUALITATIVE RESEARCH AND EARLY CHILDHOOD STUDIES

Sometimes 'qualitative research' is used synonymously with ethnography, which means a 'description of people or cultures' (Denscombe, 2010: 79). Ethnography is an approach that has developed primarily from the anthropological tradition. The terminology associated with research methodology and methods can be a little confusing, but on the whole, 'qualitative' and 'ethnographic' approaches are similar in their philosophical underpinnings. While we recognise that research that could be described as 'ethnographic' is diverse (Jenks, 2000), it is important to note that the term is traditionally employed in relation to research with a high component of observation in terms of gathering data and is carried out over a period time; indeed sometimes a long period of time is spent 'in the field' (Denscombe, 2010). You will find out more about ethnography in Chapter 9.

The kinds of research paradigms we have outlined in this chapter lead primarily to a qualitative methodological approach and associated methods, and much of this book is devoted to qualitative studies because most likely, as early childhood students and practitioners who are new to research, you will undertake a piece of qualitative research when it comes to designing and carrying out your own research. We will now examine the characteristics of qualitative research.

CHARACTERISTICS OF QUALITATIVE RESEARCH

- The focus is on gaining detailed information often about a small population as opposed to being able to make generalisations about large numbers of people or phenomena. Denscombe (2010) uses the analogy of torchlight, which we think is a useful one. If you shine a torch up close to something, you see a small area in great detail. Alternatively, if you shine a torch some distance away, you will cover more area but you will not capture the same degree of detail. The torchlight metaphor is useful in thinking about the key differences between qualitative and quantitative research.
- There is usually a focus on *words and/or images* as opposed to numbers (Denscombe, 2010).
- Arguably there is more of a concern for the people whose experiences the researcher is attempting to represent than is present in quantitative research design (Edwards, 2010).
- There is often an emphasis on the research being carried out in a naturalistic setting as opposed to a more experimental situation as used

in positivist research. This is especially important in early childhood research, as we will see later.

- There is an emphasis on the different *meanings* people attribute to different phenomena and actions (Denzin and Lincoln, 2011; Greene and Hill, 2005). In other words, as in the Reflection Point set out earlier in the chapter, there is acknowledgement of diversity of viewpoints.
- The research *process* is sometimes seen to be as important as its outcomes.
- Ethnographic researchers, in particular, tend to describe their research as providing 'thick description'– a term first used by Gilbert Ryle (Geertz, 1973). In addition, they might aim for making the familiar *strange* (Barbour, 2008), which is useful as it encourages a questioning of taken-for-granted practices and assumptions. We will see this, in particular, when we look at ethnography in Chapter 9.
- It tends to be based on inductive reasoning as opposed to deductive reasoning (see previous chapter). For example, themes are likely to be developed *from* data collected as opposed to themes being identified a priori or *before the research has been conducted* – as in the case of experimental research designs which test hypotheses.
- Finally, and importantly, there is an acknowledgement of the *self* of the researcher (Barbour, 2008) and how this impacts upon the research, as well as how the research itself impacts upon the researcher. In research methods literature this is known as reflexivity.

REFLEXIVITY

The notion of reflexivity is a very important one in research that falls within the umbrella of qualitative research. Fine et al. (2000: 108) argue that: 'There has long been a tendency to view the self of the social science observer as a potential contaminant, something to be separated out, neutralised, minimised, standardised and controlled'.

Rather than a fixed self engaged in research, Lincoln and Guba (2000) argue that the self is fluid in the research setting and is also created in the process of the research. Reflexivity, they argue, can be linked to a process of coming to know oneself better within a research project. Reinharz (1997: 5) argues that the many selves the researcher brings to the field come into three broad categories: *research-based selves*; *brought selves* (our personal and historical baggage); and our *situationally created selves*. The following Case Study aims to develop your understanding of this further, but we will continue to think about the self of the researcher in later chapters.

— 🔍 —— **CASE STUDY** ————————————————————————

Caitlin, an early childhood studies student, carried out a piece of research looking at how nursery nurses working in school settings perceive their role. She had both a personal and professional interest in the subject matter as she too had been a nursery nurse in both nursery and reception classes in a school for many years prior to going to university. This was the 'brought self', to use Reinharz's (1997) category, that Caitlin brought to the research.

Caitlin recognised that she had 'inside' knowledge of the role that gave her a degree of status and familiarity with the nursery nurses in the study that would not have been there had she not shared their professional background. While this familiarity was useful as the nursery nurses in the study seemed to be comfortable in opening up to Caitlin when being interviewed about their work, Caitlin also recognised that there was exploitative potential in their shared professional background. She felt that there were occasions when the nursery nurses were less guarded than they might have been with another researcher and noted that some of the nursery nurses in the study used phrases such as 'of course, you know what it's like too' that demonstrated a shared sense of solidarity. On some occasions she found it very difficult to maintain a degree of objectivity because she related to many of the stories told about their professional work. In carrying out research and employing her skills as an interviewer, Caitlin brought her 'research-based self' (Reinharz, 1997) to the research.

In writing up the study, Caitlin acknowledged her shared professional background and reflected on the impact it made on the research. She also acknowledged the way that the research had encouraged her to think in new ways about her previous work as a nursery nurse in a school and indeed her subsequent career in early childhood education and care. During and after the research, Caitlin herself changed, which could be linked to Reinharz's (1997) notion of a 'situationally created self'. As Lincoln and Guba (2000) observe, she came to know herself better through the process of the research.

RESEARCH IN 'NATURALISTIC' SETTINGS

Qualitative research in early childhood tends to be carried out in a naturalistic setting. But what do we mean by a 'naturalistic' setting and why might this be especially important in early childhood research?

Dunn's (2005) research looks at young children in the context of their home environment. Unlike the experimental conditions set up by theorists such as Piaget, for instance, which took children away from the environment with which they were familiar in order to conduct the tests, Dunn (2005: 87) emphasises the following:

- the need to carry out research that acknowledges how children grow and develop in complex social worlds
- the need to carry out research in situations that have emotional significance for young children
- the need to observe children in the context of their everyday lives as opposed to studying their responses to experimental situations.

These three aspects of her work would be impossible to replicate in strictly experimental conditions. While Dunn's research has sometimes involved observing children within the home, there are other contexts that could be described under the umbrella of a 'naturalistic setting'. These might include the nursery a child attends regularly, for instance. However, as Albon and Rosen (2014) have argued, it is important to think critically about the word 'natural' – hence our consistent use of inverted commas around 'naturalistic' from this point on in this book. We look at this in some depth in Chapter 9 when we examine ethnography, as conducting research in a setting which is usual or 'natural' to participants is a key characteristic of such research. However, here we wish to highlight how what is 'natural' in one socio-economic or cultural-historic context may not be in another. If we think about Dunn's (2005) research carried out in families' homes, then there will be inevitable differences between each of these homes and we should not make assumptions as to what is 'normal' or 'natural' in relation to home and family life.

This said, we can observe that, unlike an experimental situation, the child or group of children are not asked to deviate too much from *the place(s) they are used to, what they usually do or who they are usually with*. This is because the researcher tries, as far as possible, not to disturb the setting. Inevitably, however, researchers do impact upon research settings, as the earlier discussion about reflexivity encouraged you to consider. Those of you who have carried out observations in a nursery know that your presence probably has some impact on the children's behaviour. This impact might take the form of some of the following examples:

- The children may stop what they are doing and come and talk with you.
- The children may move away from the area.
- The children may appear to be self-conscious in their play, looking over at you for approval.
- The children may become highly interested in the way you are recording your observations, for example making notes or using a video camera.

There are many factors at work here, not least the degree of familiarity the children have with you as a researcher. If you are a practitioner in the setting, then the children are likely to be very familiar with you making observational notes on individuals and groups of children. Researchers who are external to a setting will often visit a nursery, for example, many times in order that the children and adults in the setting become familiar with their presence and thus their presence does not *unduly* affect the play observed (albeit that we suggest adult presence will always have some impact on play).

RESEARCH IN FOCUS

Let us now think about the importance of carrying out research in 'naturalistic' settings – or settings familiar to participants – in relation to early childhood research. We will also consider the limitations of doing this.

The work of Mary Ainsworth in relation to attachment is characterised by the need for controlling variables and standardisation with regards to conducting her research (Ainsworth and Bell, 1970; Ainsworth et al., 1978). The research involved introducing babies to a 'strange situation', which involved the following:

- A 20-minute session in which a mother and a baby are introduced to a researcher and a playroom (one they are unfamiliar with in order that it is the same for each baby and mother).
- Then, the mother is asked to leave the room for 3 minutes and the baby is left with the researcher. The mother then comes back into the playroom.
- When the mother returns and is reunited with their baby, the mother and the researcher both leave the room at the same time.
- Then, the mother and baby are reunited.

This process is videotaped and the baby's responses are given a rating. Ainsworth identified four main patterns of response:

- secure-attachment
- insecure-avoidant
- insecure-ambivalent (insecure-resistant)
- insecure-disorganised.

Holmes's (1993) book provides a useful summary of the research for those of you that wish to read further. In addition, Woodhead and Faulkner (2008) provide a thought-provoking critique of the research in terms of ethics. They question whether carrying out research where a baby is placed in a strange room, then left with a stranger (the researcher) and then left on their own is ethical. They also question the ethics of the researcher(s) dispassionately measuring the responses of the baby during what is possibly a distressing experience. We look at ethics in research in some detail in the next chapter.

(Continued)

Hatch (1995) believes that qualitative researchers would approach research in the area of attachment in a very different way to Ainsworth, studying the interactions between caregivers and children in 'naturalistic' settings such as nurseries, homes or maternity wards, for instance. Their approach would be more likely to focus on the shared meanings young children and their caregivers construct together within a particular environment. Hatch (1995: 125) states: 'The best contexts for research that takes seriously the study of childhood as a social construction are settings in which naturally occurring social behaviour is observed in natural surroundings'.

In this Research in Focus section we can see that researchers working within the positivist paradigm will differ as to how they approach and judge research about attachment when compared with those working within the paradigms discussed in this chapter. Each is likely to approach research on attachment in different ways. Positivists, as in the Ainsworth research, would be keen to control any variables in the research; for example, the environment (the playroom), the length of time the mother leaves the baby, the effect of the researcher, the sequence of the research and suchlike. This is useful in enabling others to replicate the research conditions and may be regarded as more reliable than a more qualitative methodological approach.

Alternatively, the approach that might be taken by qualitative researchers is one that is likely to prefer a 'naturalistic' setting – a setting that the baby feels comfortable in and that reflects the unpredictability of everyday life. We might regard this approach as more ethical as it is likely to involve less distress to the baby. Moreover, we might view the resulting data as more reflective of everyday attachment behaviour owing to the research being carried out in an everyday context. In this sense, it too could be regarded as valid and reliable research, albeit in a different way. It should be noted that for interpretivists authenticity is gained when the 'true' voice of the research participants shines through (Hughes, 2010). For researchers working within 'critical' theories such as feminist research, the focus of attachment-based research might be on gendered assumptions about 'attachment', perhaps also challenging the dyadic nature of attachment that is sometimes put forward (Wallbank, 2001).

Finally here, another argument in favour of qualitative research in relation to early childhood studies is that it is more in keeping with what is sometimes known as 'the new childhood studies' (Mayall, 1999). This is a perspective that sees children as social actors with their own experiences and understandings of childhood (Farrell et al., 2002) and emphasises that children are able to be competent participants in research (Albon and Rosen, 2014). Positivist research and the quantitative tradition have tended to emphasise children's 'otherness' and developmental immaturity (James et al., 1998), and, because of this, young children are sometimes viewed as less reliable research participants when compared with adults. Underpinning such a position is a view of childhood as an unstable, less fixed state compared with adulthood (Lee, 2001), which results in a privileging of adult perspectives over those of children (Robinson and Kellett, 2004) – we would add especially *very young* children. These are significant issues for early childhood research and you will find that Chapters 6 and 7 of this book explore these questions in more depth.

QUALITATIVE RESEARCH APPROACHES AND METHODS

In Chapter 4, we argued that the researcher's choice of paradigm underpins the methodological approach taken in the research, and this, in turn, influences the methods they choose to use in their research. Earlier in this chapter we noted some of the key characteristics of qualitative research. We noted that interpretivist, 'critical' and post-structuralist researchers tend to use primarily, if not exclusively, *qualitative* research approaches and methods. Edwards (2010) warns us not to consider qualitative research as a 'soft' or 'easy' option and we would certainly want to echo this view. Edwards maintains that *all* qualitative research will involve the researcher in 'getting to grips with the complexities of the social world of early childhood' (p. 117). Parts 3 and 4 of this book look at approaches to research and methods in more depth but here we want to highlight a few of those most used within the qualitative research tradition. These can be summarised as follows.

ACTION RESEARCH

Action research may employ both quantitative and qualitative methods in tandem. Action research usually involves participants as researchers, such as a group of nursery staff working together in order to make *improvements* to an area of their practice. These participants will often be led by a member of the team or possibly an outside researcher working with them. The key focus, however, is on facilitating change in a particular setting and often within the participants themselves, and in this sense it is usually *small-scale* in focus with no aim at making generalisations about the world.

ETHNOGRAPHY

Ethnographic research involves spending a long period of time immersed in a particular setting such as a nursery in order to gain detailed insights about the research participants' lives. In order to carry out ethnographic research, the researcher often becomes a participant in the setting in order to become a familiar face, able to observe people's behaviour in as 'naturalistic' a setting as possible.

CASE STUDIES

Case study research, as the name suggests, focuses on a case or a series of cases. A 'case' might be a family, a children's centre, a child or a local authority, for example. Crucially, the emphasis is on developing a detailed understanding of the 'case' under study.

OBSERVATION

Research methods such as observation may also fall within the umbrella of qualitative research, although not exclusively. Observation may involve an element of 'number crunching', such as counting the number of children who visit the book area in a given day. However, narrative observation, which focuses on the 'rich description', is *qualitative* in nature.

INTERVIEWING

Like observation, there are different types of interviewing. If interviewing a subject with a set of highly structured questions, which allow for little or no deviation beyond yes/no answers coupled with a large number of respondents, then this research may well be described as quantitative in nature, thus falling within the positivist paradigm. Usually, interviews that are carried out face to face are semi-structured or sometimes unstructured, to enable the researcher to capture as much detail as possible.

 —— ACTIVITY ———————————————————————————

What differences can you see between the qualitative approaches to research discussed here and the experimental designs outlined in Chapters 1 and 4? We have started to fill in a table for you in order to summarise the key differences. Now continue to fill this in or keep it next to you as you read further.

(Continued)

(Continued)

Table 5.1 Quantitative versus qualitative approaches to research

Experimental designs/quantitative approaches to research	Qualitative approaches to research
A concern with measurement/numbers	A concern with words
Researcher aims at objectivity – another researcher should be able to repeat the research and get the same results	Greater emphasis on subjectivity – the self of the researcher is bound up with the research (especially in 'critical' and post-structuralist paradigms)
Conducted in a carefully controlled environment – an emphasis on controlling variables	Impossible to control the environment in the 'real world' – so the aim is to research in a 'naturalistic' (or usual) setting
Will often test a hypothesis (deductive)	Will see what information emerges in the course of the research (inductive)
Seeks generalisability and the ability to predict behaviour	Usually seeks detailed and contextual data
Can you add more points here?	

COMBINING QUALITATIVE AND QUANTITATIVE RESEARCH METHODS

So far Chapters 4 and 5 of this book may have given the impression that qualitative and quantitative research cannot be combined owing to their bases in different philosophical positions. There are different viewpoints on this as this section aims to demonstrate.

Aubrey et al. (2000) argue that quantitative and qualitative research should not be viewed as in opposition with each other (see also Clough and Nutbrown, 2012). They believe that they are *complementary* to one another or might be indicative of *different stages* in the process of conducting a piece of research. Thus, some research involves a combination of quantitative methods, such as a structured questionnaire, and qualitative methods, such as semi-structured interviews. Using more than one method to obtain information is known as triangulation, whereby the strengths of one method compensate for the weaknesses of another. However, it can mean far more than this. Kasunic (2005: 15) describes the purpose of triangulation as being to 'obtain confirmation of findings through convergence of different perspectives. The point at which the perspectives converge is seen to represent reality'. This might also be done through using more than one researcher; more than one theory; or more than one methodological approach (Denzin, cited in Edwards, 2001).

There are a range of ways that combining quantitative and qualitative methods might be useful:

- Carrying out a detailed, small-scale pilot study, for example, to see how successful a new reading scheme is, then later, extending this to a large scale and carrying out a quantitative analysis to assess how successful it has been with a larger group.
- Conducting a large-scale survey, for example, to gain some general information about parents' views on paediatric services in a hospital and then carrying out some focus group interviews with small groups of parents to ascertain their views in more detail.
- In a piece of action research looking at improving the use of the block play area in a nursery class, for example, the researcher might carry out some detailed narrative observations as well as something more quantitative, such as counting the number of children who use the block play area during a week in comparison to other areas of the nursery room.

— 🔍 —— CASE STUDY

Jason is writing a research proposal and knows he wants to do a piece of research in the baby room of the setting within which he works to improve the outdoor experiences on offer to the children. Furthermore, he wants his research to tune into the perspectives of the babies in his setting through observing them closely as he is passionate about the idea of democracy in the nursery and seeing very young children as competent social actors.

But Jason is struggling to make sense of the difference between terms like 'paradigm', 'methodology' and 'methods'. How do these terms 'fit' into what he wants to do?

In terms of paradigm, we would argue that his commitment to democracy in this nursery and associated with this, his perception of the child as a competent social actor positions his research as 'critical'. He is not seeking an objective, knowable truth as positivist researchers would argue for; nor is he merely seeking a detailed understanding of a topic as interpretivists would advocate. He wants to transform practice and more particularly wants to challenge the inequitable position of children within the context of his practice. Jason is someone who works with these babies and is passionate about opening up the nursery as a democratic space, thus he is not neutral/objective about the topic; he is inseparable from the topic.

In terms of methodology, Jason has indicated that he wants to employ observations as a research strategy. But observations are a method and not a methodological approach. He uses the term 'observing them closely' which implies that he intends to undertake some detailed narrative observations with few participants (the babies) as opposed to

(Continued)

(Continued)

using a structured observation sheet with many participants. Also, the research is to be undertaken in the baby room of one setting so is small scale and 'naturalistic'; he does not intend to conduct an experiment. Taking these points together, this strongly suggests that the research is *qualitative*.

Finally, and very simply, when Jason is talking about methodology he needs to be talking about whether his research design is quantitative, qualitative or a mix of the two. When he goes on to talk about methods he needs to talk about the tools he is using to gather data. In this case, he has chosen to use *observations*. Most likely his research will employ an action research approach (you will read more about this in Chapter 11) too, which may use multiple methods. Action research is sometimes talked of as a 'method' although we tend to describe it as an *approach* to research, potentially employing a number of methods.

Like all new researchers Jason is getting to grips with some unfamiliar terminology and ideas. One of the things a tutor will be looking for is whether there is coherence between research focus, paradigm, methodology and methods. Jason would seem to have a good fit here.

However, had he had the same research focus and set up an experimental design (objective, neutral, replicable - underpinned by positivism) there would be a mismatch between his espoused intentions for the research and underpinning paradigm. Similarly, if he states his research is qualitative in terms of methodology and then goes on to say he will use structured questionnaires (e.g. to elicit practitioners' views on the topic area) the various strands of his research would not sit together comfortably. Moreover, if he did this he would be abandoning the idea that he could tune into the babies' perspectives and open up the nursery as a democratic space - perhaps challenging the idea that babies cannot speak for themselves in some way. Perhaps think of a metaphor which works for you to help you visualise this, such as a jigsaw with pieces which should fit well together.

So far in this section, we have shown how qualitative and quantitative approaches might be combined. But before concluding this chapter, it is important to note that not all writers believe it is advisable or even *possible* to combine methods from the quantitative and qualitative traditions successfully. For Denzin and Lincoln (2011), this is owing to the differences inherent in their underpinning philosophies and the greater status sometimes attributed to quantitative research methods. As you may recall, positivism and the quantitative research tradition have their basis in the idea that research can uncover *truths* about the world; that is, that the world is knowable and can be measured and categorised, with findings generalised to a large population. As the paradigms outlined in this chapter have shown, there are other ways of conceptualising claims to knowledge, which have their basis in the belief that there are multiple 'truths' and ways of seeing the world and that these are specific to particular people in particular places (Hughes, 2010).

 ——— KEY POINTS FROM THE CHAPTER ———

- Interpretivism developed as a response to positivism, which was criticised for its belief that we can make generalisations about the world. By way of contrast, interpretivism is a position that tends to focus on the meanings people attribute to phenomena and actions.
- 'Critical' theories, such as feminist theorising, aim at interrogating inequalities and oppression relating to people's economic and social position with a view to bringing about change in relation to inequalities of, for example, social class, 'race', gender, sexuality and generation.
- Post-structuralist research aims at examining the shifting relationship between knowledge and power and aims to unsettle taken-for-granted 'truths' about the world.
- The paradigms in this chapter lend themself to qualitative research approaches and methods.
- Qualitative research focuses on gaining a detailed understanding of a small sample or case and often emphasises the need to carry out research in *'naturalistic'* settings as opposed to *experimental* conditions.
- The self of the researcher (subjectivity) is viewed as important in qualitative approaches to research, which can be contrasted with positivism, which tends to aim at objectivity and the neutralising of what is commonly referred to as 'researcher effect'.
- The researcher's choice of paradigm impacts on the methodology and methods they use in their research. In qualitative research, for instance, observations (especially narrative observation) and interviewing are often employed.
- Quantitative and qualitative approaches to research may be combined successfully in order to enhance a research project – gaining 'the best of both worlds'. Triangulation is a term used to denote the way that combining methodologies, methods, different researchers and different theories can help the researcher to arrive at a reasonably clear understanding of their research area (Denzin, cited in Edwards, 2001). Post-structuralists would argue that such a 'fixed point' and certainty of knowledge is problematic (Albon, 2011).

-------------------- **FURTHER READING** --------------------

Hughes, P. (2010) 'Paradigms, methods and knowledge', in G. MacNaughton, S. Rolfe and I. Siraj-Blatchford (eds) *Doing Early Childhood Research: International Perspectives on Theory and Practice*, 2nd edition. Maidenhead: OUP. This chapter explores four paradigms using exemplars from different research projects focused on young children and the media.

Reinharz, S. (1997) 'Who am I? The need for a variety of selves in the field', in R. Hertz (ed.) *Reflexivity and Voice*. London: Sage. This is a very interesting chapter that looks at the issue of reflexivity in some depth.

Don't forget to visit the online resources at https://study.sagepub.com/mukherjiandalbon3e for access to free SAGE journal articles, weblinks, videos, exercises, mini quizzes and an interactive glossary.

6
ETHICS

- To develop an understanding of ethics and why a consideration of ethics is important in research.
- To consider ethics in early childhood research, in particular the notion of 'informed consent'.
- To develop an understanding of how ethical considerations need to be thought through in relation to the whole research process.
- To consider professional and legal guidelines in relation to ethics.

This chapter examines a crucial aspect of research: ethics. *All* research involves a consideration of ethics, and early childhood research, it could be argued, needs to be particularly mindful of ethics owing to the age and vulnerability of children from birth to 8 years. This said, alongside consideration for the vulnerability of young children, we also want to stress children's competence and ability to participate in research – something we focus on in more depth in Chapter 7. This chapter comes in this early section of the book owing to our belief that a careful consideration of ethical issues is of *central* importance to any research project.

WHAT DO WE MEAN BY 'ETHICS'?

Many of you reading this book will have heard the word 'ethics' used in relation to a wide range of contexts. You may have read about medical ethics debates in areas such as embryo technology, euthanasia and human cell cloning. You may also have thought about ethics in relation to other issues, such as testing products on animals or the responsibility human beings have in relation to exacerbating global warming.

Reality television programmes may have also encouraged you to think about ethics. There are occasions when participants in programmes such as these are put in positions of extreme stress in the particular situations they find themselves in. This might include physical stress, such as having little food, or mental stress, such as being ridiculed or being compelled to take part in activities seemingly against their better judgement. In addition to this, the participants are being filmed and observed – sometimes 24 hours a day – by a large watching public. While programme makers might argue that people give their consent to being a participant on one of these shows and are fully informed about what might happen and possibly even screened for mental illness, it is questionable whether everyone comes away from the experience unscathed.

For those of you who work or have worked directly with young children and families, you may think about ethics in relation to your professional work. Indeed Aubrey et al. (2000) argue that teachers – and we would broaden this to all early years practitioners – are making decisions every day, moment by moment, that have ethical considerations at their heart. As you can see, 'ethics' is a term that is used across a broad range of contexts.

 ACTIVITY

Reflect on the work of an early childhood practitioner working with young children and families. Construct a list of the ethical issues with which they are confronted on a regular basis. Here are a few ideas to start you off:

(Continued)

- storing information about families carefully in order to preserve confidentiality
- ensuring the practice in the nursery is anti-discriminatory
- listening and acting upon children's ideas about what they would like to do.

But our concern in this book is with *research*. So what does 'ethics' mean in relation to research? Aubrey et al. (2000: 156) define ethics as, 'The moral philosophy or set of moral principles underpinning a project'.

Over time, ethical considerations in research have become more important. Clearly, research with human and animal subjects needs to involve acting in a moral way. As Greig et al. (2007) note, the label 'researcher' does not mean we can act in ways considered not moral or ethical. Yet abuses have occurred in the name of 'research' and these have led to greater regulation over what is ethical or not in research practice. A clear example of this can be seen in the Nazi experimentation on twins in which around 1,500 sets of twins, some of them children, were subjected to horrific experiments with the aim of seeing if the Aryan race, which was considered superior by the Nazis, could multiply more quickly. Many twins died in the process of this research and many more were subjected to torturous experiments. Experimentation such as this came under scrutiny during the Nuremberg Trials that followed the Second World War from 1945 to 1949. There was public shock and condemnation at what had occurred in the name of 'research' and the Nuremberg Code was developed to make clear the legal, moral and ethical principles that should govern *any* research involving human beings (Greig et al., 2007).

But despite the Nuremberg Code and other subsequent legislation, such as the Helsinki Declaration in 1964, research still comes under the spotlight and raises questions about ethics to the present day (Greig et al., 2007). Infamous studies have drawn wider attention to the issue of ethics.

RESEARCH IN FOCUS

USA

Milgram's experiments, carried out between 1963 and 1974, have gained a level of notoriety in relation to ethics. His research looks at the issue of obedience to authority. Individuals were asked to act one at a time as 'teachers' to another person, who was, in fact, someone working with the research team unbeknown to them. The 'teachers' were required to administer an electric shock to their 'students' if they did not respond correctly to their verbal learning tasks. The electric shocks increased with severity throughout the experiment as 'wrong' answers were given. More than 1,000 'teachers' from various backgrounds took part in the research and Milgram reports how 67 per cent administered the most severe electric shock to their 'students' during the experiments, despite being told how dangerous it was.

(Continued)

(Continued)

For Milgram, this meant that people have a tendency to obey authority even if that means doing something that is regarded as wrong. The research is reported in many research methods texts, such as Cohen et al. (2000).

Of course the electric shocks administered were not real, but the 'teachers', that is the research subjects, did not know this – indeed, the 'students' acted as if they were in pain when the shocks were administered. As you read on, consider the ethical implications of a study like this and why it has become infamous in its disregard for the people who acted as research subjects.

Robson (2011a: 200) encourages the reader to reflect upon ten questionable practices in social research. These are as follows:

- involving people without their knowledge or consent
- coercing them to participate
- withholding information about the true nature of the research
- otherwise deceiving the participant
- inducing them to commit acts diminishing their self-esteem
- violating rights of self-determination (e.g. in studies seeking to promote individual change)
- exposing participants to physical or mental stress
- invading their privacy
- withholding benefits from some participants (e.g. in comparison groups)
- not treating participants fairly, or with consideration, or with respect.

Some of these ten questionable practices can be applied to the research discussed in the previous Research in Focus section. The research participants did not know the true nature of the research; they were deceived about who the other research participants were; that is, they did not know they were actors and that they were acting feeling pain; and the research is very likely to have diminished the participants' sense of self-esteem because after the research was over they had to live with themselves in the knowledge that they were capable of following orders to the extent that they might inflict pain on others (Barbour, 2008; Cohen et al., 2000).

While this example involves adults, we can apply Robson's (2011a) ten questionable practices to *early childhood* research. In doing this, we will be reflecting upon conceptualisations and the subsequent status of young children.

WHY IS A CONSIDERATION OF ETHICS IMPORTANT IN EARLY CHILDHOOD RESEARCH?

Greig et al. (2007) maintain that inexperienced researchers are able to practise designing research instruments such as questionnaires and interview schedules. However, they go on to argue that ethics is an area that should never be learned in practice. While it is important that researchers think carefully about the ethical issues that relate to their topic, research has a tendency to be more 'messy' than this suggests (Albon and Rosen, 2014; Greig et al., 2007).

Researchers also need to be especially heedful of young children's vulnerability. With this in mind, Coady (2010: 73) states that children are 'heavily represented among victims of research'. Even well-meaning researchers can cause harm to child subjects of research. An infamous example of this, cited by Coady, is that of 'Genie' (a pseudonym), a 13-year-old child from Los Angeles, who was found to have been deprived of any human contact for most of her life. This lack of human contact meant that her language skills were severely restricted. For some researchers, this meant that Genie was an 'ideal' subject for research into whether there is a sensitive period for learning a language. When the grant for the research ran out and the researchers had got what they wanted – furthering their own careers in the process – Genie was returned to poor care arrangements. Thus, the principle of beneficence to the research participants was overtaken by a concern for the research itself.

 —— ACTIVITY ———————————————————————

Investigate the website below where you can find out more about how the research was conducted, and what happened subsequently to Genie:

www.verywell.com/genie-the-story-of-the-wild-child-2795241 (accessed 16 July 2017)

There are many websites and video materials available about Genie, but we have rejected much of these as voyeuristic and sensationalist. As you think about Genie's story, reflect on the ethical issues raised by the research and her care.

It would seem that the vulnerability and 'otherness' associated with being younger, less experienced and physically smaller can also result in a view of young children as an *object* of research as opposed to a feeling *subject*. Woodhead and Faulkner (2008) seem to be implying this in relation to the research carried out by Mary Ainsworth in relation to attachment, which we discussed in Chapter 5. Coady (2010) relates this lack of consideration for research participants to research carried out on indigenous peoples in the nineteenth century, in which they were viewed as less human or as objects in some way. Thus, while the relative positionings of adult and child are not universal and are constantly changing (Albon and Rosen, 2014; Connolly, 2008), what is important to foreground here is the powerful position held by adult researchers as 'experts' in the study of young children (Woodhead and Faulkner, 2008). In addition to this, Lahman (2008: 282) argues that such power imbalances are further accentuated by 'intersecting marginalities', which are present when white, able-bodied, adult researchers, for example, carry out research on young, Black and minority-ethnic children, or children with disabilities.

Although this discussion has so far focused on the vulnerability of children, we also want to stress a view of the child as *competent*, something we explore in more depth in the next chapter, where we will be arguing that the researcher's perception of the child underpins the extent to which s/he believes they are able to fully participate in research. Lahman (2008: 285) sums up the idea that researchers can hold a view of the child as both vulnerable and competent at the same time by stating, 'I believe both the notions of competent and vulnerable, worded as *competent yet vulnerable child* may be held simultaneously as a way of considering the unique position of children' (original emphasis).

This section has encouraged you to begin to think about how conceptualisations of the child impact upon research. In particular, it has focused on the relative power of adults in relation to children. One of the ways that this imbalance of power can be seen is in the notion of informed consent.

WHAT DOES 'INFORMED CONSENT' MEAN IN THE CONTEXT OF EARLY CHILDHOOD RESEARCH?

A key term in research ethics is 'informed consent'. This means that the participants in the research give their consent to the research and fully understand the following:

- what the purposes of the research are
- why they have been asked to take part in the research
- how their involvement fits into the research as a whole
- what they will be asked to do, for example be part of a focus group interview, as well as how long this commitment is for; for instance, in a case study it may be for a few months, whereas in a one-off interview it may be for half an hour
- their right for information about the research before, during and following the data collection

- that all names of individuals and institutions will remain anonymous
- their right to withdraw from the research at any point
- how the data will be recorded
- where the data will be stored and how
- who will see the data – what it will be used for.

Initially, researchers will often do this in the form of a letter, which they ask the participants in the study to sign. The assumption that underpins this is that everyone who has signed their consent fully understands the information on the form they have signed. Robson (2011a) maintains that there are particular ethical issues raised in relation to informed consent when working with vulnerable groups such as children, particularly very young children. This is because it may be difficult for them to fully understand every aspect of the research. However, we would argue that children are far more competent than this suggests, especially if adults take the trouble to ensure they explain things in a clear and understandable way. Most very young children and babies are not in a position to *sign* a consent form and they are unlikely to understand many aspects of the research in advance of it actually happening. However, this consent should still be negotiated respectfully as we will see later in the chapter. Furthermore, ethical guidance (see British Educational Research Association, 2011) clearly puts the onus on researchers to facilitate children's informed consent.

Researchers working with children and babies usually have to ask the children's parents or guardians for written permission to carry out the research. In addition, if the research is to be carried out in a school or hospital or similar, permission will usually have to be granted by someone or a group of people in a position of power, who act to protect the individuals within their institutions.

Increasingly, researchers have to get their proposal agreed by an ethics committee (see later), for instance at the university where they are studying. The people who have the power to say 'yes' or 'no' in relation to whether research with children should go ahead or not – be they parents or professionals – are often called 'gatekeepers'. Research involving very young children will be scrutinised carefully by ethics committees owing to perceptions of the vulnerability of this group.

— 🔍 —— CASE STUDY ————————————————————

Hamdi is a university student who wishes to undertake a research project in a baby room of a nursery setting. She wishes to look at the different ways in which the babies and educators communicate in the course of a nursery day. Who might be the 'gatekeepers' in Hamdi's research?

(Continued)

(Continued)

In considering this example, there are likely to be a number of 'gatekeepers':

- Her university tutor will want to talk through the research and may insist that Hamdi fills out an ethics form. Until this is signed off she may not be permitted to undertake the research.
- Hamdi will need to write to the setting's manager to ask permission.
- There are staff members who work in the baby room with whom to negotiate access.
- Hamdi will need to ask parents for permission to undertake the observations.
- And last but not least there are the children themselves. Hamdi needs to consider how she will negotiate the consent of the babies.

Although it is important to gain the consent of key adults or 'gatekeepers' for research to be carried out (and some children may be able to understand and sign to demonstrate they consent to research being carried out), it is important to be clear that we *do* think young children's direct consent should be sought. Many research texts, when they talk about gaining the direct consent of children, do not seem to consider what this issue means for research with *very* young children and babies. Inevitably, in practice it means something different when compared with research with the majority of children of secondary school age, for instance. Christensen and Prout (2002) offer a useful conceptualisation of this in their discussion of 'ethical symmetry' in research.

The term 'ethical symmetry' (Christensen and Prout, 2002) is derived from a key principle: that children and adults should be afforded *equal considerations* in research as human beings. However, when it comes to carrying out research in situ, researchers may then have to adjust their research practice to suit the abilities and interests of research participants (children and adults alike). Thus, key principles in research are the same for children and adults but may look different in practice. An example of this might be the right to withdraw consent to research – a right which should be available to all research participants.

Many adults would be able to read and sign a consent letter making clear that they do or do not wish to participate in a research project and may do this on behalf of their child(ren). But Langston et al. (2004) demonstrate that very young children and babies are able to give or withdraw their consent to research. They might do this in a variety of ways, such as:

- refusing to engage with the researcher
- becoming abnormally quiet
- turning away and crying (or sounding distressed)
- refusing to engage with any materials used in the study.

Therefore the researcher needs to be sensitive to the moment in order to pick up on the child's cues. If engaged in research somewhere where the children do not know the researcher, it is important that the insights of parents, carers and practitioners who work there are taken into account. This is because their greater knowledge of the children is crucial in monitoring any changes in the child's behaviour. In this sense, negotiating consent with babies and young children should happen on a *moment-by-moment* basis (Langston et al., 2004). Researchers also need to be mindful that children are sometimes keen to please adults and may not obviously look as if they are distressed. Again, the insights of adults and children who know the child better are invaluable. Therefore, informed consent should be regarded in terms of *ongoing negotiation* as opposed to something that is agreed to purely in advance or 'achieved' (Albon and Rosen, 2014). In terms of 'ethical symmetry', children's right to give or withdraw consent to research as a key research principle is honoured but the particularities of children in specific situations are taken into account in the actual context of undertaking the research.

 —— **REFLECTION POINT** ——————————————

We should also remember that it is not only young children that are vulnerable in early childhood research. Many adults are vulnerable too and they may well be participants in a piece of early childhood research. Reflect on the issue of informed consent in a study in which a nursery manager asks the following individuals for their views on the quality of care for babies in the nursery:

- a parent who is an asylum seeker
- a mother who is in prison
- an early years practitioner working in the setting where the research is being carried out
- a 16-year-old woman who has just given birth to her first baby and has come into the nursery for a few 'drop ins'
- a father who has had three children come through the nursery over the last few years.

In reflecting on the issues raised in the Reflection Point, you may have thought of similar points to those that we will highlight here.

- A parent who is an asylum seeker may be worried that if they say 'no' to participating in the research, the nursery place for their baby may be taken away from them (especially if they have had poor experiences in their former country of residence).
- A mother who is in prison is quite literally captive and it may be very difficult to say 'no' to a study when so many of her other freedoms have been taken away from her.
- A different issue is presented by the early years practitioner who is working in the setting. In this instance, the practitioner might feel unable to say 'no' to participating in the research because it is her line manager who is carrying out the research – it would be easier to say 'no' to an outside researcher.
- The 16-year-old woman who has just given birth to her first baby might be vulnerable owing to issues of relative age difference and the 'expertise' of the manager. Furthermore, in a similar way to the first example, if she did not consent to the research, she may be concerned that she appears as uncooperative before she even begins to access the nursery's services regularly.
- Finally, the father who has had a few children come through the nursery may find it difficult to say 'no' because he feels he owes the nursery something – after all, three of his children have attended the nursery.

A common denominator in all five examples is the issue of power; that is, the differentials in power between the researcher and the research participants. This is something to reflect upon in any research project. However, remember too that people are often very happy to participate in a piece of research, especially if they are confident that you have their best interests at heart and that in some way their participation will make a positive contribution to something they view as important. The issue of research being of some *positive* benefit is sometimes called 'beneficence' and is an important principle to hold onto in research.

We should remember that vulnerability also extends to the researcher. In carrying out research, it is important to take care *who* you are going to see and where you will see them (Robson, 2011a). If interviewing a person who is completely unknown to you, it might be wise to conduct the interview in a public space where there are other people nearby rather than privately in the person's own accommodation. This, however, might impact on how comfortable a person feels during an interview and the type of data that might be obtained. Nevertheless, we raise the issue of researcher vulnerability because personal safety is also an ethical concern.

Before moving on to consider how ethical issues should be considered throughout the research process, we want to point out that gaining consent can raise a number of dilemmas for the researcher. Warming (2005) argues that in her research, which involved participant observation of young children in a nursery, she felt it was important, as a principle, that the children knew that she was a researcher who was carrying out a particular research project. But in practice, she came to the conclusion that she would inform children as and when they asked who she was and what she was doing. In this way, she felt she would be responding to the children's individual needs and interests in a more ethical way than by informing them as a group – the underpinning assumption being that the children would be as interested in the research as the researcher. Warming (2005: 62) discusses her dilemma, saying 'the most ethical practice might turn out to be unethical'.

RESEARCH IN FOCUS

ENGLAND

An example of Warming's notion of responding to children's individual needs and interests in relation to research can be seen in Debbie Albon's (see e.g. 2007, 2009) research looking at food and eating in early childhood settings.

Debbie has spent a few years now carrying out observations in four early childhood settings. In one setting, a child of 3 years whom we will call Avleen became very interested in the observational notes she was making. Here is an extract of the conversation held between them:

Avleen: Are you writing again? [She had often observed me writing.]

Debbie: Yes - I'm writing about what I see in the home corner again. [I have been coming to the setting for two terms.]

Avleen: Did you write about me yesterday?

Debbie: Well ... not really - not like this. To write observations of what you are actually doing I have to be able to see you.

Avleen: What does that say? [Pointing to my writing]

Debbie: It says 'K ... says "I'll go and have my drink now"'.

Avleen: K ... just said that.

Debbie: I know. I found it interesting, so I wrote it down ... here. [Avleen looks intently at the observational notes made.]

Debbie wrote about this extensively in her research journal. Here is one of many extracts that relate to this from her journal:

Avleen asked about lots of other notes in my fieldwork book and borrowed my pen to write her own notes on my pages. I must share this observation of her interest in writing with practitioners and her mum. She has shown a lot of interest in the research process and seeks me out to ask me about it - other children are keen to play with me, e.g. in the home corner, but are not so bothered about what I am writing and why - even though I do this very openly. Children, like adults, will be more drawn to some things than others and research is no different.

INCLUSIVE RESEARCH WITH CHILDREN

In research as in early childhood practice it is also too easy to ignore the perspectives of disabled children or those children who do not share the same language as the researcher and to privilege the voices of those deemed 'more competent' (Davis et al., 2008). But this raises ethical issues as the following Case Study shows.

— 🔍 —— CASE STUDY ————————————————————

Tom has been on placement in an ethnically and linguistically diverse setting. A number of disabled children attend the setting, which prides itself on its diversity and inclusivity. Tom wants to carry out a research project in which he asks children to articulate what they like about their home corner area in the nursery and also what they would like to see changed. He has chosen to focus on six children's views and intends to adopt methods including getting the children to draw pictures and participate in group interviews. The selected children were chosen, he says, because they are 'very talkative', they speak English 'well' and have 'good drawing skills'. Tom argues that he will get some lovely quotes and pictures to use as data for this study.

What is the problem with his selection criteria?

We hope you can see that there are a number of issues raised in Tom's proposed research, the key one being that he has automatically excluded children who may have communication and dexterity difficulties – perhaps owing to a disability or developmental delay – and he has also excluded non-English speakers. The assumption is they lack 'competence' to be a research participant. In the context of a setting which prides itself on its inclusivity and diversity this is also antithetical to its ethos. Yet we have heard many students say something similar when asked to justify their selection of participants for their research projects.

As with early childhood practice, researchers need to think about the inclusivity of their research. As tutors who have supported (and marked) numerous student research projects, we like to read research projects where students have thought through carefully the inclusiveness of their research. This might be in discussing any extra steps that have been adopted to facilitate the inclusion of a disabled child and reflexive commentary on the inclusivity of the research process.

Davis et al. (2008) argue that, as with researching with children as opposed to adults, the researcher needs to reflect on how dominant ideas about disability impact on the degree to which they view the disabled child and his/her capabilities as a research participant. In a context where 'vulnerability' is the dominant construction of disabled people (and in particular disabled young children) this can be difficult. Particular strategies they suggest are spending time in the field in order to find out which communication strategies – not necessarily verbal – would 'best' facilitate children's participation. It is likely, in some instances, that physical movement and noises may be more indicative of young disabled children's 'voices' than any use of words and yet are afforded less status, may not be recognised at all and at worst may even be disregarded altogether (Komulainen, 2007). Komulainen argues that rather than capturing children's 'voices' his research presents a description of 'observable action that has significant consequences to the lives of young children' (p. 24).

Thinking back to the Case Study of Tom's research, he had not considered using observation (over time) of the children in the home corner area. This might well have been a more inclusive strategy as it does not rely on verbal competence or drawing 'ability', and drawings would additionally require some verbal discussion relating to their content (Barker and Weller, 2003). Over time, observations may tell him a great deal about the kinds of home corner activity children enjoy. He could also indicate that he will spend time in the setting getting to know the children as individuals and discuss how he might make use of this greater insight into the children's interests and abilities to devise inclusive methods.

ETHICAL CONSIDERATIONS THROUGHOUT THE RESEARCH PROCESS

This section aims to demonstrate that a consideration of ethics is important at every stage of the research process. In thinking about this, we will be encouraging you to think about the following:

- research paradigm
- planning the research
- data gathering
- analysing the data and writing up.

We will go through each of these in turn.

RESEARCH PARADIGM

Aubrey et al. (2000) argue that because early childhood research has a tendency to involve human interactions, with all the complexity associated with this, it is almost impossible to predict and iron out *all* potential errors and misunderstandings. They go on to suggest that a researcher's choice of paradigm impacts upon their understanding of ethics. Chapters 4 and 5 of this book looked at some key paradigms in research. Positivist researchers, you may recall, aim at neutralising out the effect of the researcher. In a hypothetical study in which the researcher is concerned with observing young children and practitioner interactions in a nursery, the researcher is likely to try to eradicate the effect of their presence on the children and the practitioners. They might do this by quietly sitting back and taking field notes, trying to avoid doing anything that will impact upon what they are observing. By not 'spoiling the field', the positivist researcher might view their research as ethical.

Conversely, interpretivist researchers may see the positivist researcher's approach as unethical. This is because they would regard it as important to gain a range of explanations and views of the interactions taking place in the nursery. They are likely to want to elicit the views of the practitioners and the children and possibly parents too on the interactions taking place. Aubrey et al. (2000: 158) state that they might possibly view the positivist approach as constituting 'a disregard for the humanity, the "inner life", of the people involved, treating them as if they are observable and measurable, data-generating machines'. In wanting to listen to the perspectives of a range of people on the interactions they have observed, the interpretivist researcher is also acknowledging that their view is one of possibly many perspectives.

Whatever paradigm the researcher locates their work within, there needs to be discussion of the ethical considerations that underpin the study. Even a seemingly 'hands-off', positivist approach to research such as a structured, self-completion questionnaire involves ethical considerations. These might include:

- The questionnaire needs to be well-presented as this shows respect for the respondent.
- The questions should be straightforward and free of jargon. Respondents should not be made to feel stupid because they do not understand what the questions are getting at. That would be the fault of the researcher who designed the questionnaire.
- It should not take too long to complete.
- The questionnaire should not require people to spend money to return it.

The points raised here are also important to keep in mind in order to maximise the response to the research. After all, a poorly presented self-completion questionnaire that is difficult to fill in, that takes a long time to complete and needs the respondent to spend their own money to return it, is probably going to end up in the bin. You will find out more about questionnaire design in Chapter 14 of this book.

PLANNING THE RESEARCH

In planning any research project, the researcher needs to think about the initial questions they develop. Clough and Nutbrown (2012) highlight a range of ways to critique such questions, including the Goldilocks test. At one point in the story 'Goldilocks and the Three Bears' you may recall that Goldilocks tries the porridge left by the bears when they go on their walk, and in the case of father bear's porridge, declares it to be 'too hot'. Clough and Nutbrown apply the idea of 'too hot' to research. An example of a question that is 'too hot' might be: 'Which practitioner is most successful in settling children in at the beginning of a session?'

A question like this focuses on individuals and implies that the research is about judging people against each other. It would be far better to focus the question on the characteristics of good practice in the area of settling children at the beginning of sessions. In this way, the focus is not on *who* does something successfully but on *what* people do, implying that we can all develop our practice in this area. In addition, by focusing on the individual in this example of a 'hot' question, the research places practitioners outside of the structures and routines of the setting; that is, it is likely that there are organisational factors rather than purely individual traits that impact on the beginnings of sessions. These might include allowing parents to stay as long as needed at the beginning of sessions, not expecting children to sit for a formal registration period, and so on. These would not be individual decisions but would reflect the ethos of the institution as a whole.

DATA GATHERING

The methods for collecting data used in any research project will raise particular ethical issues. As was noted earlier in the 'Research paradigm' section, questionnaires – a method that may on the surface seem free from ethical concerns – have ethical implications that need to be considered. However, methods that require a greater level of face-to-face encounters inevitably carry with them a higher potential for harm.

In face-to-face interviewing, for instance, researchers need to consider where and when interviews are conducted and the general comfort of the interviewee. Furthermore, the structure and questions asked during the interview should help to put the interviewee at ease.

But we should be mindful of Oakley's (1981) criticisms of interviewing as a research tool when she states that some of the strategies designed to put the interviewee at ease are, in fact, tactics designed to manipulate them. As Fontana and Frey (2005) observe, although researchers may appear friendly and courteous, actually they are expected to remain emotionally neutral, keeping their feelings and opinions to themselves – unlike in a normal conversation.

This is an interesting point to reflect upon and is an issue raised by feminist researchers in particular. It can also be linked to the debates raised in Chapters 4 and 5 about the self of the researcher. You may recall that positivist researchers aim for objectivity, so would try to neutralise the impact of their views and feelings on the research. Conversely, researchers working within other research paradigms – and in particular, feminist researchers – are likely to acknowledge their own subjectivities. In other words, they are more likely to share information about themselves with participants in an attempt to make the research relationship more equal and responsive.

When interviewing young children, should they disclose anything that indicates abuse, it is important that the researcher shares this information with the appropriate adults – be they parents or professionals. Although it is usual to maintain anonymity in most studies, the welfare of a child who is potentially in danger must *always* take precedence. Thus, it is important not to make false promises about confidentiality in case information needs to be shared.

Observation too is not without ethical difficulties. Earlier in the chapter we highlighted the importance of informed consent, but also noted the potential difficulties Warming (2005) sees as presenting themselves when observing children at play over time. As a general principle, people who are being observed should know what is being looked at, and in the case of young children, their parents and other relevant gatekeepers should also have agreed to this. However, as observation is such a common practice in early childhood settings, it may be difficult to distinguish research practice from everyday early childhood practice, especially if the researcher and the practitioner are one and the same person (Albon and Rosen, 2014). Thus, it is important to consider ways of making clear the nature of the research: indeed some students, on reflecting on this issue, have come to question the habitual observational practices of early childhood settings.

It is usually good practice, we would argue, to share any observations and/or insights with a setting or a family, assuming the research involves observation. Not only does this make it clear what the researcher is recording and his or her reflections on it, but the people who know the child(ren) best, that is parents and practitioners, can also add their insights. This point is picked up in the next section.

ANALYSING THE DATA AND WRITING UP

Analysing data and writing up the research is also an area that needs thinking through in relation to ethics. Here are some ethical questions that might be raised by this:

- Do research participants feel the same about the way I have analysed the data gathered? What are their interpretations of the data?
- Can research participants be involved in the data analysis and if so how?
- Who is going to see the research once written up?
- Is the research written in a way that is respectful of participants?
- How can I 'give something back' to the research participants during or at the end of the research that is meaningful to them?

These questions are explored in further depth in the final two chapters of this book, but are raised here to encourage you to view ethical considerations as part of the research process as a whole. It is vital to consider ethics beyond the research 'proper' and think about the way the participants in research are represented.

ETHICAL GUIDELINES, UNIVERSITY ETHICS COMMITTEES AND LEGAL CONSIDERATIONS

Research is carried out in virtually all academic disciplines and each will have codes that are especially applicable to them. In early childhood research, the most relevant codes of ethics to refer to come from the following groups (in the UK):

- the British Psychological Society (www.bps.org.uk/system/files/Public%20 files/inf180_web.pdf [accessed 14 July 2017])
- the British Sociological Association (www.britsoc.co.uk/ethics)
- the British Educational Research Association (www.bera.ac.uk/researchers-resources/publications/ethical-guidelines-for-educational-research-2011 [accessed 14 May 2014]).

And as examples from outside of the UK:

- The National Association for the Education of Young Children (www.naeyc. org/positionstatements/ethical_conduct [accessed 16 July 2017]) – USA
- Ethical Research Involving Children (ERIC) (http://childethics.com [accessed 16 July 2017]) – ERIC is a joint project between UNICEF's Office of Research, Innocenti, the Childwatch International Research Network, the Centre for Children and Young People at Southern Cross University, Australia, and the Children's Issues Centre at the University of Otago, New Zealand.

 —— ACTIVITY ——————————————

Look up the ethical guidelines for the British Educational Research Association (BERA) on www.bera.ac.uk/researchers-resources/publications/ethical-guidelines-for-educational-research-2011. You will find the link in the online resources. We also suggest you examine the multinational group: Ethical Research Involving Children (ERIC) whose website has more of an early childhood focus – http://childethics.com.

Universities will also have their own ethics committees, which govern the types of research that are given the go-ahead under the auspices of the university. This would include research undertaken by people employed by the university and research students. Not to abide by these guidelines can be a disciplinary offence and, at worst, a criminal offence. This is an indication of how seriously ethical issues need to be taken. For those of you who are embarking on student research projects, it is important to talk through ethical issues with your supervising tutor *from the outset* and to avoid embarking on data collection without such preliminary discussions. This person will help to advise you about your choice of topic, the method(s) chosen to gather data and the data analysis and writing up. Some universities insist that all students fill in an ethics form which has to be signed off before the student can undertake any research. You should note that individual colleges and universities may have slightly different ways of doing this but they will *all* be concerned that research is undertaken ethically.

It is not just universities that have ethical committees. In addition to colleges and universities, individual institutions or local authorities may require the researcher to have their research agreed by a group or committee. Medical research generally requires that a researcher goes through a hospital ethics committee, which will scrutinise the research proposal before agreeing (or not) to the research going ahead. In hospitals, this is a process that will include proposals for drugs trials and new treatments, as well as the use of patients' records – to give but a few examples.

— 🔍 — CASE STUDY

Dimah wants to undertake some research in a baby room in an English nursery. She says she won't be alone with the children at any time and does not think she will need any special clearance. Do you think this is the case?

In the English context it is usual to expect a nursery setting to request that someone spending time with the children has a DBS clearance. DBS is the Disclosure and Barring Service, which, in essence, is a police check that an individual has nothing on record which would debar him or her from working with or coming into contact with vulnerable persons. It is an issue of safeguarding children which all settings take very seriously so it would be very unlikely that Dimah would gain access to a baby room for the research to take place. If you do not have such clearance already (either through being a practitioner or having done a placement in a setting) then you often need to allow some time for a DBS clearance to come through.

Whichever country you are located in, it is always important to check whether special clearances such as this are needed to undertake your research.

The Data Protection Act 1998 provides a legislative backdrop to some of the ethical issues raised in this chapter. In particular, the Data Protection Act legislates that researchers must do the following:

- store data securely (including electronic storage)
- ensure research participants know how the data will be used and who will see the data
- ensure data are not used beyond the life of a given research project unless express permission has been granted from participants for this.

You can look at the Data Protection Act yourself online by searching the following website: www.legislation.gov.uk.

Finally, here, it is important that in our zeal to undertake research that conforms to ethical guidelines, we do not lose sight of the fact that we are making ethical judgements all the time when researching with children. So whilst guidelines and committees, etc., have an important place in research, they cannot help us with all the situations the researcher is faced with when actually carrying out research in practice (Albon and Rosen, 2014). Research – as with life itself – is far more 'messy' than this, as we noted before. Skånfors (2009) helpfully employs the term 'ethical radar' in order to highlight the vigilance researchers need in order to 'pick up' on ethical issues in childhood research. We develop this more in the next chapter, which examines 'listening to children'.

 —— KEY POINTS FROM THE CHAPTER ——————————

- Ethical considerations should underpin *every* research project.
- Early childhood research raises particular ethical issues owing to the age and vulnerability of young children, but at the same time young children should be viewed as competent. We particularly like Lahman's (2008: 285) conceptualisation of the *'competent yet vulnerable child'* here, which might equally be applied to adults as we all experience vulnerability and competence during our lives.
- Power is an important issue to reflect upon in research, for example the relative power of a young child in relation to an adult, or a parent whose child attends a nursery in relation to a practitioner-researcher.
- The issue of informed consent is of key importance in any research project. In early childhood research, adults usually act as 'gatekeepers' to children's involvement.
- Older children in the early childhood age range, that is children up to the age of 8, are likely to be able to give prior and possibly written consent to research in a meaningful way. However, in research with very young children and babies,

(Continued)

(Continued)

informed consent *might* mean negotiating access on a moment-by-moment basis as their signed consent is likely to be meaningless or impossible. This links to the notion of 'ethical symmetry' (Christensen and Prout, 2002), as the principles underpinning any research are the same for children and adults but there is differentiation in how research is carried out; that is, it is determined by the abilities and interests of participants in situ.

- Ethical issues are present throughout the research process, in the choice of paradigm, the planning of the research, the data gathering, the data analysis and the writing up of the research.
- Finally, there are societies and research associations that have ethical guidelines that researchers working within those disciplines should be working to. Universities will also have codes of ethics that they expect researchers employed within the university and research students to abide by.

FURTHER READING

Christensen, P. and Prout, A. (2002) 'Working with ethical symmetry in social research with children', *Childhood*, 9(4): 477–97. This journal article is available in the online resources and provides greater detail about the notion of 'ethical symmetry', which has been raised in this chapter.

Lahman, M. (2008) 'Always othered: ethical research with children', *Journal of Early Childhood Research*, 6(3): 281–300. This is an excellent article that looks at the position of children in early childhood research. It is available in the online resources.

Skånfors, L. (2009) 'Ethics in child research: children's agency and researchers' "ethical radar"', *Childhoods Today*, 3(1): 1–22. An article which examines ethical issues in some depth. The term 'ethical radar' is one we find useful. There is a link to the article in the online resources.

Don't forget to visit the online resources at https://study.sagepub.com/mukherjiandalbon3e for access to free SAGE journal articles, weblinks, videos, exercises, mini quizzes and an interactive glossary.

7

LISTENING TO YOUNG CHILDREN

- To consider the growth in research involving listening to young children.
- To link this to the emergence of children's rights perspectives.
- To reflect further on ethical issues relating to involving young children directly in research.

An emerging principle that underpins research is one of listening to young children. Building on the previous chapter, where we thought through some of the ethical issues relating to research with young children, this chapter looks more specifically at how the early childhood researcher might develop creative ways of listening to young children and including them as participants in research. The preceding chapter on ethics looked at Lahman's (2008: 285) notion of the *'competent yet vulnerable child'* in research. Like Lahman, we believe these are two conceptualisations of the child that it is possible to hold simultaneously. In particular, the previous chapter looked at young children's protective rights in relation to research, whereas this chapter's focus is on their participatory rights – although inevitably, as the notion of the *'competent but vulnerable child'* implies, these are closely interwoven. Moreover, following Bath (2013), we see listening to children as strongly aligned to a more general ethic of care in early childhood practice and research.

THE DEVELOPMENT OF INTEREST IN LISTENING TO YOUNG CHILDREN

Moss et al. (2005) maintain that the development of interest around listening to children can be linked to the growth in the children's rights perspective across the globe. This perspective is one that embraces children's participation and recognises that children have their own views of what affects them directly, as well as their own perspectives of the world around them (Smith, 2011).

The United Nations Convention on the Rights of the Child (UNCRC), which was adopted by the United Nations (UN) in 1989 and has been ratified by 192 countries, champions this principle of participation alongside enshrining the need to protect children. The notion of participation can be seen most clearly in articles 12 and 13:

> Parties shall assure to the child who is capable of forming his or her own views the right to express those views freely in all matters affecting the child, the views of the child being given due weight in accordance with the age and maturity of the child ...

> The child shall have the right to freedom of expression; this right shall include freedom to seek, receive and impart information and ideas of all kinds, regardless of frontiers, either orally, in writing or in print, in the form of art, or through any other media of the child's choice. (UNCRC articles 12 and 13, quoted in Moss et al., 2005: 2)

We will return to the issue of the capability of 'forming his or her own views' as well as the issue of age and maturity later in the chapter. It is important to acknowledge that in the UK, for example, prior to the UNCRC, the 1989 Children

Act had begun to enshrine the importance of listening to children in their own right. Prior to the 1980s, international and national legislation had a tendency to view children – especially young children – as the property of their parents, as well as being incapable of expressing an opinion on matters affecting them. Thus, children were viewed as unable to form or express a view about matters affecting their lives (Taylor, 2000). This position is changing.

Underpinning the children's rights perspective is a view that children are persons in their own right – not human 'becomings' but human beings (Qvortrup, 1994). Thus, in some of the literature, children, as a group, are considered as being in a similar position to other minority or marginalised groups such as women, Black and minority ethnic groups, or people with disabilities – groups that have tended to be, 'at best under represented, more generally ignored and at worst exploited and manipulated' (Cook and Hess, 2007: 30). Thus, we might conceptualise the burgeoning interest in children's perspectives under a broader umbrella of research which actively seeks the perspectives of people from marginalised groups (Greene and Hill, 2005). To this end, Alanen (2001) develops the idea of 'generation' as a form of sociological analysis which serves to examine how children come to be distinguished as 'different' from adults and how this perpetuates inequality between these social categories. You might make a link here with the 'critical' theories discussed in Chapter 5 of this book.

Also underpinning this perspective is a view that recognises that there are a variety of different experiences of childhood according to whether the child is able-bodied or has a disability, is a girl or a boy, is living in poverty, or comes from a minority ethnic group. Other differences might relate to children's experiences of family life or whether they live in a rural or urban area, which may affect their access to early childhood services, or indeed there may be a mixture of these, such as a white boy living in an urban area who has a disability, for instance. We should recognise, then, that there is no one, universal 'child' that stands for all children (James and Prout, 1990) and that children's experiences are multiple and varied (Greene and Hill, 2005).

Increasingly, the response from public policy-makers and advocacy groups is one of developing approaches that involve listening to children, such as the 2013 UNICEF report *Child Well-being in Rich Countries* (Adamson, 2013) (see part 2 especially). In order to make a statement about children's subjective sense of their own well-being, the researchers asked children for their own perspectives on well-being, although close examination of the document shows that the children were aged from 11 years, with no younger children included in the sample. What can be said here is that there is a *general trend* towards listening to children and, as previously stated, this has its basis in children being viewed as competent in voicing their views on matters that affect them, as well as children having the right to participate in decision-making that has an impact upon their lives (Taylor, 2000). Later on in this chapter we look at the issue of 'competence' more critically.

—— ACTIVITY ————————————————————

Find out about the ways in which local government in your area attempts to gain the perspectives of children and young people about services that affect them. What areas are they interested in finding out about? What strategies are used to elicit children's views? How old are the children who are consulted – is there evidence of children under 5 years being consulted?

It is important at this point to be cautious in thinking that developments in the area of listening to children are applied equally to very young children and older children. Hyder (2002: 311) reports on the way a 'listening to children' project was caricatured as 'Babies consulted about council policy' in the local newspaper. This highlights the way young children are often viewed; as incapable of forming and expressing opinions about matters that affect them owing to their young age and immaturity.

 —— REFLECTION POINT ————————————————

'Competence' is a complex matter. How might it be defined in terms of research? Should it mean ability to understand what a research project entails in its entirety? Or perhaps the ability to answer research questions in writing or through spoken language? If we demand certain 'competencies' in order to become a 'participant' in research, *who* might be excluded?

Another interpretation of 'competence' is *experience*; that is, children having an understanding of themselves, those around them and their environment (Cocks, 2006: 255). In this sense, very young children and/or children with profound disabilities should be considered competent as they have a unique insight into their own lives. Moreover, this takes us beyond thinking about human beings according to distinct categories of 'competent/incompetent' or 'mature/immature' or 'dependent/independent' (Lee, 2001). An 'ethic of care', for instance, would emphasise our interconnectedness and dependency on each other as human beings (Bath, 2013). Furthermore, Lahman's (2008) notion of being able to hold on to the idea of vulnerability and competency at any one time adds further weight to this idea of troubling the notion of 'competency' in research and indeed human life more generally.

These are very difficult issues but they get to the heart of the 'listening' debate in relation to whose voices are elicited; whose are heard; and whose are seen as most credible.

In the previous chapter we introduced you to the work of Christensen and Prout (2002) and their idea of 'ethical symmetry'. This is an idea that starts from a position in which all children and adults are equal with respect to ethical considerations but that when it comes to research in situ, then different 'tactics' might be employed in order to research in ways that are sensitive to participants in given contexts. In order to elicit the perspectives of babies and toddlers it is highly likely that the focus group method used in the UNICEF study would be inappropriate and would, moreover, reinforce an idea of the very young child as 'incompetent' as they would be 'set up to fail' in effect. Yet babies and toddlers tell us a great deal about their lives if we take the trouble to listen, and researchers can and do endeavour to find ways of hearing their voices in research.

 REFLECTION POINT ──────────────

Before we think about research let us think about 'listening' in an everyday sense. Reflect on what we might mean by 'listening' to babies and young children. Does it have to involve speech? How do babies and young children communicate to us about what they like and dislike?

It might be useful here to think of a practical example such as meal times:

- Babies will often use their mouth and tongue to push out a teat or small spoon or draw it in using a sucking action.
- They may also move their head towards or away from a teat or spoon when being fed or change body position in a way that tells the person feeding them what they want to do.
- The baby's facial expressions are also indicative of whether the experience is enjoyable or not.
- And as the baby gets older, increasingly, their use of hands and early speech are important in communicating their feelings.
- If we add in the close relationship the child's parent or carer has with the baby, then minute changes in the above examples are likely to be noticed and acted upon.

In other words, in tuning into babies in a sensitive way we are 'listening' to them – 'listening' not only with our ears, but with our eyes, whole bodies and minds too. At this point it is also important to note that attention to body language is important when researching with adults too. If, when interviewing, an interviewee's body language suggests discomfort with a question asked, the interviewer should try to 'read' such cues and perhaps rephrase the question or move on to another question. Tuning into the body language of research participants is important, but takes on increased significance with babies and very young children as many children of this age are unable to use words to communicate their feelings.

WHAT DOES THIS MEAN FOR RESEARCH?

The growth in the children's rights perspective and its increasing impact on public policy-making has its parallels in a widening range of research. Cook and Hess (2007) note that since the late 1980s there has been a move away from seeing adults as speaking for children in research contexts towards one that seeks to listen to children's viewpoints and experiences. Crucially, adults are seen as not necessarily in the best position to represent children's viewpoints and experiences fully because children themselves have a unique perspective on their own lives. Thus, Greene and Hill (2005: 3) argue that:

> The researcher who values children's perspectives and wishes to understand their lived experience will be motivated to find out more about how children understand and interpret, negotiate and feel about their daily lives.

Such a perspective is a shift in thinking about children in research. This is because traditionally, research has been carried out on children rather than with them. For Westcott and Littleton (2005), this links to the idea of the child being passive and powerless, with the focus of the research being on adults revealing children's understandings as opposed to *creating* understandings with children. While this undoubtedly still happens, since the mid-1990s researchers have increasingly been developing participatory and inclusive research strategies in which the child, viewed as a social actor, is at the centre (Barker and Weller, 2003). Underpinning this movement in thinking about children is the criticism of developmental psychology as confining children to a position of being consistently 'less able' than adults because of their supposed location in 'earlier' developmental stages. Since the mid-1990s, writers who are sometimes known collectively as embracing the 'new sociology of childhood' have criticised this view of children as 'other' to adults and the idea of developmental stages per se, and this has led to new ways of conceptualising children and childhood in research (James et al., 1998). In short, we have begun to talk about children as being more capable than we might have done previously and this, in turn, has opened up greater possibilities for children's participation in research. Let us now examine this in relation to two research projects.

RESEARCH IN FOCUS

CANADA

There are an increasing number of studies that focus on listening to children. Rosen (2010) undertook a piece of research into children's perceptions of their role in curriculum development in a Canadian pre-school. Her key questions were: 'What are four- and five-year-old children's perceptions of how curriculum is developed in one preschool in British Columbia (BC), Canada? Do children think they have a role in developing curriculum at this preschool? Do they want to influence the curriculum and, if so, how?' (p. 92).

Throughout the article, you will see an emphasis on eliciting children's perspectives – an area we return to in depth in Chapter 17 – and this was seen in both the topic for investigation as well as the methods employed. Amongst the key findings of the study, Rosen found that the children were very capable research participants, who were keen to influence the curriculum and could talk about individual and collective curriculum goals. However, she highlights generational power and inequality between adults (teachers) and children, noting how this impacts on children's ability to exert power over curriculum decision-making. Therefore, Rosen (2010) draws our attention to inequalities which have their basis in age/generation much like researchers who draw attention to inequalities based on social class, gender, sexuality and 'race'.

Traditionally, parents, practitioners, inspectors and other adults have been 'listened to' in relation to the curriculum. However, this would restrict our understanding to a purely adult perspective. As Cook and Hess (2007) observe, this discounts the perspective of one of the 'key players' – children. Children may well have their own understandings and experiences of a particular service, which, as Rosen shows, is very illuminating.

RESEARCH IN FOCUS

NORTHERN IRELAND

We provide a second Research in Focus section here because we wish to highlight a different research project that similarly has at its core the importance of listening to young children (and hearing them!).

By way of contrast to Rosen's (2010) research into curriculum development in a nursery setting, Winter (2010) focused on ascertaining the perspectives of young children in the *care system*. Her research was carried out in Northern Ireland. Her focus on the care system is one which, she argues, is neglected in the literature. You will often notice that when reading the research of others, the researcher(s) will demonstrate how their research is positioned in relation to the work of others and how their own research will address any perceived gaps in

(Continued)

(Continued)

the literature. Winter's work is framed around the idea of children's social competence and the importance of ascertaining children's views as part of decisions made in their 'best interests'.

Winter's research involved ten case studies including 39 semi-structured interviews with young children in care, their parents and their social workers. Fourteen children – all of whom were subject to care orders (which means that responsibility for their care was held between social services and the child's parents) – aged 4-7 years participated in the study. Limits to confidentiality were shared with the children explicitly in case the children alluded to possible or actual harm and appropriate adults were on hand should the interviews cause the children distress. The interviews were based around an activity: the child's creation of a 'reality box'. These were made from a range of drawings, figures, photographs (using cutting and sticking, etc., as the child wished) and represented (on the outside) how the children thought they came across to the outside world, and the inside of the box represented their feelings and perspectives on their lives at home and in care. Thus, the methods were an unusual way of encouraging children's direct participation, which is an area we examine more thoroughly in Chapter 17.

The data give a rich and detailed insight into these young children's perspectives on their lives. One child, for instance, used card and lollipop sticks to make a fence inside his box, stating: 'I put a fence around my feelings; that's why I don't want no-one to see them' (Winter, 2010: 376). The child was clear that he did not want to be identified but was keen that his work be shared with others in order to help train other adults in their work. Winter concludes that using participatory methods such as the use of reality boxes helps to ensure that very young children are not excluded from participatory processes in research and in practice. She also argues that the method should be seen as part of a wider agenda in social work of working with young children in a transparent and respectful way. In order to protect children better, it is important to hear them.

However, we should be mindful that creative methods in research, such as the reality boxes used in this study, may not result in a deeper understanding of an issue. Spending time with children and *being available to them* (a point we raise in Chapter 17) remain very important for practitioners *and* researchers. One might also ask: Would some children see the activity purely in terms of a cutting and sticking task?

ETHICAL ISSUES WHEN INVOLVING YOUNG CHILDREN IN RESEARCH

The previous chapter was dedicated to examining the issue of ethics in research. In this section, our aim is to build on this and examine some of the particular ethical considerations that need to be taken into account when *directly* involving young children in research.

In Chapter 6 we noted that an important consideration in research is whether it is of some benefit to the participants (Robson, 2011a). In involving children directly in research and listening to their perspectives, we believe that there are many positive benefits, not least that the researcher gains access to the viewpoints of a key stakeholder group in early childhood research – the children themselves. As a consequence of carrying out research that involves listening to children, the researcher is adding to a body of research that views children as experts on their own lives, sees eliciting children's perspectives as possible and takes children's ideas seriously. By participating in research, children have the opportunity to learn a range of skills, such as those relating to speaking and listening, as well as learning about their environment and their place in it, in new and exciting ways (Driskell, 2002). In addition, participatory research methods, which we discuss further in Chapter 17, allow children more ownership over research and this can mean that they are more motivated to participate (O'Kane, 2008). But while there are positive benefits to listening to children, we should always be mindful of Woodhead and Faulkner's (2008: 35) caution that 'respect for children's status as social actors does not diminish adult responsibilities'.

Increasingly, research with children is being governed by codes of ethics, which lay down the protective responsibility researchers have towards children who are participants in research. In this sense, research that involves children can be viewed as constituting a 'risky' activity (Allen, 2005). These risks are not of the same kind as found in biomedical research; in the types of early childhood research we are discussing in this book, the risks are more likely to be 'social than physical' (Allen, 2005: 20). In other words, the child is unlikely to come to physical harm, but the researcher needs to consider the social and emotional harm they might inflict upon the child participant.

 — REFLECTION POINT —

What social and emotional harm might come to young children in a piece of research? Think about this in relation to the following hypothetical research examples:

- filming babies at lunchtime in a study aiming to look at adult-child interactions during meal times
- interviewing six children of 3-4 years as a group about what they like or dislike about coming to nursery
- carrying out research looking at children's lack of mathematical understanding in the area of conservation of number, involving children aged 5 years in various tests outside of the classroom.

If we take each hypothetical example in turn, in the first instance, the researcher would need to consider the impact of filming on the babies. S/he would need to tune in sensitively to the reactions of the babies. It is likely, for instance, that if the babies stop feeding and/or are clearly moving their faces away from the camera, they may be distressed and so filming should cease immediately and the researcher may need to move further away. The filming may also make the parent or carer feeding the baby uneasy, which might also impact negatively on the meal-time experience. As a consequence, it might also influence the findings of the research.

In the second example, what if the subject matter has little interest for the children? Possibly, traditional forms of group interviewing may be inappropriate as they may involve sitting for long periods when the children would rather be playing with their friends. In other words, there may well be a power imbalance, with adults deciding what to talk about, as well as when and where this should happen. In addition, when interviewing children as a group, the researcher would need to ensure that *all* children have the opportunity to contribute to the discussion, rather than some voices dominating. The questions asked would need to be carefully thought through to ensure *all* the children are able to understand what is being asked of them, especially given that children often feel the need to 'get it right' when asked questions by an adult. This would also need thinking through in terms of whether English is the children's first language or whether any of the children have communication difficulties. Finally here, the researcher would need to consider how a child might feel if they say something that is potentially ridiculed by the rest of the group, as well as how they would deal with this issue if it arises.

In the final hypothetical example, these mathematics tests may have little meaning for the children and take the children away from their usual activities in the classroom. The work of Donaldson (1979), although involving test situations too, emphasises the importance of tests being *meaningful* to children and demonstrates how children are able to perform at a higher level when this is the case. Hatch (1995) highlights the need to establish rapport with young children in research and make them feel comfortable. One aspect of this is the choice of place to carry out the research. Hatch argues that children are likely to be more comfortable in a familiar setting, whereas this hypothetical example sets out to put children in an unfamiliar setting, which may be unsettling and, at worst, distressing for the child. In addition to this, the research appears to be aimed at demonstrating children's lack of competence in mathematics as opposed to what they can do and could therefore be regarded as unethical. This last example, then, might also be regarded as damaging to children as a group – beyond those children involved directly in the study – because it might reinforce a view of young children as lacking or incompetent in some way (Alderson, 2000). It is far better to develop a research idea that is framed positively. So, if interested in early mathematics, the researcher could frame her question in such a way as to focus on how to support/enhance young children's mathematical thinking within the classroom, for example.

As you can see, there are many ethical implications in research with children and it is important to think this through when designing a piece of research. This can be linked to the degree of children's involvement in the research. Alderson (2005: 29–30), for instance, outlines three main levels of child involvement in research. These are as follows:

- *'Children as unknowing subjects of research'*. Here children do not know that research is being carried out and are not asked for their consent.
- *'Children as aware subjects'*. Here the design of the research is tightly within the control of the adult researcher.
- *'Children as active participants'*. Here there is flexibility over the methods used in the research. Furthermore, children themselves may become involved in planning and carrying out research projects.

Each of these levels of involvement implies a different conception of childhood, ranging from seeing the child as innocent or the child as needing controlling to the child as confident and competent (Alderson, 2005). In a similar way, Woodhead and Faulkner (2008) ask whether children in research are viewed as objects, subjects or participants, each representing changing understandings of the competency of children, as well as changing perceptions relating to the degree of sensitivity accorded children in relation to their rights and welfare.

But seeing children as competent and able to participate actively in research has ethical implications. You will recall that in the previous chapter we stressed the importance of gaining the consent of parents and other possible gatekeepers prior to research being carried out, as well as gaining the consent of the children. But this may not be as straightforward as it seems. As Alderson (2005) observes, what do we do if a parent withdraws their consent for their child to take part in a piece of research but the child is keen to participate? Similarly, what do we do if a few children object to being observed if the researcher wishes to observe a whole-class situation? Children are increasingly being seen as able to consent to participate in research as well as withdraw from research (Farrell, 2005) and, as the previous chapter noted, the notion of informed consent and the right to withdraw from research are key ethical concepts in any piece of research. Alderson (2005) does not offer any 'easy' answers to questions such as these, but she highlights the need to enter into dialogue with the children and adults involved to talk through the issues that have been raised by such dilemmas. David et al. (2005) maintain that rather than 'answering' ethical dilemmas such as those stated, we should recognise that such dilemmas are likely to multiply as awareness increases around the relative powerlessness of children in relation to adults.

Issues of power also need to be considered in relation to choice of method. It is important to recognise that there may be conceptual issues around interviewing children, for instance, which can be hidden in research. Westcott and Littleton (2005) argue that children may not be used to being listened to seriously. Further to this, Clark (2005) points out that all forms of communication between adults and children involve questions of power. She argues that an adult who views young children primarily as needing *protection* and as *vulnerable* may emphasise a strong role for adults and a relatively powerless role for children. Conversely, an adult who views children as capable of taking an active role in research is likely to have higher expectations of children in terms of the degree to which they are able to participate. An emphasis on children's communicative competence may, therefore, require a reappraisal of the relationships between children and adults (Clark, 2005; see also the discussion of communicative competence in relation to disability in the previous chapter). We explore this further in Chapter 17, which looks at creative approaches to listening.

Another compelling issue linked to the power differential between adults and children relates to tokenism. If the 'listening' is tokenistic then it merely reinforces this power differential (Brooker, 2011). Moreover, as Bath (2013) asserts, listening in the minority world is often linked to the notion of the individual as consumer, as can be seen in public consultation exercises and the like. Such exercises are premised on the idea that human beings should be viewed as individual, autonomous *consumers* as opposed to interconnected *citizens*,which seems far removed from the ethic of care that we would want to champion as important in underpinning the idea of listening to children. Hart (1992) uses the visual image of a ladder to encourage reflection on the levels of children's participation in research.

If one imagines an upright ladder with rungs, Hart (1992) conceptualises a gradual shift from the bottom rungs where children are manipulated and the listening is tokenistic to one where, at the top of the ladder, children share in the decision-making of a project. Sometimes children's involvement might only be at the level of 'decoration' such as having a balloon launch with children to showcase a particular piece of research, while the children may not have been part of any other aspect of the project. You might like to think about this in relation to the inclusion of photographs in your research projects. If your research involves children directly, for example asking them about an aspect of the nursery day, it might be appropriate (with permissions) to either take photographs yourself of the children engaged in this aspect of the day or to encourage children to take their own things of interest. However, if your use of photographs is merely to embellish the written-up study and adds no weight to any points you want to make in relation to the study you have undertaken, then we suggest it is mere *decoration* and should be avoided. We are sure you can see that these different usages of photographs represent very different rungs on Hart's participation ladder. You should note that we thread through discussion about the use of photographs elsewhere in the book.

THE CHILD AS RESEARCHER

On the face of it, it would seem that young children might be incapable of being researchers; a view that has its basis in a perspective of young children as too young, too immature and too lacking in the qualities needed to be a researcher – qualities developed with age. These might include a certain level of verbal skills or an ability to record information that can be shared.

However, Mary Kellett (2005) argues that children can be *taught* the skills that will enable them to become researchers. In early childhood literature, there are numerous examples of writers who emphasise young children's curiosity, their inbuilt desire to explore and their creativity (e.g. Athey, 2007; Bruce, 1987; Robson, 2011b). In other words, if we were talking about the motivation and ability of young children to explore the world around them, we would be saying that this is present from birth.

Alderson (2000) argues that in many schools (we would extend this to all early childhood spaces), children are engaged in research on a regular basis. However, this type of research tends to remain unpublished. Examples of this might be:

- a group of 3- and 4-year-old children going out of the nursery to conduct a traffic survey following the interest a few children have shown in the transport that passes on the main road near to the setting
- a baby exploring the different textures, shapes, sounds, tastes and smells of objects in a treasure basket
- a group of 5-year-old children investigating how they can stop a lump of snow from melting (they have brought it inside excitedly on a snowy day and want to preserve it).

Alderson (2000) points out that this type of research tends to be viewed in terms of children 'practising' being a researcher as opposed to it being important, real-life research. She argues that children are often interested in research that has a practical implication and achieves an element of change. Moreover, Driskell (2002) notes this, saying that projects about the physical environment are often highly motivating for children.

 CASE STUDY

In a module that asks students to evaluate an environment such as a local post office or local woodland as a learning environment *beyond* their workplace (that is, a nursery or school), Lina looked at the playground near to her nursery. Rather than conducting the evaluation alone, she encouraged the 3–4-year-old children to take the lead

(Continued)

(Continued)

in this. She found that very few of the children used the local playground and was intrigued why this was the case. She asked them what they would like to see in the playground and took the children there on a series of visits. The children drew pictures and she noted their comments next to the drawings. They also took photographs and took her on a tour of the playground telling her what they liked and disliked about it.

Primarily the children thought the playground was 'mostly for big kids' and felt that the equipment that was there was in a poor state of repair. However, Lina was surprised when some of the children stated that they liked the coloured lines on the playground surface (denoting the way space is used in different sports). She observed these children walking along the different lines and attributed their interest to other observations she had made relating to the trajectory nature of these children's schemas (see Athey, 2007, for a discussion on schemas).

Lina made a display of the children's evaluations of the playground in the nursery and was later encouraged to move the display to the local library as part of ongoing community efforts to improve the quality of play spaces for young children in the area. She found that the physical environment was a topic that children were keen to investigate and share their views about.

 — KEY POINTS FROM THE CHAPTER

- There has been a growth of interest in children's participation and projects that involve listening to young children. This is underpinned by the UN Convention on the Rights of the Child and a view of the child as a competent, rather than passive, co-constructor of knowledge.
- There are positive benefits to listening to children in research, not only for the researcher, but for children themselves.
- There are ethical issues that need to be thought through in relation to involving young children in research, not least the relative power of the adult researcher in relation to young children.
- Finally, there is a growth in interest about children as researchers. This reflects a more equitable balance of power between the child researcher and the adult researcher.

─── FURTHER READING ───

Brooker, L. (2011) 'Taking children seriously: an alternative agenda for research?', *Journal of Early Childhood Research*, 9: 137-49. This article makes a strong case for children's participation in research and emphasises the need to avoid tokenism.

Clark, A., Kjorholt, A.T. and Moss, P. (eds) (2005) *Beyond Listening: Children's Perspectives on Early Childhood Services*. Bristol: Policy Press. An interesting collection of contributions all concerned with listening to young children and with relevance to both early childhood research and practice.

Woodhead, M. and Faulkner, D. (2008) 'Subjects, objects or participants? Dilemmas of psychological research with children', in P. Christensen and A. James (eds) *Research with Children: Perspectives and Practices*, 2nd edition. Abingdon: Routledge. A chapter that looks at changing conceptualisations of children in research.

Don't forget to visit the online resources at
https://study.sagepub.com/mukherjiandalbon3e for access to free SAGE journal articles, weblinks, videos, exercises, mini quizzes and an interactive glossary.

PART 3

APPROACHES TO RESEARCH

If you have read Parts 1 and 2 of this book, you will already be aware that there is no 'set way' to organise research. Your underpinning assumptions, values and beliefs will be reflected in the research paradigm within which your research is positioned, and this in turn impacts on other aspects of the research, such as methodological and ethical stance and the importance that you give to enabling children to be participants in research.

Throughout the research process decisions are made and these are seldom clear-cut. There are possibilities and limitations to any approach taken in research. This part looks at four common approaches, or strategies, used in early childhood research: surveys, ethnography, case studies and action research. We will see that each approach forms the strategy of choice according to the type of research the researcher is hoping to conduct.

In Chapter 8 we start by looking at surveys. Surveys are a non-experimental research strategy that has its roots primarily in the positivist tradition, using mainly *quantitative* methodology. Usually, surveys are designed to enable conclusions to be generalisable to a whole population and they commonly use questionnaires or structured interviews as methods to collect data. Whilst it is highly unlikely that a student on an early childhood studies degree course will undertake a survey, because of the large number of participants involved, we hope to illuminate how surveys are designed and conducted in order to help provide a window into the research of others.

The other three approaches described in this section employ qualitative research methodology, and are used in situations when an *in-depth* understanding of an issue or situation is required. The findings from these approaches are usually designed to be applicable to the participants under study, that is to small groups or 'cases', but of course they may lead to lines of enquiry which could be investigated further in larger populations.

Ethnography, having its roots in anthropology, is an approach that is designed to reveal an in-depth understanding of an individual or group of individuals, paying particular attention to social relationships, culture and context. Ethnography usually involves researchers immersing themselves in a particular situation in an effort to understand the situation from the inside. In Chapter 9 we will see how ethnography offers us the opportunity to research children's worlds in a *naturalistic* setting.

In Chapter 10 we look at case studies. Some of you may already be familiar with this approach as students on early childhood studies courses are frequently required to undertake a child study, which is a form of case study. Case studies differ from ethnography as the researcher may not be as deeply immersed in the situation and, on occasions, a mixture of qualitative and quantitative methods may be used.

Finally, in Chapter 11 we discuss action research, an approach which is undertaken by practitioners with an aim of *improving practice*. Action research is collaborative, in that it seeks to involve all participants in a situation and often aims to develop a shared understanding of measures that can be taken to improve an aspect of practice. In doing this, there is often an emphasis on a shared implementation of changes to practice and a group evaluation of the effectiveness of any changes.

When reading through this part of the book we would ask you to keep in mind that we have chosen to use the word 'approach', as the approaches to research design we refer to are not actual *methods* but will employ different methods as appropriate. Methods, as you may recall from earlier chapters, refer to data-collection techniques such as questionnaires and interviews. You will find out more about methods in Part 4 of this book.

8

SURVEYS

───────────── CHAPTER OBJECTIVES ─────────────

- To gain an understanding of what surveys are and their uses in research.
- To consider how surveys are designed and conducted.
- To look at how surveys have been used in the field of early childhood care and education.
- To reflect upon the possibilities and limitations of surveys.

ᴜrvey approach is the first of several different approaches to research described Part 3 of this book. Surveys lie within the positivist paradigm, using primarily quantitative methods to obtain information from large groups of participants. Although widely used in the fields of marketing, politics and demography, surveys have been a useful research tool in studies of *early childhood*. It is, however, very unlikely that students will choose this approach for their research project as surveys generally involve large numbers of participants. In this chapter we will be looking at how surveys are constructed and we will investigate examples of well-known surveys involving children and their parents.

WHAT IS A SURVEY?

The word 'survey' has a number of different meanings, but common to them all is the concept of investigation or examination. You may remember what it was like being a new student in your first lecture. As you sat down, you examined or *surveyed* the other students around you, to see if you recognised anyone or just to take a close look at others starting the learning journey with you. In geography the term is used to describe the process of investigating and mapping physical features of a locality, and the term is also used in the construction industry; some of you may have paid for a survey on a house that you were thinking of buying.

In research methods, a survey is a way of obtaining information usually from a large number of people. Very often students think that a survey is just another way of describing the use of questionnaires; however, a survey is a *process*, and a questionnaire is just one of a variety of methods that may be used as part of this process. This said, Hutton (1990: 8) describes surveys as a method of 'collecting information by asking a set of preformulated questions in a predetermined sequence in a structured questionnaire to a sample of individuals drawn so as to be representative of a defined population'. Therefore, if a survey is designed well, the findings should be applicable to a larger population; that is, you should be able to generalise your findings. In addition to the use of structured questionnaires, Greig et al. (2007) describe how information can be collected by using rating scales or interviews. Surveys are, therefore, an example of non-experimental research that can make use of both qualitative and quantitative methods in the same research project, using a mixed research design. These different ways of obtaining information are described in detail in Part 4 of this book.

In a more detailed look at the characteristics of surveys, Backstrom and Hursh-César (1981) identify six main features. They consider surveys to be:

- *Systematic.* That is, they are designed according to a commonly agreed set of procedures.
- *Impartial.* The participants are chosen carefully, so as to avoid any prejudice or preference on behalf of the researcher/research team.

- *Representative*. The sample of participants to be surveyed is selected carefully so that the findings generated can be generalised to a wider population. Later on in the chapter we will look at sampling in more detail.
- *Theory based*. The survey should be based upon underpinning theoretical principles that both guide the formation of the research objectives and guide the choice of methodology and methods.
- *Quantitative*. Most surveys are primarily quantitative in nature, although as previously discussed qualitative methods can be used as well.
- *Replicable*. Other people using the same methods should be able to get similar results. Of course, as we have noted elsewhere in this book, this assumes that it is possible to neutralise the effect of the researcher(s).

WHY ARE SURVEYS USED?

Coolican (2014) outlines two main purposes for surveys: descriptive and analytical.

DESCRIPTIVE SURVEYS

A descriptive survey is one that sets out to discover what people from a particular target population think and do. There are many examples of descriptive surveys in everyday life:

- *Public opinion polls*. Around election time it is hard to escape media reports of the findings of the latest public opinion polls. These polls are usually undertaken by specialised organisations that are paid by political parties, or the media, to find out people's views on which way they intend to vote. Since it is not possible to contact everyone of voting age, the pollsters ask a sample of the population for their views and hope that these views represent the population as a whole. The polls are made more reliable by choosing the sample of people to be interviewed very carefully. As far as possible, the sample is constructed to represent the demographic make-up of the population, and is chosen according to characteristics such as age, gender, social class, education and ethnicity. No poll can be totally accurate, and far from being predictive of possible voting behaviour, can only reflect opinion at the time the poll was taken.
- *The UK national census*. This is a survey of all households in the UK, held every ten years. It is designed to give detailed information about the whole population, rather than taking a sample, asking everyone the same set of core questions. The questions are designed to help the government better plan for housing, transport, health and education. At the time of writing the next census is planned to be held in 2021.

—— ACTIVITY ——————————————

Explore the census information that is available for the country you live in. A few examples have been included here:

- For the UK: www.ons.gov.uk/ons/guide-method/census/2011/index.html.
- For the USA: http://census.gov/library/publications.html.
- For New Zealand: www.stats.govt.nz/Census.aspx.
- For India: www.censusindia.gov.in.
- For the Republic of Ireland: www.cso.ie/en/census/index.html.

Investigate the methods used for collecting census information and the main findings for the latest census. How is this information used?
   (All websites accessed 16 February 2017.)

- *Market research.* Market research is used by businesses to find out information from consumers about products and services. The information used helps producers refine their product to meet a 'recognised need' and to target promotional material accurately to those likely to use the product. The three main ways of collecting market research information are by postal survey, telephone interview or face-to-face interview. Supermarkets and big stores also collect information from till receipts and often target promotions to individuals on the basis of this.
- *Descriptive surveys.* These are used in childcare and education to find out information on such topics as availability and cost of provision, achievement (results of Standard Attainment Tests [SATs]), nutrition, health and attitudes of parents and practitioners on a variety of issues.

RESEARCH IN FOCUS

In this Research in Focus section we will look at an example of a descriptive survey (Kavanagh et al., 2012).

This study investigates the knowledge, attitudes and prior exposure to breast feeding in a group of 248 undergraduate students (both male and female) in the USA. A cross-sectional descriptive survey design was used. The students were all attending nutrition classes in the

(Continued)

university and filled in a questionnaire designed to reveal their knowledge and attitudes towards breast feeding.

Findings revealed that although the students had good knowledge of breast feeding, they had rather negative attitudes towards it. So although they 'knew' that breast feeding was 'best' for baby, it was seen to be painful and inconvenient, especially if the mother was working. The students were generally unsupportive of breast feeding in public, with men being slightly more supportive than the women.

Key questions

- Why did the researchers look at so many students? Would a similar study of 20 students be a large enough sample from which to make generalisations? Do you think the sample size used in this study was sufficient?
- The students were all undergraduates attending classes on nutrition. Do you consider that the findings can be used to tell us anything about young people in general?

In responding to the questions posed in the Research in Focus feature, you may have reflected that in a study such as this, the more participants there are in a survey, the more likely it is that the results will be generalisable to a wider population. Later on in the chapter you will find a discussion about the factors that need to be considered when choosing participants for a survey. In addition, the sample is not 'representative' of the population of young people; that is, the students are studying nutrition so the finding that their knowledge was good is to be expected. Also, students at university are, by definition, better educated than the general population.

ANALYTICAL SURVEYS

Surveys can be used to test a hypothesis or to answer specific research questions.

RESEARCH IN FOCUS

INDIA

According to De Souza et al. (2006) early intervention can improve the outcomes of babies who are born at risk of growth and developmental problems. In India and other developing countries parents may fail to keep up with treatment programmes for their children because of lack of money, poor education or lack of communication with the various agencies involved. It was hypothesised that if treatment was provided closer to the babies' homes and supported

(Continued)

(Continued)

by local health workers then parents would be more likely to adhere to the treatment that their babies needed. To test this hypothesis De Souza et al. (2006) undertook a survey of 152 new babies and their parents who were part of an early intervention programme designed to improve the outcome of the infants who were considered to be at high risk. The families were followed up until the babies were 1 year old.

The findings suggested that although approximately 60 per cent of families attended three or more sessions, 40 per cent of parents failed to comply with the intervention programme. Looking at the characteristics of the families that showed good compliance, it was revealed that families who were better educated and lived closer to the centre were more likely to adhere to the programme.

Key questions

Look at the De Souza et al. (2006) article which can be found at: http://onlinelibrary.wiley.com/doi/10.1111/j.1365-2214.2006.00576.x/full (accessed 16 February 2017).

1. What criteria were used to decide which families to include in the study?
2. What did the intervention programme consist of?
3. What information was obtained about the families and the babies throughout the study?
4. Did the findings prove, partially prove or disprove the original hypothesis?

Johnson and Christensen (2012) have outlined five objectives for educational research: exploration, description, explanation, prediction and influence; surveys can be used to obtain information to fulfil all five objectives.

1. *Exploration.* This is where a researcher is trying to generate ideas about a particular issue. It is useful at the beginning of a project, helping to throw up questions that can be looked at in more depth. For instance, a survey of parents' views about a particular issue may point to a common attitude or idea that needs to be looked at in more depth than a survey will allow.
2. *Description.* As noted previously, this is one of the most basic activities of research. Surveys are an ideal tool to provide descriptive data, as we saw in Kavanagh et al.'s (2012) research.
3. *Explanation.* This is where a researcher tries to explain why a particular observed phenomenon occurs. For example, Coolican (2009) describes how survey data have been used to show that poor reading levels in children from the lowest socio-economic class in the UK can be attributed to poverty and disadvantage rather than class per se.

4. *Prediction.* This is when the researcher attempts to forecast a particular phenomenon. The De Souza et al. (2006) study is an example of this, where the authors formulated a prediction (hypothesis) and used survey material to confirm their predictions.
5. *Influence.* This is when researchers attempt to use research findings to make changes in practice and/or policy. An example of this is the importance attached to the results of the evaluation surveys of the US Head Start programme. This is a programme designed to support very young children and their parents in disadvantaged areas. Ongoing research, including the use of surveys, has shown the many positive benefits of the intervention and this research was one of the factors underpinning the adoption of the Sure Start initiative in the UK (Glass, 1999).

DESIGNING A SURVEY

The design stage of the survey process will determine if the results will be useful (Kasunic, 2005), and it is at this stage of the proceedings that the researcher needs to bring into play three distinct kinds of knowledge. In the first instance, it is important to have a degree of expertise in the subject matter under investigation as this will inform the aims of the research and the information to be obtained. Secondly, the researcher needs to have an understanding of how to design a reliable and valid survey and, finally, it is important to have skills to analyse the survey data.

Deming (1960) points out that there is considerable skill required in devising a survey. In addition, there are considerable limitations to the survey approach, which tend not to make it a method of choice for students undertaking a piece of small-scale research. Kasunic (2005: 6) outlines these limitations as follows:

- One of the characteristics of surveys is that they are designed to obtain data from a *sample* population with the expectation that the findings will be generalisable; that is, applicable to the population from which the sample is drawn. For this outcome, the survey must follow *strict* procedures in defining which participants are to be studied and how they are selected. In order to do this, it is likely that a form of probability sampling will be used, which is where participants are chosen at random from the population being studied or have an 'equal and independent chance of selection in the sample' (Kumar, 2014: 320). This reduces the possibility that the results of the survey could be influenced, consciously or unconsciously, by human choice. For example, the De Souza et al. (2006) study did not use probability sampling. Although *all* babies discharged from a special care baby unit who were identified as being at high risk were eligible for the study, they were only entered if their parents gave permission. The survey's findings could have been different if they had been included. For example, parents may have refused to enter the study because they knew beforehand that it would be impossible for them to find the transport or money to enable their child to enter the intervention programme.

- Far from being a quick and cheap option, designing a reliable, valid survey can be very *expensive* of both time and money.

- Because of the potentially large numbers of participants involved, and the need to ensure reliability, survey data are usually *superficial*. In the Kavanagh et al. (2012) research that we looked at earlier there were 248 participants. In-depth interviews would have provided the researchers with a more 'in-depth' understanding of the students' attitudes, etc., but resources may have been limited.

- Surveys can be *intrusive*, asking participants to reveal aspects of themselves that they may be reluctant to reveal. If the main method of collecting data is a self-administered questionnaire the response may not be truthful. However, this could also be said of other data-collection methods, such as interviewing.

To overcome some of these limitations Kasunic (2005) suggests that a seven-stage process is undertaken when designing a survey.

THE SEVEN STAGES IN DESIGNING A SURVEY

1. Identification of objectives

It is essential that the researcher is clear from the beginning what it is they want to find out. Without clear objectives, the survey will not be very effective. For example, in the Kavanagh et al. (2012) study the researchers wanted to find out about students' knowledge of, attitudes to and prior exposure to breast feeding. It is at this stage of the process that the researcher needs to decide if the survey is to follow a set of participants over a period of time (a *longitudinal* survey) or to survey the participants at one point in time only (a *cross-sectional* survey).

- *Longitudinal surveys*. These are surveys where information is collected at more than one point in time. Johnson and Christensen (2012) describe two main types of longitudinal study. One is the trend study where different samples of people from a population are asked the same questions at different times. For example, in the UK there was a longitudinal study of infant feeding practices, called the Infant Feeding Survey. Every five years, from 1985 until 2010, mothers with babies aged 0–9 months were surveyed to elicit information on infant feeding practices (McAndrew et al., 2012). The other main type of longitudinal survey is the panel survey, where the same groups of participants are studied at different points over time. This type of study is also known as a prospective study, because the researcher starts in the present and moves forward in time (Johnson and Christensen, 2012). The group of individuals studied is called a 'cohort'. Some longitudinal studies follow just one cohort, while others study successive cohorts of participants. The De Souza et al. (2006) study is an example of a prospective study.

Longitudinal studies are very useful for looking at how individuals change over time; for instance, it is possible to see if the chances of becoming obese increase as the participants get older. However, there are disadvantages as participants may be lost from the study. These surveys are relatively expensive and time-consuming, and once started it is difficult to make modifications to the survey design, as the researcher would no longer be comparing 'like with like'.

- *Cross-sectional surveys*. In this type of survey information is collected from participants at one point in time only, and comparisons are made between different groups within the study. For example, if a researcher wanted to see if levels of obesity change with age, they would include participants of different ages in the study. However, as they would not be following the same individuals over time, differences between the participants may influence the results.

Some large, prospective studies introduce a cross-sectional element when questions are asked in one year when the cohort is surveyed, but not in other years.

2. Identification and characterisation of the population

The 'population' of a survey is the group to which the researcher wishes their findings to be applicable. The 'population' can be defined in terms of any variable that is relevant to the study. For example, in the De Souza et al. (2006) study the 'population' consisted of newborn babies considered to be at high risk. Out of these 278 infants only 152 babies completed the intervention programme and it was this group of children who formed the final sample. This is sometimes known as the 'sampling frame'.

Once the population of the survey has been identified then the researcher tries to understand as much as possible about the target audience. For instance, in the De Souza et al. study, the population was the children, but the target audience included the children's parents as well, because the researchers aimed to find out what factors within the families would promote or hinder compliance with the intervention programme. Therefore, when designing the survey researchers needed to take into consideration such things as:

- the best way to communicate with parents (many in the study would not be able to read so relying on written information would be difficult)
- social customs (would mothers feel comfortable talking to a male researcher?).

Understanding the target audience will help in designing information-gathering instruments that the participants can both understand and will be motivated to complete.

CASE STUDY

Yolande is an early years practitioner in a large UK inner-city school with 120 children in the nursery and reception classes. The school has found that it is increasingly difficult to arrange consultation times with parents that suit their domestic and working arrangements. Yolande intends to carry out a survey of *all* the parents to find out their preferred way of keeping in contact with school staff.

1. What is the population of her survey?
2. In this case will there be any difference between her population and the target audience?
3. What characteristics of the population does she need to know to help her design her survey?

Yolande's target population is all the parents of children in the nursery and reception classes. As she intends to include every family there is no difference between the target population and the target audience. In a survey such as this, Yolande will need to know as much as possible about the target population so that she can design a survey that will give useful information, such as how many parents may need help accessing written material. She may need to think about providing translations in community languages and using clear, bold text that is easy to understand.

3. Design of sampling plan

Unless the target population is very specific, as in the Case Study, it is unlikely that the researcher can survey everyone; they have to choose a *sample*. There are two main decisions to be made:

(a) How will the participants of the survey be selected?
(b) How many participants will be needed?

If the researcher intends the results of the survey to be generalised out to the *whole* population then the sample must be chosen in such a way that every member of the population has an *equal chance* of being selected and the sample size has to be large enough for there to be a reasonable chance that all the relevant variables are accounted for. In a survey of parents, for instance, a large sample chosen at random is more likely to include mothers and fathers, of all social classes, with representatives from Black and minority ethnic groups in the proportion that they occur in the population, and parents with different levels of education. There is a more detailed look at sampling in Chapter 1.

4. Design and writing of the questionnaire/and or designing the structure of interviews

The success of a survey depends upon *what* questions are asked and *how* they are asked. Most surveys have a questionnaire at their core, to find out key information. However, some surveys also include a more qualitative measure, such as semi-structured interviews. Whatever measure is chosen, the design process must be equally as rigorous, especially if the researcher intends the results of the survey to be *generalisable*. Using more than one method to obtain information is a type of triangulation, whereby the strengths of one method compensate for the weaknesses of another. You will find information about how to design a questionnaire and how to conduct an interview in Part 4 of this book.

5. Pilot the test questionnaire/interview format

Before the researcher embarks on a *full-scale* survey it is always wise to test or 'pilot' the questionnaire and/or interview format with a small group of participants, who are as representative as possible of the larger sample. Many potential difficulties with the questions, layout, procedure and any technology used can be ironed out at this stage. It is also wise to practise analysing the results of the pilot study using the techniques that will be used in the main survey. This will tell you if the questions asked are actually giving you the information that you are seeking and, in addition, any procedural difficulties can be resolved.

6. Distribution of the questionnaire/conducting the interviews

The researcher may have had to modify their questionnaire/interview format because of issues that arose at the piloting stage, but all being well s/he can move on to distributing the questionnaire and/or conducting the interviews. For questionnaires the main issues to think about are:

- controlling distribution (such as email or by post)
- deciding how long to give participants to respond

- monitoring the response rate
- deciding if and when to send out reminders to participants.

If the researchers are using interviews, they need to decide if this will be face to face or via the telephone. Often several interviewers will be used and they will have to be trained so that the same procedure is used for all participants. You will note that this links to positivist concerns about the ability of the study to be replicated and the need to neutralise the effect of the researcher.

7. Analysis of results and writing the report

When the data have been collected they then need to be analysed. This needs to have been thought about at the design stage. If the questions have been formulated well and relate directly to the main research objectives, then analysis should be relatively straightforward. If you are using an online tool then the analysis will be done for you, but you still have to make sure that the results make sense and are in the format you expect. The various ways of analysing information from questionnaires and interviews will be discussed later on in this book. Finally, the report needs to be written.

THE USE OF SURVEYS IN EARLY CHILDHOOD

The use of surveys to obtain information about early childhood issues is well established, and in this section we will look in more detail at some examples. You will recall that there are two main kinds of survey: *longitudinal prospective studies* that follow a cohort of children until adulthood and beyond, and *cross-sectional surveys* that tend to have a more limited focus.

LONGITUDINAL PROSPECTIVE STUDIES

There have been three main birth cohort studies in the UK. Cohort studies involve following a particular group or 'cohort' of individuals from birth, throughout their lives. This involves the use of multiple surveys undertaken at regular intervals on the same group of people. The surveys collect a huge and varied amount of information about the individuals, from the moment they are born through to adulthood. In addition, information is collected about their families. The information collected includes:

- details about the individual's birth, health and all-round development
- details about the individual's education and employment

- details about the individual's attitudes and beliefs
- demographic details about the individual's parents and their parenting style.

Because the same individuals are studied throughout their lives, it is possible to see the effect of different circumstances on their lives. For example, such a survey would be able to show if children born of wealthier parents had better outcomes in terms of health, education and employment as adults.

The three main large-scale cohort studies in the UK are:

- the 1958 National Child Development Study, which looked at 17,500 children born in a single week in 1958 (in England, Scotland and Wales)
- the 1970 British Cohort Study, which looked at 17,200 children born in one week in April 1970 (in England, Scotland, Wales and Northern Ireland)
- the Millennium Cohort Study, which looked at 18,800 children from the age of 9 months living in the UK, who were born in 2000.

Because there are now three separate cohorts being studied it is possible to see if there have been any changes across generations. For instance, it is possible to see if children's health has improved since 1958.

The organisation of these studies, together with the collation, dissemination and storage of all the information collected, is now in the hands of the Centre for Longitudinal Studies (CLS), based at the Institute of Education in London. The data that are collected are made available to the wider research community and are a valuable national resource. According to the CLS (2007), the findings produced evidence for a number of government inquiries such as the Plowden Committee on Primary Education (Central Advisory Council for Education, 1967), the Warnock Report on children with special educational needs (Warnock Committee, 1978) and the Acheson report on inequalities in health (Acheson, 1998).

RESEARCH IN FOCUS

The Millennium Cohort Study included as its sample 18,800 babies born in 2000, the first survey (first sweep) being undertaken when the babies were 9 months old. As well as being designed to obtain data about children born in England, the study is particularly interested in outcomes for children born in Northern Ireland, Scotland and Wales, children from Black and minority ethnic groups, and those living in disadvantaged areas. Children were drawn at random from areas in the UK chosen to represent these characteristics. As well as concentrating on particular geographic areas and upon specific groups, the study is designed so that findings

(Continued)

(Continued)

can be compared with those from the earlier cohort studies. One difference is that in this study information is being gathered from the children's fathers as well as from their mothers.

Further surveys were undertaken on the children when they were aged 3, 5, 7, 11 and 14.

So far findings show the great diversity of families that children are born into; from families where both parents, in their thirties, are graduates and earning, to lone mothers in their teens with no employment and no qualifications. The survey has shown that there are great differences between the different groups in the survey, with Asian mothers being more likely to breast feed than other groups and less likely to return to employment after the birth of their baby.

Key questions

1. What are the advantages and disadvantages of having a sample of nearly 19,000 children?
2. Look at the CLS website. What is the main difference in the way in which the sample was drawn, compared with the 1970 British Cohort Study? www.cls.ioe.ac.uk/Sitemap.aspx (accessed 16 February 2017).

The advantage of having such a large sample is that findings can be generalised to a wider population with some confidence, but administering such a large survey is costly in terms of time and money. It is difficult to keep in touch with so many families and there will always be some families who cannot be contacted. The main difference in the way that the samples were drawn for the Millennium Cohort Study and the 1970 British Cohort Study is that the Millennium Cohort Study included children from Northern Ireland and particularly targeted areas of disadvantage, whereas the British Cohort Study looked at every child born in a particular week in England, Scotland and Wales in 1970.

Other examples of longitudinal prospective studies

- *The Avon Longitudinal Study of Parents and Their Children (ALSPAC).* This is a longitudinal study of 14,000 children born in 1991–92 in the West of England. The study began with their parents, before the children were born, and continues to monitor the children, who are now young adults. The study has a health focus, specifically looking at the interaction between environmental and genetic factors on children's health and development (Golding et al., 2001). The website can be found at: www.bristol.ac.uk/alspac/about (accessed 16 February 2017).

- *The Christchurch Health and Development Study.* This New Zealand Study is similar to the Avon Longitudinal Study in the UK. The Christchurch study has followed 1,265 children born in the mid-1970s. Details of the study and the many publications arising from it can be found at: www.otago.ac.nz/christchurch/research/healthdevelopment (accessed 16 February 2017).
- *The Effective Provision of Pre-School Education Project (EPPE).* This is a longitudinal study of 3,000 children in the UK that was designed to look at the effectiveness of different types of pre-school education on children's development and later achievement in school. The project started in 1997 and has followed the children through pre-school, primary and secondary school. The project intends to follow the children as they become young adults and enter post-compulsory education and employment. It has been re-named the Effective Pre-School, Primary and Secondary Education (EPPSE) project. The website can be found at: www.ucl.ac.uk/ioe/research/featured-research/effective-pre-school-primary-secondary-education-project (accessed 16 February 2017).
- *The NICHD Study of Early Child Care and Youth Development (SECCYD).* This is a US longitudinal study of a cohort of children aged 1 month old in 1991. The study gathered information on the children at 4 different points in time and concluded in 2009 when the children were in 9th grade. The data remain available for researchers to analyse and findings are still being reported. The prime goal of the NICHD study was to investigate how children's social, emotional, intellectual, and language development, and their physical growth and health are influenced by differences in child care experiences. Information on the SECCYD can be found at: www.nichd.nih.gov/research/supported/seccyd/Pages/overview.aspx (accessed 16 February 2017).

--- ✈ --- ACTIVITY --

The Fragile Families and Wellbeing Study is a longitudinal prospective study of nearly 2,000 children born between 1998 and 2000 in the USA.

Details of the study can be found at: www.fragilefamilies.princeton.edu/about (accessed 16 February 2017).

1. What are the aims of this study?
2. What data-collecting methods have been used?
3. Look at the publications section and summarise the main findings to date.

CROSS-SECTIONAL SURVEYS

These studies endeavour to find out information from a sample of participants at one point in time.

An example of this kind of survey is the survey of parents' views about childcare (Booth et al., 2013) undertaken for the Department for Education in England, which looked at the childcare arrangements made by 1,000 families in 2012. The survey was conducted by telephone in September of that year using parents who were originally recruited using child benefit data.

 REFLECTION POINT

Before leaving this chapter, reflect for a moment on what surveys can tell us and what they cannot tell us. In doing this, think back to some of the debates we introduced you to in Chapters 4 and 5. In what ways are surveys limited as an approach in early childhood research?

We are sure that in reflecting upon surveys as an approach to early childhood research, you can see the advantage of being able to 'speak with confidence' about large numbers of children and families. However, you may also have noted that there are other aspects of early childhood that surveys cannot illuminate. You may have thought that they would be inappropriate if the research was aiming for a detailed, holistic insight into a setting, or wishing to focus on the minutiae of early childhood practice, or if the aim of the research was to elicit the children's perspectives directly. It is highly unlikely that any undergraduate student would undertake a survey as a research project as they can be a *huge* and *time-consuming* undertaking, often requiring a high level of skill in statistics, and are usually conducted by a team of researchers as opposed to one individual.

The next chapter looks at a very different approach to research, which is qualitative in nature: ethnography.

 KEY POINTS FROM THE CHAPTER

- A survey is a way of collecting information from individuals, often in large numbers, using primarily quantitative methods such as questionnaires. Qualitative methods, such as semi-structured interviews, are sometimes used if there is a mixed approach.
- Generally, the findings of surveys are designed to be *generalisable* from the participants being investigated to the whole of the population to whom the research is relevant.

(Continued)

- For findings to be generalisable, the sample of participants to be studied has to be *representative* of the population as a whole.
- Surveys can be longitudinal, following a cohort of individuals over time, or *cross-sectional*, where a group of individuals is studied at one point in time only.
- Surveys are not useful if the researcher wishes to focus on the minutiae of practice, gain detailed data on a small sample or elicit children's perspectives directly.

FURTHER READING

De Vaus, D. (2013) *Surveys in Social Research*, 6th edition. London: Routledge. This is a 'classic' text that takes the reader through the practical steps of designing a survey and analysing the results.

Johnson, B. and Christensen, L. (2012) *Educational Research*, 4th edition. Thousand Oaks, CA: Sage. Chapter 9 has a good section on sampling.

Don't forget to visit the online resources at https://study.sagepub.com/mukherjiandalbon3e for access to free SAGE journal articles, weblinks, videos, exercises, mini quizzes and an interactive glossary.

9

ETHNOGRAPHY

———————— CHAPTER OBJECTIVES ————————

- To gain an understanding of ethnography as an approach to research.
- To consider how ethnographic research is used in the field of early childhood.
- To think about the research methods that are appropriate in ethnographic research.
- To reflect on the possibilities and limitations of this approach to research.

This chapter is in marked contrast to the previous chapter, which looked at surveys. Here we will be thinking about research that falls firmly within the sphere of qualitative research. Ethnography, as we will see, has a long tradition in research, especially in the field of social anthropology. In particular, ethnography has been used in studies of children and childhoods in many sociocultural contexts and has been important in highlighting the multifaceted nature of childhood (James, 2007). In addition to this, ethnographic research has been employed in *early childhood* research illuminating a wide range of areas, such as children's play cultures (Corsaro, 1985). In terms of the process of doing ethnographic research, we will see that ethnographic research aims at 'immersion' or becoming a member of a setting or group in some way and stresses the keeping of a detailed fieldwork diary and participant observation. It is this level of fieldwork that distinguishes ethnography from case study research, which may or may not involve this. The next chapter on case studies discusses this distinction further.

WHAT DO WE MEAN BY 'ETHNOGRAPHY'?

You may recall that in Chapter 5 we observed that ethnography can be defined as a 'description of people or cultures' (Denscombe, 2010: 79). In addition, ethnography can be described as 'the study of people as they go about their everyday lives' (Buchbinder et al., 2006: 47). These descriptions of ethnography tell us that it relates to research about people going about their everyday activities, but more than this, ethnography is also associated with 'thick description' and the interpretations made of this (James, 2007). You will find out more about this key feature of ethnography as you read the chapter.

But ethnography is not as simple to define as this suggests. Pole and Morrison (2003) note that ethnography is sometimes used as a synonym for *all* qualitative approaches to research, something we highlighted in Chapter 5. This can be seen in the way 'ethnography' is used to refer to the product of the research as well as the activity or process of carrying out the research. Despite this ambiguity, Pole and Morrison (2003) maintain that in reading a wide range of studies there are some features that studies deemed 'ethnographic' have in common:

- There is a focus on a specific location, setting or event.
- Within this specific location, setting or event, there is a focus on the *full* range of social behaviour.
- A range of methods might be employed – although, in general, the emphasis is on observation – in order to understand this social behaviour from *inside* the location, setting or event.

- Data analysis involves a movement from rich description to identifying concepts and theories that are grounded in the data, which are collected in that location, setting or event.
- There is an emphasis on capturing as much detail as possible and in so doing, not shying away from the *complexities* of the issues in the research location, setting or event. This is viewed as more important than the ability to make generalisations in ethnographic research.

(Adapted slightly from Pole and Morrison, 2003: 3.)

Thus, we can see that rather than aiming to test hypotheses or establish causality between variables, ethnographers focus on individuals' understandings of their social world as well as gaining an insight – at first hand – into the everyday habits, beliefs and language of the group they are studying (Edmond, 2005). There is also an emphasis on observation in a 'naturalistic' setting in ethnographic research, with the researcher or 'ethnographer' traditionally aiming for a position where they do not 'disturb the field'. By 'field' researchers are talking about the context in which their study is located such as a nursery, hospital, playground or home and the people who are part of that context. More recent approaches to ethnography recognise that it is impossible *not* to disturb the field and stress the importance of acknowledging the subjectivity of the researcher; that is, who they are in relation to the group they are studying – the notion of reflexivity (Angrosino, 2005; Coffey, 1999).

In tracing the history of ethnography, we can see that it evolved as a result of colonialism when the British colonialist administration wished to find out information about indigenous peoples in the countries they had colonised (Fielding, 2008). In social anthropological research, ethnography was used to study indigenous peoples and their cultural practices in a wide range of places around the world. Writers such as Margaret Mead and Claude Lévi-Strauss are regarded as classic scholars in this respect and lived among diverse communities in different parts of the world in order to gain an understanding of people's lives as lived in those communities.

More recently, in the 1960s, ethnography developed a more critical edge in what is known as the Chicago School of Sociology. Sociologists within this school used ethnographic methods to help them to see the world from the perspectives of those they were studying, often with an emphasis on groups who were deemed powerless in some way, such as urban youth (Deegan, 2007). They believed that by blending into the setting in which the research was carried out and carrying out research in the 'real world', with all the 'messiness' this entails, they would be able to see the world through the eyes of those they were studying. Later on, when leaving the field, they similarly believed that they would be able to interpret and write about the setting in a detached way (Fielding, 2008).

—— REFLECTION POINT ——————————————

Pause for a moment and think about what has just been said. Imagine you are going to study a group of people in a particular context that is unfamiliar to you. This unfamiliarity might be due to economic wealth, professional activity, cultural and religious practices, trauma experienced and suchlike.

How possible is it to see the world through someone else's eyes? Also, reflect on whether it is possible to represent this 'Other' world in some way – as you might try to do when making field notes, analysing and writing up a piece of research. These are important questions in relation to ethnographic research and ones we will return to later in the chapter as they have been the basis of some strong criticisms of ethnography.

Crucially, ethnography involves the intensive and continuous study of a setting or small group over a period of time in order to gain detailed insights into the particular setting or group (Corsaro, 1996; Fielding, 2008). Often, this will be via a case study example, such as a school, but, as noted previously, while case study research and ethnography are sometimes used synonymously, a case study does not *necessarily* involve the same level of fieldwork, particularly the length of time in the field. We will discuss what is meant by 'fieldwork' later in the chapter.

In summing up this first section it is important to highlight the emphasis on the in-depth analysis of everyday practices of given groups in 'naturalistic' settings as key characteristics of the ethnographic approach. These practices that come to the attention of the ethnographer might be regarded as so commonplace that the community under study hardly notices them. Indeed, the notion of making the *familiar strange* is a common one in ethnographic studies (Coffey, 1999). Thus, Gallagher and Fusco (2006: 302) maintain that, 'the real power of ethnographic study, then, lies in its ability to observe and trouble such everyday practices, the ordinary and habitual moments in given cultures'.

RESEARCH IN FOCUS

The work of Shirley Brice-Heath (1983) is a good example of ethnographic research. Although quite old now, it is still considered to be influential today. Brice-Heath spent ten years living and working among two communities in the Piedmont Carolinas in America, studying their language use. The communities were known as 'Trackton' and 'Roadville'; the former being a Black working-class community and the latter a white working-class community. Among her many

(Continued)

findings, Brice-Heath found that ways of talking and interacting in one community that seemed 'natural' to its members were culturally unfamiliar to the other community. She stresses the need to view language acquisition and conventions within a *sociocultural* context.

In terms of the research conducted, Brice-Heath engaged in 'long-term participation and observation' in the two communities (Brice-Heath, 1983: 9). She goes on to say, 'The reader should see *Ways with Words* as an unfinished story, in which the characters are real people whose lives go on beyond the decade covered in this book, and for whom we cannot, within these pages, either resolve the plot or complete the story' (1983: 13).

- In what ways does this differ from quantitative research?
- What might be the benefits of spending such a long time engaged in participation and observation in the life of these communities?
- Can you see any limitations relating to this approach to research?

In reflecting on the differences between Brice-Heath's qualitative research study and quantitative research, you may have thought about its lack of concern for controlled measurement and researcher effect, as well as the impossibility of replicating the study exactly. You may also have felt that there is a seeming lack of concern for generalisability. More pragmatically, you may have reflected that the study was highly time-consuming. However, as with all research, it is important to see that different research questions and topics lead to different methodological approaches – after all, Brice-Heath's study aimed to focus on a 'naturalistic' environment at a particular time in order to gain an insight into the *everyday* language use of two communities as opposed to their language use in an *experimental* situation. By engaging in the 'everyday life' of the two communities over a very long period, she gathered extensive observational data offering a rich description of the communities under study that could never be possible in a large-scale study such as a survey. Moreover, Brice-Heath's study does not purport to offer any neat and tidy 'solutions' to the complex study of language use but tells us a great deal about the importance of sociocultural context in language acquisition and in conventions used. In this sense, *Ways with Words* provides a powerful message that has relevance beyond the two communities studied.

ETHNOGRAPHY AND EARLY CHILDHOOD RESEARCH

James (2007) documents how social anthropologists have carried out ethnographic research into the study of childhood for over a century. While she acknowledges that some of the early anthropological studies can be criticised for their questionable assumptions about the group under study, she highlights how they documented the play and social lives of children in great detail. James (2007) also observes the way that throughout the twentieth century social anthropological studies such as those carried out by Margaret Mead in New Guinea have attempted to study the process of growing up in particular societies. As a consequence, they detail a range of things that relate to children's childhoods, not least children's family life, their early education, relationships between adults and children, and children's social lives.

James (2007) demonstrates that although these studies did not involve the children as participants, as might be more usual in studies carried out today, they *did* show that childhood is experienced differently according to the particular sociocultural group within which the child belongs. By studying children in particular sociocultural contexts – in their 'real' worlds – ethnographers have been able to show that children *actively* shape their own childhoods. Indeed Corsaro (1985: 286) goes as far as to argue 'child development ... cannot be fully documented unless it is studied as it occurs in the life-worlds of children', highlighting the importance of researching children in 'naturalistic' contexts. This can be contrasted with the search for universal generalisations about children and childhood through the use of highly controlled, experimental methods, as in many studies in the field of psychology (James, 2007).

More recent ethnographic studies of children have continued to focus on socialisation, and while direct participation 'in the field' continues to be a feature, studies carried out in areas such as early childhood do not necessarily involve *living and working* among a particular community in the way that Brice-Heath's (1983) study, outlined earlier, entailed. Corsaro (1985), for instance, has undertaken research that focuses on children's friendships and peer cultures in a *nursery*. The following Research in Focus section outlines his study and some of its key findings.

RESEARCH IN FOCUS

USA

Corsaro's research was carried out in a nursery school in the USA over a period of a year. He kept detailed field notes, carried out participant observations, video-taped the children's interactions and talked to staff. Corsaro (1985: 3) argues that to carry out his research, it was important to free himself from 'adult conceptions of children's activities, and enter the child's world as both *observer* and *participant*'.

Among the study's many findings, Corsaro found that young children are active agents in their socialisation, who begin to see themselves as 'children' - a distinct group from 'adults'. He states, 'peer culture in the nursery school was characterised by the children's persistent attempts to gain *control* of their lives through the *communal production* and *sharing* of social

(Continued)

activities with peers' (1985: 272, original emphases). In their role play with peers, Corsaro argues children are reproducing their own perceptions of the adult world as opposed to directly imitating them. He also identifies themes of sharing and control as key aspects of children's experience of nursery life.

Try to get hold of Corsaro's book *Friendship and Peer Culture in the Early Years* (1985) because it is a good example of an ethnographic study. Its first chapter 'Entering the child's world' documents in detail how the research was carried out and many books do not provide this level of detail on the methodology used. If you cannot get this book, try to find something else written by Corsaro as he has written extensively about the various ethnographic studies he has been engaged in. Later in the chapter, however, we will see that there are strong criticisms of Corsaro's approach and we will also examine another example of research on peer cultures, carried out in Sweden, which makes reference to Corsaro's ideas.

So far in this section we have thought about the ways in which ethnography has been used in studies carried out some decades ago and the ways in which it has demonstrated that children's childhoods are differently experienced. We now wish to outline why ethnography is important in *early childhood* research.

THE IMPORTANCE OF ETHNOGRAPHY TO EARLY CHILDHOOD RESEARCH

- As ethnographic studies take place over a sustained period of time, they can be particularly useful in illuminating children's development over time and capturing critical periods in childcare environments such as transition points (Buchbinder et al., 2006).
- As ethnographic research is carried out in 'naturalistic' settings as opposed to experimental conditions (we later critique the idea of 'naturalistic'), it is particularly appropriate for early childhood research (Aubrey et al., 2000). A key rationale for this is that a 'naturalistic' environment is likely to show children in a more positive light than experimental situations. This is because generally children feel more comfortable in a context that is familiar to them than one that is not, such as is the case in experimental research.
- Ethnographic research provides researchers with opportunities to gain an intimate understanding of a setting owing to the possibility of developing close relationships with children (and adults) over time. Moreover, the emotional dimension to the daily work of an early childhood setting can be more readily explored in ethnographic research than in a superficial, one-off experiment (Buchbinder et al., 2006).
- Owing to its emphasis on long immersion in the field, ethnography can empower children because, if carried out with sensitivity, children are able to

manage the participation of the researcher. Rather than their presence being imposed on the children, as in observing children at a distance, participant observation allows for the researcher's engagement with the children to be negotiated (Edmond, 2005).

- Ethnographic research in settings enables the researcher to study early childhood practice at both micro and macro levels, as early childhood settings embody a complex weaving together of government policies and sociocultural beliefs about childcare within families and institutions, as well as individual practitioners' beliefs about early childhood practice (Buchbinder et al., 2006).

- Finally here, because ethnographic research emphasises the 'naturalistic' context of its fieldwork, it illuminates everyday practices and, consequently, enables the researcher to analyse the way everyday cultural activities are organised (Buchbinder et al., 2006). Given the number of daily activities that are of significance to early childhood practice, this might be especially important. These might include meal times, sleep times and/or the development of peer relationships (Ben-Ari, 1997). In addition, ethnographic studies enable the researcher to document the sense children make of their cultural worlds.

RESEARCH IN FOCUS

SWEDEN

Löfdahl and Hägglund, like Corsaro, have explored children's peer cultures extensively in their research, employing an ethnographic approach. In the Swedish study: 'Stability and Change in Social Knowledge Domains amongst Children in Pre School Settings' they gathered data in the school year of 2004-5 about 3-5-year-old children through observing them in their daily activities and through informal conversations.

In one article from this study, Löfdahl and Hägglund (2007) explore the ring game: 'The Farmer's in His Den', which has variants across the world. In the Swedish variant, the last child in the middle becomes 'the cheese', who then becomes the next farmer. The game involves – in the first instance – the 'farmer' (in the middle of the ring) choosing the next child to join him/her in the middle, and there are seven roles in total in the game. Löfdahl and Hägglund (2007) became interested in the way that, despite the teacher's pedagogical intentions for the activity, aimed at fostering a sense of collectivity in the group, the children appropriated the game to confirm social positions and status in relation to their peer group. In particular, children chose children of the same sex and age when asked to choose someone to join them in the middle. Thus, the game produced and reproduced the social knowledge the children had of their peer group. You may wish to recall your own memories of childhood ring games (assuming you played them) and the extent to which 'choosing' reinforced social positionings, including the exclusion of some children.

Like Corsaro's (1985) research mentioned earlier in this chapter, Löfdahl and Hägglund (2007) employed an ethnographic approach in their study of children's peer cultures, and we might well have drawn on a range of other studies which have explored the peer cultures of children. These include Marsh's (2012) study on playground games in the 'new media age' in two primary schools in England, and Scott's (2002) study (in the USA) which examines intersections of gender and 'race' in the peer relationships of African-American girls, playing with and without boys, in two schools. We could have mentioned numerous other studies here.

A key question, then, is: 'Why have researchers been especially drawn to employing an ethnographic approach when researching the *peer cultures* of children?'

In answering the question above, you may have considered:

- the complexity of researching peer cultures
- the need to try – as far as is possible – to learn from and with children 'from the inside'
- the need to establish relationships with participants (children and adults)
- the importance of the 'naturalistic' context in order to observe what 'really' happens, as opposed to setting up an artificial experiment
- the need to examine changes in the peer culture over time.

When looking at any piece of research, always try to scrutinise the justification the researchers make for their research design.

It would seem, then, that ethnography offers a lot of possibilities for the researcher wishing to find out about children's different experiences of childhood. We will now look in more detail at some of the key features of carrying out ethnographic fieldwork. When talking about 'fieldwork' ethnographers are describing their experiences of being immersed in the setting which is the focus for the research. In early anthropological studies the 'setting' often amounted to living among a group of indigenous people, whose culture was very different or 'other' to the ethnographer's own. More recently, this conceptualisation of 'other' culture has been applied to groups *within* minority world countries, such as individual nurseries or urban gang cultures (Edmond, 2005).

CARRYING OUT ETHNOGRAPHIC FIELDWORK

Traditionally, and maybe in its 'purest' form, ethnographic fieldwork involves participant observation as its main research tool (Pole and Morrison, 2003). This means that the observer, that is the researcher, is part of the context they are observing and there is *direct contact* between the researcher and the people being researched. However, we should be mindful that there are various levels of involvement when carrying out observations; they might also be carried out in a way that allows the researcher to retain some detachment from the activity being observed (Edmond, 2005). You will find out more about observation in Part 4 of this book where we look at a range of methods that are used in research.

Researchers employing an ethnographic approach will use qualitative research methods (James, 2007) as these are more in keeping with the spirit of naturalism that underpins ethnography. Thus, interviews may also be used in ethnographic research, but they are likely to take the form of 'naturalistic' conversations as opposed to those involving a highly structured interview schedule (Fielding, 2008). Finally, documents might be used in ethnographic research as they can tell the researcher a great deal about the values of the setting they are studying.

 —— REFLECTION POINT ————————————————

A lot has been said so far about the 'naturalistic' context in relation to ethnography. Albon and Rosen (2014) unsettle this notion by asking the reader to consider just how 'natural' early childhood settings are. You might want to think about the following points here:

- Early childhood settings are governed by a set of rules/policies that reflect a particular society's idea of what and how young children should learn and how they should be cared for, and these change over time.
- The adults will generally have had some sort of specialist training in accordance with the above point.
- Only children of a particular age can attend and there are often rules around how many children can be grouped together in a particular space or with a particular adult.
- Young children are the majority of the participants in the setting.
- In minority world contexts especially, there is likely to be special equipment made with young children in mind and much of the furniture is likely to be on a far smaller scale than is usual outside of spaces designed for young children.

Of course the word 'naturalistic' in relation to ethnography relates to the idea of what is *usual* for a child or group, and if regular attendance at an early childhood setting is 'usual' for that child or group then this might become equated with 'natural'. However, Albon and Rosen (2014) are keen that researchers continue to question what is regarded as 'natural' and how it comes to be viewed as such. When we come to examine anything deeply in relation to social life, it is difficult to apply the word with a high degree of confidence.

Fieldwork is a key aspect of ethnography. In carrying out ethnographic research, the researcher becomes a temporary part of the setting and this immersion in the field is viewed as enabling him or her to gain an understanding of the use of language and the cultural practices of the setting, which in turn will enable inferences to be made about the kinds of rules that govern behaviours in the particular setting under study as well as underlying patterns of behaviour (Fielding, 2008).

In becoming part of a setting, albeit on a temporary basis, the researcher using an ethnographic approach will keep detailed field notes in an attempt to try and understand the perspective(s) of the group under study. Later on in this book we devote a chapter to journaling as a research tool, but also highlight its importance in documenting thoughts and feelings as research progresses. This is very important in ethnographic research. Ethnographic field notes will also contain detailed observations and reflections on these, which when pieced together, form a detailed picture of the setting under study. Usually field notes are written up on a daily basis to ensure things are not forgotten, even though much of the material in a fieldwork diary will not be written up in the final publication or report. Emerson et al. (2007: 353) describe field notes as a 'loose collection of possibly usable materials' and assert that in writing field notes, the researcher is constructing the field of their inquiry according to their ethnographic gaze. You may recall the Reflection Point near the beginning of this chapter, which encouraged you to think about whether it is possible to 'know' the 'Other'. Inevitably, *who we are* impacts on *how we see* the research setting – it directs our ethnographic gaze.

But becoming 'part of a setting' or 'entering the field' is not as easy as it might at first appear. It can involve lengthy and ongoing negotiation (Albon and Rosen, 2014). Clearly, in early childhood research, if you wanted to carry out an ethnographic study in an early childhood institution, for instance, you would need to do a lot of work in gaining access, working with a range of adult gatekeepers such as the nursery manager, parents and staff, and being clear about the kinds of things you will be looking at and how you will be gathering the data. You will recall from Chapter 6 that this is an essential part of 'informed consent'. In doing this, it is important to be aware that having negotiated access with these adult gatekeepers, the researcher still needs to think carefully about negotiating access with *children* (James, 2007). After all, we should not assume that adults 'speak' for all the children in the nursery and negotiating relationships with very young children requires at least the same degree of respect and consideration as it does with adults. Moreover, relationships require constant negotiation, which reflects the 'messiness' of undertaking ethnographic fieldwork. This 'messiness' is reflected in the way that any research relationship with a participant needs to be seen as part of a 'web of encounters' in that setting, involving, for example, children, practitioners and parents, each of whom may have particular 'calls' on the researcher (Albon and Rosen, 2014). The idea of research being 'messy' was also raised as an issue in Chapter 6.

— 🔍 —— **CASE STUDY** —————————————————————

Let us consider the idea that in ethnographic research the researcher's relationships with the children are part of a wider web of encounters within a particular setting or community, as Albon and Rosen (2014) assert. Earlier in the chapter, we noted how researchers have often employed an ethnographic approach when researching children's peer cultures and play. Maria – an early childhood studies student – was interested in exploring this area in relation to superhero play in a nursery, which she visited once a week for eight months. The following is an account of one of the ethical dilemmas she encountered.

When observing and participating with a group of children at play, sometimes Maria heard a child use language that would not be sanctioned by the practitioners (she was the only adult within earshot). Maria pondered over whether she should join in the play, perhaps reinforcing that language or the idea expressed in that language? However, alternatively, should she pretend not to hear? Should she reprimand the child? Should she inform the practitioners but perhaps break any trust she had formed with the children?

Maria decided that she would adopt a strategy of pretending not to hear whilst not informing the practitioners in the setting what she had heard unless what was said related to a child protection issue or if she felt a child was being subjected to, for example, a racist comment. Maria did not want to compromise the 'different' position she had within the setting – she was not, after all, employed as a practitioner and so did not have the same power and responsibility for the children.

In reflecting on what Maria decided to do and not do, consider the consequences of her actions (or *inactions*) on that child, the group of children, the practitioners, the setting and her as researcher.

We hope that in reflecting on Maria's research and exploring these questions you can see how 'messy' research can be and how ethical issues can emerge throughout a study. The more you read about how established researchers have tackled such issues and the more you reflect on such issues yourself (particularly with a supervising tutor if currently undertaking a research project) the more insight you will gain. Ethnographic research throws into sharp relief these kinds of questions as it tends towards fostering closer relationships between the researcher and research participants, unlike, for example, a large-scale survey conducted at a distance.

Whilst 'informed consent' is an important principle in any research project, ethnographic studies have been carried out more covertly. An example of a covert ethnographic study is Fielding's study of the racist organisation, the National Front, described in Fielding (2008). In this study, he infiltrated the group covertly in order to allow him access to the group's activities and documentation. He argues that he would never have been accepted into the group if his status as a researcher had been known. In early childhood research, we would argue *very strongly* that a covert study in an early-childhood-related institution, for instance, is highly unethical. Even highly experienced researchers would find it difficult to justify covert ethnographic research to an ethics committee. Whilst we might recall watching some of the exposés of poor practice in a few nurseries that have been televised in the past, which have involved a person pretending to be an early childhood practitioner as a 'cover story' and covertly using video equipment, this is journalism and *not* academic research. Therefore, if you have seen any practices of serious concern occurring in an early childhood setting – particularly if you feel they compromise the safety and well-being of young children – you should report these concerns *immediately* to the relevant authorities. You should not try to 'build a case' as if you were an undercover reporter. Should this situation arise and if you are in any doubt as to what you should do, talk to your tutor as soon as you are able.

Owing to ethnography's focus on ongoing participation in the field, the researcher has to consider what role they will adopt in the setting. Fielding (2008: 271) uses the phrase 'front management' to describe this process, whereas Coffey (1999: 23) refers to this as the 'negotiation or crafting of ethnographic selfhood in the process of fieldwork'. Crucially, the onus is on the *researcher* to initiate, establish and maintain a good working relationship with the setting (Coffey, 1999). As noted in the previous Reflection Point, this is not always easy to navigate.

Fielding (2008) argues that this is easiest when the researcher is in tune with the values of the setting. We wish to stress the importance of this because if the researcher's own values are at *significant odds* with the values of the research setting, there is likely to be a degree of deception involved in the data collection. This is because there is a high probability that fieldwork notes will highlight this clash in values and, consequently, the researcher may not feel able to share her/his observations and reflections on these with the research setting. As you will know from Chapter 6, deception is rarely viewed as acceptable in research.

Whatever role is adopted, it is important to remember that the researcher is a 'semi-participant' in the setting and needs to present a 'true self' (Edmond, 2005: 131). A concrete example of this can be seen in Debbie Albon's research. While she is a qualified nursery nurse and teacher of more than 20 years, when she carries out research in early childhood settings she is *not* the teacher or nursery nurse of those children. However, she does draw upon her professional skills in the course of participating in the everyday life of the setting and tries to support the work of the setting in whatever ways she can. Not to do so would mean pretending to be something she is not and would feel uncomfortable. Children are also wise to people they see as acting in inauthentic ways (Edmond, 2005).

An example of another role that might be adopted in a setting is that of 'not knowing', which can be useful as members of the group under study feel the need to explain what they do and why they do it, even if it seems obvious to them. In early childhood research, Mandell (1988) advocates the adoption of a 'least adult' role, which involves taking on the social position of a child in order to gain an insight into their perspectives. Buchbinder et al. (2006) argue that while differences between adults and children cannot be fully overcome, not least in terms of physical size, the adoption of the 'least adult' position does treat children as experts on their own lives as the adult researcher is not adopting a position of power. This is a point we return to later.

ITALY

RESEARCH IN FOCUS

In a study Corsaro conducted into peer culture in a nursery in Modena, Italy, his lack of competence in speaking Italian gave him the persona of an 'incompetent adult' in the eyes of the children, who sought to educate him in the ways of their language and the cultural life of their school. He feels that this lack of knowledge enabled him to gain an insight into the relative powerlessness of children in society, not least owing to the teasing he experienced from the children and adults. Corsaro's 'incompetence', arguably, enabled him to be readily accepted by the children. In other words, he was able to 'enter their world' as he was seen as less threatening. Another example of how Corsaro negotiated access to the children's worlds was in the children's use of seemingly risqué jokes about 'poo-poo', through which they tested how he would react. As his reaction was deemed positive, he was further accepted into the children's peer culture (Corsaro and Molinari, 2008).

You might like to reflect upon the conceptualisation of 'children's worlds' as if they are somehow very different to the 'world of adults'.

In thinking about the role the researcher might adopt within a setting, we should also remember that settings change (Angrosino, 2005). If we imagine an ethnographic study being carried out in a nursery, we might envisage a huge number of things that could change within a given time span – let us say six months. These might be:

- new children starting
- children leaving for other settings and schools
- staff members coming and going
- the themes of the children's talk and play changing owing to newly co-created group interests
- new working practices introduced – maybe as a result of new policy
- changes made to the layout of the nursery environment
- an outbreak of chickenpox or other disease.

We are sure that you can imagine many other things that might change over time. Try also to envisage what might change in relation to the self of the *researcher* over time. Look at the following Case Study as an example of this.

— 🔍 —— CASE STUDY ——————————————————

Debbie Albon's Doctoral study examined food and eating 'events' (to use the term coined by Douglas and Nicod, 1974) in four early childhood settings. She spent four to five months, one day a week, in each setting, adopting an ethnographic approach. When carrying out the fieldwork in setting three, Debbie decided to go on a weight loss pro- gramme and over the ensuing months, gradually lost three stones in weight. In doing this, she feels she had a different relationship to the practitioners in this setting because she did not join in with their snack-eating of cakes and biscuits brought in from home, which seemed to serve as a means of binding the group together.

Without intending to, she seemed to develop a role as someone of immense will-power, something many of the practitioners felt they personally could not sustain. This seemed to mark her out as 'other' or different in a way that had not been her experience in the previous two settings. Not only this, but her physical experience of being in the set- ting felt different as the small furniture in the nursery began to feel less small as her physical size diminished. It was important for Debbie to document her reflections on the impact her weight loss seemed to have on both her and the setting because she felt it impacted on the data she was gathering. Angrosino (2005) argues that an understand- ing of the self of the ethnographer is essential in enabling the reader to interpret the written research or 'product'.

You might like to think further about the issue of physical size in relation to a study such as this, and indeed early childhood research in general – after all, a key feature that marks adults out from babies and young children is relative size. Albon and Rosen's (2014) book explores issues such as this, particularly in Chapters 3 and 4.

What we can see from this is that it is not only the setting that is constantly changing; the self of the ethnographer in relation to the setting is also dynamic and ever changing (Angrosino and Perez, 2000). Similarly, Coffey (1999: 1) high- lights the way that fieldwork is 'personal, emotional and identity *work*', which involves the researcher in an ongoing reflexive engagement of their own position in relation to the research context (original emphasis).

A final point that needs to be made about fieldwork relates to the notion of 'leaving the field'. The date when the researcher will finish data gathering should be negotiated at the beginning of the study, albeit that there may be some flex- ibility in this. Inevitably, all research comes to an end and while the ethnographer may feel they 'belong' in the setting they have been studying owing to their long immersion in the field, s/he has to think carefully about this, knowing that the process of leaving the field is most likely to be more difficult for the ethnographer than their host (Coffey, 1999). Coffey (1999) argues that it is more likely that the ethnographer remains as a 'friend' of the setting.

POSSIBILITIES AND LIMITATIONS OF ETHNOGRAPHIC RESEARCH

This chapter has outlined a number of benefits to employing an ethnographic approach in early childhood research. In short, these relate to the potential it offers for researching children's social worlds in the context of a 'naturalistic' setting over time, with all the possibilities for developing relationships and observing the everyday practices of a setting it affords. For this reason, ethnographic research has been used in a wide range of studies in early childhood (Buchbinder et al., 2006).

But ethnographic research is not without its critics. The notion of 'entering the field' as used in traditional ethnographic approaches, where the researcher views the subject(s) under study as exotic or 'Other' in some way, is problematic. Coffey (1999) points to the way that ethnographers set about constructing the 'field' for their study as something alien to them, with their own position akin to being a stranger or tourist. She says, 'it suggests a distant and remote site, which the ethnographer must learn about and endure' (Coffey, 1999: 19). In doing this, the ethnographer is expected to become increasingly familiar with the values of this culture, coming to 'know' it or becoming enlightened, but at the same time remaining coolly distant in order to achieve professional objectivity. This treatment of the setting and the participants within it as 'exotic' or 'Other' in some way has been likened to the way colonialist powers viewed the societies and cultures of the groups they colonised. Some would argue further, that ethnographic studies into children and childhood have sought to 'colonise' children's bodies in the same way that minority world countries sought to colonise majority world cultures, conceptualising children as if they are a different *species* to adults (Viruru, 2001).

Similarly, Alldred (1998) is critical of the use of ethnographic approaches in childhood research, such as Corsaro's (1996), which talk of 'entering the child's world'. This is because they seem to imply that children and adults occupy different social spheres, with the child constructed as 'Other' to the dominant *adult*-centred culture. You may recall that we asked you to reflect on this at the end of one of the previous Research in Focus sections (see p. 174). For Alldred (1998), such research ignores cultural meanings assigned to 'children' and 'childhood', and disregards the unequal power relationships that exist between adults and children and between researcher and research subject/participant. This masking of unequal power relationships could be applied to the notion of adopting the 'least adult' role (Mandell, 1988) discussed earlier. As James (2007) asserts, a researcher is *not* a child and is able to refer to their 'adult' and thus more powerful role as and when they choose. Albon and Rosen (2014) prefer the use of 'least educator' here when discussing their respective research projects in early childhood settings, as it gives some sense of being a differently positioned adult within the setting (when not a practitioner-researcher).

A different criticism can be levelled at ethnography in terms of objectivity. Researchers coming from a more positivistic position might criticise its potential for bias – sometimes known as 'going native' in older anthropological studies. Given the importance placed on the self of the researcher, it could be argued that ethnographic research is less reliable or valid than studies such as surveys, because different researchers are likely to obtain different results. This is why importance is placed on the keeping of detailed field notes – they can act as a crucial source of verification of what has taken place in ethnographic studies as they offer an insight into what decisions were taken and why (Fielding, 2008). Finally here, because ethnographic research is carried out over time, it generates a huge amount of material that needs to be sifted through and analysed (Edmond, 2005). This is a key strength, but it can also be daunting, particularly if it is your first experience of carrying out research.

Despite these criticisms, ethnography *is* considered a useful approach to use in the study of children and childhoods (James, 2007). Indeed Buchbinder et al. (2006) believe that ethnography is under-used in early childhood research. When carrying out ethnographic research, it seems that an ongoing reflexive discussion about your own perspective in relation to the setting under study is vital, as is a detailed description of the setting. If you are deciding what to do for a research project, we suggest that ethnography is most likely to be useful if you have a length of time in which to develop relationships within a setting. It is also an appropriate approach to employ if the aim is to attain *rich* and *detailed* data in relation to a setting, such as a nursery or health centre. As with any approach or method adopted in research, what is crucial is its 'fitness for purpose' (Sylva, 1999).

 —— **REFLECTION POINT** ————————————————————

Steven is a full-time, final year student at a university, who is studying for an Early Childhood Studies degree. He is considering undertaking an ethnographic research project looking at social interactions between babies and caregivers in an early childhood setting. He has to be in the university three days a week and works in a coffee bar another day of the week and at weekends. Inevitably he has other coursework demands than his research project. It is the beginning of January and his written-up dissertation is due in at the end of April.

(Continued)

(Continued)

Given his circumstances and timescale, would you advise Steven to undertake an ethnographic piece of research? Think of what you might suggest to him.

- He has little time in a week to undertake the fieldwork.
- He has a short time period in which to undertake the fieldwork (by the time he has negotiated access to a setting, which may not be straightforward, and allowing for a period of final data analysis and writing up at the end he will only have a few months at best in the setting. A setting may also be closed for a period over the Spring/ Easter break.
- His research topic (social interactions between babies and caregivers in an early childhood setting) could perhaps be investigated through other means. For example, Steven could do a case study of one setting, doing some observations of interactions and interviews over a shorter, defined period. He would not get the depth of an ethnographic study or the sense of development over time of the relationships between caregivers and babies that an ethnographic study would afford, but he would still get some interesting data. He might also consider doing a piece of research interviewing early childhood practitioners about the kinds of social interactions they engage in with babies in their care, the value they place on these and the challenges they face in maximising opportunities for such interactions in a group care setting. This would not involve having to negotiate access to observe babies in a setting and the interviews could be completed over a shorter time period; but of course the additional, detailed observational data gleaned over time, which is emblematic of the ethnographic approach, giving some sense of the babies' perspectives would be lost.

— —— **KEY POINTS FROM THE CHAPTER** ———————

- Ethnography is a qualitative approach to research that aims to provide rich and detailed data about people in particular sociocultural contexts.
- It emphasises the importance of research being carried out in a 'naturalistic' rather than experimental setting.
- Ethnography has a long history, particularly in the tradition of social anthropology, which has demonstrated how children's experiences of childhood are different according to sociocultural context.
- In early childhood research, ethnography has been used in a wide range of studies looking at areas such as children's peer relationships and the daily routines that happen as part of nursery life.

(Continued)

- Fieldwork is an important part of ethnography. Immersion 'in the field' is seen as allowing the researcher a gradual understanding of the everyday lives of particular groups of people in particular contexts.
- Participant observation is usually seen as a key tool in ethnographic research. However, other tools, such as unstructured interviewing, are likely to be used and the keeping of detailed field notes is considered very important.
- Like any other approach to research, ethnographic studies can be criticised. The positioning of the setting and the participants within it as 'Other' in some way is seen as problematic and when applied to children seems to ignore the many aspects of the world that adults and children share. In addition, owing to the emphasis on the self of the researcher, different researchers might obtain different results in the same setting, which might impact on the research's reliability. Therefore, in ethnographic studies, it is essential to document ongoing reflections about the impact of the self of the researcher in relation to the research as this acts as verification of what has taken place in the study.

FURTHER READING

Albon, D. and Rosen, R. (2014) *Negotiating Adult-Child Relationships in Early Childhood Research*. London: Routledge. Throughout this book, the reader is encouraged to examine the 'messy' nature of negotiating relationships with research participants in two ethnographic research projects.

Corsaro, W. (1985) *Friendship and Peer Culture in the Early Years*. Norwood, NJ: Ablex. This book is a classic example of early childhood ethnographic research – Chapter 1 is especially useful as Corsaro discusses the research methods used in some detail.

James, A. (2007) 'Ethnography in the study of children and childhood', in P. Atkinson, A. Coffey, S. Delamont, J. Lofland and L. Lofland (eds) *Handbook of Ethnography*. London: Sage. A very useful chapter because it highlights anthropological studies into children and childhood carried out over many years that focus on a wide range of children's experiences – not just those in institutions such as schools.

Don't forget to visit the online resources at https://study.sagepub.com/mukherjiandalbon3e for access to free SAGE journal articles, weblinks, videos, exercises, mini quizzes and an interactive glossary.

10

CASE STUDIES

CHAPTER OBJECTIVES

- To consider what is meant by a 'case study' in early childhood research.
- To reflect on the historical context of the use of case studies.
- To explore the relationship between case study design and purpose.
- To consider some of the methods used to collect data for case studies.
- To reflect on the possibilities and limitations of the case study approach.

Case studies are a useful tool for early childhood researchers. This is especially the case if you are a small-scale researcher with limited resources (Blaxter et al., 2010), a description that might be applicable to many students. Case studies can be used to study an individual child, a group of children, an early years setting (which could be a place of work), or an organisation. They are one of the most common forms of qualitative research and can generate rich information, allowing for an in-depth understanding of the people and/or context being studied (Stake, 2000).

WHAT IS A CASE STUDY?

Greig et al. (2013: 187) define a case study as 'an investigation of an individual, a family, a group, an institution, a community, or even a resource, programme or intervention'. In early childhood research, a 'case' could be an in-depth child study focusing on a particular child's development and learning or an investigation into a group of children in transition from a nursery class into reception. A researcher could undertake a case study about the setting up of a new early years setting, or investigate one aspect of a setting's work, such as the implementation of a 'healthy eating' programme. Case studies are undertaken in a 'naturalistic' setting and can give information on both relationships and processes (Denscombe, 2014).

It is important to note here that a case study, in itself, is not a *method* of collecting information, but is an *approach*, within which one can choose to use a variety of data-collecting instruments. Stake (2000: 435) argues that it is a 'choice of what is to be studied' as opposed to a methodological choice, owing to its focus on a 'case' – be it one child or a local authority or a series of 'cases'. As the previous chapter noted, a case study may differ from ethnographic research. A case study, while detailed, could be carried out at arm's length, without the expectation of participation in the life of the setting or community under study as in ethnographic research. This said, a case study might be carried out this way but it does not have to be. Stake (2000), for instance, argues that case studies that are highly qualitative in nature will involve researchers in spending extended time 'in the field' as a participant in the life of the setting. Another difference would be that the 'case' in case study research might be one child, as opposed to a place or community as in ethnographic research.

It is up to the researcher to define the limits of the case study. For example, a case study could be conducted on a child being treated with cancer, with the aim of investigating how the child is coping with cancer treatment. The case study will probably look, not only at the child, but also at the child's relationship with his or her parents and siblings. If one of the aims of the study is to investigate the effects of the hospital experience, it may also be appropriate to observe interactions between the child and the hospital staff. The researcher has to set 'boundaries' to the case study, and for this reason case studies are sometimes referred to as 'bounded systems' (Edwards, 2010). Used in this context, the word 'system' is defined as 'a set of interrelated elements that form an organised whole' (Johnson and Christensen, 2012: 395). In a case study, therefore, the researcher is looking at the various aspects of a system and how they interrelate; in order to answer the question 'What is going on here?' (Edwards, 2010: 164).

Most case studies are qualitative in nature and allow the researcher to gather very detailed information with a narrow focus. Stake (2000: 438–9) maintains that it is important to demonstrate the *particularity* of the 'case', which might include:

1. The nature of the case.
2. The case's historical background.
3. The physical setting.
4. Other contexts (e.g. economic, political, legal, and aesthetic).
5. Other cases through which this case is recognised.
6. Those informants through whom the case can be known.

Although the approach can be criticised for its lack of generalisability, with the information obtained often seen as only being applicable to the 'case' under investigation, some qualitative researchers consider that case studies are the *bedrock* of scientific investigation (Bromley, 1986). Many scientific discoveries and advances in theory have been spurred on by case study research. Inferences can be drawn and applied (albeit with caution) to 'cases' which resemble closely the 'case' in the research, e.g. a similar local authority or a nursery with a similar intake of children. But this can only happen if there is sufficient descriptive detail to allow some level of comparison to be made (Stake, 2000).

HISTORICAL BACKGROUND

The roots of using the case study approach in the study of children lie in parents' reports of their children's progress, sometimes known as 'baby biographies' (Arnold, 2003). These were written by people such as Darwin (Darwin, 1877) and Piaget (Fawcett, 2009). Psychoanalysts from the beginning of the twentieth century used child studies of individual children to advance their understanding of psychoanalytic theory. One famous case study was undertaken by Freud in 1909, of a 5-year-old child called Hans. Hans had a fear of horses and Freud was able to use the case study to help him develop his theory of the Oedipus complex (Greig et al., 2013).

—— ACTIVITY ——————————————————

Investigate this website. It has a good description of the 'Little Hans' case study and the methods used: www.holah.karoo.net/freudstudy.htm (accessed 17 February 2017).

Using the information on case study design outlined later in this chapter, classify the type of case study used by Freud. What were the strengths and weaknesses of the methods used in this case study?

The father is reported as asking the child 'leading questions'. In what way could this have adversely affected the validity of the conclusions that were drawn from the case study? You will find a discussion about validity in Chapter 1.

In the 1950s, a series of case studies were conducted by James and Joyce Robertson on young children who were separated from their main carers. The plight of one 2-year-old girl, who was filmed as she embarked on a brief stay in hospital without her mother, was instrumental in allowing parents to stay with their children on hospital wards (Bowlby et al., 1952). In this sense we can see that although the emphasis in a case study is on the particular 'case' under study, the information gained can still be very influential in furthering our understandings of an issue and improving practice.

Another well-known case study was of a 5-year-old child called Dibs who was undergoing play therapy because of his aggression, 'temper tantrums' and anti-social behaviour. The case study describes how, through play and over a period of time, he was able to communicate his underlying feelings, resulting in a positive change in behaviour (Axline, 1971).

The case study approach can also be used to look at the work of early years settings. An example of this approach is the work of Bertram and Pascal (2001), who published a series of case studies of early years settings in the UK, focusing on the quality of practice. The research undertaken has been influential in supporting other settings in improving their practice.

CASE STUDY DESIGN

We have already looked at several examples of case study research; from studies of single children, to studies that include a range of different early years settings. The type of case study chosen can vary across a number of dimensions, and there have been various attempts made to classify case study design (Blaxter et al., 2010). Knowledge of the different designs available is important as it helps the researcher choose the most appropriate design for their research and gives them the terminology to be able to describe their design to others.

Blaxter et al. (2010) cite Yin's 1993 classification which they find helpful. According to this classification, case studies can vary across two dimensions:

1. *Number of case studies*: whether there is one case or multiple cases.
2. *The purpose of the study*: whether the purpose of the case is exploratory, descriptive or explanatory.

In addition, Coolican (2014) suggests a third dimension:

3. *Time frame*: whether the case study is longitudinal, with the case studied over a period of time, or is conducted as a 'snapshot' at one particular point.

It is clear that the type of case study design you choose is dependent on the overall aim of your study. Edwards (2010) identifies two broad differences. In one type of case study, the aim is to find out more about the case in question, with no expectation that the information can or will be applied more widely. Edwards gives the example of the introduction of a new way of working in an early years setting. The other type of study is designed to be an example of a phenomenon that has a *wider* interest, the expectation being that the findings from an in-depth study of one case can be generalised across to similar cases/settings. An example of this would be the case studies undertaken by Bertram and Pascal (2001), outlined previously. The findings from these studies were used by other settings to improve the quality of their practice.

Stake (1995) identifies case studies as being *intrinsic*, *instrumental* or *collective*. We will now look at these in turn.

INTRINSIC CASE STUDIES

These are single case designs, where the aim of the research is to obtain a deep understanding of the case. Students on early childhood courses are sometimes asked to undertake case studies on children to help them gain an understanding of an aspect of child development. These case studies, or child studies, usually entail undertaking a series of observations on a child, together with, perhaps, details of conversations about the child with the parents and the child's key person. Child studies are not just a description of a child's development, but include reflections and analysis, often using theory to explain observed behaviour. Depending on the aim of the child study, recommendations for the care and education of the child may be included. *Observing Harry* (a child study written up as a book by Cath Arnold) is an example of an in-depth child study that not only provides a deep understanding of a particular child, but also contributes to our understanding of ways to extend learning for other children (Arnold, 2003).

The intrinsic case study can be used as an evaluative tool to examine how a programme is working; for instance, you may want to review how a 'walk to school programme' initiated some time before, is operating several months later. Sometimes researchers use a single case study to explore a particular phenomenon in detail. Restricting resources to a single case can mean that a very deep understanding can be obtained. Often an exploratory, in-depth study of one case can give direction to a larger research project.

THE INSTRUMENTAL CASE STUDY

In an instrumental case study the 'case' is an instrument or tool used to help the researcher understand more about a general phenomenon. Johnson and Christensen (2012: 408) describe this as using the case as a 'means to an end'. For example, you may want to find out what factors contribute to the effective leadership of children's centres. An in-depth case study of a children's centre deemed successful and its leader may allow you to identify features that can then be used to assist in the professional development of other centre leaders. In this way case studies can be used to investigate an important issue in depth or to develop or test a theory.

RESEARCH IN FOCUS

USA

Oller (2010) presents a case study of a trilingual toddler, living in the USA, which examines the child's language development between the ages of 11 months and 24 months. The author of the article is the child's parent. The child was living in a household where she was exposed to three languages: English, German and Spanish. The child's language was recorded by a small battery-powered device that was attached to her clothing which recorded both her vocalisations and the language that was spoken around and to her. The recordings were made on 11 days during her second year of life and were undertaken as the child went about her normal activities in and around her home (a 'naturalistic' setting). After a day of recording, the information was downloaded onto a computer for analysis. The study had two main aims. One was to test the feasibility of recording and analysing language development in this way, and the other was to find out if the child's developing vocabulary was influenced more by speech being directed to her than just being in a situation where she heard language being spoken around her.

The findings showed that the method used for recording and analysing language development worked well. In addition, the results clearly demonstrated that the child's expressive language was hugely dependent on the language that was directed to her. Most of the language that was directed to her was in German and she used more German words in her own speech, despite hearing English and Spanish being spoken by the adults around her.

(Continued)

This is an example of an instrumental case study. It was designed to help the researcher understand more about using this particular method of recording and analysing language and to evaluate the effectiveness of direct as opposed to indirect speech in supporting a child's language development.

In Chapter 6 we looked at the ethical issues involved in conducting research with and about very young children. There are inherent ethical issues to be considered in this sort of study. The recording device was unobtrusive and was designed to record any language uttered by or near the child. Although the main people in the child's life will have given consent for the recording, it is unlikely that everyone with whom the child came into contact realised that a recording was being made.

COLLECTIVE CASE STUDY

As it implies, a collective case study, or multiple case design, is one that contains more than one case. The Bertram and Pascal (2001) series of case studies outlined previously is a good example of this. The number of in-depth cases that are studied is dependent on resources. In general, the greater the depth required about each 'case', the fewer the number of cases that are studied. Johnson and Christensen (2012) note that up to ten case studies within one particular design are common if there are the resources available and less depth is required.

In collective case study design there is usually a focus on the *instrumental* rather than *intrinsic* value of the case, as the aim is to find out information that can be generalised out to a wider population that shares the characteristics of the cases. In the Bertram and Pascal (2001) series of case studies, for instance, the information was used to improve the quality of early years settings throughout England.

It would seem, then, that there are advantages to the collective case study design. These can be summarised as follows:

- Comparisons can be made between cases; for example, you could compare the quality of provision for children under 3 years of age provided by different early years settings.
- If the aim of your research is to test a theory, the findings will be more valid if you look at more than one case.
- You are more likely to be able to generalise your findings to a wider population by looking at more than one case.

The disadvantage of the collective case study design is that resources will be spread more thinly than in a single case study design, adversely affecting the depth and quality of the data that can be obtained. This is the 'depth versus breadth trade-off' (Johnson and Christensen, 2012: 398). In addition, Stake (2000) argues that an emphasis on making comparisons takes attention away from the particularities of a single 'case'. In other words, the *comparison* rather than the *'case'* becomes the defining feature of the research design. After all, we should remember that in reading intrinsic and instrumental case studies, we are making connections with our existing knowledge about other cases (Stake, 2000).

RESEARCH IN FOCUS

Tay-Lim and Gan (2013) used a collective case study approach to investigate peer rejection in pre-school children. Eight children, four girls and four boys aged 4 years to 7 years, were chosen from a pre-school in Singapore where one of the authors worked; the aim being to ascertain their understanding of, and subjective feelings about, peer rejection. The research entailed in-depth interviews which included asking children for their reactions to a 'story' where a child experienced rejection, as a trigger to elicit their views and experiences. As part of the interview process children were encouraged to represent their ideas by drawing and talking about their drawings. The findings revealed that the children all identified incidents of rejection, which they mostly experienced as being excluded from activities, and they all found these events stressful. However, there were individual differences in the degree of sensitivity to these events shown by the children, with some children's well-being being more compromised by rejection than others.

This research shows that listening to children's experiences, even at a very young age, can give valuable insight into their lives, a topic which was raised in Chapter 7 and is investigated in more detail in Chapter 17.

 — ACTIVITY

Using the classifications described earlier in this chapter, how would you describe the design of these case studies?

1. The case study of Dibs.
2. The Robertsons' study of the 2-year-old going to hospital.
3. The Bertram and Pascal study.

METHODS THAT CAN BE USED IN CASE STUDIES

In the same way that it is left to each individual researcher to decide on the 'bounds' of the 'case' or 'cases' to be studied, it is also left to the researcher to choose whatever methods are thought to be appropriate to collect the data that are required. Case studies will often make use of qualitative methods such as semi-structured interviews, documentary analysis and narrative observations. However, when there are many participants involved, more use is likely to be made of quantitative methods such as questionnaires. The use of different methods of collecting data within a case study, such as observations, interviews and questionnaires, is an example of triangulation and can improve the validity of the information gathered. Validity and triangulation are discussed in more detail in Chapter 1. If the 'case' is large, a team of researchers might be used, but this inevitably raises difficulties in terms of maintaining a degree of uniformity in the data collection and analysis across the team (Stake, 2000). As you will recall from other chapters you have read so far in this book, the self of the researcher has an impact on research (Coffey, 1999), and it can be very difficult, if not impossible, to homogenise the behaviours and 'selves' of the researchers.

Care also needs to be taken when using a collective case study design to ensure that the same methods are used for each case. This helps with making a reliable comparison. For example, if using questionnaires, the same questionnaire needs to be used and administered in the same way for each participant.

POSSIBILITIES AND LIMITATIONS OF USING CASE STUDIES

This chapter has shown that case study research offers a number of possibilities for researchers. It can provide in-depth information and allow an insight into the special circumstances that have affected the 'case' in a way that is not possible with quantitative approaches to research such as conducting surveys. In child studies, such as *Observing Harry* (Arnold, 2003), this information can assist us in planning to meet the needs of the child concerned. Insights gained from studying one subject may cause us to rethink our position on a certain topic or area of theory.

Case studies can be used in the exploratory phase of a larger research study. The depth of information obtained can point the way to issues that can be followed up with a wider population. Collective case studies may be particularly useful when used in this way as the information from a number of studies can be pooled, often allowing common patterns and features to be identified. Moreover, case studies can be used to confirm or refute theory. In particular, case studies are useful in challenging a theory, as all it takes is one case study that does not confirm predictions based on a particular theory, to allow for the validity of the theory to be questioned (Denscombe, 2012).

Case studies can also have ecological validity (Tobin et al., 1989); that is, the findings observed reflect what happens in 'real life', as opposed to laboratory studies, where participants may not behave in the same way as they would in their 'natural' or usual setting. In this sense, case study research shares many characteristics with ethnographic research and can be particularly useful in early childhood research as it might look at children in a more holistic way. In addition to this, case studies are a good approach to use when exploring sensitive areas. In an in-depth study the researcher is more likely to become aware if the participant is uncomfortable and can be proactive in protecting their well-being.

Finally, case study research is a good way of investigating the development of a child or an area of development, such as their language skills, over time. In early childhood, as we have seen in this chapter, the close focus on *one child* and their development has a long tradition in research.

While there are many possibilities for case study research in early childhood, there are limitations. Because case studies are an in-depth study of one or very few cases, the findings cannot be applied to a population as a whole; they are not *generalisable* (Gilbert, 2008a). In addition, the nature of case study research means that the findings may not be easily replicable by others. The researcher may bring bias to the proceedings by being selective in the case they decide to study, as well as in what and how they record, and in analysing the data. This is especially the case if the study is undertaken by a close family member, as in some of the 'baby biography' kinds of studies. If we are not careful, it is easy to see what we *want* to see.

ETHICS

As with all research with and about children it is vital that case study research is conducted with due regard to ethical guidelines. Issues of consent, confidentiality and the children's comfort and well-being are just a few of the considerations that need to be thought through. In Chapter 6 you were introduced to the case study of 'Genie', a 13-year-old child who was discovered living in very neglectful circumstances, to the extent that lack of meaningful communication with others had severely affected her speech development. Although the researchers started the study of Genie with the best of intentions, Genie was very vulnerable and lack of funding led to Genie being returned to inadequate care arrangements. It is doubtful if Genie ever had the competence to give consent to being studied or the ability to ask to be withdrawn from the study. In addition there are real concerns about confidentiality; Genie was not her real name, but photographs of her were published which meant she was identifiable.

Stake (2003) considers that case study researchers have special responsibilities, saying that 'Qualitative researchers are guests in the private spaces of the world. Their manners should be good and their code of ethics strict' (p. 154). He is of the opinion that researchers using case studies should seek to *exceed* the standard ethical requirements and aim to reduce potential harm to participants by engaging in ongoing and active dialogue, providing feedback and by 'listening well to signs of concern' (Stake, 2003: 154).

—   —— **ACTIVITY** ———————————————————

Flewitt (2005) undertook an ethnographic video case study of four 3-year-old children over a period of a year as they entered pre-school. She drew up a list of ethical guidelines under the following headings:

- Negotiation of initial consent.
- Negotiation of ongoing consent.
- Anonymity, confidentiality and visual data.
- Participant consultation and research outcomes.

Take each heading and reflect upon the ethical issues involved in such a study, taking care to think through the specifics of this research, i.e. use of video, research conducted over a year, and the participants – young children who have just entered pre-school. For example, under 'Negotiation of initial consent' you may reflect that consent needs to be obtained from the setting staff, the parents and the children involved. How could you ensure that the children *really* understood that they could choose not to take part?

You may be able to access an online version of the full article (Flewitt, 2005) through your institution.

RESEARCH IN FOCUS

ENGLAND

In 2010 Iram Siraj-Blatchford published the results of a collective case study designed to investigate, in depth, the factors leading to a highly rated home learning environment (HLE) and high attainment for 21 children from a range of ethnic backgrounds living in England. For comparison three families were included who were disadvantaged and where the children had received a poor home learning environment and had low levels of achievement. Children and parents were interviewed by trained interviewers who spoke the main language of the family.

The findings indicated that:

Families tend to make the extra efforts required in developing a rich HLE when they believe their efforts will be rewarded. When parents are aware that their child has as much potential as any other to be successful, and when they recognise that they have an active role to play themselves in realising this potential, then early social disadvantages may be overcome. (Siraj-Blatchford, 2010: 476–7)

This collective case study would be considered as having an 'instrumental' approach as it was designed to help us understand more about the factors influencing children's home learning environment.

CASE STUDY

In order to consolidate your learning in this chapter, consider the following Case Study: Ameena is a student on an undergraduate early childhood studies course. She attends a 'mornings only' nursery class in a primary school, once a week. She is very interested in investigating the relationship between the staff in the setting and the children's parents. She has decided to use a qualitative methodological approach, reasoning that she is interested in the ideas and attitudes of staff and parents in this particular setting, with no expectation that the findings would relate to other nurseries. Her initial thinking was to undertake an ethnographic approach to her study.

What other approaches are available to Ameena and which would you advise her to take? Explain your reasons. You may find reviewing ideas from the previous two chapters helpful here.

Ameena could have considered undertaking a survey, but with the small number of practitioners and participants involved, this approach would not be suitable. In addition a survey generally (although not always) falls into the category of quantitative research rather than qualitative research. An ethnographic approach would involve the total immersion of the researcher in the life of the setting, with the emphasis on observation as a data-collection method. It aims to produce 'thick' descriptions of people as they go about their everyday lives (Coffey, 1999). Ameena only attends the setting for one half-day a week and this will not give her the opportunity to totally immerse herself in the culture of the setting. A case study approach is more relevant because there is no opportunity for Ameena to spend the time needed to fully capture the full range of social behaviour in the setting. In any case, Ameena has delimitated the aspect of the life of the setting in which she is interested: the way that the staff and parents relate with each other. If Ameena had been a permanent member of the staff team, and the team were interested in improving the way that they work with parents in the setting, then action research may have been an option. Action research is always a collaborative approach, with all the staff team participating to transform practice. You will find out more about action research in the next chapter.

 KEY POINTS FROM THE CHAPTER

- Greig et al. (2013: 187) define a case study as 'an investigation of an individual, a family, a group, an institution, a community, or even a resource, programme or intervention'.
- Most case studies are qualitative in nature, although some employ mixed methodology and methods.

(Continued)

- The use of case studies has a long history in research with and about children – the child study is a particular type of case study used in early childhood research.
- Case study research can include only one 'case' or several.
- Case studies can be a 'snapshot' of one point in time or longitudinal.
- *Intrinsic* case studies are usually single case studies where the aim is to obtain a deep understanding of a case, the findings may be particular to the case, or may give direction to a larger research project (Stake, 2000).
- *Instrumental* case studies are used to help researchers understand more about a general phenomenon (Stake, 2000).
- 'Collective case studies' is a term used to describe when more than one case study is used in a research design. Sometimes known as a multiple case study design.
- A variety of methods can be used in a case study including observation, interviews and questionnaires.
- Case studies can give in-depth information about the 'case' under study, but it is difficult to generalise the findings of case study research to larger populations.

————— FURTHER READING ——————

Arnold, C. (2003) *Observing Harry: Child Development and Learning 0–5*. Maidenhead: Open University Press. This is a fascinating child study which gives real insights into the holistic development of a child.

Denscombe, M. (2014) *The Good Research Guide for Small-Scale Social Research Projects*, 5th edition. Maidenhead: Open University Press. Chapter 3 gives a good introduction to case studies.

Schwandt, T. and Gates, E. (2017) 'Case study', in N.K. Denzin and Y. Lincoln (eds) *The Sage Handbook of Qualitative Research*, 5th edition. London: Sage. This chapter looks at the topic in greater depth than Denscombe.

Don't forget to visit the online resources at https://study.sagepub.com/mukherjiandalbon3e for access to free SAGE journal articles, weblinks, videos, exercises, mini quizzes and an interactive glossary.

11
ACTION RESEARCH

CHAPTER OBJECTIVES

- To consider what is meant by action research.
- To reflect upon the idea of the practitioner as researcher.
- To gain an understanding of action research as a cycle.
- To consider research methods that are appropriate in action research.
- To consider the possibilities and limitations of this approach to research.

As with the other chapters in Part 3 of this book, this chapter explores an approach to research rather than specific research tools such as interviews or questionnaires. Action research, as we will see, may employ a range of different research tools. Action research has gained popularity as an approach to research owing to its focus on improving practice in particular contexts and with particular people. In this way it differs from case study research, for instance, because it aims primarily to create *change* rather than produce new knowledge. Owing to its focus on improving practice, action research is often used in educational research and in research into other areas of professional practice, such as nursing.

WHAT IS ACTION RESEARCH?

Action research can be described as a 'living inquiry' owing to the way real-life experiences underpin the research (Wicks et al., 2008). Kemmis and McTaggart (2005: 564) also emphasise the way that action research focuses on *actual* rather than *abstract* practices, saying, 'It involves learning about the real, material, concrete, and particular practices of particular people in particular places'. However, it should be noted that Kemmis and McTaggart qualify this by observing that, inevitably, in describing and analysing the data gained in action research, there is a level of abstraction that occurs. Central to action research, though, is the focus on change (Greenwood and Levin, 2000). It is this which makes it an attractive research approach for practitioners to employ. With this in mind, McNiff and Whitehead (2011) define action research as involving practitioners in investigating and evaluating their work with a focus on improving their own practice and the practice of others.

This is not new. From its inception in the mid-twentieth century, action research has aimed to bring about improvements to practice in some way. Kurt Lewin, who is generally credited with developing the idea of 'action research', saw action research as a tool for bringing about democracy, as practitioners are central to the process (Robson, 2011a). However, we should not see action research as having remained static as an approach to research or as something that can be viewed in one way only. Kemmis and McTaggart (2005) argue that action research has a range of guises. They argue that recent developments in the approach are *participatory* research and *critical* action research. Participatory research emphasises community action and shared ownership and analysis of research. Critical action research shares the commitment to collective participation towards change but also focuses on injustice and disadvantage owing to social class, gender, sexuality, ethnicity, and so on. As with any approach to research, there are a range of interpretations and emphases that might come under the broad umbrella of 'action research' and we should always be mindful that different writers use the term in different ways.

Despite the multiple ways action research can be viewed and the differences in the terminology ascribed to it, improvement and change could be regarded as its key components. This will often mean that the research involves planning, acting upon, observing and reflecting upon an issue or problem that has some relevance to practice. We will look at the process of action research in more depth when we consider the action research cycle.

So, what kinds of problems with relevance to early childhood practice might form the basis of a piece of action research?

- A nursery practitioner may wish to examine the way s/he supports (or does not support) a child with a particular disability through a particular activity with a view to enhancing his/her practice.
- A health visiting team may wish to develop its practice in relation to supporting young parents – a parent group which rarely accesses services and which they feel is inadequately supported at present.
- A reception class team may want to develop its practice so that the children have free-flow outdoor and indoor play – something that does not happen at present.

Thus, action research is an approach to research that emerges from real-life, practical problems rather than focusing on the development of theory or understanding of an issue. For Elliott (1991: 52), action research develops 'practical wisdom', which he defines as 'the capacity to discern the right course of action when confronted with particular, complex and problematic states of affairs'. The issue of complexity in relation to the contexts in which such professional problems arise is also expressed by Wicks et al. (2008: 17) when they argue:

> It is evident that each person's understanding and practice of action research does not stand in isolation from other aspects of their being-in-the-world; instead, action research both emerges from and contributes to a complex and panoramic view of the world in which one lives and one's own particular place within it.

Let us consider this complexity further by thinking about a concrete example such as a reception class practitioner and her team who wish to reflect on the ways that they develop close emotional attachments in their work with children and families. Let us imagine that they are working to develop a 'key person' approach (see Elfer et al. [2012] for a full discussion of what is meant by 'key person'). In this context, there are likely to be a range of factors that weave together in intricate ways:

- the present way of working in the reception class
- published material on this topic, for example, books and journal articles

- the personal and professional histories of the individual practitioners in the reception class team and wider Foundation Stage team
- the views of the children in the reception class and the rest of the school
- the ways in which the team work together
- the physical environment
- the opportunities for professional development in this area
- the generally accepted view(s) of what school should be about and how children should be supported within it at this point in history and in this geographical and cultural context
- the views of parents whose children attend the reception class
- government policy
- the views of the senior management team in the school, as well as of other staff members and school governors
- the funds available to support this new development
- the local authority advisory team.

The interplay between these factors, which are ever changing – and this is not an exhaustive list – is likely to be highly complex. It reflects the intricacies and realities of early childhood practice. Another way of thinking about the complexities of practice is in thinking about the types of change that action research might hope to achieve. In action research, there may be changes to the following:

- what people do
- how people interact with the world and with others
- what people mean and what they value
- the discourses in which people understand and interpret the world (Kemmis and McTaggart, 2005: 565).

In thinking about action research in this way, we can see that it can mean far more than trying to improve a specific area of practice at surface level. Brown and Jones (2001), for instance, point to the way action research can encourage practitioners to problematise areas of practice that have seemed 'common-sense' and encourage them to seek alternative stories as explanations of classroom events. Jones does this by reflecting in detail on her own practice as a former nursery teacher, using reflective accounts written during this period with a particular focus on gender (Brown and Jones, 2001).

Rather than aiming for simple solutions to complex problems, Jones challenges whether this is possible or even desirable, given her preference for a post-structuralist theoretical position. In other words, she does not believe in the possibility of linear progress and universal, knowable 'solutions' to complex issues, which she suggests is sometimes the lure of action research. Rather, she favours a position that embraces multiple, uncertain and shifting viewpoints, with a recognition that movements forward in one's own practice are always contingent and contextual and cannot be generalised (Brown and Jones, 2001; see also Swantz, 2008). This links back to some of the discussion in Chapters 4 and 5. Reflection such as this can be viewed as a form of self-study in that it does not aim – at least initially – to change the practice of a team towards a clear goal, as is the case with many guises of 'action research', but seeks to interrogate one's own thinking and actions over time, and in the process re-envision early childhood practice.

 REFLECTION POINT

Think about the ideas being expressed here. Is there a tension between seeing action research in terms of its possibility of improving practice (in the sense of making progress towards some predetermined, measurable goal) and the idea that certain and knowable outcomes are possible or even desirable? Think back to some of the ideas you were introduced to in Chapters 4 and 5 and reflect on some of the ideas about research that might underpin these two positions. Also consider which conceptualisation of action research might be most attractive to government institutions and why – it is a point we pick up later in the chapter.

It would seem, therefore, that despite the focus on improving practice in action research, the researcher's theoretical stance is still important. Taylor (2010), for instance, discusses how her action research design was rooted in her commitment to emancipatory ideas about learning, which were inspired initially by the works of writers such as hooks and Freire. Taylor wanted to think about professional learning in terms of how it might promote individual and social change in early education and she drew on critical theory and feminist and post-structuralist thinking to help frame her research. In this sense, action research can be regarded as praxis. This is because theory and practice are viewed as inseparable, with theory informing practice and practice supporting the development of theory (McNiff and Whitehead, 2011). Thus, praxis supports the notion of *informed* practice because ideas are understood in terms of the way they relate to the *lived world* as opposed to purely existing in the abstract (Kincheloe, 1991).

For Freire, in particular, praxis is linked to consciousness-raising and transformation from the bottom up (Christians, 2005). Applied to an early childhood context this might mean raising the consciousness of the practitioners and children in a given setting, for instance, in relation to conceptions of 'childhood' and 'adulthood'. Through developing an understanding of their own positions and disrupting commonly held views about the relative subject positionings of 'child' and 'adult', practitioners might develop more respectful ways of working that acknowledge the rights of adults and children alike. From small beginnings – in this case an early childhood setting – Freire would argue that wider social change takes place (Christians, 2005).

Not only does action research focus on making changes to practice, it also focuses on the *process* of the research (MacNaughton, 2001). We will see this in more detail when we discuss the action research cycle, but first we will look at *who* carries out action research.

WHO DOES ACTION RESEARCH? THE PRACTITIONER AS RESEARCHER

In order to carry out action research, researchers need to spend a considerable amount of time in a setting, such as a nursery, or be able to meet regularly with a group of practitioners from a range of different settings if leading a larger-scale action research project (most likely this will not be the case for a beginner researcher). Therefore, it is an approach that is particularly suited to those of you that are working in a setting or for those of you that are able to spend a substantial length of time in a setting, for example if you are studying part-time and have access to a setting that is willing to work with you. The reason for emphasising the importance of having a close, long-term relationship with a setting can be seen in the following bullet-pointed list that outlines some of the key features of the action research approach:

- It is a social process.
- It is participatory.
- It is practical and collaborative.
- It is emancipatory.
- It is critical.
- It is reflexive.
- It aims to *transform* both theory and practice (Kemmis and McTaggart, 2005: 566–8).

Action research, then, is carried out by practitioners or sometimes by researchers working closely with a group of practitioners, who, as noted previously, have a desire to change and improve their practice in some way. Thus, it is rooted in the idea that research is not the preserve of those working in academia, such as professional researchers within universities (Greenwood and Levin, 2000). Therefore, Elliott (1991: 45) believes that action research should be regarded as 'cultural innovation' because it threatens the traditional divide between professional learning and academia.

Elliott (1991) also notes that it is practitioners themselves, with their desire to improve their practice, who initiate action research. This differs from other changes that are made in professional practice.

REFLECTION POINT

Let us continue to think about the reception class team and the development of the key person approach. *Who* is likely to impact on the professional practice of these practitioners? In what way(s) might they do this?

As noted earlier, there are a range of people who might impact upon the reception class team's practice in relation to developing a key person approach. These might include the headteacher of the school or Foundation Stage/early childhood coordinator; or possibly the local area's early years advisory team. In some areas of practice, government policy might have a direct impact. This can be seen in the requirement to have a key person in place to support young children and their families in the Foundation Stage.

The focus on the practitioner as researcher has been promoted as invigorating the practitioner's professional development. Sachs (1999) believes that this is because teachers (we would broaden this to include all early childhood practitioners) are at the centre of producing and disseminating the knowledge about practice they have gained through their research.

CASE STUDY

We have emphasised the practitioner as researcher, but some students – not yet qualified as practitioners or possessing the status that comes with being an employee – may well have work placements in early years settings. Although it is unlikely that a student will be able to initiate and sustain a larger-scale action research project, there may be small-scale action research projects that are possible. Here are two examples:

Example one

Nadiya (a third-year Early Childhood Studies degree student) wanted to improve the home corner (role play) environment for the toddlers in the nursery where she was on placement with respect to reflecting the home cultures of the families who attended that nursery. Her question was: 'How can I enhance the home corner environment in the toddler room to reflect the home cultures of the children? What impact does this have on children's involvement in the home corner?'

Her research design involved doing an initial audit of existing resources in the home corner area (with a focus on cultural diversity) and over a period of a few days she

(Continued)

(Continued)

monitored the use children made of the existing home corner, making brief observational notes as to who went in the home corner, how long they stayed and the activity she observed. She also conducted a short focus group interview with practitioners to share her initial findings and to see what they thought could be improved. She then asked families and practitioners to help her to develop the home corner further and then monitored (through observations) the area to see if the changes in resources impacted on the children's play in the area. At the end of the research, she conducted a final focus group interview to see if practitioners thought the change in resources had made any difference and also asked families to comment on the 'new look' area.

Initial work involved negotiating carefully with the practitioners to see if this was possible and they agreed. Nadiya made it clear that she would use pseudonyms for the setting and all participants, but as she aimed to share the findings with the team and because there were few practitioners, children and families in the room, she was aware that within the setting itself it would be difficult to achieve complete anonymity even when using pseudonyms. Sensitivity at this stage was vital, as implying the setting was doing something wrong may well have impacted negatively on relationships between Nadiya and the setting. Nadiya also had to ensure that she asked all families for their consent to her research as she wanted to observe children and include the written observations in the finalised project. She also needed to negotiate the consent of the children when observing them, being sensitive to their cues as to how happy or not they were about her sitting close by and making written notes, and also to ensure any favourite items that existed in the home corner were not removed (to name but two ethical concerns).

Negotiated carefully, the practitioners were happy for Nadiya to develop the home corner by asking families if there were items they might bring in or suggest for inclusion in the area. Many families brought in empty food packets, football programmes, etc., and the home corner gradually changed over the weeks of Nadiya's placement. Careful monitoring through observation showed that more children were using the area and their play was observed to be more sustained; however, Nadiya was careful not to attribute this too simplistically to the changes in resources as the increased interest adults were taking in the area was also – potentially – a very significant factor. At the end of the project, Nadiya wrote up her key findings in a newsletter which went out to all families in the setting. She also thanked everyone again for their participation and support.

Nadiya was able to evidence that she had taken a lead on making a small but significant change to practice and the practitioners in the setting were impressed with the sensitivity with which she negotiated with practitioners in the team, children and families, as well as the effort she put into effecting change and reflecting on the changes made. But more

(Continued)

important than this, it is sometimes easy for students to forget the bigger picture when working towards a particular qualification: Nadiya's small-scale action research project made a *positive impact* on the practice of the setting.

Example two

Another student, Hannah, was on placement in a children's centre and had the opportunity to shadow a range of different professionals including the nursery practitioners, family support workers and health visiting team. Her research questions were: 'How do different professionals work together in my placement setting? How might this impact on my future work as an early years practitioner?'

Although Hannah was unable to effect an *obvious* improvement in the practice of the setting in relation to multi-professional working, she kept a reflective journal of her observations of the practices of the professional groups whom she shadowed (including conversations with individuals), and alongside this noted her thoughts and feelings about what she observed. Although a journal can be seen as a private document, it is important to note that Hannah asked the head of centre (initially) and then all the professionals for their written permission to write down notes about her conversations with them about their role and also to note down any relevant observations of practice in relation to multi-professional working. As these observations were to be shared with a wider audience in the finalised research project for her assignment, it was vital to negotiate consent and be 'up front' that she was undertaking a piece of research. Hannah was also clear with participants that she would anonymise both the name of the children's centre and individuals in the written-up project and would ensure her notes were kept on an encrypted memory stick, being mindful of data protection.

In carrying out the research, Hannah began to notice subtle differences in professionals' approaches to working with children and families, such as in the way they communicated with parents, and her reflective journal showed the development of her ideas over time. Notes from her journal were used directly as data in her project. Thus, Hannah was able to evidence a shift in her *thinking*, which she felt would feed forward into her future work as an early years practitioner. In the conclusion of her research project, she detailed what she had learnt from undertaking the research.

Some of the examples we have discussed so far have focused on *individual* practitioners as change agents – but of course early years practitioners rarely work in isolation. Another characteristic of many action research projects is the *collaborative* nature of the inquiry. The democratic nature of action research is put forward by some writers as a challenge to traditional models of research, which are led by academics in universities. Greenwood and Levin (2000: 96), for instance, employ the term 'co-generative inquiry' in relation to action research to highlight the way that knowledge is co-generated through the collaborative processes of the research and the way that the diversity of experience, knowledge and skills within an action research team is valued. Early childhood practice, like other professional work, is a social practice involving many people. Thus, in order to transform practice/praxis, change is necessarily a social and political process (Kemmis, 2008). For this reason, Kemmis (2008: 124) argues that in action research, practice needs to be understood 'not solely from the perspectives of the individuals involved, but also in terms of the collective understandings and collective efforts of those involved or affected by the practice'.

THE ACTION RESEARCH CYCLE

The process of action research is best regarded as a process that works in spirals of self-reflective cycles (Kemmis and McTaggart, 2005). Figure 11.1 shows what these action research cycles might look like.

Movement through the action research cycle occurs as the practitioners engaged in the study reflect critically on what they are doing, the changes they have made and the changes in their understandings. MacNaughton (2001: 212) views critical reflection as the 'motor that drives the research process' – without it an action research project grinds to a halt.

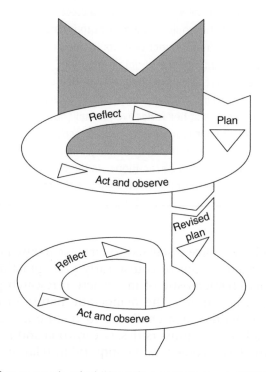

Figure 11.1 The action research spiral (Kemmis and McTaggart, 2005: 564)

Schmuck (2006: 18–19) sees action research more in terms of moving from the present situation towards a particular desired goal in a series of seven problem-solving steps:

1. *Specify the problem.* This involves a consideration of what the actual situation is like and the position the practitioner is hoping to move towards.
2. *Assess the situation with force-field analysis.* This means a consideration of the forces that help to facilitate change and those that restrain change.
3. *Specify multiple solutions.* This step involves being creative in brainstorming a range of solutions to the perceived problem and considering the factors that act to restrain the change from happening at the present time.
4. *Plan for action.* Here, the researcher looks critically at the ideas generated by the brainstorming process and develops a more coherent plan in terms of what to do, who will do it, in what order, and when to do it.
5. *Anticipate obstacles.* In this step it is important to think through the things that may stand in the way of the plan working. This may involve modifying the plan in some way.
6. *Take action.* This step involves implementing the action plan, carrying out the planned changes and reflecting on them in action.
7. *Evaluate.* The final step involves reflecting on the strengths and weaknesses of the actions taken so far and then using this evaluation to identify a new problem.

The new problem then forms the starting point for the next set of seven steps of problem-solving, which Schmuck (2006) views as crucial in continuous self-improvement. Therefore, we can see that Schmuck sees these seven steps as operating in a cyclical way. A common denominator in much of the literature about action research is how it operates in a series of cycles.

However, we want to suggest that the process of moving through these cycles (or Schmuck's 'problem-solving steps') is messier and more fluid than suggested thus far. Stages have a tendency to overlap and by reflecting on experience, some initial ideas are changed or modified (Kemmis and McTaggart, 2005). This also seems to reflect the nature of early childhood work as there are rarely easy answers to improving practice. In addition, given the multiple and fluid perspectives that exist in relation to different aspects of early childhood practice, it is unlikely that universal 'answers' to improving practice are possible or knowable.

Further to this, Kemmis and McTaggart (2005: 566–8) argue, there is a tendency to get fixated with the cyclical nature of action research; that is, its methodology and methods, at the expense of its other features. You may recall that earlier in this chapter we highlighted the following features of action research:

- It is a social process.
- It is participatory.
- It is practical and collaborative.

- It is emancipatory.
- It is critical.
- It is reflexive.
- It aims to *transform* both theory and practice.

While we agree that the values and ideas that underpin action research are of central importance, we also think a brief discussion of the methods that might be employed in action research is useful here as it also further underlines the distinctiveness of action research.

METHODS USED IN ACTION RESEARCH

Action research is an approach to research that might employ a range of qualitative and quantitative methods depending on what the researcher wants to find out about their own particular setting/practice (MacNaughton, 2001). Indeed, Greenwood and Levin (2000: 93) argue that action research should use any methods, from a range of disciplines if necessary, in order to 'address the problem in hand'. Therefore, any of the methods discussed in Part 4 of this book might well be used. However, as noted previously, in considering action research we should not become overly preoccupied with the technical aspects of research methods (Kemmis and McTaggart, 2005).

Let us continue to think about the reception class team who are beginning to adopt a key person approach to working with children and families. We will do this in order to highlight the methods the practitioners might employ as part of the action research.

- The team might use *journaling* in order to document their initial and changing thoughts about adopting this new way of working. Brown and Jones (2001) particularly emphasise writing as a research tool in action research and we will think about this further in Chapter 19.
- They might send a *questionnaire* to parents in the initial and maybe later part of a cycle to elicit their views on this aspect of practice.
- The practitioner leading the action research might facilitate a focus group *interview*, or even interview the practitioners in the team individually, in order to elicit their initial and subsequent feelings about the key person approach. It is likely that any changes to practice will be monitored by the team and then discussed in team meetings, which might also be recorded in some way.
- The team might analyse and review any *documents* they have in this area.
- The team might carry out timed observations to gain an understanding of the number of adults a child has contact with in a given period, such as a day or week, in order to gain a picture of the initial situation prior to adopting a key person approach (assuming they think this should be kept to a minimum).

They might also use observation to monitor whether the number of adults a child is expected to interact with decreases once the key person approach is adopted. Another way of using observation might be to carry out some detailed, narrative observations of registration and story times at the initial planning, sometimes called 'reconnaissance' phase of the action research cycle (let us imagine that these classroom events happen as a group of 30 children with one teacher, with other members of the team, such as a nursery nurse, engaged in setting-up tasks). The team might instigate a change to practice that involves going into smaller key groups for registration and story times and could monitor the impact of this new practice through observation.

 REFLECTION POINT

Given what has been said so far in this chapter, how does action research differ from a practitioner's usual professional practice? Is it not usual for a practitioner or group of practitioners to try to improve their practice when they perceive something is not working as well as they would like or if they have to implement something new?

The question raised in this Reflection Point is one we will consider in more detail in the next section as it is a criticism sometimes levelled at action research.

Action research sometimes gets confused with case study research too and although there is some blurring we hope Table 11.1 makes the distinction clear:

Table 11.1 Some differences between action research and case study research

Action research	Case study
The focus is on *change or improvement* in a particular area of practice including early childhood settings	The focus is on developing a *detailed understanding* of a particular 'case' or series of 'cases'. These 'cases' might be children or families or countries as well as schools and nurseries
An action research study is usually conducted as a cycle or spiral (or series of these). Often it will begin with a reconnaissance exercise to see what the current situation is and this – in effect – is like conducting a mini case-study. From this, ideas are developed to enhance practice and these are implemented, monitored and evaluated. Documenting the process of change is important to action research	A case study generally stops at gathering a detailed understanding of the case in question. People may use evidence from case study research to help them to improve their practice but the research itself does not involve systematic monitoring and evaluation of the process of change

(Continued)

Table 11.1 (Continued)

Action research	Case study
The researcher is often an 'insider' who wishes to enhance her own practice, perhaps supported by a more experienced researcher. Thus, there is often a very personal engagement in the research	Case studies are often conducted by 'outsiders', i.e. researchers who do not work in a setting (but not exclusively). Whilst they most likely hope their work will have implications for practice, the researcher's aim is not to enhance practice (and document this process) in the course of the research
It is likely that an action research project will try to involve other members of an institution as the emphasis is often on collaboration and co-inquiry. These people (adults and perhaps children too) would be encouraged to be active participants in the research, trying out ideas in their practice, observing and reflecting on what they do, etc. In other words they would in effect be co-researchers	Case study research can be carried out by one person or many. The key difference is that there is not the same impetus to work collaboratively to change something, which requires practitioners to work together in some way. A case study researcher may work in a team of other researchers but is unlikely to need the help of practitioners in quite the same way, but would hope to be able to observe practice, examine documents and interview relevant people (if the 'case' is a nursery or school)
It is very likely that an action research project will take time (e.g. some months) as any project that aims to change or enhance something takes time to develop.	A case study may take some time too – the more time one has the more detail that is possible. However, a case study may also be less detailed and may be concluded in a far shorter timescale

POSSIBILITIES AND LIMITATIONS OF ACTION RESEARCH

Much could be said about the possibilities and limitations of action research – indeed it would be a chapter in itself. We will, however, confine ourselves to a brief discussion of what we feel are the key issues.

Action research is generally conducted by practitioners in areas that relate directly to their own practice. It therefore offers a challenge to the idea that research is the preserve of traditional academia. It is also context specific (Greenwood and Levin, 2000). This, as has been suggested, is the strength of action research, but it is also a limitation – not least because the findings cannot be generalised. However, further to this, Campbell et al. (2004) point out, as we have done, that issues relating to professional practice are complex and there are rarely easy solutions, if indeed 'solutions' are possible or even desirable (Brown and Jones, 2001). Possibly, there is a danger that practitioners might naively think that action research can solve all the problems that manifest themselves in their professional work (Campbell et al., 2004).

In addition to this, it might be easy to confuse action research with what practitioners do anyway – reflecting upon and improving their practice. Like the previous Reflection Point noted, this is a charge that could be levelled at action research. We believe, therefore, that it is important to reflect upon some of the underpinning premises behind any project undertaken. A distinction between action research and what practitioners do routinely in their practice, for instance, can be seen in the idea of praxis. This is because an understanding and application of theory to practice and practice to theory is important to action research but is not necessarily a *routine* part of every practitioner's daily work. Our hope, though, is that those of you who work with young children, and are studying on early-childhood-related courses, apply your professional work to the ideas you are introduced to in your studies and, equally, apply your studies to your practice.

 —— **ACTIVITY** ————————————————

Note down anything further that you can think of that distinguishes research from practice. In doing this, we hope that you can see that a number of ethical issues emerge pertaining to action research in particular.

Examples of some differences include issues relating to dissemination, i.e. sharing information. Research projects involve presenting the findings in a way that can be shared with a wider audience such as writing up in a particular format for your university tutors or even for wider publication or presentation at a conference. In so doing, detailed information about a child or group of children will be shared beyond a particular family or setting, although it should be stressed that it is important to maintain confidentiality and anonymity. This is a clear difference to everyday practice in an early childhood setting and thus requires the informed consent of those people participating in the research. We know of students who have reflected that practitioners often share information about their practice – with specific exemplars of identifiable children – with other professionals from other settings in the spirit of practitioner development and sharing good practice (notably if working nearby). And they do this with no such careful negotiation of consent.

We would argue that reflecting on matters pertaining to research – especially action research – can often flag up ethical issues in relation to early childhood practice too. By way of a further example, we have argued that consent should be given to observing children in research (the consent of children and their parents/carers), but as Albon and Rosen (2014) note, observation is so widely embedded in the practice of early childhood settings in the minority world that it may be difficult to distinguish the difference between research and practice. Is consent negotiated with children and their families for such observations, conducted as part of 'practice', to take place? We suggest that this is rare, and yet, as Grieshaber and McArdle (2010) have shown, some parents attribute a sinister interpretation to detailed observational notes about their child – one parent using the word 'dossier' in this respect. As with all research, we need to constantly attend to ethical considerations.

We should also be cautious about emphasising the claim that action research is empowering to practitioners, owing to the way they themselves identify and initiate change. Campbell et al. (2004) discuss practitioner research and professional development in education, with a focus on teachers. They argue that the growth in evidence-based practice, with teachers conducting school-based research, has had a tendency to focus on raising standards rather than empowering the teachers themselves. Moreover, they draw upon Elliott's work to argue that the promotion and funding of such research has served to legitimise the government's agenda – one of driving up educational standards. In an earlier Reflection Point, for example, we asked you to consider how action research might be conceptualised and which conceptualisation might be most attractive to governments.

Another issue relates to the democratic and collaborative nature of action research inquiry, discussed earlier (Greenwood and Levin, 2000). While we believe this is a positive feature of action research, it can also be problematic. On a very practical level, it can be difficult to stimulate interest in a research topic in a team, especially if the research is perceived as an add-on to their ordinary work. One's position within an organisation may be important here. A manager, for example, may be able to use her or his leadership position to engender support for a particular action research project but on ethical grounds would need to reflect on issues of power in relation to the research – for example, whether the team would feel able to say 'no' to participating in the project or feel able to withdraw from it part of the way through. Further to this, there is an assumption within the notion of collaborative inquiry that the person leading the research is able to facilitate a group to work together effectively. Inevitably, managing group dynamics can be difficult, especially if the practitioner-researcher is inexperienced in this.

There are also advantages and disadvantages to being an 'insider': defined here as a person who works in the setting where the research is carried out. On the positive side, it can be easier to gain access to a setting or a group of children – whatever the sample is for the research. The ongoing relationship a practitioner has with his or her colleagues may engender support that would be impossible for an 'outsider' to muster. An 'insider' is also more likely to be in tune with the issues that are pertinent to the particular context where they are planning to carry out the research when compared with an 'outsider'.

However, being an 'insider' can also be difficult. Examples of these difficulties are as follows. It may be easier for colleagues to ask for interviews to be postponed as they may feel comfortable enough with the practitioner to say 'no' in contrast to research participation with 'outside' researchers. This point links to power issues in research. In addition, when carrying out research as an 'insider', it is important to set boundaries around what you will and will not document. It would be very easy to document the comments of colleagues in unguarded moments in the staffroom, if pertinent to the study, but the practitioner-researcher would have to consider the ethics of doing this – after all, in a one-off interview situation, the interviewee is clear about the boundaries of the interview in terms of the time and space in which it takes place. This is less clear in action research, especially when one is an 'insider'. We would want to add here that the notion of 'insider' and 'outsider' in relation to research is less clear than it might appear on the surface (see e.g. Gregory and Ruby, 2011). For instance, one might be considered an 'insider' when working in the same setting, but may not share the same professional heritage, gender, ethnicity, sexuality, linguistic or class background. Simple distinctions such as 'insider/outsider' will often need further reflection and elaboration when writing up a research project.

Finally, action research may not necessarily change the world, but it does not claim to do this and this would be a huge claim for *any* research! But as Kemmis and McTaggart (2005) note, it does have the potential to improve things for 'particular people in particular places and in many other places where their stories have travelled' (p. 600). Thus, there may well be a gradual shift in practice as other practitioners become familiar with the research. This can be seen in the following example of Penny Holland's (2003) research.

RESEARCH IN FOCUS

ENGLAND

Penny Holland's (2003) research, carried out in England, into young children's war, weapon and superhero play did not result in an *immediate* change in early childhood practice beyond that of herself and the practitioners engaged in the research. Indeed she rejects strongly what she describes as 'a neatly packaged alternative strategy to zero tolerance of this area of play' (2003: 95). Over time, her work has been disseminated to a worldwide audience through her writings, workshop sessions with practitioners, conference papers and interviews with the media. Gradually, many practitioners are coming to know her work and are beginning to ask similar questions of their *own* practice, but, owing to their different subjectivities and different contexts, may come to different understandings and alternative ways of developing their practice. Thus, the uncritical acceptance of an unwritten rule that 'you can't play with guns here' is beginning to be questioned widely as her story has travelled.

We would add a final note here that the Department for Children, Schools and Families in England (DCSF, 2007) – now the Department for Education – recommended Holland's work in relation to raising the achievement of boys in the early years. Perhaps a new orthodoxy is forming around permitting and providing supportive environments for superhero play as equating with the 'greater achievement of boys'. Although this is important, we need to be careful of such a simplistic interpretation: assuming boys (as a group) differ from girls (as a group) on the basis of their biology – Penny Holland would say this too! Moreover, we might also challenge the pedagogisation of play that such a view engenders (see e.g. Rogers [2011] on the way play is increasingly being viewed as instrumental in learning as opposed to other conceptualisations of play). As with any area of practice, we should always open up our supposedly 'common-sense' understandings of practice to scrutiny, as what is deemed 'common-sense' shifts over time.

KEY POINTS FROM THE CHAPTER

- Action research is concerned with changing and improving *practice* in some way.
- It is initiated and carried out by practitioners working in a setting, sometimes with the help of a facilitator such as a professional researcher.
- It is particularly appropriate for those of you who are working in a setting or have the opportunity to spend a considerable length of time in a setting that is willing to work with you on an action research project.
- Action research is often regarded as democratic and emancipatory owing to its focus on collaborative working and the focus on the *practitioner* as researcher as opposed to a more traditional research model where a researcher outside of professional practice initiates, carries out, analyses and evaluates a piece of research.
- Action research operates in a series of cycles, each involving reflections on practice.
- A variety of methods or combinations of methods may be used in action research depending on the focus of the project being undertaken.
- Despite the cyclical nature of action research, some advocates of the approach argue that the primary focus of action research is not its methodology but its capacity to transform practice.
- While action research does not try to effect change on a grand scale – it is particular to people and contexts – it has the capacity to make changes on a wider scale as people tell the stories of their research and share their reflections on practice.

FURTHER READING

Brown, T. and Jones, L. (2001) *Action Research and Postmodernism: Congruence and Critique.* Buckingham: Open University Press. This is a challenging read if you are new to research methods but we recommend it as highly thought-provoking with some interesting early childhood exemplars of action research in practice from Liz Jones's own research in a nursery classroom.

McNiff, J. and Whitehead, J. (2011) *All You Need to Know about Action Research*, 2nd edition. London: Sage. Primarily concerned with action research in schools, this book is a very useful overview of action research with some practical examples of action research in action.

PART 4
METHODS

In Part 3 we learned that there are a variety of strategies or approaches that can be used in research design; we discussed surveys, ethnography, case studies and action research. This part of the book looks at the data-gathering instruments or methods that might be employed in research.

Although some research studies will only use one method to collect data, it is common for more than one method to be used. Sometimes this is a pragmatic decision; for example, if you wanted to investigate the understanding of parents and practitioners about role play, it may be practical to interview all the staff but impractical to interview *all* the parents, so a questionnaire may be used. Using more than one method can also be used to enhance the validity of a study by looking at a topic from a variety of different perspectives (a form of triangulation).

You may recall from Chapter 5 that there is some debate as to whether one should mix methods that 'belong' to different methodologies, in the same research study. For instance, highly structured questionnaires lie within quantitative methodology, underpinned by the positivist paradigm, whereas informal or less structured interviews lie within qualitative methodology and – for example – interpretivist or post-structuralist paradigms; some researchers would consider that combining methods in this way is inadvisable (Denzin and Lincoln, 2011).

In this part we begin by looking at three methods with which you may already be quite familiar: observations, interviews and questionnaires. We also look at theoretical and practical issues to do with these methods and give examples of how these methods have been applied in early childhood research. In Chapters 15 and 16 we look at using documents and other visual texts, and journaling as a research tool. Using documents as a method of obtaining data has a long tradition, especially in disciplines such as history, but is also useful in early childhood research. In the chapter on journaling we introduce you to the idea that 'you' as the researcher are a legitimate source of information. For example, reflections recorded immediately after conducting an interview can add powerful contextual information and insights. In ethnographic studies, the interactions between the researcher and the individual, or group being studied, may reveal additional and salient levels of understanding.

Finally, in Chapter 17 we look at creative ways of involving children in research. These include ways of giving children 'voice', by giving them cameras, looking at their drawings, listening to their narratives and stories and sharing in their play. This chapter is the practical application of one of the principles outlined in Part 2 – listening to children (Chapter 7) – although we recognise that interviewing and observation, in particular, continue to be important methods in early childhood research.

12

OBSERVATION

CHAPTER OBJECTIVES

- To consider how observations have been used as a classic method in early childhood research.
- To discuss the different types of observational methods available and their uses in research.
- To look at the possibilities and limitations of using observations in early childhood research.

One of the characteristics of early childhood care and education is the emphasis that is placed on the role of child observation as a tool to help practitioners understand the children they care for, so they can provide appropriate experiences that will promote the children's learning and development. When used in this way, observations can supply information about a particular child or group of children, which can be used for planning and assessment. You may have used observations of children as part of a course, to help you learn more about child development.

In early childhood *research*, observations are used as a way of gathering primary data as part of both qualitative and quantitative methodologies and, although they may appear similar to the observations practitioners undertake in the workplace, there are profound differences, not least because in research, observations will be shared with others in the publications and reports produced. However, observation is such a commonplace practice in early childhood settings that for early childhood practitioners undertaking research it can be difficult to distinguish one's research practice from one's everyday practice (Albon and Rosen, 2014). This is an ethical consideration that is worth reflecting upon if you are in this position.

Observations related to your practice have a different focus, that of promoting children's learning and development either to inform planning or assessment or to supply information that will improve the quality of the work within the setting. Observations for research purposes may be of no direct benefit to individual children or the work of the setting, although they *may* be beneficial. Observations used in research are designed to supply data related to the overall aim of the study or answer specific research questions. There are always ethical issues involved in observing children, whether this is part of your professional work or for research purposes. However, there are additional ethical issues that need to be considered when using observations for research purposes and these will be discussed later on in the chapter.

The decision about which observational method to choose will depend upon the research question that is being investigated and the use to which the findings will be put. In this chapter we will look at a variety of observational methods that are available and their possibilities and limitations.

HISTORICAL OVERVIEW

Human survival depends upon individuals being able to observe the world around them accurately. At its most basic level, accurate observational skills help us to avoid dangers and keep us safe. As social beings, much of our learning depends on us observing what others are doing – the actions and reactions of people around us. As Rolfe and Emmett (2010: 309) comment, 'Observation is something we do all our waking lives'.

Children became a focus of *systematic* observation in the eighteenth century when Rousseau suggested that children's behaviour was worthy of study in an attempt to promote their 'natural development' (Fawcett and Watson, 2016: 48). Of course people were observing children prior to this, as parents commonly made anecdotal records of what their children were doing and how they were developing. Following Rousseau's lead, there were a succession of publications by educationalists, such as Pestalozzi, who recorded their children's early development, leading to what may be considered one of the most important forerunners of child study: the observations undertaken by Charles Darwin of his son (Darwin, 1877).

 —— **REFLECTION POINT** —————————————————

Charles Darwin's work can be viewed online: http://darwin-online.org.uk (accessed 8 March 2017).

Read 'A biographical sketch of an infant'. (Use the search facility.) What similarities can you find between this observational study and observations about children you may have read or conducted yourself?

The child study came to be seen as a legitimate tool for the study of child psychology, and Fawcett and Watson (2016) describe how, at the beginning of the twentieth century, universities in the USA opened up child study centres where parents were encouraged to bring their children so that they could be observed under 'controlled' laboratory conditions. Some psychologists, however, expressed concern that behaviour observed under controlled laboratory conditions may not be a true reflection of how children behave in their 'natural' environment. As a response to this there was a move to undertake observations of children in their normal, everyday settings. Fawcett and Watson describe this as the 'ecological approach' as it takes account of 'the child's real habitat: the location, other people present, and the expectations and rules under which the child is operating' (Fawcett and Watson, 2016: 52).

In Europe, psychoanalysts such as Freud, psychologists such as Piaget and educationalists such as Susan Isaacs all used observations on children to further their knowledge (Fawcett and Watson, 2016). Observations and measurements of children continue to inform the work of developmental psychologists. Without systematic child observation:

- Piaget (Wadsworth, 1996) and Bruner (2006) would not have been able to formulate their theories on cognitive development.
- Bowlby (1969) and Ainsworth (Ainsworth et al., 1978) would not have been able to recognise the importance of human attachment.
- Athey (2007) would not have developed her ideas about children's schemas.

Child observations have also contributed to the compilation of schedules of development or developmental norms (descriptions of sequential steps, or milestones, that most children pass through as they mature). Perhaps one of the most well-known of these schedules of development was devised by Mary Sheridan. Originally published in the 1960s, the most recent version was published in 2014 (Sharma and Cockerill, 2014). The developmental norm approach has been the subject of much criticism for advocating a 'one size fits all' view of child development and because it can fail to take into account the wide variety of factors that might impact upon the development of children around the world, including culture and economic disadvantage. These variations can mean that using checklists or a milestone approach may be unhelpful as 'the unique individuality of every growing person can easily be devalued by over concentration on measurement and the achievement of norms' (Fawcett and Watson, 2016 :56).

WHEN IS IT APPROPRIATE TO USE OBSERVATION IN RESEARCH?

Before we investigate when it is appropriate to use observation in research we need to look a little closer into what we mean by the term 'observation'. When we observe something we use all of our senses, as this is the way that we take in information about the world around us.

 REFLECTION POINT

It is lunchtime at a nursery. Joe is sitting with his key children around the table, interacting with the children as they eat their pasta and sauce. Fumi, a girl aged 18 months, is eating with obvious enthusiasm and, at the same time, is experimenting with the food on her plate. She is laughing and tries to feed him with her spoon.

What senses might Joe be using to take in and process (perceive) this information?

You may reflect that Joe is using his eyes and ears, his sense of touch, taste and smell. In fact Joe is using all his senses.

We use the same processes whether we are interviewing, administering a questionnaire or making a direct observation, and Rolfe and Emmett (2010: 312) suggest that 'if we define observation broadly as one person's perception' then we could say that all research is based on observation. However, in this chapter, we will be focusing on *direct observation* of participants' behaviour, be they children, parents, early years practitioners or other individuals relevant to a piece of research.

Coolican (2014) makes the distinction between observation being used as a method of data collection *within* the overall research design, or *as* the overall research design. When observations are used as the overall design of a piece of research, the study is often known as an 'observational study' to make it clear to the reader that they are not looking at experimental research. You will find information on research design in Chapter 1.

An example of observations being used as a method of data collection are the structured observations focusing on the 'quality' of pre-school settings as part of the EPPE project (Sylva et al., 2004). Within this longitudinal study there were a variety of methods of data collection used, including structured observations. An example of observations being used as the overall research design is the work conducted by Plowman and Stephen (2003) where in-depth observations of pre-school children's use of information and communications technology (ICT) were conducted in seven pre-school settings. Observations are also a key part of ethnographic studies. These are often known as 'participant observations', which are discussed later on in this chapter.

Rolfe and Emmett (2010) consider that observations are useful when researchers want to understand or explain everyday behaviours, or examine the effect of something on everyday behaviour. Often, with very young children and babies, it may be the only way of obtaining information because they may lack the communication skills needed to give an interview or fill in a questionnaire.

TYPES OF OBSERVATION

Observations can vary across a number of dimensions. Already in this chapter we have made the distinction between observations undertaken within a laboratory and those undertaken in a 'naturalistic' environment. We will now look at a few of these different types of observation.

LABORATORY OR 'NATURALISTIC'?

Laboratory observations are carried out in a controlled environment that has been set up by the researcher in an effort to make the situation as similar as possible for all participants. When studying children, a laboratory may be a room set up like a nursery, with a one-way mirror on one wall through which a researcher can observe what is going on in the room, but with the participants unable to see the researcher. The advantage of laboratory observations is that all participants are observed in conditions that are, as near as possible, the same, reducing the effect of confounding variables. This is the 'scientific' or experimental approach and you can read more about this in Chapter 4. The disadvantage is that researchers may not be seeing 'normal' behaviour, as the participant is not in their everyday environment (Hayes, 2010).

'Naturalistic' observations are undertaken in the everyday setting of the partici-pant, which for young children might be their home or nursery setting. These are the type of observations that most practitioners are familiar with and are not without limitations. However, as we have noted in earlier chapters in this book, 'naturalistic' is a term which – when you think about it – can be questioned. After all, there are many things which could be considered quite 'unnatural' about homes and nursery settings. Perhaps 'usual environment', i.e. the environment with which a child is most familiar, is a more useful term to use.

 REFLECTION POINT

In a 'naturalistic' observation it is *impossible* to ensure that all the participants are observed under the same conditions. If a child is being observed in his or her own home, or in a nursery, what sort of variables might have an effect on the child's behaviour? Does this matter?

The kinds of variables that might have an effect on the child's behaviour could include the physical environment, the people with whom the child is interacting and the presence or not of the observer. In experimental research this would be considered problematic, because it is difficult to control variables in a 'naturalis-tic' situation. However, as you may recall from Chapter 5, it could also be argued that researchers should try to observe children in a 'naturalistic' environment in recognition of the fact that children grow and develop in complex social worlds – not worlds that can be easily controlled. Thus, researchers should try to observe children in the context of their everyday lives (Dunn, 2005).

QUANTITATIVE OR QUALITATIVE?

Observations can either be quantitative in nature or qualitative. We have looked at this classification several times already in this book as it is one of the main methodological distinctions in planning research.

- *Quantitative observations*, sometimes known as structured observations, are designed to give standardised, numerical data, in an effort to reduce the number of variables and improve reliability of the findings. Johnson and Christensen (2012: 206) suggest that the following variables could be standardised in quantitative observations: who is observed, what is observed, when observations are to take place, where the observations are to be carried out, and how the observations are to be done. Very often, in large studies involving several observers, training is given beforehand to increase the reliability of the observations.

- *Qualitative observations* are often undertaken for exploratory purposes and exactly what will be observed is not specified beforehand. Qualitative observations are usually undertaken in 'naturalistic' situations, with what the researcher records being guided by the overall aim of the research and interesting things that they see at the time.

PARTICIPANT OR NON-PARTICIPANT OBSERVATION?

Another dimension to the type of observation being used is the degree to which the researcher/observer is *part* of the actual observation. Consider the scenario outlined previously when Joe was observing Fumi as she ate her lunch. Joe, while observing, was also fully participating in the exchange. You may recall that participant observation is a key component of ethnographic research and is discussed in Chapter 9. Although the degree to which an observer is a participant or not lies on a continuum, for convenience's sake, Johnson and Christensen (2012) have identified four conditions:

- *Complete participation* is where the observer is a full member of the group being studied. If the researcher is a complete participant it is not usual to inform the group about the research aim, as this may alter the group's behaviour towards the researcher. This aspect of complete participation is considered unethical as it involves deception and the participants have not been given the right 'not to participate'. In Chapter 9 we discussed this in relation to Fielding's covert study of the National Front, described in Fielding (2008). Students should not be engaging in research that involves deception.
- *Participant as observer* is when the researcher spends a considerable amount of time with a group and attempts to become a full member of the group, but explains to the group from the beginning that they are conducting research. This is similar to practitioner research in early years settings. The staff team will be fully aware that the researcher is undertaking observations (and for what purpose) and may give insightful comments on what has been recorded or even help with data collection. If observing children, it is important to gain the written permission of parents too.
- *Observer as participant* is when the researchers spend only a limited amount of time with the group they are observing, seeking permission from the participants to join in only with the activities that they wish to observe. This is similar to a student on a course attending a nursery setting for a limited amount

of time a week. The advantage of this is that it is easier to remain objective, but a complete understanding of what is happening may be difficult to attain because the observer remains an outsider (Johnson and Christensen, 2012).

- *The complete observer* does not involve themselves with the group being observed at all. S/he remains anonymous and endeavours not to be noticed by the participants. An example of this may be a researcher observing children playing in a public place, where Johnson and Christensen (2012) consider that the participants do not need to be informed that they are being observed. The advantage of this type of observation is that the participants' behaviour is less likely to differ from their usual behaviour, but the information obtained will lack the insider's point of view.

— —— REFLECTION POINT ————————————————

Now reflect upon the advisability of observing children in this covert way. Although your intentions may be innocent, your behaviour may be misinterpreted by others. Is it ethical to carry out research without informed consent? Could you call the people being observed 'participants' in this type of study? Chapter 6 on ethics will help you think through the issues.

NARRATIVE METHODS

Narrative observations are those where the observer endeavours to write down, in everyday language, (or otherwise record) what the participant says or does. Narrative methods are qualitative in nature, although it may be possible to reduce the information obtained to allow a quantitative analysis if this is thought appropriate.

We will be describing four main methods: 'naturalistic' observations, target child observations, the clinical interview and diary entries. There is no real agreement about what each method is called and you will find different sources will use different terms to describe similar methods. Rolfe and Emmett (2010) suggest that to avoid confusion it is best to focus on what the method *involves*, rather than its *name*.

'Naturalistic' observations

'Naturalistic' observations are also known as narrative observations, descriptive narratives, running records and written observations. These observations are commonly used by practitioners in early childhood settings as part of their everyday work, but when used for the purposes of research, the rationale for doing them will be different. Although this is a reasonably straightforward method, and often the one that students of early years care and education are introduced to first, it is by no means an easy skill to acquire. This method involves observers writing down exactly what they see and hear as it happens. Observers usually use a notebook to record what they see, often using abbreviations to speed up the process, writing up the observation neatly as soon as is practical, while what has been seen is still fresh in the memory (Table 12.1).

There are several points to remember when writing a 'naturalistic' observation:

- The present tense is usually used; however, this is a convention and some practitioners and researchers prefer to use the past tense. The use of the present tense implies that the observer is recording things as they happen, whilst the use of the past tense implies that the observer is remembering what happened. In reality it is often impossible to write everything down at the time and a degree of retrospection is inevitable.

Table 12.1 Excerpt from a 'naturalistic' observation

Date: 25-08-08	**Time observation starts:** 07.55
	Time observation finishes: 08.05
Child's name: Freddy (a pseudonym)	**Gender:** M
Age: 1:3	**D.O.B:** 25-05-07

Main language of child: English

Context: Children's centre in inner city London, toddler room. Freddy is being brought into the centre by his mother, Mona. He has been attending for 2 weeks. Freddy's key person has seen the family arrive and is waiting for them.

Number and age of other children: 2 children 1:6 and 2:1.

Number of adults: 2: Freddy's key person, Kate, and 1 other.

Mona pushes open the door and ushers Freddy into the room. He has tears on his face and holds on to Mona's legs, burying his head in her skirt.

Mona: 'What's all this about? You enjoyed yourself yesterday. Don't cry. Look, here is Kate.'

Mona picks Freddy up, he buries his head in her shoulder.

Kate approaches Freddy, she touches his shoulder gently.

Kate: 'Hi Freddy. Don't you want to play with me today? Mona, why don't you help Freddy take off his coat? Shall we see if Freddy remembers where his peg is?'

Mona puts Freddy on the ground and Freddy lets her take his coat off.

Mona: 'Can you show me your peg, Freddy?'

Freddy points to where the pegs are, he walks towards them and Mona finds his peg.

Mona leaves the room. Freddy looks at her going and begins to cry loudly. He goes towards the shut door. He tries to open it, but can't. He sits on the floor, banging his feet on the door. He is crying loudly.

- Only behaviour is recorded – the observation will be analysed at a later date – so you would not write 'F was upset when he came into the nursery' because that is an interpretation of his behaviour.
- Using initials instead of using participants' names can be confusing. You can use pseudonyms instead. As long as the real names of the setting and the participants are not used you will be able to maintain confidentiality. If you work with young children and you are carrying out observations as part of your *professional* work, you would retain the child's real name so that the information can contribute to the child's record. This is one of the distinctions between undertaking research and carrying out observations if employed as a practitioner. Of course if you are both the practitioner and the researcher – as in action research – this blurring of boundaries can throw up ethical issues around confidentiality.

The main advantage of using 'naturalistic' observations is that behaviour can be recorded as it happens and little advance preparation is needed. The disadvantage is that decisions have to be made about exactly what to record; if there is a lot going on something might be missed. This assumes greater importance if there is more than one researcher. Moreover, the data that are produced are *unstructured* and will require careful analysis later on, and, although they will give you information about that particular event, it is hard to *compare* observations.

Target child method

This method was developed during the 1970s as part of the Oxford Pre-School Project (Sylva et al., 1980) and was used as a research tool in the EPPE project (Sylva et al., 2004), where it was originally used to discover the situations which promoted children's concentration. Green (2000) argues that the target child method is also useful for noting social interactions and the child's use of language. The method involves the use of a pre-prepared template on which to record the observation, which makes use of pre-decided abbreviations. This is particularly useful if more than one observer is involved in data collection. The following is a list of commonly used codes, but any code can be used as long as it is decided beforehand and every observer uses the same codes.

- Activity codes:

  TC = target child (the child's name or initials are not used)

  C = child

  A = adult

- Language codes:

  To record language (what the child is saying), you would simply write: TC>C, if the target child is speaking to another child, or TC>A, if they are speaking to an adult.

- Task codes:

  LMM = large muscle movement

  LSC = large-scale construction

  SSC = small-scale construction

  MAN = manipulation

  SM = structured materials

  PS = problem solving

  SVT = scale-version toys

  IG = informal games

  SINP = social interaction, non-play

  DB = distress behaviour

  (This is just an example of what can be an extensive list.)

- Social codes:

  SOL = the target child is playing on their own (solitary)

  PAIR = the child is with one other person, child or adult

  SG = the target child is within a small group (three to five children)

  LG = the target child is within a large group (six or more children)

  PAIR/P = the target child is playing parallel to one other child

  SG/P = the target child is playing parallel to a small group

  LG/P = the target child is playing parallel to a large group

  (If there is an adult interacting with an activity, there would be a circle drawn around the social code.)

In the short example of a target child observation in Table 12.2, the target child (TC) is playing in the sand with another child (C).

Once observers have memorised the codes, this method is a time-efficient way of observing children's behaviour. It is useful for identifying children who are not socialising with other children or who rarely communicate.

Table 12.2 Excerpt from a target child observation

Details of the child and the setting (note: these details will be similar to the ones recorded for the 'naturalistic' observation described previously)

Activity record	Language record	Task code	Social code
TC takes cup in right hand. Pushes it under the sand and brings it up filled with sand. Holds funnel in left hand. Pours sand from cup into funnel.	TC>C Look it's falling	MAN	PAIR
C adds water to the sand. TC stirs it around. C puts the damp sand into the cup. TC takes cup and tries to pour the sand into the funnel.	C>TC it won't go	MAN PS	PAIR

The clinical interview

Jarvis et al. (2004) describe how this method of observation, involving a mixture of observation and interview, was developed by Piaget as a way of trying to understand young children's thinking and reasoning. Piaget would watch children playing or trying to complete a task and then ask them questions about what they were doing and why they were doing it. In clinical interviewing there are no set questions because the questions depend on what the child is doing and later questions depend on the answers to the earlier ones. The disadvantage of this method is that children are not all asked the same questions so the findings are not generalisable. In addition, there is a danger that the children's intentions can be misinterpreted. For example, Jarvis et al. (2004) describe how clinical interviews were used to suggest that children believe in animism: a belief that inanimate objects are alive and can understand the children. Jarvis et al. point out that if a child hits a teddy and calls it 'naughty', it may not mean that the child believes the toy is alive; the child may just be engaged in imaginative play.

The diary method

Diaries contain records of significant events that have been observed over a period of time and may contain observational material together with personal reflection and analysis. There are no hard and fast guidelines as to what should be recorded in a diary, as the observers decide for themselves what is worthy of inclusion. Coolican (2014) considers that diaries can be a rich source of information as they can document change; however, they can become highly subjective, making any comparison with other diary studies very difficult. Chapters 9 (ethnography), 15 (documents) and 16 (journaling as a research tool) in this book provide further information about the use of diaries and field notes in research.

STRUCTURED METHODS

In narrative observations, children's behaviour is recorded in some detail, often with no prior decision as to exactly what should be observed. *Structured* observational methods narrow down the focus of the observation and are often guided by a very precise aim. Most structured observations are quantitative in nature and can generate numerical data. We will be looking at three different types of structured observation in this section: the time sample, the event sample and the checklist.

Time samples

Time samples involve observing a participant (adult or child), a group of participants or an area of the nursery at regular intervals during the day. Before observing, it is important to be clear about:

- the *aim* of the observation
- *who* or *what* is being observed
- exactly *what* will be recorded
- how *often* the recordings will be made
- the *length* of each recording.

Before starting to observe, a grid should be drawn up. For example, it may be that the aim is to investigate what proportion of the day staff members are interacting with children as opposed to being involved in other activities. The recording grid may look like Table 12.3.

Table 12.3 Extract from a time sample recording adult–child interaction

	Total number of staff in room: 5		
Time	No interaction	Interacting with 1 child	Interacting with more than 1 child
09.00	3	1	1
09.15	3	0	2
09.30	1	2	2
09.45	0	3	2
10.00	4	0	1
...			
11.45	4	0	1
Total			

Time samples need to be repeated at different times of the day and different days of the week, as just one observation will not help you reveal if there is any consistent pattern. Enough time samples need to be made to enable the researcher to make some generalisations about the behaviour of individuals or groups.

Time samples can be used to look at individual children, such as observing a child every 5 minutes to see what the child is doing. This can be very time-consuming, and the researcher is unlikely to be able to do much else, unless some sort of timer is used as a reminder for when to look up and find the child. The advantage of time samples in research is that they are repeatable and it is possible to 'measure' the success of an intervention by undertaking 'before' and 'after' observations (as long as it is remembered to keep variables such as the time of day and day of the week constant). The disadvantage of time samples is that examples of the behaviour under observation could be missed because they fall in-between two time points. In addition, the information recorded may lack detail.

Event samples

Event samples are similar to time samples, except that instead of sampling at regular times, a particular event is chosen, whenever it occurs (Rolfe and Emmett, 2010). This type of observation is very useful for looking at aspects of children's behaviour, for example, the researcher may wish to find out what is provoking a child's frequent 'temper tantrums', or why a particular area of the nursery appears to provoke conflict among the children. When investigating instances of challenging behaviour it is useful to know the ABC of the event (Mukherji, 2001):

- *Antecedent*: what was going on immediately beforehand that may have provoked the event?
- *Behaviour*: what the child/children did, possibly as a response to what was going on beforehand.
- *Consequences*: what followed on immediately after the event?

Table 12.4 is an example of an event sample used to investigate a child's 'temper tantrums'.

If this event sample was undertaken throughout a day it might be possible to detect that Anil's 'temper tantrums' occur in situations when he cannot get his own way. He may have learned that such behaviour might get him what he wants. The disadvantages of event samples are that observers need to be alert to what is going on around them, so that they are aware of the events as they occur. It is also necessary to be clear beforehand about exactly what constitutes an 'event' (Mukherji, 2001). In addition, if there is more than one observer, then training in recognising salient events will be necessary.

Table 12.4 Excerpt from an event sample

Time	Record of event	What was happening immediately beforehand?	What was the outcome of the event?
09.15	Anil looks around and sees that his mother is leaving the room. He runs after her, holding onto her skirt. He yells and screams. He kicks her legs with his feet. 'Don't go', he cries.	Anil was playing in the sand tray. His mother, who was watching, quietly moves towards the door.	Anil's mother picks him up, cuddles him and says, 'Don't worry, I will stay a bit longer!' Anil stops crying.
09.43	Anil is lying on his front on the floor, crying loudly. He is beating the floor with his fists. An adult goes towards him. He lashes out at her with his arm.	Anil was playing with the farm animals with another child, Harry. He grabbed a toy from Harry's hand, saying that he wants it. Harry asked an adult for help. The adult explained to Anil that he should give the toy back to Harry.	Harry gives the toy to Anil. 'Here, you have it'. Anil stops crying. The adult finds another toy for Harry.

Checklists

Checklists are commonly used in recording aspects of child development and are commonly based on schedules of development, such as Mary Sheridan's 'From Birth to Five Years' (Sharma and Cockerill, 2014). The use of checklists to record children's development in early years settings used to be very popular, and many local authorities provided settings with developmental booklets that could be used. However, the use of these checklists has fallen out of favour in recent years as it is recognised that a checklist approach contains very little information and checklists should really be thought of as *summaries* of observations (Fawcett and Watson, 2016: 90). Checklists are still used as a guide for health professionals (Table 12.5), and parents are invited to fill in checklists about their children's development in their personal child health record (NHS, 2016).

It is possible to make up checklists for practically any aspect of development or work procedures. You may be familiar with checklists that are used by staff to record when a task has been completed. Data from checklists tend to be quantitative in nature and easy to analyse numerically.

Table 12.5 Excerpt from a checklist to assess vision in babies aged 2 months

Behaviour	Yes	No
Baby opens his/her eyes and looks at parent.		
Baby follows the movement of the parent's head by following with his/her eyes or by moving his/her head.		
Do the baby's eyes look normal?		

THE LEUVEN SCALES FOR WELL-BEING AND INVOLVEMENT

The Leuven scales are an assessment instrument designed by Ferre Laevers to help settings become aware of their strengths and weaknesses when it comes to creating the best possible environment for children to develop (Laevers, 2005: 3). Children's levels of well-being (feeling like a fish in water) and involvement (being completely absorbed in the moment) are assessed using two scales where children are given scores from 1 (low) to 5 (high) for both well-being and involvement, based on observations of their behaviour. For example, if children exhibit all or most of the following behaviours they will be assessed at level 1 for well-being.

- whines, sobs, cries, screams;
- looks dejected, sad or frightened;
- is in panic;
- is angry or furious;
- shows signs feet [sic], wriggles, throws objects, hurts others;
- sucks its thumb, rubs its eyes;
- doesn't respond to the environment, avoids contact, withdraws;
- hurts him/herself: bangs its head, throws him/herself on the floor (Laevers, 2005: 13).

Once assessments are completed, the staff team analyse the findings and implement interventions to improve the quality of provision.

Although designed as a self-assessment tool the scales have also been used to monitor the well-being and involvement of individual children.

 ACTIVITY

Investigate this website which is the link to Laevers's *Well-being and Involvement in Care Settings. A Process-oriented Self-evaluation Instrument*: /img/sics-ziko-manual.pdf (accessed 8 March 2017).

 CASE STUDY

Farida works in a private day care setting for children from 3 months to 5 years old. She works with 18-months- to 2-year-olds and is studying for her early childhood degree part-time. Farida and her colleagues want to improve the settling in process for children

(Continued)

and families joining the centre. Farida is about to embark on her undergraduate research project and decides to use the opportunity this presents to undertake a piece of action research in her setting. As part of the research she wants to observe three children who are soon to join the setting, from first contact through to when the children are settled in their new environment.

As action research is a collaborative process she talks to the other practitioners in a staff meeting who have agreed to support her and help her with the observations. It is agreed that the children's key persons will conduct the observations, with other staff contributing observations if they 'see' something that they think will contribute to gaining an all-round picture of how the children settle.

The parents of the children have given informed consent which was obtained when the key person undertook the home visit.

1. What would you suggest would be useful to observe?
2. What observation techniques could be used?
3. What ethical issues are there in this sort of study?

Because Farida and the staff team want to get as complete an understanding of the settling in process for these children (and their families) as possible, it is decided that observations will include observations of the children in their home setting, as well as the initial visits to the setting and the first four weeks of the children's full-time attendance. The children's behaviour at the beginning and end of the day will be noted, together with how they cope with routines such as meal times, nap times and nappy changing (if appropriate). The children will be observed as they play on their own, interact with the other children and interact with their key persons and other adults.

Farida suggests that a variety of observational techniques could be used, from narrative observations through to time samples following the children through a typical day, and event samples recording when children show distress. The staff team are clear that observations will also include observing the family members and practitioners as they interact with the children.

There are ethical issues involved in this study, as there are in all early childhood research. In this case parents may feel pressurised to give consent as they may assume that the staff will think badly about them if they say 'no' and that this may result in unfavourable treatment of their children. This is particularly likely at the beginning of their relationship with the setting. One way to overcome this (although it will always be an issue) is to give the parents full information about the research and why it is being done; that the aim is to improve settling in for children, whist acknowledging that *their* children may not benefit immediately. Parents should be clearly informed that they do not have to agree to research observations being conducted and that their children will only be observed as part of the normal practice of the setting. Practitioners may also feel uncomfortable since their interactions with children and families may also be recorded. This needs to be discussed in the staff meeting and practitioners should also be given the opportunity not to be involved. Although if more than one or two staff want to be excluded from the project it may be that action research is not appropriate in these circumstances. Consideration of the children is of paramount importance too, so sensitivity should be shown to individual children's cues as to whether they are comfortable with being observed closely (see Chapters 6 and 7 for more detail).

RECORDING INFORMATION

DATA-GATHERING DEVICES

Most of the techniques we have looked at lend themselves to paper-and-pen methods of recording, although a checklist could be entered electronically. Some researchers like to use digital recording devices such as a video camera. The advantage of this is that you have permanently captured an event and can review it over and over again, as Tobin et al. (1989, 2009) did in their study of pre-schools in three cultures. Unfortunately, unless recording under laboratory/studio conditions, it is often difficult to hear what is going on because of interference from the noise in an early years setting. The human ear is very good at screening out background noise, allowing you to concentrate on the event you are observing, but camcorders record everything, making analysis difficult at times.

The same applies to electronic sound recorders, such as Dictaphones, as trying to decipher what has been heard can be difficult. The other drawback of these methods is that participants may behave differently with recording devices around. Researchers tend to introduce these devices some time before using them in their research, to give participants a chance to get used to them and to allow their behaviour to return to 'normal'.

It is important to consider the additional ethical responsibilities that digital recording of observations presents. In recording observations in this way, it is imperative that participants have agreed to this method of recording and know how the recording will be used; that is, *who* will see it and *how long* the recording will be kept. However, this is not so simple in practice. Robson (2011b) highlights how in 'raw' video data, participants are recognisable and that, although blurring of individual identities is technically possible, it simultaneously blurs out detail of facial expression, which might be important data, in the instance Robson discusses, of metacognitive activity. In addition, as consent should be regarded as ongoing or provisional, Robson also highlights how there can be a tension between trying not to be obtrusive when filming but also ensuring that the consent of children to be filmed is negotiated. This is a tension which can be extended to the observational method more generally owing to the ubiquity of observation in early childhood practice – a point we noted at the beginning of this chapter. As children may be so familiar with staff undertaking observations as part of their day-to-day practice, it may be very difficult to make clear when 'research' is taking place. This also raises issues about 'consent' in relation to many aspects of early childhood practice which are beyond the remit of this book.

RESEARCH IN FOCUS

SWEDEN

Björk et al. (2006) undertook an observational study in Sweden of 12 children, under the age of 7, who were receiving treatment for cancer on a paediatric oncology ward. The aim of the study was to describe the needs of the children as they were being treated, as revealed by what they expressed verbally, their behaviour and body language. Björk, a paediatric nurse, was the observer. Non-participant, unstructured observations were used whereby the researcher sat quietly and observed what was happening, without joining in. The observation periods varied from 20 minutes to 80 minutes. No recording was made at the time of the observation, but field notes were made immediately afterwards and later written up as a narrative text. The observations were analysed using content analysis to identify recurring themes and concepts. (Chapter 18 looks at content analysis in some detail.) The findings revealed that the primary need expressed by the children was to have their parents nearby and that this then helped the children express the other needs that they had.

Ethical considerations are issues in any research and the use of observations as a method to collect data has specific challenges in this area. In the Björk et al. (2006) research, ethical considerations were a key feature in designing the study, both children and parents being at a time in their lives when they were particularly vulnerable. Because the research was undertaken in a hospital, the research proposal had to go in front of the ethics committee before the researchers were given permission to proceed. Staff involved in the care of the children in the hospital were given information about the research process. Parents were fully informed about what the research entailed, both orally and in writing, and gave written consent if they agreed to be included in the study. Before they gave consent parents were told that they could withdraw from the study at any time and that the observer would withdraw at any time if requested. For children over 2, the research was described in a 'developmentally appropriate' way and they were asked for their assent. The article describing the research does not inform us about how assent was obtained from the younger children, but it is assumed that this was an ongoing process whereby children's behaviour was monitored for signs that they were not at ease with the situation.

RECORDING CONTEXTUAL INFORMATION

When undertaking observations, it is important to have all the relevant details about the participants and the setting, as there is nothing worse than realising, when it is too late, that a vital detail has not been recorded. The details that you need to record will vary according to the aim of your research study, but should include information that may have an influence on what you have observed. It may be pertinent to include items from the following list:

- details of the child/children observed, such as age, date of birth, gender, ethnicity, language spoken, length of time at setting
- date, time and length of observation
- method of observation used
- details of the setting; for example, a playground, child's home or playgroup
- details of the area in which the setting is located (rural/affluent suburb/ multicultural inner city, etc.)
- immediate context, for example, in the garden
- what was happening immediately before the observation
- details of the adults involved (numbers/roles, etc.).

Clearly, if researchers are undertaking a series of observations in the same setting, or on the same child, many of these details only have to be recorded once. It is important to remember that permission should be sought from *all* involved and that you should maintain confidentiality. In addition, due consideration must be taken of data protection. Please see Chapter 6 where these aspects are looked at in some detail.

OBSERVER BIAS

In this chapter we have looked at a variety of techniques, ranging from 'naturalistic' observations where observers attempt to write down everything that they see, to the checklist approach where all that is required is a tick in a box if a particular event/aspect of development is seen. Observers are different. They have all had different life experiences or 'brought selves' (Reinharz, 1997) and these differences affect what they focus on when they are observing. For example, if you asked two observers to write a 'naturalistic' observation of children playing outside, one person may have focused on the children's gross motor skills and their confidence in using the play equipment, while the other observer may have focused on how the children cooperated together. Physical characteristics of the observers, such as whether they are tired, too hot or cold, hungry or unwell may also contribute to their attention span and their ability to make accurate recordings. These considerations are important as they affect the reliability of observations. The use of some of the more structured forms of observing and the prior training of observers may overcome these effects to some extent.

In addition to the differences in what observers may record, different observers may interpret what they see in very different ways (Coffey, 1999). In the research discussed in the Research in Focus feature above (Björk et al., 2006) the authors reflect that their previous experiences as paediatric nurses, mothers and child psychologists may have influenced the way that the observations were interpreted. During the analysis of the observations these experiences were reflected upon and discussed.

 REFLECTION POINT

Ashu is 3 years old and has just started nursery. He lives with his parents who are of Indian descent, and his grandmother, who came to the UK as a young woman. Ashu communicates well in both Bengali and English. It has been observed that Ashu is reluctant to feed himself and is still unable to put his coat on independently.

One observer is very worried about his development, fearing that he is lacking in independence skills. Another observer considers that his behaviour is completely normal. Why are there such different interpretations?

Factors such as culture, class, religion, level of education and past life experiences all contribute to the way we interpret what we see. We bring to the observation process our opinions and prejudices (Coffey, 1999). To increase objectivity, the researcher should aim to avoid including 'evaluations, judgements, impressions and personal speculations' when recording observations (Nicholson and Shipstead, 1998: 13, cited in Rolfe and Emmett, 2010). For post-structuralist researchers in particular, it is important to be constantly reflexive of one's position in relation to the research and the impact this may have had on the collection and analysis of data, which might mean keeping an ongoing reflexive journal (see Chapter 16).

The ways in which observations can be analysed are discussed in Chapter 18. However, we would like to include a word of caution here about the risk of 'over analysing' observational material. By this we mean going beyond what has actually been observed and reading into a situation something that is not there.

KEY POINTS FROM THE CHAPTER

- There has been a long history of using child observations to further our understanding of child development and education.
- Observations can be undertaken in a laboratory or in 'naturalistic' surroundings.
- Observers can be placed somewhere along a continuum, with complete participation in the situation being observed at one end, and complete non-participation at the other.
- Observations can be used to generate both qualitative and quantitative data.
- There are a variety of different methods of observation that can be used, from unstructured narratives to more structured methods.
- The self of the researcher impacts on what they see and how they analyse observations; therefore, reflexivity in relation to observational data is important.
- Some would argue that observational bias can be overcome with research training and the use of more structured observations.

FURTHER READING

Dunn, J. (2005) 'Naturalistic observations of children and their families', in S. Green and D. Hogan (eds) *Researching Children's Experience: Approaches and Methods*. London: Sage. In this chapter, Dunn draws on her considerable experience of using observations as a way to study children's lives.

Fawcett, M. and Watson, D. (2016) *Learning through Child Observation*, 3rd edition. London: Jessica Kingsley. This is a good basic text on child observation, covering both theory and practice.

Rolfe, S. and Emmett, S. (2010) 'Direct observation', in G. MacNaughton, S. Rolfe and I. Siraj-Blatchford (eds) *Doing Early Childhood Research: International Perspectives on Theory and Practice*, 2nd edition. Maidenhead: Open University Press. In this chapter, Rolfe and Emmett describe the decisions made when planning a research study involving child observation and give an excellent overview of the topic.

13

INTERVIEWS

CHAPTER OBJECTIVES

- To consider the use of interviews as a method in early childhood research.
- To outline the different types of interview and the research paradigms that underpin them.
- To reflect on key issues, which need to be considered when designing and conducting interviews with adults as well as children.
- To consider ways of recording interviews.
- To reflect on the possibilities and limitations of using interviews in early childhood research.

It has been said that we live in an 'interview society' (Silverman, 2014: 55). It is difficult to open a magazine or newspaper, or turn on the television without being made aware of how many interviews are conducted, not only to find out about current events and the world of celebrities, but also in more 'scientific' research. Interviews are a highly versatile research tool; they can be used in quantitative or qualitative research involving adults and children, as individuals or in groups. All of the approaches discussed in Part 3 of this book could involve the use of interviews as a way of obtaining data.

In this chapter we will outline the various types of interview that are available as tools for researchers to use and we will discuss some of the decisions that have to be made to ensure that interviews are reliable, valid and ethical.

WHAT IS AN INTERVIEW?

Fundamentally an interview is a method where one person asks questions of an individual or group of people with the expectation of getting answers to a particular question or an elaboration of their views on a particular topic.

 —— REFLECTION POINT ————————

It is the first day of a course. You, and everyone else in your class, are new to the university and to each other. In a break from lectures you sit with another student in the student cafeteria. You tentatively start talking to her, revealing that you had felt anxious before you entered the classroom and asking her if she felt the same way. You find yourself asking questions to find out her name and how far she has travelled to get to university, while sharing these details about yourself. Gradually you begin to get to know each other.

In the developing conversation you both ask questions of each other, but one would not describe this as an interview; it is a conversation. What is the difference between an interview and a conversation?

Johnson and Christensen (2012: 198) define an interview as 'a data collection method in which an interviewer asks an interviewee questions'. In a conversation we frequently ask questions of each other; it is one of the ways we form and maintain relationships, and at first glance it is possible to conceive of these sorts of conversations as interviews. However, Denscombe (2010) notes some important differences:

- There is consent to take part in an interview – the interviewee should know the purpose of the interview, how it will be recorded, how the data will be stored and what the information will be used for. This relates to the issue of 'informed consent' discussed in Chapter 6 and is clearly different from the informality of ordinary conversation.
- In addition, the words of the interviewee are likely to be analysed and written about in a way unlike usual conversation. The interviewee is 'on the record'.
- A conversation will often happen by chance and at the whim of the participants. Interviewing, on the other hand, needs more planning and even in unstructured interviewing (a term we will discuss later), there is an 'agenda' on the part of the interviewer.
- In an interview, the interviewer usually has some grasp of the subject under discussion, maybe through carrying out a thorough review of literature related to the topic, and the interviewee has lived experience of the issue being researched, which the researcher hopes to tap into (they may, of course, also share this experience). This is different to a conversation (Denscombe, 2010). We are sure you have had conversations where some or all of the participants have little knowledge or experience in relation to the topic under discussion but are happy to air their opinions.

In Chapter 14 we discuss another method of data collection – questionnaires. One of the fundamental differences between a questionnaire and an interview is that interviews are always *interpersonal* in some way; that is, there is always personal contact between the researcher (interviewer) and the participant (the interviewee). The interpersonal contact may not always be face to face as interviews can be conducted by telephone or video link. The extent to which the interview relationship develops is dependent on the research paradigm within which the research is located. As we will see, for positivist researchers, it is important to neutralise the effect of the interviewer, whereas interpretivist researchers tend to value and analyse the effect of the researcher on the interviewee's responses (Fielding and Thomas, 2008).

WHEN TO USE INTERVIEWS

When discussing research proposals with students, it is our experience that often the first choice of data-collection instrument is a questionnaire. This is because using a questionnaire seems to be viewed as less time-consuming when compared with interviewing. The perception is often that all that has to be done is to write out a list of questions, distribute the questionnaire and wait for the completed questionnaires to return. Chapter 14 will argue that it is nowhere near as straightforward as this, but it is true that a student could potentially obtain the views of many more people using a questionnaire than interviewing. However, it is important to stress that the information obtained from using questionnaires is likely to be more superficial than that obtained through an interview. Interviews are used when 'in-depth' information from participants is needed. Depending upon the type of interview used, the interviewer can clarify what the interviewee is trying to say, and can investigate areas of interest as they emerge, probing and teasing out strands of thought. This is a key advantage of interviewing as a research method (Robson, 2011a). In all of the approaches described in Part 3 of this book (surveys, ethnography, case studies and action research) interviewing can be included as a way of collecting data.

TYPES OF INTERVIEW

Interviews can vary according to a number of dimensions:

- The underlying research methodology. Is the interview designed to produce quantitative or qualitative data?
- The degree of flexibility of the interview.
- The number of interviewees being interviewed at one time.
- The elicitation of photos and the use of other resources in interviews.
- Whether or not the interview is conducted face to face or via telephone or video.

We will look at each of these in turn.

QUANTITATIVE OR QUALITATIVE?

In Chapters 4 and 5, the main approaches to research methodology were discussed. You may recall that positivism usually leads to a choice of quantitative methodology and is primarily concerned with obtaining data that can be converted into numbers. On the other hand, interpretivist research, although different, tends to lead to a choice of qualitative methodology and is primarily concerned with finding out participants' thoughts, ideas and opinions in more detail. Interview design reflects this state of affairs. This is because:

- Interviews can be highly structured and aimed at collecting information that is easily converted into numbers.
- Interviews can be completely unstructured with no intention that the results should be subjected to numerical analysis. This is often the case in biographical or life-history interviewing.
- Interviews can be semi-structured including elements of both the quantitative and qualitative approaches, but primarily focusing on the former.

THE DEGREE OF FLEXIBILITY OF THE INTERVIEW

Interviews are frequently classified according to the degree of flexibility that the interviewer has to probe and ask additional questions, and the degree of flexibility that the participant has to say what they want, in the way that they want (Johnson and Christensen, 2012; Kumar, 2014).

Structured interviews

This kind of interviewing is linked to the positivist research paradigm. Structured interviews, sometimes known as standardised interviews (Fielding and Thomas, 2008), consist of mostly 'closed' questions where only a limited number of responses can be given. You will find that Chapter 14 contains a discussion on the difference between open and closed questions. The researcher is given an interview schedule, a written list of questions that have to be asked in the same way and in a specific order, which looks very similar to a questionnaire. This type of interview is used in large studies such as surveys, where it is seen as important to control variability, so that the results of the study can be generalised to the wider population.

Often a team of interviewers may be used in this type of interviewing, but inevitably the way an interviewer behaves (what they do and say) is a major source of variance. Therefore, interviewers will be trained to administer the interview in exactly the same way – using exactly the same words and question order (Fontana and Frey, 2000). This written 'script' is known as the interview *protocol* (Johnson and Christensen, 2012) or *schedule* (Fielding and Thomas, 2008). However, it is questionable as to whether it is possible to completely control for the effect that different interviewers will have on the interview situation (Fielding and Thomas, 2008; Robson, 2011a).

 —— ACTIVITY ——————————————————————

If you are an early childhood studies student you may be able to try out this Activity in your university or college. Choose a topic that everyone will be able to say something about, such as what people remember about playing as a child, and write a series of questions about this. Then ask a few students in turn if they would be willing to answer your questions - try to choose students who have different backgrounds to yourself or students you do not know well. You will need to have worked out exactly how you will introduce yourself and the interview topic before you conduct the interview, so that you say the same thing to everyone.

As you are interviewing the participants, take note of how you react, feel and behave towards them, and how they react to you. Reflect upon how the characteristics of the participants may have had an effect on the interview proceedings.

The characteristics of both the interviewer and the participant are likely to have an effect on the interview process (Fontana and Frey, 2000). The interaction between two students of roughly the same age, gender, sexuality and ethnicity may well be different than when these characteristics are not shared between the interviewer and interviewee. Not only do we tend to act differently depending on characteristics such as age, ethnicity and gender (Fielding and Thomas, 2008), but power relations between the interviewer and the participant can also have an effect. You might like to consider this in relation to an adult interviewing a child and a nursery manager interviewing a parent whose child has just started nursery.

Patton (1987) refers to structured interviews as 'closed quantitative interviews' because the questions are fixed and the responses that the participant can give are limited. The data collected are easy to convert to numerical data for statistical analysis because the responses are often pre-coded. Here is a typical excerpt from a structured interview.

Q1 How many children do you have?

1. none
2. one
3. two
4. three
5. more than three

Q2 Do your children attend any of the following schools?

1. Sheldon primary school
2. Wexfield middle school
3. Armitage infant school
4. Seacole primary school
5. Middleworth infant school

As you can see, with structured interviewing the response categories are fixed and the information obtained is likely to be limited in nature. In addition, the interviewee is given little room to elaborate on their responses to the questions or statements. On this basis, we would argue that this type of interviewing is of little benefit when interviewing young children, as there is no room for them to talk about the things of interest to them, in a way that is meaningful to them.

Westcott and Littleton (2005) argue that structured interviewing of children is underpinned by a view of the child as powerless and passive in the research process. This is because this kind of research, located within the positivist paradigm, focuses primarily on trying to reveal children's understandings as opposed to creating understandings *with* children. When conducting any of the interview types discussed in this chapter we should remember that children may not be used to being listened to. Moreover, their lack of experience in being interviewed, especially if carried out in a formal way designed for older, more experienced children and adults, may be a barrier to their participation rather than their lack of age and maturity (Westcott and Littleton, 2005).

Semi-structured interviews

Semi-structured interviews or 'structured conversations' (Cannold, 2001: 179) contain a mixture of both open and closed questions but are primarily used in qualitative research. For example, an interview may start off by asking the participant about details such as the number of children they have, and then continue to ask questions on a particular topic where the participant can respond freely. An example of an open question might be 'How did you feel when you started back to work after your maternity leave was over?' Although open questions are mostly used, the same questions are asked of everyone, so some degree of standardisation is achieved. However, unlike structured interviewing, there is greater flexibility to probe for detail in relation to a particular response. Furthermore, the interviewer can adapt the questioning to suit the needs of the interviewee, such as their level of understanding (Fielding and Thomas, 2008). This type of interviewing may be appropriate for some children, particularly the oldest children in the 0–8 years age range. However, when interviewing young children, we believe that unstructured and focus group interviewing offer the most potential.

It should be noted that writing questions for structured and semi-structured interviews requires careful consideration. The next chapter, looking at questionnaires, gives detailed guidance about avoiding common pitfalls in question design that applies equally to interviews.

Unstructured interviews

Unstructured interviews are also qualitative in nature and are designed to provide in-depth information about participants' beliefs, thoughts and feelings. Kumar (2014) refers to these interviews as '*in-depth*' interviews and Fielding and Thomas (2008) refer to them as '*non-standardised* interviews'. The main difference between structured interviews and unstructured interviews is that the aim of structured interviews is to explain behaviour within categories that have been decided beforehand (*deductive*), whereas unstructured interviews are seen as trying to understand complex behaviour, without deciding beforehand what categories of response may emerge (*inductive*) (Fontana and Frey, 2000).

In unstructured interviewing, the topics to be investigated are not decided in full detail beforehand. Thus, it is often an approach to interviewing that is used in biographical or life-history interviewing. The interview proceeds more like a conversation or a discussion, with questions being asked as themes and topics emerge naturally and the participant being free to respond as well as lead the discussion as s/he wants. Thus, control during the interview does not lie permanently with the interviewer (Fontana and Frey, 2000). For this reason we believe that unstructured interviewing is the most appropriate tool when interviewing young children because it allows children to set the pace and the direction of the interview on a range of topics that have meaning for them.

We can see, then, that an unstructured interview is a research tool that is characterised by its flexibility and sharing of power between interviewer and interviewee. This can also be seen in the possibility that the interviewer may add their own opinions on the topic under discussion in a way that would be unthinkable in structured interviewing (Fielding and Thomas, 2008). Although this means that it is difficult to compare responses between individuals, what is lost by not being able to generalise the results is gained by the richness of the information obtained. Unstructured interviews are fundamentally different from other types of interviewing that seek a degree of standardisation, since the aim is to establish 'human to human contact with the desire to understand rather than to explain' (Fontana and Frey, 2000: 654).

Increasingly, new trends in interviewing see the interview as a 'negotiated text' (Fontana and Frey, 2000: 663) as there is growing recognition that researchers are not 'invisible, neutral entities; rather, they are part of the interactions they seek to study and influence those interactions'. Thus, there is acknowledgement that the direction the interview takes is influenced not only by the interviewer but also by the interviewee. This relates to the idea that 'reality is an ongoing interpretive accomplishment' (Holstein and Gubrium, 1995: 16). We hope you can see that it is a perspective that is far removed from the positivist position outlined in Chapter 4.

Looking at the types of interview we have discussed so far, it is possible to identify that there is significant difference in the amount of interpersonal rapport between interviewer and interviewee according to the type of interview used. In the structured interview it is important that the interviewer remains as objective as possible and adheres very closely to the 'script'. In the less formal, unstructured interview, where the aim is to obtain an 'in-depth' understanding, there needs to be an interpersonal exchange between the interviewer and the participant. This method relies on the interviewer contributing something of themselves, which would be considered undesirable in structured interviewing (Fontana and Frey, 2000).

RESEARCH IN FOCUS

USA

Encouraging friendships between children in early childhood settings has long been considered to be part of good early childhood practice. In this American article, Hollingsworth and Buysse (2009) explain that in the USA (as in the UK) there have been a growing number of children with developmental delay attending inclusive early childhood settings. This arrangement benefits both children with developmental delay and those without. One of the hopes

(Continued)

behind including children with developmental delay in 'mainstream' settings is that there will be increased interaction between children with and without developmental delay. In this study, Hollingsworth and Buysse aim to look at the strategies parents and practitioners use to support friendships between children, the importance that they attach to these friendships, and whether or not parents and practitioners talk to each other about these friendships.

Twelve pairs of friends (dyads), one of whom had a developmental delay and the other who had no delay, were chosen. Their practitioners and parents were interviewed using semi-structured interviews. The following are examples of questions asked (Hollingsworth and Buysse, 2009: 295):

How did [child] meet [friend]?

What kinds of things do you see or hear that let you know they are friends?

How long have they been friends?

How important do you think this friendship is for [child]?

Open-ended question: Are there things that you do to help [child] and [friend] stay friends? What kinds of things do you do?

Tell me more about [strategy named].

a. How often do you do this?
b. Can you tell me about a time when you did this?
c. Do you think [strategy] worked?
d. How and why did you decide to do this?
e. How did [child with developmental delay (DD)]'s disability affect the decision to [strategy], if at all?

Probing question: Do you ever arrange times for [child] and [friend] to play together?

(follow-up questions a.-e. as above)

Probing question: Do you ever help [child] and [friend] play together by participating in the play yourself?

(follow-up questions a.-e. as above)

The interviews were recorded and transcribed. They were then analysed to uncover underlying themes. This way of analysing qualitative data is examined in Chapter 18. The findings indicated that the children obtained huge enjoyment from their friendships, that parents and teachers supported these friendships using a number of different strategies, and that parents and practitioners communicated together about these friendships.

This is a good example of a study which uses a qualitative methodological approach. Although semi-structured interviews were used, many of the questions were open, allowing participants to freely express their views.

INTERVIEWING MORE THAN ONE PARTICIPANT AT ONCE

So far we have looked at interviews that involve just one interviewer and one participant. There are, however, situations where it is desirable to interview several participants together. Group interviews, commonly called focus groups, are where an interviewer, sometimes called a moderator or facilitator, leads a discussion with a small group of people (Johnson and Christensen, 2012). It is a method very commonly used in market research.

Stewart et al. (2008) and Fontana and Frey (2000) identify many uses of focus groups, including:

- finding out background information about a topic
- generating ideas that can be tested using more systematic, quantitative methods
- evaluating a new process or product
- generating impressions of a product, organisation, etc.
- interpreting results obtained from other research methods
- pre-testing questionnaires, tests or interviews for use in further research
- as a method of triangulation, aimed at increasing the reliability of a research study.

Characteristically, a focus group consists of between six and 12 participants, who are likely to be selected because they are relatively similar to each other. Johnson and Christensen (2012), for instance, consider that homogenous groups are more likely to promote discussion than groups which are dissimilar to each other. However, one of the disadvantages of holding a focus group with comparable individuals is that their views are likely to be similar. In order to get around this problem it is usual to hold a series of focus groups, containing participants selected according to different criteria. For example, Penny Mukherji, one of the authors of this book, was involved in finding out what students in a further education college felt about the quality of student support. In order to get a range of opinions, she selected groups composed of:

- students under the age of 18 studying for A levels
- students under the age of 18 on vocational courses
- adult students studying vocational courses
- adult students studying part-time.

Before the focus group is held the researcher needs to have decided on the format the interview will take. As with individual interviews discussed previously, there are decisions to be made about the degree of flexibility the moderator will have in conducting the interview, but, usually, focus group interviews are semi-structured in nature. In order to conduct the focus group interview, the group moderator needs a high level of interpersonal skills because s/he has to be able to promote discussion between individuals who may not know each other. It is the role of the moderator to make sure that everyone has a chance to give their views and that the conversation is not dominated by one or two individuals. In addition, unless a completely flexible approach is to be taken, the groups must be brought back to the topic under discussion if they start to wander too far from the research agenda.

 ACTIVITY

If you conduct an Internet search for 'guidelines for focus groups' you will find a variety of resources. Most of these resources are designed for businesses that undertake focus groups for other organisations; so you need to be selective.

The following is an excerpt from one of these guidelines written in 2005 by Eliot and Associates. The whole document can be found at: http://datainnovationproject.org/wp-content/uploads/2017/04/4/_How_to_Conduct_a_Focus_Group-2-1.pdf (accessed 10 November 2017).

Conducting the focus group:

- Before asking the first focus group question, an icebreaker can be inserted to increase comfort and level the playing field. Example: 'How long have you worked in early childhood?'
- The focus group moderator has a responsibility to adequately cover all prepared questions within the time allotted. S/he also has a responsibility to get all participants to talk and fully explain their answers. Some helpful probes include: 'Can you talk about that more?' 'Help me understand what you mean' 'Can you give an example?' It is good moderator practice to paraphrase and summarise long, complex or ambiguous comments. It demonstrates active listening and clarifies the comment for everyone in the group.
- Because the moderator holds a position of authority and perceived influence, s/he must remain relatively neutral, refraining from nodding/raising eyebrows, agreeing/disagreeing, or praising/denigrating any comment made.
- A moderator must tactfully deal with challenging participants. Here are some appropriate strategies:

  o <u>Self-appointed experts:</u> *'Thank you. What do other people think?'*
  o <u>The dominator:</u> *'Let's have some other comments.'*
  o <u>The rambler:</u> Stop eye contact; gently, look at your watch; perhaps jump in as they inhale.
  o <u>The shy participant:</u> Make eye contact; call on them; smile at them.
  o <u>The participant who talks very quietly:</u> Ask them to repeat their response more loudly.

(Excerpt taken from Eliot and Associates, 2005: 10)

Focus group interviewing is considered to be particularly appropriate in research with older children in the early childhood range. Lancaster and Broadbent (2003) see the main strengths of focus group interviewing with children as follows:

- Focus group interviews are especially useful when children (of around 5–6 years) know and like each other.
- Interaction between children is encouraged.
- Focus groups help to build confidence and can be empowering.
- Children are able to raise issues that they would like to discuss.
- Children are recognised as experts in their own setting.
- An insight is gained into children's shared understandings of everyday life.
- New ideas and meanings are generated through the interaction of different members of the group.
- It is more akin to the kind of conversations children are used to having than the question–answer style of interviewing.
- Children are familiar with taking part in shared discussions through story-times or circletimes.

(Based on Lancaster and Broadbent, 2003: 46.)

However, we should not see focus group interviewing with children as devoid of problems. Lancaster and Broadbent (2003) seem to echo Robson's (2011a) concerns when they argue that children can be influenced by individuals within a group and it can be difficult to identify individual children's perspectives. Furthermore, as in any group situation, some individuals' voices may dominate. Possibly, then, focus group interviewing with children is best employed by researchers who are used to working with children in groups. Those of you who are practitioners may be particularly well placed to do this as you are likely to be used to managing a group at story times, for instance, and ensuring that all children have the opportunity to have their say.

RESEARCH IN FOCUS

ENGLAND

Mayall's (2008) research looked at the extent to which children promote, maintain and restore their health at home and at school, and involved spending time with children in their homes and school (in England). One of the groups in the study consisted of 5-6-year-old children, the other group consisted of children aged from 9 to 10 years. Mayall spent two days a week for two terms in the school so the children would come to accept her as a familiar figure. Mayall's rationale for this was that it would enable the children to talk to her with confidence and would lessen the possibility of disrupting their usual behaviours in their classroom. You may recall in the chapter on ethnography that becoming a familiar part of the group is considered important.

(Continued)

As well as interviewing key adults for the study - that is, parents and school staff - Mayall engaged with the children undertaking their usual activities and began to hold discussions with the children in pairs or threes, drawing pictures and encouraging the children to talk about them. She calls these interviews 'research conversations'. Mayall states, 'I aimed to engage with them in conversations, where an opening gambit could lead wherever children wished' (2008: 112).

To increase individual children's confidence she asked the children to choose a friend and talked to the children in pairs, something she believes the children found both supportive and enabling. The children stayed in the classroom for the interviews rather than being taken away from their usual environment, because their teacher and the researcher (Mayall) believed it would be a more familiar and comfortable context for them. As the children grew in confidence, they began to talk between themselves about points made rather than the conversation developing in the mode of adult question-child answer.

In the home interviews, Mayall gradually involved the children's parents as lead interviewers in the study, briefing them beforehand about the research purposes and topics. Children were encouraged to discuss their school day with their parents, with Mayall present and providing occasional prompts. As these interviews took place in their home the children were surrounded by familiar objects and were able to leave the room if they wanted to. Having parents interview their own children was helpful because their shared history of people, places and events of significance to the children enabled a greater understanding to be gained about the issues raised.

In both the home and school, 'research conversations' enabled children to take some control over the research agenda, such as controlling the topics to be explored as well as the pace and direction of the conversations. Mayall sees a key advantage in interviewing children together as it enables them to share their experiences of being a child and learn about different experiences of childhood. This is similar to the argument that interviewing women as a group allows them to collectivise their experiences (Mies, 1993). Finally, Mayall highlights the high degree of social skills the children demonstrated in listening to each other's viewpoints, replying and adding to the discussion, and the importance of helping to facilitate discussion with children who find it difficult to communicate for one reason or another.

This Research in Focus section has raised a number of important issues in relation to interviewing that are pertinent to interviewing adults *and* children. These relate to:

- where and when to conduct an interview
- establishing rapport in an interview
- how the interview 'works' in practice.

We will look at these areas later in the chapter when we think about carrying out and recording interviews, but before we do this we will discuss photo elicitation and use of other resources.

PHOTO ELICITATION AND THE USE OF OTHER RESOURCES IN INTERVIEWS

In addition to asking participants to reflect upon questions posed by the interviewer there are other techniques that researchers can use to elicit responses, such as the use of photographs, audio or visual recordings and the introduction of written documents or other artefacts. The use of photographs is known as photo elicitation (Harper, 2002) or photo ethnography (Schwartz, 1989). Harper (2002) considers that the use of photographs and other visual representations in interviews can evoke a different type of information than verbal questions. He suggests that this is because the parts of the brain responsible for processing visual information are, in evolutionary terms, older than the parts of the brain which process verbal information. This, according to Harper, 'evokes deeper levels of human consciousness than do words' (Harper, 2002: 13).

When introducing visual material such as photographs it is important to realise that representations are viewed differently by people, depending on the characteristics of both the image and the person. Schwartz (1989) makes the point that historically photographs have been viewed in two ways: as works of art or as true records of a scene or a subject. Harper (2002) talks about a continuum with 'scientific' 'true' records at one end of the continuum, images that represent part of a collective or communal past in the middle, and images that show intimate aspects of participants' social/family life or even their own body at the other end of the continuum.

Schwartz (1989: 120) reminds us that 'viewing photographic imagery is a patterned social activity shaped by social context, cultural conventions, and group norms' and that having an idea of the way that participants view photography will enable us to refine how the interviews are conducted. It is not always possible to predict the kind of response an image will elicit and piloting the visual representations may prevent you conducting interviews where very little conversation is generated. Harper (2002) gives the example where he wanted to find out farmers' reflections on their relationship with the land, their identity as farmers and their changing roles in farming. The first set of photographs elicited very little reflection. Harper considered that this was because the images were too like everyday images the farmers saw in the agricultural press. When he changed the photographs to aerial images of farms and of farmers in everyday situations such as sitting together for a meal, he found that 'suddenly previously taciturn farmers had a great deal to say' (Harper, 2002: 21). He describes this as 'breaking the frame', enabling the participant to see themselves in a different way.

Photo elicitation has been used in interviewing young children, either as an ice breaker or as a focus for discussion. In some studies the children have been given cameras and taken pictures which have been discussed later, in other studies the researchers have produced the photographs. For example Diamond and Hestenes (1996) used photographs of children with disabilities with 3–6 year olds to find out young children's ideas about physical and sensory disabilities and Down Syndrome. Findings indicated that, at this age, children had a good understanding about how a physical disability may affect a child, but were not so clear on what the effects of other types of disabilities might be.

 ACTIVITY

Photo elicitation, especially auto photo elicitation where the participants take the photographs to be used in the interviews, is a method which can raise ethical concerns, especially about informed consent of those in the photographs. The following article by Miller (2015) investigates the use of auto photo elicitation in a research study on children as they make the transition to school. Read the article and note the ethical issues that were raised by ethics committees and how the author was able to show that her study conformed to ethical guidelines. This is an open access article and the link is given in the reference.

Miller, K. (2015) 'Dear critics: addressing concerns and justifying the benefits of photography as a research method,' *Forum Qualitative Sozialforschung/Forum: Qualitative Social Research*, 16(3): art. 27. www.qualitative-research.net/index.php/fqs/article/view/2434/3874 (accessed 15 March 2017).

REMOTE METHODS OF INTERVIEWING

So far in this chapter we have described face-to-face interviews; however, telephone interviewing is increasingly used as a method of collecting information both for market research and surveys. For example, the National Child Development Study 2004/5 follow-up used a 30-minute computer-aided telephone interview (Centre for Longitudinal Studies, 2007).

In computer-aided telephone interviews, interviewers located in a call centre read out a structured questionnaire from a computer screen and enter the participants' responses directly into the computer. Generally these sorts of interviews tend to be short, less than 30 minutes, and do not require participants to give personal information, as it has been suggested that interviewees are reluctant to do this over the telephone (Carr and Worth, 2001). More recently, telephone interviews have been used for smaller-scale qualitative studies, especially where contact has already been made with the participants. Research has found that telephone interviewing produces data that are comparable in quality to face-to-face methods (Carr and Worth, 2001).

One criticism of telephone interviews is that the sample cannot be selected at random, because it relies on the participant having a telephone at home.

Recently, then, there has been an increase in the number of studies using mobile phones and email as ways of reaching more people. McCoyd and Kerson (2006), for instance, suggest that email interviewing, if it occurs in 'real time', compares favourably with telephone interviewing. Email interviewing should not be confused with sending a structured questionnaire by email; using email to conduct an interview in real time involves a degree of personal interaction between the interviewer and the interviewee which is absent if email is used as a means of sending out a questionnaire instead of using the postal service.

CARRYING OUT AND RECORDING INTERVIEWS

When carrying out an interview, it is important to think about the time and location in which the interview will take place. Interviewees should feel comfortable in their surroundings, and interviewers should always be mindful that the interviewees have been good enough to give up their time for the interview and try to make the experience a pleasant one. Robson (2011a: 282) argues that the interviewer should aim to:

- listen more than speak
- put questions in a straightforward, clear and non-threatening way
- eliminate cues which lead interviewees to respond in a particular way (but see the earlier section on unstructured interviews)
- enjoy it (or at least give the appearance of enjoyment).

Robson (2011a) argues that usually, an interview will follow a similar pattern, as follows, although for unstructured interviewing this may well vary from interview to interview.

- *Introduction.* Here, researchers will introduce themselves, explain again the purposes of the interview and restate assurances in relation to confidentiality. They will also check that interviewees are comfortable and are happy with the method of recording the interview.
- *'Warm up'.* The first few questions should aim at putting interviewees at ease. Often interviewers using any type of interviewing method will ask some non-threatening questions that do not require long answers at the beginning of an interview.
- *Main body of interview.* This is the part of the interview when the interviewer will ask the key questions in their study. Depending on the interview type, the question order might be varied and the interviewer might probe for further information if the interviewee says something interesting that could be explored further. An example might be as follows. In a study looking at how nurseries celebrate individual children's birthdays, a practitioner might be asked 'Do you do anything in the nursery when it is a child's birthday?' Let us

say the practitioner responds with 'We don't let children bring in cakes from home as it goes against our new healthy eating policy'. As an interviewer, you might like to probe for her views on the nursery's position; probe what the policy contains and who contributed to its development; or probe how parents and children have reacted to this policy.

- *Closing comments*. This is another important phase in the interview. This is the point when the interviewee is thanked and recording stops. Sometimes, interviewees continue to talk about issues raised during the interview so it is important that the interviewer asks for permission to make notes if they wish to use this material. In addition, any promises that are made at this point, such as having the opportunity to see the interview transcript or finished research project, should be adhered to and the interviewer should clarify how the interviewee can be reached in order to do this.

 —— **REFLECTION POINT** ——————————————

We have looked at Robson's thinking about the pattern an interview should take, with its warm-up and in-depth questions later on. How do you feel about it? Fontana and Frey (2000: 658), for instance, draw on Oakley's work and argue that the friendly manner of the interviewer is a 'ruse to gain the trust and confidence of the respondent without reciprocating those feelings in any way' – we noted this in Chapter 6. In structured interviewing, the researcher is expected to ask the questions in exactly the same way to each interviewee. Is this good research practice, owing to its emphasis on objectivity and minimising researcher effect, or is it unethical in its lack of reciprocity and lessening of the importance of relationships? These questions are much debated in research and link back to the discussions in the earlier chapters of this book about paradigms and principles.

The method of recording an interview depends upon the type of interview used. Where interview questions are closed it is possible to record pre-coded responses onto a written questionnaire, or into a computer. For example, we have discussed the use of computer-aided telephone (usually 'structured') interviews where the findings are entered directly into a computer, ready for data analysis. More flexible interviews make direct recording of responses very difficult. Interviewers could try to make rough written notes, but this distracts from the interview process. For this reason it is recommended that the interviewer records the interview electronically and writes up a transcript of the interview later (Fielding and Thomas, 2008). This is because note-taking is not only slow, but can be questionable in terms of validity. Fielding and Thomas (2008) argue that by offering to give interviewees a copy of the full transcript of their interview, audio recording it might seem more palatable. It is also useful in terms of gauging the reliability and validity of the responses, acting as a further check on the data. Recording interviews systematically is important, as the record acts as 'the best index of the interviewer's effect on the respondent's testimony' (Fielding and Thomas, 2008: 256).

Recording can be via an audio-recording device or by using a camcorder. The advantage of using a camcorder is that you not only record the words spoken but also aspects of non-verbal communication. The disadvantage of more obtrusive methods of recording an interview is that the participant is likely to find it difficult to act naturally. When using equipment like this the researcher needs to be completely at ease with the technology, and should have had a trial run before conducting their first 'real' interview. Choosing the right place for an interview is essential if using electronic methods, such as a camcorder, as too much noise or lack of light will all have a negative effect. The positioning of the device in relation to the participant and the interviewer is also important.

Whatever means of recording the interview you choose, the participant should be told beforehand the method that will be used and s/he should be given the opportunity to decline to be interviewed or to have the interview recorded in a different way. This is all part of 'informed consent', a term we discussed in Chapter 6. Finally here, before recording starts, decisions need to have been made about how confidentiality will be maintained and how the recordings, whether they are written or in digital format, will be kept secure.

PILOTING THE INTERVIEW PROCESS

However you decide to conduct your interviews or focus groups, it is strongly recommended that you have a trial run first. You will be able to find out:

- If the interview questions elicit the information that you are expecting, or need modifying.
- How long the interview is likely to take.
- The suitability of the room you have chosen.
- How to use the recording equipment.

TRANSCRIBING INTERVIEWS

Students frequently underestimate the time it takes to transcribe an audio recording of an interview, often assuming that it just involves copying the words that the participant has used during the interview. However, conversation is never just words; there is a great deal of information in the way that words are said, in terms of speed, pitch, intonation and loudness.

REFLECTION POINT

Let's think of an example that you may have captured on an audio recording. The participant may have said 'she told me to do it'. Depending on the way it is said the statement could indicate:

- SHE told me to do it [that person told me to do it].
- She TOLD me to do it [I only did it because she told me to].
- She told ME to do it [she didn't tell anyone else to do it. Just me].

In addition, the pitch and tone of the participant's voice will indicate the emotions attached to the words. One can imagine that the words could be interpreted as an upset child laying the blame on another 'She TOLD me to do it'. Or the words could be said with real pride, 'She told ME to do it'.

Crucially these words need to be seen within the context of the interview as a whole, including the context in which the interview took place.

There are various ways to deal with this, one of which is to transcribe the words first and then go back and indicate on the transcript additional information contained in the way that something is said. This will also involve indicating pauses and sounds that we all make while we are trying to think. The 'ums' and the 'ahs'. This aspect of transcription involves a degree of subjectivity. No two people will transcribe an interview in the same way, although in large research studies transcribers are trained to use the same techniques and notation to remove subjectivity as much as possible.

All this takes time, even experienced transcribers will take two hours to transcribe a 30 minute interview and time needed to transcribe interviews should be factored into your research timeline.

ACTIVITY

Undertake an Internet search for tips on transcribing qualitative interviews.

You will discover that you can pay someone to do the task for you. Not something we would recommend, as the process of transcription will also help you become familiar with the data, and actually becomes the first stage of your analysis.

You can also make use of free transcription software, which may be helpful if you have very many interviews to transcribe. However it is our experience that, in an undergraduate research project, the number of interviews to transcribe is generally manageable without resorting to computer packages.

 —— REFLECTION POINT ——————————————

As with all research, using interviews will highlight ethical issues. Read Chapter 6 on ethics and reflect on whether or not there are ethical issues that are specific to using interviews. You may like to reflect upon:

- the effect of the personality/age/gender/culture of the interviewee and interviewer and the power relationship between them
- the 'personal' nature of interviews and their similarity to conversations
- issues related to informed consent when the themes that emerge cannot be predicted beforehand.

 —— KEY POINTS FROM THE CHAPTER ——————————

- Interviews are a common way of finding out information. They are used in the media, politics and consumer research, as well as in scientific research.
- Interviews can be used both in quantitative and qualitative research studies.
- Interviews always involve a degree of personal interaction (not always face to face) between the interviewer and the interviewee.
- Quantitative interviews are very structured and may resemble questionnaires. To reduce variance interviewers are trained to deliver the interview in exactly the same way.
- Qualitative interviews are less structured and are used to obtain 'in-depth' information from participants with the aim of understanding as much as possible about the research situation, theme or topic.
- Interviews with less structure may be especially useful when interviewing children as they are able to take some control over the pace and direction of the interview and talk about topics of meaning to them.
- Focus group interviewing is also a useful strategy with children because they may be familiar with taking part in group discussions, such as during story times, and many are able to share their experiences with other children.
- Thought should be given to how interviews are carried out. Recordings of interviews can be made directly into computers, on paper or recorded using electronic means.

FURTHER READING

Fielding, N. and Thomas, H. (2015) 'Qualitative interviewing', in N. Gilbert (ed.) *Researching Social Life*, 4th edition. London: Sage. This chapter looks at the practicalities of conducting focused interviews 'in the field' and takes the approach that interviews can be likened to a 'guided conversation'.

Mayall, B. (2008) 'Conversations with children: working with generational issues', in P. Christensen and A. James (eds) *Research with Children: Perspectives and Practices*, 2nd edition. Abingdon: Routledge. This chapter looks at some of the key issues that relate to interviewing children and draws upon the author's own research.

Don't forget to visit the online resources at https://study.sagepub.com/mukherjiandalbon3e for access to free SAGE journal articles, weblinks, videos, exercises, mini quizzes and an interactive glossary.

14

QUESTIONNAIRES

CHAPTER OBJECTIVES

- To reflect on the use of questionnaires as a research tool.
- To consider the different ways that questionnaires can be designed.
- To gain an understanding of the different ways of administering a questionnaire.

In Chapter 13 we looked at interviewing, which involves a researcher asking questions or directly engaging with participants, either face to face or via a computer or telephone link. In this chapter we look at another way of eliciting information from participants: the questionnaire, which generally does not involve direct communication between the researcher and the respondent. Questionnaires are a common way of obtaining information from respondents. They are a versatile and cost-effective research tool (Walliman, 2001) and are primarily used for collecting quantitative data. At first glance, designing a questionnaire may appear a relatively simple task. However, producing a questionnaire that will provide the information wanted from a group of respondents has to be undertaken carefully if the questionnaire is to be valid and the findings reliable.

Anderson (1998: 170) warns that 'the questionnaire has become one of the most used and abused means of collecting information'. Therefore, in this chapter we will look, in some detail, at how to design and administer a questionnaire, pointing out some of the possible pitfalls that may render a questionnaire invalid or unreliable.

Before we look at questionnaires in detail we need to clear up a commonly held misunderstanding; that questionnaires and surveys are synonymous. In Chapter 8 we looked at surveys, a research approach which commonly uses questionnaires as a data-collection method. Previously in Chapter 5 we discussed the difference between methodology and method. Methodology refers to the ideas about how to approach research based on an underlying paradigm. Surveys are an approach guided by quantitative methodology located within the positivist paradigm. Method refers to the data-collection technique used in research. So, although surveys can use questionnaires as a data-collection method, they may also use other methods such as structured interviews. Questionnaires and surveys are not the same thing.

PARTICIPANT OR RESPONDENT?

You may have noticed that at the start of this chapter we used the words participant and respondent to describe people who answer questionnaires. Generally the term participant is used to describe people involved in qualitative studies and respondent is used to describe people involved in quantitative research. This distinction recognises that participants in qualitative interviews or qualitative questionnaires are required to share much more of themselves with the researcher, than someone who responds to a structured questionnaire and just gives the precise information asked for. Participants have more control over where the discussion 'goes' and the issues that are discussed.

WHAT IS A QUESTIONNAIRE?

Very few of us will have escaped completing a questionnaire, so it is likely that you already have a good idea about what constitutes a questionnaire. In its simplest form, a questionnaire is a piece of paper on which is printed a number of questions or statements, with space for someone to respond. It is a 'written list of questions, the answers to which are recorded by respondents' (Kumar, 2014: 177). Nowadays many questionnaires are not paper based, but come to us via the Internet or via our email, but the principle is the same.

WHY ARE QUESTIONNAIRES USED IN RESEARCH?

As we saw in Chapter 8, questionnaires are often used as a data-collection method in surveys. An example of this would be Schum et al.'s 2002 study which used questionnaires to ask parents of over 250 infants about the progress of 'toilet training' and the Avon Longitudinal Study of Parents and their Children (Golding et al., 2001) which used questionnaires filled in by parents to collect data.

 REFLECTION POINT

Think about the occasions that you have been asked to fill in a questionnaire. What sort of information was the questionnaire designed to collect? How was it given to you: by post, by hand, by email or the Internet?

Sometimes we are more motivated than at other times to fill in questionnaires. What factors influence how enthusiastically you respond to them?

We find that we are motivated to fill in questionnaires if they are seen to be relevant in some way; that is, to do with work or a cause we are interested in. We also tend to complete questionnaires if they are conducted by colleagues, friends or students (when we have time) as we have a personal and/or professional commitment to them.

Johnson and Christensen (2017) have identified that typically questionnaires are designed to find out information on the following aspects of individuals' lives:

- Knowledge about a particular topic, such as asking early years practitioners about their understanding of what constitutes healthy eating for toddlers.
- Attitudes, beliefs, opinions and values, such as parental attitudes towards having their children immunised or the value of working in partnership with their children's early years settings.
- Experiences, such as the experience of a parent taking their child to an early years setting for the first time, or asking early years practitioners about their experiences of implementing a new policy.
- Behaviour, such as the number of times parents read to their children or whether or not parents smoke in front of their children.

In addition questionnaires commonly include questions on demographics and background information, such as age, gender, social class and number of years of education.

It is clear that the design of the questionnaire very much depends upon its intended use. For example, asking someone for his or her age will require a different type of question than a question designed to elicit an attitude. It is therefore essential that, before attempting to design a questionnaire, there is clarity about what it is you want to find out. There is nothing more disheartening than carrying out a questionnaire only to find out later that an important piece of information is missing because a relevant question was not asked. For this reason, large-scale surveys allow considerable time for consultation with all interested stakeholders to ensure that the appropriate questions are included.

 —— REFLECTION POINT ————————————————

Mary is undertaking her undergraduate research project and is looking at healthy eating in early years settings. Her research question is: 'To what extent does early years practitioners' knowledge of the healthy eating guidelines for toddlers correspond with the advice given by the Food Standards Agency?'

The areas included on her questionnaire are as follows:

Name:

Age:

Male/Female (please state):

Please outline what you consider a healthy diet for children:

Please describe the meals that are provided in your setting:

Please supply a typical menu for a week:

The questionnaires were sent out to a variety of different settings and when they were returned she realised that she had not got all the information she wanted. What further information do you think would have been useful?

The main omission was that Mary did not ask the settings to specify what type of setting they were, or the age of the children involved. In addition, she wanted to find out what practitioners knew about *healthy diets for toddlers*, and this questionnaire would not elicit this information specifically. There was nowhere for respondents to indicate

(Continued)

their role within the setting, or their qualifications. This may have been important as, afterwards, Mary wondered if members of staff who were qualified teachers knew more or less on the topic than the practitioners who possessed lower-level, vocational qualifications. In addition, she had asked questions that were not really relevant. For instance, did Mary really need to know the name of the respondent?

We strongly recommend that students show questionnaires to their research supervisors and any gatekeepers to the research, such as headteachers, before sending them out. Piloting a questionnaire with someone (or a few people) who shares characteristics with the intended group can also help to iron out difficulties, as we will see later in this chapter.

TYPES OF QUESTION USED IN QUESTIONNAIRE DESIGN

When designing questions to be included in a questionnaire, one of the main decisions is whether to use open questions, closed questions or a mixture of both. This will relate to the underpinning paradigm and methodology within which the research is located. Chapters 4 and 5 look at this in some detail and we also raised the issue of open and closed questions in the previous chapter, which looked at interviewing.

OPEN OR CLOSED QUESTIONS?

Open questions are ones that encourage the respondent to answer the question in any way they want, using the language that they want. Closed questions are ones where the respondent has to choose from a number of answers that the researcher has chosen beforehand (Kumar, 2014).

Very often the same question can be written in both open and closed versions. For example, if you wanted to find out the qualifications of a respondent, the question could be asked directly as an *open question*:

What qualifications in early years care and education do you have?

Or in a more *structured* way:

What qualifications in early years care and education do you have? (You can tick more than one box)

❏ NVQ level 2 or equivalent

❏ NVQ level 3 or equivalent

❐ NVQ level 4 or equivalent

❐ NNEB

❐ Foundation Degree in Early Childhood Studies

❐ Early Childhood Studies Degree

❐ PGCE Early Years

In looking at these examples, we can see that the more structured approach does not allow respondents to contribute qualifications outside the categories put forward by the researcher. Sometimes, a questionnaire will have a category 'Other (please state)' at the end of a list like this to enable respondents to contribute another category (Simmons, 2008). Given the number of qualifications that exist in early childhood, the list could potentially be very long.

Open questions are often used when a researcher is trying to find out respondents' views in some depth. In the previous Reflection Point, Mary wanted to know the level of knowledge that practitioners had about healthy eating guidelines for toddlers. She could have chosen closed true/false questions, but this would have supplied the practitioners with prompts as to facts that were important. For example, a question such as: 'A two-year-old child can be given skimmed milk to drink. True/False?' could be correctly answered by guesswork. By stating 'Please outline a healthy diet for toddlers' – an open statement – the respondent's knowledge of healthy eating is more likely to be revealed. However, Simmons (2008) notes that if a question requires a lot of thought from respondents, they may not make the time to write their response in full.

Using open questions can often produce 'rich' information about ideas, attitudes and values that would not have been provided by using a closed question. Open questions give primarily qualitative data; however, if there are a number of similar responses, then the number of times a particular issue is mentioned can be counted, thus converting qualitative data into quantitative data. Chapter 18 looks at data analysis in more detail.

Closed questions, on the other hand, give responses that are easy to count and convert into numbers, thus they tend to elicit quantitative data. Because there is the same choice of responses (owing to pre-coding), the resulting data can be compared and analysed reasonably easily (Simmons, 2008). This allows for hypotheses to be tested and the influence of specific variables to be examined. In reality, many questionnaires contain a mixture of both open and closed questions and fall somewhere on a continuum with qualitative at one end of the continuum and quantitative at the other.

Blaxter et al. (2010: 203) list seven different types of question:

1. Quantity or information.
2. Categories.
3. Lists or multiple choice.

4. Scales.
5. Ranking.
6. Complex grids or tables.
7. Open ended.

We will look at each of these in turn.

QUANTITY OR INFORMATION

This is a simple, direct question such as:

How many years have you worked in childcare and education? _____

CATEGORIES

As it suggests, this type of question invites participants to decide which category they belong to, for example:

What is the highest level of education you have achieved?

GCSE or equivalent ☐   A level or equivalent ☐   Degree or equivalent ☐

LISTS OR MULTIPLE CHOICE

A list or multiple choice is similar to the category type of question, except that there are more possibilities. Respondents may be asked to check the categories that are relevant to them and usually more than one response is permitted. There are disadvantages with presenting people with a list of categories, because there is a tendency for individuals to tick the first items on the list (Johnson and Christensen, 2017). One way of getting over this tendency is by using a rating scale.

Here is an example of a list or multiple choice:

How do you keep up to date with current initiatives in childcare and education? Please tick as many as apply.

Information from your manager   ☐

Reading a journal such as *Nursery World*   ☐

Receiving regular email newsletters from organisations   ☐

Going on short professional development courses   ☐

Attending college or university to study for an award   ☐

SCALES

Unlike the types of question looked at previously, scales do not pose a question; rather, they give a statement to which there are a number of responses to choose from set out along a continuum. For example:

Please indicate the extent to which you agree with the following statement.

I am happy with the opening hours of the library.

1	2	3	4	5
Strongly disagree	Disagree	Neither agree nor disagree	Agree	Strongly agree

In numerical scales only the end points are given descriptors, for instance:

How satisfied are you with the quality of food on offer in the university canteen?				
1	2	3	4	5
Very dissatisfied				Very satisfied

Whatever type of scale used, there are some important points to remember:

- The descriptors must agree with the statement. For example, if you want the respondents to rate things according to the degree that they agreed with a statement, it would not be appropriate to use an evaluative scale such as 'Excellent, Good, Fair and Poor'.
- Make sure that the scale items are placed exactly the same distance apart.
- Ensure that there is no bias towards one end of the response continuum.

 REFLECTION POINT

Consider this item in a rating scale. Why do you think it may render results invalid?

Indicate the extent with which you agree with this statement.

Children should be formally introduced to phonics by the age of 3.

1	2	3	4	5
Very strongly disagree	Strongly disagree	Disagree	Neither agree nor disagree	Agree

You may have identified that there are three descriptors that are about disagreement and only one that allows the respondent to say that they agree with the statement. In situations such as this, it is reasonable to assume a degree of bias on the part of the researcher.

Other factors that need to be considered in the use of scales are to avoid using too many points on the scale, usually no more than five. Respondents should be able to discriminate easily between, for example, 'strongly disapprove' and 'disapprove'. The more points used, the harder it is for respondents to choose where to make their response, and the more inaccurate the results will be.

In addition, there is no real agreement as to whether an odd or an even number of descriptors should be employed. It could be argued that respondents should be allowed the option to be neutral about a particular topic, whereas leaving out a middle point forces a response in one direction or the other.

RANKING

Questions that use ranking are generally used when the researcher wishes the respondents to indicate the *importance* they place upon a particular issue or concept. Respondents might be asked to rank using either open or closed questions; an open question often being used in a preliminary study to reveal items that can be used in a subsequent study using closed questions. The following are examples of both the open and closed approach.

A closed question

Below is a list of suggestions about what can be done to help a toddler settle into an early years setting. Please rank them in order of importance, using the numbers 1 to 5, where 1 is the most important suggestion and 5 is the least important.

❒ Make sure the setting is warm and welcoming for the child and parent(s).

❒ Visit the child and family at home so that you can begin to get to know them and they can get to know you.

❒ Have a flexible settling-in policy that encourages a parent to gradually introduce the child to the nursery over a period of time.

❒ Operate an effective key person policy to enable the child to build a close relationship with a member of staff.

❒ Give the family a booklet all about the setting and how they can prepare the child beforehand.

An open question

What do you consider to be the three most important things early years settings can do to help a new toddler settle in? Please write them in rank order with the most important thing first and the least important last.

Now carry out the following Activity.

 ACTIVITY

For each of the issues below, devise an open and a closed question. When using closed questions try to use a range of question types; that is, scales, lists and ranking.

- The importance of a play-based curriculum.
- Parental views on the MMR vaccination.
- Creating a quality environment for babies in early years settings.

COMPLEX GRIDS OR TABLES

These are used when the researcher wishes to explore respondents' views about an issue in some depth while retaining control over the range of possible responses. For example, a grid could be used for exploring how students studying for a Foundation Degree in Early Childhood Studies perceive the level of support they have had from a range of people.

Please indicate how supportive the following people have been while you have been studying for your foundation degree. Please tick the relevant boxes.

	Very supportive	Quite supportive	Neither supportive nor unsupportive	Quite unsupportive	Very unsupportive
Your line manager					
Your work colleagues					
The college staff					
Your friends					
Your family					

Another type of grid is the *semantic differential*. This was first used in the 1950s by Osgood and is sometimes called an Osgood Semantic Differential (Heise, 1970).

In this grid, the respondent is asked to rank an idea or concept on a number of scales that use opposite adjectives at each end of the continuum. It is a useful way of finding out information about complex ideas and attitudes. In the following example, a semantic differential is used to explore attitudes held by early years practitioners about parents. As suggested previously, the items that make up the scale could have been obtained by asking open questions to a group of practitioners in an exploratory study.

Please rate the parent group who use your setting on the following scales. Place a tick on one of the lines between each pair of words to indicate your feelings.

Helpful	—	—	—	—	—	—	Unhelpful
Supportive	—	—	—	—	—	—	Unsupportive
Punctual	—	—	—	—	—	—	Unpunctual
Authoritative	—	—	—	—	—	—	Permissive
Friendly	—	—	—	—	—	—	Unfriendly

OPEN ENDED

These are questions where the participant is not prompted in any way. For example: 'What ways do you use to promote parental partnership in your setting?'

The advantage of this type of question is that respondents are free to write whatever they want. This can often provide very 'rich information' throwing up ideas that you may not have thought of. The disadvantage is that these questions are more difficult to analyse than those with a numerical answer. Chapter 18 gives advice as to how to analyse this type of question.

PUTTING A QUESTIONNAIRE TOGETHER

So far in this chapter, we have investigated various ways that questions can be formulated and we have emphasised how important it is that the questions match the aims of the research. This is vital in order that the questions used elicit the information wanted. In this section, we will give some thought as to how to present a questionnaire in order that it will give reliable results. The following points are developed from suggestions by Johnson and Christensen (2017).

KNOW THE CHARACTERISTICS OF THE POTENTIAL RESPONDENTS

One of the first considerations is who the respondents are likely to be. A good understanding of their characteristics is important as it may affect how the questionnaire is constructed.

 REFLECTION POINT

What factors might you need to take into account when devising a questionnaire for the following two groups?

1. A questionnaire about the Early Years Curriculum targeting early childhood practitioners.
2. A questionnaire about parental involvement within an early years setting, targeting Bangladeshi families in an inner city area.

In the above examples, you may have considered that early childhood practitioners have more knowledge of the curriculum than parents and that a questionnaire directed towards the practitioners can contain 'technical terms' that they use every day. For parents, such terms may be unknown to them and would need explaining. A questionnaire about parental involvement intended specifically for Bangladeshi families may not be understood if it is written in English. A straightforward translation may also cause difficulties because some families may be unfamiliar with written Bengali. In this case, it may be appropriate to ask a translator to read the questionnaire out to the parents. When producing a questionnaire, the researcher should use language that is familiar to respondents and pay due regard to their expected reading age; a questionnaire that is too complex will mean that a respondent is unable to complete it, whereas one that is too simple may lead respondents not to take it seriously and to give superficial responses.

BE CLEAR AND PRECISE

If items in a questionnaire are long-winded or unclear, respondents may not give the information wanted. It is a good idea to get someone unconnected with the research but who shares some of the characteristics of the respondent group to read through the questions to see if they can understand what is being asked. In addition, it is important to avoid questions that are ambiguous or imprecise (Blaxter et al., 2010).

NEVER ASK BIASED QUESTIONS

A biased question is one that is written in a way that increases the likelihood of a particular response. One way of influencing how people respond is by including words that may elicit a strong negative reaction in individuals. The use of highly emotive words can be so powerful that individuals may make a negative response to a questionnaire item when a more emotionally neutral word would produce a different result. Using a phrase such as 'drug *addict*' may produce a different response than 'drug *user*', for instance.

The use of *leading* questions is another way that a questionnaire can become biased, as they suggest a certain response.

— 💡 —— REFLECTION POINT ——————————————

Can you identify the bias in these questions?

1. Please tick the appropriate response.

   The new Early Years Curriculum is:

   A great improvement on the old curriculum ☐

   A slight improvement on the old curriculum ☐

   Not an improvement on the old curriculum ☐

2. Some people suggest that fast food is leading to both tooth decay and an increase in obesity in children. Do you agree?

   Yes   No

The main difficulty with question 1 is that the respondent is not given the opportunity to say that they think the new curriculum is worse than the old one. In addition, the use of the words 'old' and 'new' introduce an emotive element, as 'new' generally conjures up positive images, whereas 'old' *may* conjure up more negative thoughts. In question 2, it is likely that the response will always be 'yes' because some people do suggest that fast food leads to these ill effects. Can you think of ways that this question could have been better expressed?

AVOID THE USE OF DOUBLE-BARRELLED QUESTIONS

Double-barrelled questions are those where two or more issues are combined into one question. In question 2 in the previous Reflection Point feature, respondents were asked to consider the effects of fast food on both dental health *and* body weight. It may be that respondents would agree with one association, but not the other.

AVOID DOUBLE NEGATIVES

Consider the following sentence: 'I do not want children not to have a healthy diet'. The sentence contains a double negative and could be better written as: 'I *want* children to have a healthy diet'. Occasionally when writing a questionnaire it is possible to find oneself in a 'double negative' situation that may lead to respondents making mistakes.

AVOID OVERLAPPING CATEGORIES WHEN USING NUMBERS

Overlapping categories are confusing because a respondent could put their response in more than one category. For example, if asked to tick a box to indicate age, it would be confusing if the options were written like this:

0-10, 10-20, 20-30, 30-40, 40+

The categories should be written 0–9, 10–19, 20–29, and so on, in order that the response can only fit into one category.

BE AWARE THAT RESPONDENTS MAY GET INTO PATTERNS OF RESPONDING

Not all respondents will respond to a questionnaire with focus and concentration. Lack of concentration may result in them responding according to a pattern. The authors both have considerable experience of reading module evaluation forms where students are given a five-point scale to rate various aspects of a module. There is a strong tendency for students to tick the same response for all items, even though they are asked to evaluate such disparate items as the suitability of the rooms in which teaching was held and the quality of tutor support. In a similar way, some respondents will have a tendency to either agree or disagree with items, regardless of the content of the item. One way to counteract this is to use a variety of types of question in one questionnaire and to keep the number of items to be rated in a similar way to a minimum.

BE AWARE THAT RESPONDENTS MAY GIVE A SOCIALLY ACCEPTABLE RESPONSE

In questions about behaviour and attitudes, respondents may feel embarrassed to respond truthfully. For example, if you wanted to find out how many hours of television parents allow their children to watch a day, you are likely to get an underestimation, because many parents now know that too much television is viewed as detrimental to children's development. If the parent knows who is administering the questionnaire, and that person is a person in authority, then the tendency is strengthened. This is important to consider if sending out a questionnaire to people with whom you are familiar (Anderson, 1998).

DECIDE ON HOW YOU WILL INTRODUCE YOUR QUESTIONNAIRE

Questionnaires are either introduced by means of a covering letter, or the details are contained on the questionnaire schedule itself, by means of an introduction. Denscombe (2014) recommends that the following information is included:

- Who is responsible for the questionnaire. Is there a sponsor or organisation involved? If the questionnaire is for a student research project then this needs to be explained. Full contact details of the researcher/organisation should also be given (Cohen et al., 2011).
- The purpose of the questionnaire. The reason why the questions are being asked needs to be explained.
- The return address and date.
- How confidentiality will be maintained. This should include an explanation that respondents' identities will not be revealed and that there will be due consideration paid to the secure storage of data.
- The voluntary nature of the questionnaire. Everyone who is asked to respond has the right to say 'no'.
- Thanks. Respondents will have chosen to give up valuable time to help fill in the questionnaire and a sincere statement of thanks should be included either at the beginning of the questionnaire or at the end.

DECIDE ON HOW TO PRESENT YOUR ITEMS

There is some evidence that the response rate improves if the items that respondents consider to be important are placed at the beginning of a questionnaire (Robertson and Sundstrom, 1990). Bell (2010) argues that personal data, such as income, should be put towards the end of a questionnaire.

- Start with positive, non-threatening items first (Bell and Walters, 2014) that can be answered easily (Simmons, 2008).
- Limit the number of questions that direct respondents to another question depending on how they answer a previous question (Johnson and Christensen, 2017). An example of this type of question is: 'Do you use the Internet? If yes, go to question 3; if no, go to question 6'.

- Include clear instructions and indicate where a new topic starts by using an introductory sentence. Examples can be included to help respondents see exactly what you mean (Denscombe, 2014).
- Give the questionnaire a title, number each question and include page numbers.
- Consider ending your questionnaire with an open question, asking respondents if they have any other comments they want to contribute.
- Finish with a couple of straightforward questions to allow the respondent to 'cool off'.
- Finally, thank the respondents for completing the questionnaire.

Check that the questionnaire looks professional. Is it laid out well? It should not be overcrowded and the text should be easily readable. Using the typeface 'Arial' and a font size of at least 12 will make text clear. Bell and Walters (2014) suggests that the font and style of the typeface for instructions should be different from that of the main questionnaire. It is also vital that the questionnaire is proofread carefully for errors in spelling, grammar and punctuation.

PILOT THE QUESTIONNAIRE

It is unwise to send out a questionnaire without testing it out on a few people first; initially family and friends might be helpful, and once any obvious modifications have been made it can be piloted with people who are representative of the group you want to study. Respondents in a pilot group could be asked to 'think aloud' and verbalise and record their thoughts as they are filling in the questionnaire. Anderson (1998) suggests using a focus group approach, where 6–12 volunteers are gathered together to fill in the questionnaire and are encouraged to write comments in the margins. Afterwards the researcher could conduct a discussion about how the questionnaire worked.

Feedback from the pilot phase helps to identify if the questionnaire is too long or confusing, for instance. The researcher can ask for comments on presentation and any proofreading errors may be identified. Looking at the responses will also indicate whether the questionnaire has elicited the information expected – a key factor for validity. If not, the questions will need amending.

THE RESPONSE RATE

Decisions made about putting together a questionnaire and how to distribute it can have a profound effect on the number of questionnaires that are completed and returned. The proportion of questionnaires returned is commonly known as the *response rate*, and is calculated as the percentage of completed questionnaires returned compared with the number sent out; calculated as:

$$\frac{\text{Number returned}}{\text{Number sent out}} \times 100$$

 — ACTIVITY

Conduct an online search to find out average response rates for questionnaires. You will find that there are many sites, all of which give different answers. That is because the number of completed questionnaires you receive is dependent on so many factors. The following is from the University of Texas and gives various response rates according to the method of distribution.

Mail: 50% adequate, 60% good, 70% very good

Phone: 80% good

Email: 40% average, 50% good, 60% very good

Online: 30% average

Classroom paper: >50% = good

Face-to-face: 80–85% good

Taken from Saldivar, 2012.

Cohen et al. (2011) suggest that the response rate can be increased by ensuring the questionnaire is attractive and easy to use, it is clear how to return it (and it does not require the respondent to spend money on postage), and if follow-ups and reminders are sent. Sometimes researchers use an identification code on questionnaires so they can identify who has returned them. This helps to identify if a specific group has chosen not to return the questionnaire. For example, if you wanted to find out information about school–parent links, it would be important to know that parents whose first language was not English failed to respond. Clearly, non-response does need to be thought about, because this can impact on the validity of the findings, but being able to identify respondents will impact on their anonymity.

Students often ask how many questionnaires they should aim to receive back. What is the minimum number needed for analysis? This is a difficult question to answer and depends upon the aim of your study and your methodology. If you are conducting a quantitative study and subjecting your data to statistical analysis then one of the aims of the research will be to produce findings that are generalisable. You will have chosen your sample carefully so that the respondents represent the population that you want to study. The larger the sample, the more reliable will be the findings. Market research companies often aim for 400 completed questionnaires to try to ensure findings are reliable. However, with an undergraduate research project, the aim is to show that you understand the principles behind research design and analysis, and we have often accepted as few as 15 to 20 completed questionnaires as long as students can demonstrate an understanding about how this small number of respondents will affect reliability.

For qualitative research, where questionnaires use open questions and the data are not subjected to statistical analysis, the requirements for large data sets are less important. In most instances there is no expectation that the findings will be generalisable, as the research is specific to a particular situation. What is important here is that students read the questionnaires as they come in and see if there are sufficient data to answer their research question. This is an individual judgement. It is often better to have fewer questionnaires which have been analysed really well, than to have many questionnaires that have not been properly analysed. As a rule of thumb we would expect to see ten or more qualitative questionnaires, so long as there is no element of statistical analysis involved. Any less and one would wonder why the student has not conducted face-to-face interviews. Whether or not you are using structured questionnaires, which will be subject to statistical analysis, or qualitative questionnaires, which will be subject to thematic analysis, you are strongly advised to seek guidance from your research supervisor, as each institution will have different guidelines on this. Chapter 18 looks at how one analyses questionnaires.

ADMINISTERING A QUESTIONNAIRE

There are a variety of ways to administer a questionnaire, which all have advantages and disadvantages. The aim in choosing a method should be to maximise the *response* rate. As noted previously, before sending out a questionnaire a covering letter should be written introducing the researcher and the aims of the study and providing details about how to return the questionnaire. Let us now think about some different ways of administering a questionnaire in turn.

HANDING OUT QUESTIONNAIRES DIRECTLY

This is a very common way of distributing questionnaires, especially if carrying out a piece of small-scale research such as in the workplace. It has the advantage that the respondents are known to the researcher and they may be predisposed to help. It also has the advantage that the research can be explained in person and the procedure for returning the questionnaires explained (Walliman, 2001). The disadvantage is that there is an increased risk of respondents telling you what they think you want to know. In addition, the respondent may be too embarrassed to respond to questions on sensitive issues. An added disadvantage of the personal approach is that it can be especially annoying if questionnaires are not returned; it is easy to personalise this process and be disappointed that someone you thought would help, has let you down. It is best to remember that people lead busy lives, and if, after a couple of prompts, the questionnaire has not been returned, nothing more should be said. Often it is possible to take advantage of a group of respondents being in the same place at the same time, such as a class of students. Kumar (2014: 197) describes this as 'collective' administration.

USING THE POST

This is a common way of sending out a questionnaire. The advantages of using the post are that it is a relatively effective use of time and it is a good way of reaching a large number of respondents. However, it is not always that easy to get an accurate database of addresses of potential respondents owing to data protection issues. In addition, sending out questionnaires by post can be expensive and the response rate is often low (Bell and Walters, 2014).

USING OTHERS TO DISTRIBUTE YOUR QUESTIONNAIRE

Sometimes it is possible to enlist the help of other people in distributing questionnaires. This can improve the response rate, although it does not negate the need to obtain direct permission for your questionnaires to be distributed if they are going to be distributed via these 'helpers' in settings such as in a range of nurseries. In this instance, permission would still need to be sought from the nursery managers.

SENDING OUT A QUESTIONNAIRE ELECTRONICALLY

Email can be an effective way of reaching a large number of people, particularly if they are all members of a network and it is easy to send a group email. The disadvantage is that the method is limited to those individuals for whom there is an email contact. Placing the questionnaire on an Internet website is another way of reaching potential respondents, but access needs to be gained to a site whose users fit the profile of the sample you wish to reach. Crucially, both email and Internet distribution will automatically exclude individuals with no access to this technology and complete anonymity may be difficult to achieve.

There are free software packages, such as Survey Monkey (www.surveymonkey.com) which help you both design and disseminate your questionnaire. Bell and Walters (2014) consider that this is a useful resource, one which is used by 16 million users throughout the world. Their experience using Survey Monkey leads them to recommend that you plan your questionnaire yourself first before you use the survey design tools provided by the software package.

 ——— ACTIVITY ————————————————————

Explore these resources:

1. A briefing paper from Exeter University (UK) on creating and using online questionnaires: https://as.exeter.ac.uk/media/universityofexeter/academicservices/educationenhancement/cascade/Creating_and_using_online_surveys.pdf (accessed 16 February 2017).
2. Information from Harvard University (USA) on Qualtrics, the online survey tool available to Harvard students: http://huit.harvard.edu/services/survey-tool (accessed 16 February 2017).

Now investigate the resources that are available to you through your institution and/or on the Internet.

TELEPHONE AND FACE TO FACE

It is possible to administer a questionnaire over the telephone, or by asking the questions face to face. It is a common method used by market researchers and has the main advantage of getting an instant reply, thus increasing the response rate. The main disadvantage of this method is that you may well meet with refusal because people do not have the time to talk. In addition, Cohen et al. (2011) point out that sometimes, the person taking a phone call is not the most suitable one to answer the questionnaire. Telephone and face-to-face administration of questionnaires is also both costly and time-consuming. There is very little difference between administering a questionnaire face to face and a structured interview.

RESEARCH IN FOCUS

In Sweden, Lefèvre et al. (2015) used web-based questionnaires to find out the views of child health care nurses on running groups for parents with children under 1 year of age. The aim of the groups was to offer parenting support and to encourage social support among group members. The questionnaire, which was piloted beforehand, consisted of 30 questions. Most questions were multiple choice with an invitation to add additional comments. The questions were designed to find out how the groups were run, the respondents' understanding of parental support, and their own personal group leadership skills.

SWEDEN

Of the 311 nurses who were invited to respond to the questionnaire by an email letter, 156 filled in the questionnaire. Two email reminders were sent and there was a final reminder by telephone. Thirteen nurses declined to participate, 14 didn't run groups and 113 nurses did not answer. This gave a response rate of 55 per cent which is high for this type of study. The questions which gave numerical data were analysed using SPSS (a computer program) and the comments were analysed using qualitative methods. (Chapter 18 looks at analysing data.)

The findings indicated that nurses would benefit from more training in leading groups and that this should be incorporated into their education. Research is needed to find out how to involve more parents in the group support initiative.

CASE STUDY

Susan is studying for her early childhood degree. Previous to this she obtained a qualification as an early years educator in a local further education college. This gave her the qualifications needed to go into employment as an early years practitioner or progress to university, which she did immediately after she completed her course. However, she noted that very few of the other students on the course took this step and she wondered where the students had decided to go after they completed their course and what were the factors that influenced their decisions. Susan is no longer in touch with many of the students she studied with so has decided to look at students coming to the end of their course now.

Susan has visited her old college and has asked the course tutor if she could hand out questionnaires to the students who are just finishing their course and have been thinking about 'next steps'. There are two groups of final year students with 30 students in each class. The tutor has suggested that Susan uses group tutorial lessons to talk about herself and explain about her research project. She will give out the questionnaires during group tutorial time for each class and collect them back at the end.

1. What sort of questionnaire is likely to get the information Susan is asking for?
2. What are the ethical issues that Susan should consider?
3. What methodology underpins this research?

Susan's questionnaire is likely to be semi-structured. It would most likely include questions to elicit information such as a respondent's age, previous qualifications, caring responsibilities and educational background of parents. All of these factors could have an effect on individuals' decisions. For example, students whose parents have been educated up to university level may be more likely to progress to university than students whose families have had no previous background of higher education (see e.g. Crawford et al., 2016). Susan should be careful not to include questions about aspects of the respondents' lives which are not relevant; political affiliation may be an example of this.

Questions about the factors influencing choices are best written as 'open questions', where participants are free to give their responses. For example, Susan could ask 'What do you plan to do with your qualification once the course is over?' 'What factors have influenced your choice?' 'What job do you see yourself doing in 5 years' time?'

There are always ethical issues involved when conducting research. Chapter 6 looks at ethics in detail. In this situation you would need to think about informed consent, confidentiality and data protection. In addition you should be aware that at the end of their course some students may be anxious about next steps. The questionnaire should be written and introduced in such a way that no particular option is valued over another. Students may be worrying that they haven't found employment yet or a place on the course that they want to progress to in order to build on their qualifications. Susan could discuss this with the course tutor beforehand and have information available about where students can go for advice about progression. After the students have handed back their completed questionnaires Susan could discuss the career decisions she made. Students may also feel uncomfortable if they think that their course tutor will see what they have written. It is not unusual for students to reach the end of their course and decide that they are really not suited to working with young children and that they will be taking another direction.

Questionnaires can be used in both quantitative and qualitative research studies. Structured questionnaires are generally quantitative in nature, and unstructured questionnaires are usually qualitative. This will be a semi-structured questionnaire and looking at the aim of the study can help us decide on the methodological approach. Susan wants to understand the factors which underpin participants' decisions about 'next steps'. The closed questions, which can be reduced to numerical data, can be analysed statistically and it may be possible to show that the educational background of parents has an effect. This is a quantitative approach. The open questions are designed to elicit participants' thoughts, feelings and opinions. These responses are likely to be analysed using thematic analysis. (Chapter 18 looks at analysing data.) So Susan's research can be described as using mixed methodology. As you may have read in Chapter 5, there has been much debate as to whether or not it is legitimate to use mixed methodology. Some would say that the underpinning paradigms for the two methodological approaches are so different that it is not possible for the two approaches to be used in the same study. However, using a mixed methodological approach is common practice, and many, such as Aubrey et al. (2000) believe that the approaches can be viewed as complementary to each other, rather than in opposition.

POSSIBILITIES AND LIMITATIONS OF QUESTIONNAIRES

Questionnaires are a popular way of collecting information as they can be administered to a large number of people and can glean a lot of information, albeit not in any great depth. Topics involving feelings and attitudes, for instance, are better explored using qualitative methods. Questionnaires are usually cost-effective in terms of time, as opposed to interviews, because they are generally not administered face to face. However, for a student, they can incur high photocopying costs.

The main disadvantage is that the design process is not straightforward, and that without care and attention to the suggestions contained within this chapter, questionnaires can be rendered unreliable and invalid. Bell and Walters (2014: 130) go so far as to suggest that questionnaires can be 'fiendishly difficult to design'. Finally, as a method to use directly with *young* children, they are unlikely to be useful.

 —— KEY POINTS FROM THE CHAPTER ——————

- Questionnaires are a common way of obtaining information but they are difficult to design.
- There are a variety of ways questions can be asked including questions designed to find out information about quantities and numbers, categories, lists, multiple choice, scales, ranking and complex grids and tables. Questions can also be open or closed.
- When putting a questionnaire together it is important to think about the characteristics of the respondents so that the questions are accessible to them. Questions need to be clearly written, unbiased and designed to reduce response bias. Ethical considerations also need to be taken into account.
- Questionnaires should be piloted so that any potential problems are picked up before the final questionnaire is sent out.
- Questionnaires can be sent out by post, via the Internet or email, delivered by a third party, or by the researcher, or read to respondents over the phone or face to face.

———————— **FURTHER READING** ————————

Bell, J. With Walters, S. (2014) *Doing Your Research Project: A Guide for First Time Researchers*, 6th edition. Maidenhead: Open University Press. Chapter 9 contains a good discussion on questionnaires.

Johnson, B. and Christensen, L. (2017) *Educational Research: Quantitative, Qualitative, and Mixed Approaches*, 6th edition. Thousand Oaks, CA: Sage. Chapter 8 contains a clear and comprehensive explanation of how to construct a questionnaire in more depth than the Bell and Walters's text.

Don't forget to visit the online resources at https://study.sagepub.com/mukherjiandalbon3e for access to free SAGE journal articles, weblinks, videos, exercises, mini quizzes and an interactive glossary.

15

USING DOCUMENTS AND VISUAL TEXTS

───────── CHAPTER OBJECTIVES ─────────

- To consider what is meant by documents and visual texts in research.
- To reflect on why we might use these in research.
- To consider how access to different types of texts might be gained.
- To gain an understanding of how we might evaluate different texts in terms of their usefulness in research.
- To begin to think about how we might analyse documents and visual texts.
- To look at the possibilities and limitations of using documents and visual texts in research.

So far, in this part of the book, we have looked at observation, interviewing and questionnaires. Each of these involves direct engagement with people – even a self-completion questionnaire is designed with a specific audience in mind. Documents, by way of contrast, may be centuries old and may not have been written or designed with an audience in mind, such as in the case of personal diaries. In this chapter, then, we are thinking about analysing documents as a research tool as opposed to using written documents as background reading for a literature review. We will also be reflecting on the term 'document' in its widest sense, including the use of a wide range of visual texts in research. These, such as photographs, may not always be in written form but nonetheless 'speak' to us in ways akin to a written text. We will not be exploring the creation of visual texts as part of a piece of research in this chapter – as opposed to those already in existence. However, for a good example of such work, we would suggest you investigate the online resources and look at Kate Pahl's work on exploring the relationship between narratives and objects, which included the creation of digital stories (see www.everyobjecttellsastory.org.uk).

WHAT IS A DOCUMENT?

 —— ACTIVITY ————————————————

At the beginning of this chapter it is important to think about what we might mean by a document. Make a list of things you consider to be documents before moving on to look at this section.

When you do move on to read this section, compare your own list to the examples considered below. Do some of the items included challenge your own definition of documents?

We might expect to list journals and books as important documents. Indeed they are an important starting point for researchers in helping them to find out about studies that have been carried out in their area before. The Internet also provides an enormous amount of information, some of it more credible than others. We reflected upon the usefulness of a range of sources of information in Chapter 3 when we considered reviewing the literature.

However, in terms of actual *methods* that a researcher might employ, alongside the inclusion of questionnaires, interviews and observations, we could also include documentary research as a research *tool*. Indeed Macdonald and Tipton (1993) argue that documentary research has a long history and is valuable as a research tool in its own right, as well as in conjunction with other methods as part of the researcher's attempt at triangulating their study.

Denscombe (2010) summarises the types of documents that might be used as:

- newspapers and magazines
- records
- letters
- diaries
- government publications and official statistics.

Let us look at each of these in turn.

NEWSPAPERS AND MAGAZINES

Newspapers and magazines are useful to researchers because they are up-to-date documents. While some might be considered more reliable than others as sources of information, all are useful in gaining an insight into how a story is reported and the kinds of language used in the reporting of particular stories.

RECORDS

Denscombe (2010) notes how the bureaucratisation of industrial societies has produced a range of documents. These might include records of transactions and the decision-making of committees, minutes of meetings, and suchlike. This type of documentation often serves to enhance public accountability – for example, the minutes of a parents' committee meeting in a nursery will be publicly available so all parents whose children attend the nursery, those who attended the meeting and those who did not, can see what was said and not said, agreed or not agreed. For a researcher, these types of documents may be useful for a range of purposes, such as tracking the development of a new policy or possibly by using discourse analysis – something we return to in Chapter 18 – to investigate the way language is used to promote the power of particular individuals or groups, for example. If these types of documents are publicly available, they are often easy to access by researchers. However, as Duffy (2010) warns, it should never be assumed that all existing records are available to researchers. Sometimes such documents are regarded as highly confidential and access to them is restricted.

LETTERS

Private correspondence such as letters can be interesting but differs in many ways from the kinds of publicly available documents such as minutes of meetings.

Letters are written to specific people and will often contain detail about people's personal opinions on an issue as opposed to giving an impartial account of something that has happened as, some would argue, might be contained in the minutes of a meeting. Their value lies in the way they allow us to enter the private world of the writer and gain their perceptions of an issue or event and the way they share this with another person. However, in terms of research, as letters are private documents, they can be difficult to access unless the person is well known and their letters form part of an archive. In the early childhood field, there are archives of writings by people such as Margaret McMillan as their work was so influential on the development of early childhood provision.

Sometimes, private correspondence is made available to a more public audience owing to a sense of duty to add further information about a particular person's life and work or to shed light on an important event and make this information available to the public. Examples of this might be the letters exhibited in the Imperial War Museum in London that highlight the experience of child evacuees in the Second World War, or the notes exhibited in the Thomas Coram Foundling Museum in London, which were written by mothers and pinned to their babies when they left them at the foundling hospital in the knowledge they would not see them again.

DIARIES

Diaries can be a rich source of data to researchers. Denscombe (2010) notes the way that they might contain detail about factual data, for example, a log of things that have happened, significant incidents and personal interpretations. Like letters, diaries should be seen as subjective accounts of things that have happened, affected by the identity of the diarist. However, this is also their strength.

Sometimes, researchers ask people to keep a diary as part of the research. Bell (1998: 73) refers to this type of diary as a 'solicited diary' as it is produced at the request of the researcher. An example might be asking a parent to keep a diary of books read with his or her child or food eaten over a given period. This can be very useful in allowing the researchers some insight into the research participants' world when they are not together, as in an interview. Inevitably, though, it is a research tool that involves a lot of commitment from the participants, who complete much of the data collection themselves away from the researcher. This can impact on their reliability (Bell, 2010).

GOVERNMENT PUBLICATIONS AND OFFICIAL STATISTICS

These types of documents are sometimes seen as having greater authority or credibility than documents such as letters or diaries, because they are produced by, or on behalf of, the state by expert professionals (Denscombe, 2010). The kind of statistical, that is quantitative, data produced in such documents are often seen as 'hard facts' and objective. However, we should always be wary that there may be vested interests in producing the statistics and be mindful that statistics may well mask other information. Moreover, we should always be mindful of how reliable the figures are: Who was counted? What was counted? Was it counted accurately? When, where and how did this take place and by whom? (Duffy, 2010: 125). In addition, you may recall that in Chapter 5 we argued that the real-life social world that we live in is a complex place and the positivist approach of reducing this to numerical data can be problematic.

If we think of a practical example such as bed-turnover in hospitals, official statistics might show a decrease in time that patients stay in hospital after their operations and an increase in patients treated. However, possibly those patients are being discharged from hospital before being fully recovered and are being re-admitted to hospital at a later date. The statistical evidence might mask the way the same patients are being re-admitted and seem positive in demonstrating a high bed-turnover. We have to remember that statistics, like other sources of data, can be open to alternative interpretations.

Researchers also use qualitative methodological approaches to analysing documents. Government documents can be open to many interpretations and some researchers use discourse analysis to interrogate such texts to explore – for example – shifts in government thinking or dominant narratives at a particular time, for our purposes in relation to early childhood education and care. Put very simply, researchers examining texts in such a way are far less concerned with statistics and more interested in examining the *uses* of words within the text and the *meanings* behind those words. You will think about this in more detail in Chapter 18.

RESEARCH IN FOCUS

AUSTRALIA

Ailwood (2008) analyses documents produced by the government of Queensland in relation to the development of a preparatory year in Queensland government schools in 2007. For children about to reach their fifth birthday, this is a non-compulsory but universally available year of schooling. She argues that: 'The groundwork on which this agenda has emerged is related to a complex mix of global, national and state-based discursive trends' (p. 536) and her article examines these trends in detail. The following extended quotation (from p. 546) is indicative of the approach taken throughout the article:

The conditions of possibility provided through advanced liberalism and knowledge economies in Queensland have produced a preparatory child that is predominantly thought of as a potential adult *learner* or *earner* rather than the previously more dominant *developer*

(Continued)

(Continued)

who is a potentially modern, rational adult. *The Early Years Curriculum Guidelines* for the preparatory year opens with a statement to the effect that a central focus of the preparatory year is the 'valuing and highlighting [of] the contribution of early childhood education to lifelong learning' (QSA, 2005: 1). Rather than 'job readiness' (Rose, 1999: 162), young children are to be judged on their 'school readiness', as indeed are their preparatory teachers whose job it is to 'make' them ready.

You will notice Ailwood's (2008) use of italics to highlight the shift towards seeing children as 'learners' or 'earners'. This shift, evidenced in the documents she draws to our attention, impacts on early childhood education and care (ECEC) as emphasis is placed on 'school readiness' and on young children in terms of their potentiality as *future* learners or earners (note our emphasis in italics on the word 'future' – a discourse of what children will become as opposed to what they are now). This can be contrasted with a notion of the young child as 'developer' (another word you see Ailwood emphasise in italics). In ECEC, the idea of child development and theories of developmental psychology have dominated the field. Ailwood is not saying that such theorising is 'correct', but is noting the shift from one particular way of constructing early childhood to another and this is a key point to bear in mind when reading an article such as this. Moreover, she is also examining the implications of such discourses on the work of early childhood practitioners when she states that it is 'preparatory teachers whose job it is to "make" them [children] ready'.

So far in this section you may have found that the list you made of items you consider to be documents is similar to those discussed. We will now move on to think more broadly about the term 'document'.

As well as text-based documents there are other documents available to researchers that are based on visual images. Just as the number-based information contained in official statistics and the word-based information contained in diaries and letters are considered as documents, visual images can also be considered as 'documents' (Denscombe, 2010). In this sense they can be viewed as different forms of 'text'. Hodder (2000: 703) calls written texts and artefacts 'mute evidence' as, unlike an interview, they may well exist long after their creator or user is available for comment. They are therefore invaluable in historical research – one might, for instance, look at the development of children's toys here. Toy museums are likely to exhibit toys that were produced and played with many years ago, even beyond living memory. These toys can still, however, tell us something about children and childhoods in the era(s) they were designed and used.

Researchers, who base their research on the use of visual images, see images as containing information in the same way as numbers and words do. They are often concerned with the way images serve to represent different attitudes, ideas and values. In other words, their focus will often be on the meanings and symbolism that appear to be behind an image (Denscombe, 2010). This type of research would be regarded as falling within the umbrella of qualitative research. However, as you will see in Chapter 18, there are also ways of analysing documents in a more quantitative or number-based way, such as in content analysis (Jupp and Norris, 1993).

 ACTIVITY

Look at the cover design of this book. It has an image of three 'slinkies' on it. Make some notes about what this suggests to you.

In looking at the front cover of this book, you may have thought of similar things to our friends, family and colleagues when they looked at the design prior to publication. Here are some examples of their comments:

- 'It seems to represent the learning curve the students might take when reading the book.'
- 'It makes you think research is fun.'
- 'It seems to represent the shifting nature of research.'
- 'There are three slinkies to represent the way the book is in its third edition – the first edition had one slinky on the cover.'

We included this example to encourage you to think about documents in their widest sense. But more broadly, what can be described as an image-based document? We might include the following as examples of image-based documentary data, which in turn can be grouped into whether it is a 'still' such as a photograph; a 'movie' such as a film; or an 'object' such as a building or item of clothing (Denscombe, 2010: 227):

- photographs
- films and videos
- archive film footage
- drawings
- the built environment and places

- clothing and fashion items
- cultural artefacts
- body language/signs
- advertisements
- graffiti.

In addition to the above, Macdonald and Tipton (1993: 188) encourage us to think about documents in terms of whether they were meant for public or private records. They add,

> But in addition to the purposeful record, there are those things which may be overtly intended to provoke amusement or admiration or pride or aesthetic enjoyment – songs, buildings, statues, novels – but which nonetheless tell us something about the values, interests and purposes of those who commissioned or produced them.

As examples of image-based documents or visual texts examined in research, Chang-Kredl's (2010) work is fascinating as she examines cinematic representations of childhood and the ways in which such films position the adult viewer. Her work does not necessarily comprise interviewing actual adults or indeed children, but involves an examination of films from a variety of different genres, each representing childhood in some way. In other words, *the films themselves* are the source of data.

By way of another example, researchers, whose work is framed within what is sometimes called the 'geographies of childhood', explore spaces for children. Fielding (2000: 242), for example, examines the use of space in a primary school and focuses on the 'connections between space, identity, schooling and pedagogy'. In so doing, not only does he draw on data from children and teachers (e.g. gained through interviews), but he also examines the school building as a visual text, as it too 'speaks' – for instance about the degree to which children are encouraged to work together. He argues that the school space can be viewed as a 'hotbed of moral geographies – of moral codes about how and where children ought to learn and behave' (Fielding, 2000: 231).

In our experience, students rarely undertake research which examines visual texts in such a way. Examining visual texts such as films or advertisements in terms of how they 'speak' about childhood could be an interesting option for student research. Moreover, for those of you who are finding it hard to access a placement setting to undertake research, it might be a practical and interesting alternative. The online resources give some ideas for student projects with this in mind.

Before we move on to think about how we might use this vast array of documents, you might like to reflect on the degree to which you considered the above as examples of documents when you started to read this chapter.

— 💡 —— **REFLECTION POINT** ————————————————————

Think about a document that is personal to you - it might be a photograph that you keep with you or on display at home. Consider the following in relation to it:

- Why is the photograph important to you? Does it remind you of people or a place or an event that is special in some way?
- Why do you keep it in the way that you do? Is it with you at all times so you have a constant reminder of the people/place/event with you at all times? (This is often the case with family photographs.) If on display, does the type of frame used or positioning of the photograph tell people something about the value you place on the photograph?

These questions are intended to encourage you to begin to think about how you might 'read' a photograph as you might another sort of text. You will learn more about why and how documents might be used in research as you read on in this chapter.

PHOTO ELICITATION

It is useful at this point to examine photo elicitation in some more detail: you may recall we thought about this in Chapter 13 when we looked at interviewing. A number of researchers have used photo elicitation to examine aspects of family life which would be difficult to observe on a regular basis but more particularly to help provide a basis for interviewing. Very simply, 'photo elicitation' refers to the use of photographs in the course of research interviews (Miller, 2016). Thus, unlike other aspects of this chapter which rely on the interpretation of the researcher of the document or visual text, here photographs (or visual text) form the basis of discussion. In Miller's research in the USA, which examined how families prepare their children for school, this was useful because:

> Instead of relying solely on a one-time interview, it allowed families to spend a week documenting and reflecting on readiness activities and allowed them to visually and orally communicate their ideas to the research team. (Miller, 2016: 265)

Thus, the photographs served a purpose as a prompt for discussion as opposed to merely being data in themselves.

Other researchers have used photographs to give an additional perspective on interview data. O'Connell (2013), for example, suggests that the use of visual methods in a study examining food practices within families was important because, in addition to being a useful prompt for discussion, they provided additional evidence of families' eating practices. When families talked about the difficulty of sitting around a table to eat together, the photographs of the dining space and child eating from the floor gave evidence of this and added additional verification of the account given.

 — ACTIVITY —

Imagine the usefulness of photographs as part of the following hypothetical studies:

- A study looking at how space is organised for new babies in the home.
- A study looking at the use of corridor displays in a nursery over a period of time.
- A study looking at how time spent at nursery fits in with the rest of a child's day.

In thinking through the Activity above you may have thought that it could be intrusive to visit a family home, particularly (potentially) the bedroom spaces. Photographs would be useful to prompt discussion on choices of equipment, how space has been (re)organised for the new baby and the choices made. In a study looking at corridor spaces over a year, it would entail a lot of visits to the setting, which may or may not be within easy distance, and it may be difficult to know when the spaces are freshened up with new displays. Photo elicitation would be useful as it could provide a record of displays over the year as a prompt for discussion during an interview. Finally, a study examining children's lives within and outside of nursery settings might ask children and families to take photographs at key points when away from the nursery, and the nursery could take photographs of how time is used in the setting. Individual timelines of photographs across home and nursery might prompt some very interesting research discussions. We hope you see there is potential for a number of avenues for using photographs, always with the caveat that ethical issues relating to the use of photographs are thought through carefully.

SOCIAL MEDIA AND NEW TECHNOLOGIES

So far in this chapter we have focused on fairly tangible documents inasmuch as they mostly have a presence in the physical world. The virtual world has expanded our notion of 'text' to include online blogs and social networking such as Twitter and Facebook, and these open up different possibilities in terms of research. Newspapers and journals are usually available now in an online format; however, the medium of documents should not really be the prime concern. After all, websites, with their mix of images and text can be regarded as a 'document' in the same way as a paper-based text (Denscombe, 2010), but, as we will see in Chapter 18, if used as a source of information – such as when reviewing the literature in a project – they should be treated carefully.

Some researchers focus on new social media and the technologies associated with this in their research and make use of such technologies to help them to gather data. Once such example can be seen in Ringrose et al.'s (2012) work on 'sexting' – a topic a little outside of the youngest children in the bracket 'early childhood', but nevertheless a topic that is important to childhood studies as it troubles notions of 'innocence' in childhood; the sexualisation of childhood; and the uses of technology in childhood, including online safety. Ringrose et al. (2012) examined the phenomenon of 'sexting' amongst young people, i.e. the sharing of sexual images and/or messages via the mobile phone and/or via the Internet. As part of their research strategy, the researchers asked the participants to friend them on Facebook with a research Facebook profile, and then monitored (with participants' awareness) their online activity. Key findings were that, as opposed to strangers, the prime technological threat to children and young people comes from their peers. They also found that sexting can often be coercive and that girls are more likely to be adversely affected by it.

The use of social media in research has been employed in studies pertaining to early childhood, as can be seen in the following Research in Focus. You will see that it raises some complex ethical issues around researching online chat forums.

RESEARCH IN FOCUS

Researchers in Scotland and England (Skea et al., 2008) analysed an online chat forum to ascertain parents' views about vaccination for measles, mumps and rubella (MMR). The MMR vaccination was developed to prevent the development of these diseases but there has been much controversy surrounding its safety. The researchers analysed archive discussions on mumsnet: an online chat forum for parents without actually posting any commentary themselves (mumsnet.com – launched in 2000 by two UK parents, now attracts thousands of 'visitors' a month). Non-members of the website are able to search discussion forum archives via keywords. In particular, the researchers analysed the kinds of discussions parents were having with regard to MMR vaccination. Skea et al. (2008) highlight one dominant perspective that emerged from their analysis of the online chat forum, which related to 'avoiding harm to others'. Parents wanted to both protect their own child but also ensure the development of 'herd immunity' (protection for all children).

 SCOTLAND

(Continued)

(Continued)

Whilst the research is interesting in terms of its findings, for our purposes here, we suggest it also raises some complex issues regarding ethics in research. Skea et al. (2008: 1383) state:

> The archives of discussion threads on 'mumsnet' are accessible without any request to register or 'log on' to the website. The venue is thus perceived as a 'public' rather than a 'private' sphere (Eysenbach & Till, 2001). Mumsnet members are told that their postings on the discussion forum will be publicly available, and are asked to anonymise their postings by using a 'chat nickname' and adopting codes when referring to members of their family.

With this in mind, the researchers felt that both: (1) the information was in the public domain and that everybody who posts something is aware of this; and (2) that all people who posted something online were anonymous – indeed the researchers did not ask for any personal information and note that their reasoning was to minimise intrusiveness. So they did not take part in any online discussions, which would have declared them publicly as researchers, but neither did they regard themselves as 'covert participants' (p. 1383) such as pretending to be a parent and posting a comment about the MMR vaccination in order to provoke and then analyse any response.

Reflect on whether you think the researchers should have alerted mumsnet and its online community about their intentions. What might have been the consequences of alerting people? If you have ever posted a question or comment on an online chat forum (a supposedly 'public' space), have you ever considered that you might be contributing data for someone's research? How do you feel about that possibility? Finally, can we rely on information posted on an online forum – do you think it is more or less reliable than information gained through, for example, interviewing face to face? What reasons do you give for your position? Finally, we should remember that all data are produced in a particular context – whether via an online discussion forum, a face-to-face interview, or an observation of a group activity. This context is likely to impact on the 'data' gathered by the researcher, so remaining vigilant as to how data are 'produced' is important.

WHY MIGHT WE USE DOCUMENTS AND VISUAL TEXTS IN RESEARCH?

Some documents, such as letters and diaries, can give the researcher an insight into how an issue or event was perceived by individuals or groups at a particular point in history (Barbour, 2008). Another important use of documents – here we are talking about artefacts – is that some areas of experience do not involve language. Many of the tools used in research are dependent on the use of language, notably questionnaires and interviews. Hodder (2000) draws on research that has looked at how slaves working on plantations in the American South expressed their feelings about and made sense of their oppression through the food and pots they used. Thus, a group whose perspective is often silent has a 'voice' through the study of their artefacts. We should remember, though, that inevitably, in this instance, the *interpretation* was done by the researcher years later, and was not done by those living in slavery themselves. This is an important point to bear in mind and can also be applied to the following example.

We might also think about the artefacts pinned to babies left at the foundling hospital again, as we did earlier in this chapter when we considered the notes left. These artefacts included items such as buttons and could be 'read' as symbolising the love, care and hope these mothers had for their babies when they left them to the care of others in the hospital owing to the dire financial and personal circumstances they found themselves in. It is likely that many of these women could not read and write, given their poverty and the lack of education available to them at that time, making letter-writing impossible. Thus, the items pinned to the babies' clothing still have the power to 'give voice' to the intense emotions these particular mothers may have experienced centuries after they left their children at the hospital. However, as Hodder (2000) reminds us, it is important to consider that in using documents, both written texts and artefacts, researchers are not only looking at the context in which the document was produced, but they, themselves, are looking at the document through the lens of their own particular context.

Hodder (2000) also argues that we should view artefacts as important components of social relations. Uniforms, for instance, are often developed with a view that they create a common identity among those who wear them – be they adults or children. Thus, if carrying out a study looking at the ethos of a particular school, while one might interview staff, children and parents about this – to name but one strategy – one could also examine the 'mute' material such as the clothing the children and staff are expected to wear. This would add another dimension to the study.

There are other advantages that can be put forward in relation to using documents. Unlike interview data, for instance, looking at documents (in the widest sense of the term) enables the researcher to look at 'material traces' of human life. This can be important because what people *say* they do may well be different to what people *actually* do (Hodder, 2000).

RESEARCH IN FOCUS

NORTHERN IRELAND

An interesting approach to using artefacts was applied in research carried out by Bunting and Freeman (1999) in North and West Belfast, Northern Ireland. Their research aimed to look at what children eat at school during break times. Rather than interviewing parents or children about this, the research team asked the children to place any empty food packaging and leftover

(Continued)

(Continued)

foods (writing down their name if there was no wrapping) into a labelled plastic bag and at the end of the allotted time they analysed its contents. By doing this, the researchers were able to gain an account of what was consumed without relying on the memory or perceptions of those who had produced the snack (the parents), those who had consumed it (the children), or indeed those who had supervised the break time.

They found that girls were more likely to eat fruit when compared with boys and that children from economically disadvantaged backgrounds were more likely to eat sweets during break times. They concluded that gender and poverty are associated with children's snack choices and recommended that efforts should be made to increase the availability and afford-ability of healthy foods.

HOW MIGHT WE EVALUATE DOCUMENTARY SOURCES?

Macdonald (2008) argues that there are a range of problems a researcher might come across when carrying out documentary research. He groups these under four main headings: authenticity, credibility, representativeness and meaning. We will now look at each of these in turn.

AUTHENTICITY

Authenticity is clearly important in research that uses documents. It is important that if using diaries or letters, for instance, the researcher knows that they are the work of the person who is credited with writing them.

CREDIBILITY

In considering the credibility of a particular document, the researcher needs to think about whether the document is free from distortion and error (Macdonald and Tipton, 1993). Of course this is affected by a range of factors:

- who produced the document
- who it was produced for (it may never have been intended for public gaze)
- when it was produced
- in what context it was produced.

But this is not as clear-cut as it seems. After all, what source counts as more credible than another?

REFLECTION POINT

If carrying out a piece of research looking at the area of inclusive practice, are government statistics on the number of children with special educational needs (SEN) and local authority statistics relating to the amount of money spent on provision in this area *more* credible than a mother's personal diary of her experiences of being a parent of a child with SEN?

We are sure that in thinking about the issues raised in this Reflection Point you might have reflected that the government statistics offer some general, quantitative information but give no indication of the thoughts and feelings associated with being a particular parent of a particular child with SEN in a particular context. As you know from Chapters 4 and 5 of this book, numerical data such as government statistics do not aim to do this.

The diary, however, would allow access to such a partial account, but it is unlikely to have been kept in a systematic way; the mother may have written in the diary only on days when she was exasperated at something that had happened rather than logging her reflections every day whether or not they were negative. Also, crucially, the mother's diary is one account among *many* possible accounts of this same situation. Other family members – not least the child with SEN – his or her siblings and staff in the setting the child attends will also have their own perceptions of inclusive practice in this particular instance. In addition, the diary is a document that is unlikely to have been written with an audience in mind and is highly context specific. After all, we could not generalise this person's account in order to 'speak' for *all* parents of children with SEN.

REPRESENTATIVENESS

Representativeness is a key issue in any piece of research. Just as in carrying out interviews or questionnaires, when the researcher needs to think about the relationship between the participants in her research and the population as a whole (which is essential in quantitative research), in documentary research the researcher needs to consider whether the document is representative of the entirety of documents that exist from which the sample was drawn. Sometimes a full archive of documents may exist, but there may well be missing documents; some may have been destroyed. In addition, relevant documents may be held in a range of places.

We might think about the range of information held about key early childhood pioneers here. The Froebel archive at Roehampton University would be a key source of information about Froebel, but does not contain *all* the documents that exist about him. Researching documents is akin to being a detective (Macdonald and Tipton, 1993) as the researcher needs to 'sniff out' new leads on information and be able to identify anything that might be suspect.

MEANING

Macdonald (2008) argues that there are two levels of meaning when looking at a document: its surface and its deeper meaning. To a certain extent, surface and deeper meaning are not so distant from each other. After all, when in conversation with someone, we understand the message the speaker wishes to convey; that is, the deeper meaning alongside the grammar. We do not usually separate these out, but it is useful to think about the way we 'read' different forms of text (Macdonald, 2008).

Deeper meaning is arrived at through analysis and interpretation. You will learn more about this in Chapter 18, which looks at analysing and presenting data. We will show that for post-structuralists such as Foucault, a 'text' might be a visual image, an object, an event or process (Woolfitt, 2008). An example of such a 'text' might be a card that is sent to parents to celebrate the birth of their new baby. We might look at the card and, owing to our knowledge of the cultural practices of a particular group of people at a given point in history, might recognise the object as a 'new baby card' and recognise the practice of sending cards. We could look at other more superficial aspects of the card, such as whether it says 'boy' or 'girl' on the front. However, there are deeper meanings that could be elicited. What colours are used in the image – what are they meant to signify? What is the baby doing in the picture – is s/he active or passive? Does the baby seem to be expressing emotion – if so, what? Is the baby alone or with someone else in the picture? What does the image say about children and childhood in a particular culture, such as the way new babies are welcomed into a family or community or issues of gender in relation to childhood? Who benefits from the perpetuation of the discourses that inform the text; that is, the card? In undertaking such an analysis, it is important to be aware that any interpretations will always be formed through our own sociocultural and historical lens.

Holland's (2004) book, for instance, is a fascinating look at the way childhood and children are portrayed in popular visual imagery. She argues that we need to look at lots of visual material in order to draw inferences from it. We would not say that *all* new baby cards depict girls as passive and dressed in pink clothing on the basis of one card, for example.

This chapter has moved a long way from the idea that documents are letters, diaries, minutes and other forms of written text. We have ended here with the idea that almost anything can be read as a 'text'. This idea is open to criticism, not least because it is far easier to 'read' these many forms of 'text' (used in the widest sense of the word) than actually achieving real and lasting *change*. After all, in the real world of human interaction, some ideas dominate and repression is *real* (Bordo, 2003; hooks, 1990). Thus, we might 'read' new baby cards for their portrayals of gender, but achieving real movement towards gender equity is far more difficult to accomplish. However, a reading of such 'texts' is useful in encouraging us to look again at some of the taken-for-granted assumptions we might hold about the world around us.

—— KEY POINTS FROM THE CHAPTER ———————

- There are many different types of document. These might include written texts such as diaries and newspapers as well as artefacts such as toys, clothing and photographs. Changes in technology, such as the increased use of social media, show that what can be regarded as a text and the format of such texts is ever changing.
- Documentary analysis can be employed as *part* of a research project but can also be used as the primary research tool.
- Care needs to be taken to ensure that if documents are used in research, they are authentic and credible. However, the issue of credibility does not preclude the use of partial sources, such as personal diaries. Different types of document allow the researcher different insights and it is important to acknowledge this when writing up the research.
- Documents can be analysed for their surface and deeper meanings – a point we pick up in more detail in Chapter 18.

———————— FURTHER READING ————————————

Hodder, I. (2000) 'The interpretation of documents and materials culture', in N.K. Denzin and Y.S. Lincoln (eds) *Handbook of Qualitative Research*, 2nd edition. London: Sage. A more challenging read than the others noted here, but an excellent chapter looking at the use of documents and visual texts – in their widest sense – in research.

Holland, P. (2004) *Picturing Childhood: The Myth of the Child in Popular Imagery.* London: Tauris. This book is a fascinating look at how popular cultural images of children and childhood can be analysed and interpreted.

Macdonald, K. (2008) 'Using documents', in N. Gilbert (ed.) *Researching Social Life*, 3rd edition. London: Sage. A useful introductory read about using documents in research in a general research methods text.

16

JOURNALING AS A RESEARCH TOOL

CHAPTER OBJECTIVES

- To consider how an examination of oneself can be legitimate in research.
- To develop an understanding of how journaling can be employed as a primary mode of data collection.
- To outline some of the tools that can be used to enhance reflection in journal writing.
- To gain an understanding of the possibilities and limitations of journaling as a research tool.

Rather than thinking about research as something carried out with *other* people, in this chapter we think about how the *self* can be a legitimate subject for research. As you will see, this is an area of research that has been a feature of qualitative feminist research in particular. But it has also been employed by professionals who are interested in examining aspects of their practice and responses to these with a view to gaining greater insight into their work. Therefore, there is a link to the action research chapter, which was also concerned with an examination of one's own professional practice.

In this chapter, we will be introducing you to the use of journaling in research and will consider how it can be employed as a research tool. A key concept that we return to in this chapter is 'reflexivity'. It is a term we looked at in Chapter 5. In writing this chapter, we debated whether to include it in Part 3 of this book as it is strongly linked to Chapter 11 on action research and can be regarded as an approach to research. In addition, owing to its usefulness in the research process, we might have included this chapter in Part 1 of the book. We eventually decided that it should be included here as its focus is primarily on using journaling as a research tool.

THE SELF AS A LEGITIMATE SUBJECT FOR STUDY

For some of you reading this book, looking at oneself as legitimate research may seem strange because traditional models of research have tended to emphasise the need to neutralise the self of the researcher. You may recall this from Chapter 4. Indeed, control, restraint and even the silencing of the researcher's own voice is often pursued in order to attain 'respectability' as a researcher in a particular academic discipline (Charmaz and Mitchell, 1997; Papen, 2008). Furthermore, in the academic world, the 'proper' subject for research has traditionally been seen as someone *other* than the researcher him/herself (Mykhalovsky, 1997).

This is changing. Increasingly, the self of the researcher is being seen as important in research. Wasserfall (1997) argues that this, in part, has been due to the increasing recognition that the self of the researcher is a key instrument in research. The personal history, subjectivities and biases of the researcher are seen as inevitably impacting in some way(s) on the research, from initial design to writing up. In addition, there is acknowledgement that the self of the researcher is in constant flux, impacting upon the research and changing as a result of it (Coffey, 1999; Reinharz, 1997). You may recall, from Chapter 5, that this is known as reflexivity.

The corollary of this is that there has been a growth in research that puts personal writing at the centre of its analyses (Emerson et al., 2007; Jones, 2005). Sometimes this is known as *autoethnography*. As the term suggests, it is a combination of the words 'autobiography' and 'ethnography', and refers to research that places the self of the researcher firmly within the narrative of the research.

However, although the self of the researcher takes centre stage, the social and cultural context which impact on the individual's experience is a significant part of the analysis (Papen, 2008). Etherington (2004) views it as both a method and the resulting text. In the following Research in Focus section, you will see how one researcher used this approach when researching her own pregnancy.

RESEARCH IN FOCUS

ENGLAND

Uta Papen is a researcher at Lancaster University, England, who used an autoethnographic approach to document her experience of becoming a mother as a 'textually mediated' experience (Papen, 2008). Thus, rather than researching the lives of other pregnant women, she turned her researcher's gaze towards herself. She discusses the significance of her 'Green Notes' or official maternity records during pregnancy; her own reading and writing practices, which enabled her to make sense of her experience of pregnancy; and finally, the significance of reading and writing in 'difficult moments' during her pregnancy.

She kept a diary for seven months as well as any written material she looked at or created during that period, e.g. leaflets, emails and notes – some of which were 'official' literature in relation to pregnancy. When reflecting on the Green Notes, Papen (2008: 388) states:

> the Notes were associated more with the professionals – my carers – than with me. As a literacy practice, they were shaped by the needs of the health care providers and the culture of work of the NHS. Reflecting on them now, with the more distanced eye of a researcher who is familiar with current health policies and debates, I see them as an only partially successful step in a new patient-centred health communication policy (NHS, 2000). At the time, I did not feel that because I possessed my own record I was empowered or could 'control' my own case.

Papen (2008) observes that she learnt a lot about herself in the course of her research but also argues that there were important things learnt about textual practices during pregnancy beyond herself: indeed she counters the charge sometimes made against autoethnography that it veers too far towards self-indulgence on the part of the researcher. From her very personal account, Papen makes some more general points about becoming a mother and the textual practices associated with this. We can see this in the following extended quotation, where Papen argues:

> Antenatal care is a highly structured social world, populated with norms and conventions which every pregnant woman in England encounters. As do other pregnant women, I had to negotiate my place within this world. My desire to belong and to be accepted without

(Continued)

(Continued)

being fully constructed and constrained by its parameters is a conflict all too common in many contexts of contemporary life. Working on my diary and other data, I became aware that I had wanted the midwives to like me and to think of me as a good, easy patient. If possible, I avoided conflict. This is a personal experience, but it also stems from gendered social expectations and is likely to be shared by other women. It is an example of how the personal is socially shaped. I also expect other women to have similar feelings towards their Green Notes, feeling only partly involved and empowered by the current structures. (p. 398)

Autoethnographers sometimes present their writing in texts that could be regarded as more 'experimental' than those described elsewhere in this book, such as through the use of poetry or dance. For Jones (2005), this marks a shift in focus from representation to one of presentation or performance. While we would not want to dismiss the use of such presentations of people's research, owing to their possibilities for creative expression, we think this might be difficult for a novice researcher to justify and achieve within early childhood studies as a field at the present time. And we certainly think you should be guided by your tutor in any choice you make about presenting your research.

What follows in this chapter is further discussion of some of the uses that can be made of journaling in a research project. Journaling can be employed as a tool to help the researcher reflect upon his or her research as and when issues arise, but may not be the main data-gathering instrument. It can also be used as the primary research tool in itself. It is this latter usage of journaling that we will be concentrating upon.

WHAT DO WE MEAN BY A 'JOURNAL'?

A journal is a private document that is used by the writer to document their thoughts and feelings about any number of issues that seem important to them (Etherington, 2004). In other words it can be viewed as a 'vehicle for reflection' (Moon, 2006: 1). Moon (2006) refers to journals as 'learning journals' but recognises that they are variously referred to as 'diaries' or 'logs'. For Moon, 'learning journal' is a useful term to employ because it gives a sense of the journal reflecting the writer's ongoing processes of reflection and learning. However, for the purposes of this chapter we will use the terms 'journal' and 'journaling'.

The writer of a journal will use whatever they are most comfortable with or whatever is available to them for the purpose. Thus, it might be a pad of paper, an attractively bound book, a Dictaphone or audio-recorder if writing is difficult, or it may be kept on a USB memory stick. At some point, it may be useful to develop an index or means of accessing the information contained in the journal in order to ease access to specific entries as well as help with the reflection process (Clough and Nutbrown, 2012; Moon, 2006).

Entries into a journal may include small notes about something or extended discussions about an issue or situation. There may be entries made every day or only occasionally. These entries might be in the form of notes, stories, diagrams, poetry, and so on (Bolton, 2005; Etherington, 2004). In addition, journaling may include a revisiting of past entries with additional journal entries made in relation to these. We discuss the importance of this later in the chapter. Bolton (2005: 167) exhorts her readers to 'experiment!' Seen in this spirit, a journal is a personal document that is kept in an idiosyncratic way (Clough and Nutbrown, 2012). Moon (2006: 27) encapsulates this idea by employing a driving metaphor, saying, 'the writer is at the wheel and is steering'. Bolton (2001: 155) similarly describes a journal as an 'organic tool' that aids the reflective process as opposed to it being a 'created product'.

It is likely that the writer of a journal would not want their journal to be open to scrutiny in its entirety but may choose specific entries to share with others. However, when using journaling as a *research tool* as opposed to purely for personal use, some of its contents inevitably become part of an assessment process. This might be at a university where the researcher is studying or through a peer-review process when writing a paper based on the research for a journal.

WHY USE JOURNALING AS A RESEARCH TOOL?

Journaling is used in a variety of different spheres. It is increasingly being suggested as a tool for professional development. This can be seen in the growth of the idea of the 'reflective practitioner' (Bolton, 2005; Moon, 2006; Schön, 1983). Many writers encourage researchers to keep a reflective journal throughout their research (Clough and Nutbrown, 2012; Roberts-Holmes, 2011). Other writers emphasise writing as a *primary* research tool or data-gathering instrument (Brown and Jones, 2001; Richardson and Adams St Pierre, 2005). Researchers are variously encouraged to document their thoughts and feelings in a journal and use these writings to:

- act as an aide-memoire for points to think about further or to note things to explore later or that have been useful in some way
- help with sorting out an initial focus for the research
- document any thoughts and feelings during the research; this might involve the researcher in reflecting on their impact on the research and the impact the research is having (and has had) on them
- form the main basis of the data.

We will think about each of these points in turn.

JOURNALING AS AN AIDE-MEMOIRE

This is probably the least interesting use of journaling, but it is nonetheless useful. While this use of journaling cannot make claims to being a data-gathering instrument or research tool as such, a journal is beneficial to researchers as a central point for jotting down things s/he would like to look up, such as a reference and suchlike. You may have experienced losing notes made on scraps of paper or Post-it notes and therefore value the idea of having a location such as a journal to keep such information. Thus, there is a very practical reason for keeping a journal (Etherington, 2004).

JOURNALING TO HELP FIND AN INITIAL FOCUS FOR RESEARCH

Journaling may be useful at the initial stage of carrying out a research project as it can help to develop an idea for the research. Tripp (1993) discusses how journaling what he describes as 'critical incidents' can be useful in providing starting points for research. The term 'critical incident' refers to how one interprets a given event and is highly individual. In this sense, the practitioner-researcher *creates* an incident as 'critical'. Critical incidents may seem like commonplace events that occur in one's practice, but on deeper reflection they trouble the writer who journals about them in some way.

In looking at one's journal, the researcher may be able to identify areas that they would like to explore further in their research. Possibly a similar issue keeps coming up in their journal. An example might be a practitioner reflecting that s/he keeps writing about the way sleep times are organised in his/her early childhood setting. However, it should be noted that Tripp (1993) maintains that what moves an event from the 'typical' to the 'critical' is the detailed analysis one undertakes of it. We will find out more about analysing critical incidents later in the chapter.

JOURNALING TO DOCUMENT THOUGHTS AND FEELINGS DURING THE RESEARCH PROCESS

Journaling can be a useful tool in encouraging the researcher to document the *process* of their research. It can encourage the writing down of personal feelings alongside the keeping of field notes and observations, for instance. This, in turn, can encourage greater empathy with participant(s) in the study as well as attunement with oneself (Etherington, 2004; Moon, 2006). This material might be drawn upon at the writing-up stage of the research in order to account for any decisions made in relation to research methods, for instance. DeVault (1997) argues that this documenting of the research story is usually done in order to establish the authority of the researcher; that is, 'why they did what they did' in the research process. In carrying out a piece of early childhood research at a college or university, you are usually expected to justify any decisions that were taken in relation to the research.

RESEARCH IN FOCUS

USA

Vivian Gussin-Paley writes extensively about her experiences as a kindergarten teacher in Chicago, USA (e.g. Paley, 1990, 1991). Her work documents the importance of fantasy and story-telling for young children (see Lee [2011] for an overview of the importance of her work). You will come across the work of Paley later on in this book (in Chapter 17) when we discuss 'creative methods' in research and explore 'storying' as a research tool.

Here, we wish to highlight the way in which Paley uses personal reflection on the children's stories and story-making throughout her work in order to try to make sense of the children's thinking. Although not describing this as a journal to document thoughts and feelings throughout her research – indeed 'research' and 'practice' are conflated in her work – in effect Paley's work is littered with thoughts and feelings about the significance of storying and fantasy in the lives of young children in a kindergarten classroom. The reader is left in no doubt as to Paley's personal commitment to continuing to try to make sense of the children's stories and to the importance of reflecting on practice.

JOURNALING AS THE MAIN TOOL IN DATA GATHERING

While journaling is a useful tool in documenting the researcher's feelings and thoughts during the research process, it is also a useful tool in itself, as a prime method of data gathering. The Research in Focus section earlier, which highlighted Papen's work, illustrated one such example. It is to this that the chapter now turns.

Brown and Jones (2001) see writing as central to action research as opposed to the use of other methods such as questionnaires. Through writing, they argue, the writer (practitioner-researcher) is commentating on and responding to changes they have made to their practice as well as reflecting on what any future actions might be. They maintain that the practitioner-researcher evolves in the context of their ever-evolving place of work. As you can see, this is a far cry from the positivist concern with developing a universally agreed understanding of an issue that is relevant for all time and in all contexts.

We can also see this rejection of positivism in Richardson and Adams St Pierre's (2005: 961) discussion of writing. They claim that 'language does not "reflect" social realities but rather produces meaning and creates social reality'. In addition, they argue that 'language constructs one's subjectivity in ways that are historically and locally specific' (2005: 961).

— 💡 —— REFLECTION POINT ———————————————

There are some complex ideas being expressed here about writing and language, not least that its meaning is not fixed in a way that can be understood by everyone in the same way for all time in different contexts. It is a viewpoint that is strongly allied to the post-structuralist position on language. Let us think about this in relation to a concrete example: smacking young children. There are many discourses that exist around this, with some occupying a more powerful position for particular individuals owing to a range of factors such as their childhood experiences, experience of parenting, work with young children in some capacity, locally accepted practice at that point in history, and so on. Here are some you may have come across:

- 'A smack never did me any harm when I was a child.'
- 'It's OK to smack *young* children - it's all they understand.'
- 'Professionals should not smack young children but it is alright in the context of a loving home environment.'
- 'It is children's right to be protected from harm just like we would protect adults from harm.'
- 'It's the right of every parent to care for their children in their own way - it is not the job of professionals to tell families what to do in the privacy of their own homes.'

(You should note that these are but a few of the many discourses that are taken up [or rejected] in relation to smacking - we are sure you could add to these.)

Reflect on the different ideas being expressed here about what it is to be a child and a parent and the role of the state in supporting children and families. You might also like to reflect on the issue of smacking in relation to different aspects of your life; that is, some early years practitioners would be horrified at the idea of smacking children in their professional work but believe it is acceptable to smack their *own* children. You may also like to deepen your reflection on this issue, if you feel able to, by journaling your thoughts and reflecting on why you hold the position(s) that you do. Try also to journal some competing positions to disrupt your initial thoughts on this issue in order to offer an alternative story. Journaling, as we shall see, can be a very useful tool in doing this.

A key advantage of journaling is that it enables the researcher to re-enter the same story and reinterpret that story in the light of new understandings and experiences. This might be an ongoing process as you might look at a piece of writing many times and interpret it differently each time. You may, for example, look at your journaling about the issue of smacking on another occasion and think differently about what you had written previously. The new insights and interpretations could also be noted in the journal in order to deepen your understanding of this complex issue. As Richardson and Adams St Pierre (2005: 962) note, writing enables us to know ourselves and 'explore new ways of knowing', acknowledging that we are all constantly in a process of creating ourselves. Moon (2006) also emphasises the way that a journal reflects the changing ideas and ongoing learning of the writer. In essence, inevitably, we change!

It would seem, then, that the use of journaling in research acknowledges the complexity of issues, in our case in relation to early childhood. In Chapter 11 we noted this in relation to early childhood practice. In writing, the 'up close and personal' nature of the inquiry is rarely easy and the use of journaling also welcomes data into the research that may not always be written about. Adams St Pierre (in Richardson and Adams St Pierre) variously refers to this as 'dream data, sensual data, emotional data, response data and memory data' and discusses how she uses writing to think by writing her 'way into particular spaces' (2005: 970). She highlights the importance of this because she maintains that other data-collection methods such as interviewing, on their own, do not document *everything* that is important in a research project. The next section looks at some tools that might enable the writer to write their 'way into particular spaces' and deepen their reflection on the issues with which they are concerned.

TOOLS TO HELP DEVELOP REFLECTIVE JOURNAL WRITING

So far in this chapter we have discussed a range of ways that journaling might be used in research. In this section, the aim is to provide an introduction to some of the many creative ideas that have been developed to encourage deeper reflection in journal writing. A couple of these are outlined in the following Activity section.

 ACTIVITY

Richardson and Adams St Pierre (2005) offer a range of interesting ideas for creating what they term 'analytical writing practices'. We think some of these could be useful in early childhood research. You should note here that we are relating these tasks to those of you that *work* with young children and families, but the tasks could easily be amended to other contexts.

(Continued)

(Continued)

Activity 1

Consider a particular setting, for example, a children's centre. Think about the range of subject positionings you have or have had in that centre. As an example, this might include being a parent of a child in the centre, taking the lead in running parenting classes, organising fund-raising events in the evenings in the centre, and studying for an early childhood qualification. Thus, one might (*now or in the past*) be a team leader, a parent, a fund-raiser, a student. We could also add being a Black woman or a lone parent or 'green' activist (whatever subject positionings you might apply to yourself). Write about the children's centre from these different perspectives and consider what you 'know' from these various subject positions. Richardson and Adams St Pierre (2005: 975) then recommend that you let these different points of view enter into dialogue with each other and reflect on what you learn through these dialogues. But more than this, they ask the writer to consider what this tells them about social inequities in the particular context chosen - in this instance, a children's centre.

Activity 2

Another analytical writing practice suggested by Richardson and Adams St Pierre (2005: 975) is one which consists of writing about something that has happened to you from your own perspective - we are suggesting that it might be something that relates to your work with young children and families. Then interview another participant in this story - it might be someone from a different professional group or another person in your team, for instance, depending on the story chosen to write about. As the writer, you need to try to see yourself as part of the participant's story in the same way as they are part of your own story. Now think about how you could rewrite the story from the participant's point of view and the challenges this raises.

The analytical writing practices outlined in the Activity box may certainly prove challenging, but could offer valuable opportunities to interrogate practice and recognise alternative avenues for interpretation. This might be especially important in the area of multi-agency working, which is recognised as being complex owing to variations in the way different agencies and professionals understand and put into practice issues relating to – in our case – working with children and families (Anning et al., 2006).

Moon (2006) devotes a chapter to activities designed to enhance journal writing. In one section she encourages the writer to work on self-improvement and problem-solving through journaling. Through writing about solving a problem, the writer also learns about the *process* of problem-solving. This might be a useful strategy to employ as part of an action research project where improving practice is central as its aim. She also suggests strategies such as using a SWOT analysis of an event, project or situation. By this, she means reviewing this event, project or situation in terms of its strengths (S), then weaknesses (W), then thinking through the opportunities (O) it offers and the threats (T) to making possible changes.

Earlier in the chapter we looked at how 'critical incidents' might be useful in deciding on a focus for a research project. Tripp (1993: 44–54) outlines a range of ways in which they might be used. Here are some of them:

THE 'WHY?' CHALLENGE

This, as the title suggests, involves subjecting the incident deemed 'critical' to ongoing 'why?' questions. This can help the writer to progressively challenge their beliefs relating to a particular incident.

DILEMMA IDENTIFICATION

Tripp (1993) maintains that many critical incidents involve a dilemma or a series of dilemmas. An examination of these can be helpful in enabling the practitioner to deal more effectively with it next time but, importantly, it helps her/him to see that the source of these dilemmas is not always of their own making. In early childhood, an example might be that a practitioner writes about a critical incident when s/he was torn between meeting the needs of an individual child, who wanted her or him to read a particular story near to home time. The practitioner felt unable to do this because of the perceived competing demands of ensuring the nursery room was tidied up and the children got ready for home time.

PERSONAL THEORY ANALYSIS

This can help deepen the analysis of the dilemma identification because here the writer reflects on their personal theories and the way they influence their professional judgements. Any decisions made in relation to dilemmas have their basis in a range of often unstated values and these can be opened up to scrutiny through reflective writing. If we take the example outlined in the previous section – a practitioner torn between meeting the needs of an individual child and the need to get a task done in a particular time frame – this might involve reflecting on fundamental questions about the individual vs. group and children vs. tasks to be done.

POSSIBILITIES AND LIMITATIONS OF USING JOURNALING AS A RESEARCH TOOL

So far in this chapter, we have thought about how a journal might be used as an *aid* to the research and as an actual *method* in itself. We have also explored some of the tools that might be useful in encouraging the writer to develop a greater degree of reflection in their journaling. This final section summarises some of what we see are the possibilities and limitations of using journaling as a research tool.

First, the action of writing enables the writer to slow down their thoughts and in so doing it may seem as if the world slows down long enough to take stock (Brown and Jones, 2001). This can be very useful, but the time this takes up can also be its downfall (Moon, 2006). After all, if something takes time it can be easy to think of excuses for not doing it. But we should remember that any methods that are employed in research will take time. The use of any data-gathering instrument will involve time and effort, not least in developing the understanding and skills needed to be able to use it effectively. This leads to our second point.

We should be mindful that keeping a journal in itself does not necessarily mean that the entries will be reflective. It may well be that early attempts at writing are descriptive and the writer may need to practise journaling in order to improve the level of reflection it might engender (Moon, 2006). The use of a range of different tools to enhance the reflection is recommended in this chapter as this enables writers to go beyond merely outlining an event, situation or project to a position that asks questions of it and, crucially, asks questions of them personally.

Thirdly, the use of journaling as a research tool could be regarded as narcissistic or overly self-indulgent. DeVault (1997: 225), for instance, expresses a concern that 'the recent emphasis on the personal may signal a retreat from the attempt to interpret a wider social world'. However, the corollary of this is that voices that are sometimes excluded or on the margins might be given a central platform. Examples of groups of people whose experience has often been marginalised might include lone parents, Black women or travellers. But while journaling seems a highly promising avenue for research, we should recognise that this might reinforce journaling as a tool for those marked out as 'others' (DeVault, 1997). DeVault goes on to argue that it is important that personal writing is located within a larger picture – the situations that produced and continue to produce the story. Sometimes people talk about this as 'situating oneself' (Letherby, 2003: 143). Letherby (2003) is positive about writing about oneself in research, drawing upon Okley's work to make a distinction between 'self-adoration' and 'self-awareness and a critical scrutiny of the self' (p. 143). We believe this is an important distinction to emphasise as a justification for using journaling as a research tool.

Therefore, on a positive note, journaling is attributed with developing greater self-awareness in researchers in relation to their thoughts and feelings, biases, responses and behaviours (Etherington, 2004). However, Etherington also acknowledges that in autoethnographic approaches to research, which put the self firmly at the centre, there is an inevitable *telling of the stories of others*. If we think about a concrete example here, in journaling about one's experience of working in an early years setting, a practitioner is likely to be telling a story about the children, families and colleagues with whom s/he works. Thus, there are ethical implications associated with doing this in terms of consent and anonymity.

 —— **REFLECTION POINT** ——————————————

Shahrusaad used journaling extensively as a research tool in her student project examining the process of change in her nursery (for 3–5-year-old children) as it moved to admitting 2-year-old children. Her own role in the nursery was as a practitioner responsible for a small group of children: she did not hold a leadership position in relation to other members of staff, e.g. as a line manager. Shahrusaad was especially keen to document her own feelings towards this process – both towards the shift of focus to include 2-year-old children in the provision and how this change was managed.

In documenting her thoughts and feelings, her journal contained detailed entries which were both positive and negative about the shift towards including 2-year-old children in the provision and the process of change. Shahrusaad found herself at odds with many other practitioners, who were often disparaging in relation to extending their provision to include this younger age group. She had promised from the outset to share her written project (not her personal journal, it should be noted) with the participants in the study, but was torn between wanting her written project to reflect the difficulties in making this shift in practice but also writing in such a way that it did not offend the participants, who were also members of her team. Shahrusaad had to tread a fine line here because, although anonymised, when talking about 'the manager', for example, the identity of the manager would be clear to all. Moreover, she took pains to recognise that she was writing an academic piece of work, which requires a high degree of reflection and rigour as opposed to writing something analogous to a rant about her colleagues.

An example of the way she incorporated her journal entries into her written-up project is as follows:

It has been documented that practitioners working with the birth to three age group are often viewed as 'less professional' than those working with older children. This harks back to long-standing debates about the status of 'care' in relation to 'education' in early childhood practice (Manning-Morton, 2006). My research journal (11.11.13 entry) noted:

(Continued)

(Continued)

> 'At a team meeting today, two practitioners said they didn't want to be spending all day changing nappies. It's as if they only see working with children aged 2 years in negative terms but also in terms of care routines. Whilst I think care routines are very important, I found myself arguing that there is far more to working with 2-year-old children than just nappy-changing.'

You can see from this short extract that Shahrusaad has included some reference to academic debates about professionalism in early childhood as well as the status of the birth-to-three practitioner. Her journal entry is written like a quote which could have been taken from an interview transcript and is dated but she omits the names of the practitioners involved. The text also makes it clear that this snippet of data comes from her *journal* (particularly important if you are using a mix of methods). Finally, the journal extract is clearly linked to the topic she has introduced. When you are writing up your research findings, whatever source of data you are drawing from, this is essential.

A consideration of ethics also needs to be thought through in terms of the researcher. In becoming the *subject* for the research, there is no anonymity for the researcher. In this sense, opening oneself up to scrutiny in research could be regarded as emotionally dangerous (Letherby, 2003). Letherby (2003) notes this in relation to her own work, stating that this has an impact upon the decisions she takes as to what to include and exclude in her published work. This might impact on any research findings. However, this charge could also be levelled at other methods such as interviewing and questionnaires. Research participants will pick and choose the aspects of their lives they want to share with a researcher. In doing this, they will inevitably leave some things out.

We hope you can see that there are many ideas about using journaling as a research tool. As with any other method, journaling is a tool that has possibilities as well as limitations for the researcher. We believe that journaling is useful for *all* researchers in order to document their feelings and thoughts in relation to a range of issues to do with their research. In terms of being a central mode of data collection, it may be particularly useful in action research studies in relation to early childhood where the researcher is also a practitioner.

 KEY POINTS FROM THE CHAPTER

- The self of the researcher is now considered to be a legitimate subject for research.
- Journaling during the research process can help the researcher to reflect on thoughts and feelings related to the research as and when they arise.

(Continued)

- Journaling itself can also be seen as a research tool. This is especially the case in research that is linked to professional practice, such as in action research.
- A key use of a journal is the way it can enable the researcher to re-enter stories and reinterpret them in the light of their new experiences and understandings – in the recognition that ideas are in constant flux. In this way, journaling can act in a way to disrupt 'common-sense' or present thinking about a given topic or situation and encourage the writer to consider alternative or competing stories.

FURTHER READING

Etherington, K. (2004) *Becoming a Reflexive Researcher: Using Ourselves in Research.* London: Jessica Kingsley. An interesting book on the subject from an author with a counselling and psychotherapy background.

Papen, U. (2008) 'Pregnancy starts with a literacy event: pregnancy and antenatal care as textually mediated experiences', *Ethnography*, 9(3): 377–402. This article (discussed in this chapter) provides an example of autoethnography and how journaling can be used in research.

Richardson, L. and Adams St Pierre, E. (2005) 'Writing: a method of inquiry', in N. Denzin and Y. Lincoln (eds) *The Sage Handbook of Qualitative Research*, 3rd edition. London: Sage. A far more challenging read than the other texts mentioned here, but a chapter that is highly thought-provoking about the uses of writing in research.

Don't forget to visit the online resources at
https://study.sagepub.com/mukherjiandalbon3e for access to free SAGE journal articles, weblinks, videos, exercises, mini quizzes and an interactive glossary.

17

CREATIVE METHODS FOR LISTENING TO CHILDREN IN RESEARCH

CHAPTER OBJECTIVES

- To further develop the idea that research can involve children directly as participants.
- To consider what might be meant by the idea of 'creative methods'.
- To think about a range of research methods that might directly elicit young children's views.
- To reflect upon the possibilities and limitations of such methods.

In Chapter 7 of this book, we discussed the development of research that involves listening to and engaging directly with children in research. This is linked to the growth of work which stresses the need for children's views to be sought on matters that affect them, following the UN Convention on the Rights of the Child. Crucially, the emergence of participatory research can be viewed as a challenge to thinking that has positioned children as passive in research (Veale, 2005) or has regarded children – especially young children – as incompetent and unreliable research participants (Warming, 2005). Indeed, Malewski (2005: 221) argues that children often offer the 'cleverest voices' in research.

The development of research in this area can be seen in the increasing number of publications that focus on the use of children-centred methods that involve children *directly* in the research process, as well as research that reports on studies that have been carried out *with* children. You will read about a few of these studies as you work through the chapter.

Our purpose in this chapter is to outline some of the 'creative' approaches to listening to young children in research that have been developed – with a focus on early childhood. In doing this, we recognise that there has been significant growth in this area over the past few years and there are likely to be many other interesting methods that have been used but not reported here. We include a discussion about children's drawing and photography here rather than in the chapter that looks at using documents in research because here we want to focus on using these tools as an *active* strategy rather than what Robson (2011a: 347) describes as an 'unobtrusive measure'.

LISTENING TO YOUNG CHILDREN IN RESEARCH: DEVELOPING AN INCLUSIVE APPROACH

We begin this chapter by reiterating our commitment to the development of strategies that involve young children as participants in research. Before looking more directly at methods that might be used in order to do this, we will outline what 'creative listening' might mean. We will then think about this in relation to research carried out with young children and make the case for developing inclusive methods in research.

Roberts-Holmes (2011) links the notion of 'creative listening' to young children to the Hundred Languages of Children – a term used in Reggio Emilia to denote the many ways that children 'speak' to us about their experiences, perceptions and concerns using music, talk, sculpture and painting, for example. He argues that researchers need to be receptive to these many languages in order to elicit children's perspectives.

A commitment to not only listening to but also to *hearing* young children is a theme that also runs throughout Soto and Swadener's (2005) edited book on research with children. With this in mind, Malewski (2005: 219) argues for 'precocious methodologies' in research with children. By this, he is referring to methods that empower children and young people and offer a challenge to traditional practices in research that have had a tendency to ignore the lived experiences of particular children in particular sociocultural contexts. For Veale (2005), participatory or creative methods that involve children in research offer a challenge to traditional ideas about research, such as positivism, because they combine both scientific rigour with imagination and creativity.

Before we move on to discuss some of these creative methods, it is important to note that we are aware that the development of innovative approaches to involving young children in research can also be criticised, at times, for falling into the trap of being a 'gimmick approach' (Dockett and Perry, 2007: 50). As with any methods chosen, they need to be 'fit for purpose'. It should also be noted here that we believe that interviewing children continues to be a significant method in early childhood research, once young children are able to do this. Similarly, we think that observation continues to be a key research tool, particularly when carrying out research with very young children and babies. Chapters 12 and 13 looked at these research tools.

Malewski (2005) is critical of methods that are underpinned by a belief that children's perceived unpredictability and naivety should be compensated for in some way. This is also a position Christensen and Prout (2002) critique in their notion of 'ethical symmetry' (also discussed in Chapters 6 and 7), as there is an assumption a priori that children require something different from adults in research. While we agree that researchers should not underestimate children's abilities, we do think the researcher has a responsibility to develop methods that are suited to children's current or persistent interests and their perceived level of knowledge and understanding, and this requires particular knowledge of particular children in a particular context – the 'tactics' of research (Christensen and Prout, 2002). This has resonance for *early childhood* research owing to the vulnerability of young children and, on occasions, their parents/carers (Langston et al., 2004). An example of this might be that we would not usually expect a child aged 2 years to be able to participate in an interview that includes complex questions worded with an older, more experienced person in mind. Similarly, we would not expect a 2-year-old child to sit in one place for an extended length of time for an interview as we might most adults (although we should not assume this is impossible for *all* 2-year-olds). This also links to Alderson's (2005) work on ethical research with children and her belief that it is wrong to put children in a position which is difficult for them – one that possibly highlights what they do not know and cannot do as opposed to what they do know and can do. Therefore, the researcher needs to ensure that the methods they choose to use are appropriate for the particular children participating in the research (Greene and Hill, 2005). We would add the caveat here that this is important for adults too.

We would also want to note here that what might work with one group of children or one child on one occasion, might not be a successful research strategy on another occasion. For those of you who have had direct experience of caring for young children, this might seem like a truism. This is not an argument for the 'special' or different nature of young children, but a recognition that adults and children alike are not fixed entities, with fixed emotions and fixed ideas. Research participants, like the researcher and the context in which the research is carried out, are ever changing.

REFLECTION POINT

What challenges does the argument that people and contexts are changeable hold for researchers?

In thinking through the question raised in this Reflection Point, you may have reflected that the changeable nature of human ideas, feelings and behaviours is problematic for researchers working within the positivist paradigm, who aim for uncovering 'truths' about the world.

So far we have made the case that researchers might employ a range of creative methods in order to involve children directly as *participants* in research. Before looking at some of these methods, it is important to stress the importance of developing research methods that are inclusive of *all* children. This can be difficult in research where collective participation is the chosen approach, such as in the use of drama and role play, because inequities can be masked by the research process (Veale, 2005). An example might be a child who does not participate equally in a particular aspect of a research project owing to differentials in class, gender, ethnicity or ability in comparison with other group members. As with any method employed in research, if some children – and indeed adults – are unable to participate in the research for some reason, this may result in a silencing of their perspectives. This, in turn, is likely to impact on the validity of the research findings.

What follows in this chapter is a discussion of a range of creative methods that might be employed when carrying out research that involves children *directly*.

PHOTOGRAPHY

Photography is a tool that has been employed creatively in research projects with young children. Cook and Hess (2007: 32), in their discussion of three research projects involving children using cameras, summarise the key benefits as:

- Using cameras is an engaging strategy for children.
- Acceptable results can be produced by young children with modern equipment.
- As young children are able to operate many modern cameras, they are able to be in control of what they take pictures of. Thus, the resulting pictures are likely to reflect the children's interests and concerns.
- Using photographs is a more tangible strategy than direct interviewing, particularly if the topic under discussion is complex or abstract. This is an important point to consider in research with young children.
- Photographs enable the researcher to return to a topic at a later date as they act as a visual prompt for the children.
- Photographs can be used when writing up a research project, making the resulting work accessible and interesting to the children.

However, we need to be cautious in using cameras. Roberts-Holmes (2011) argues that a delay in printing out photographs can mean a loss of interest in the subject matter by the children. He points to the ethical issues involved in taking photographs of children, advising that permission is sought from practitioners (including the manager), parents and carers and children themselves. In addition, when thinking about photography, the researcher should also consider ownership of the photographs. Children should be given a copy of photographs they have taken or that have been taken of them.

 CASE STUDY

Anna's research for her Early Childhood Studies degree project aimed to look at the benefits of using a forest school on a weekly basis for a term with a reception class. She decided to adopt a multi-method approach to address issues of triangulation, including using children's drawings, observations of the children, discussions with the children in small groups, parent questionnaires before and after the forest school programme, interviews with practitioners, and making use of digital cameras with the children.

Anna encouraged the children to use the digital cameras to take photographs of the things they were interested in on their visits to the wooded area. She used the photographs as points for discussion on return to the classroom, asking the children to tell her why they had taken a particular picture. Here are some examples of comments children made:

- Daniel had taken a photograph of a large red flower. He said 'I like it – it's really beautiful'.
- Seema had taken a photograph of some rubbish and stated 'There shouldn't be rubbish in *our* wood'.

(Continued)

(Continued)

- Thomas had taken a photograph of a pile of sticks and assorted materials with a group of children building a den from them. He observed that the picture was of 'my friends making a den'.
- Hamdi had taken some photographs of children jumping from a large log, noting, 'I like jumping off the logs'.

From these comments and other data gathered with the children, such as drawings and interviews, Anna began to identify a few themes. These were as follows:

- Children appreciated the aesthetic quality of the wooded area.
- Over the period of the project, the children began to talk of the wood as 'our wood' as opposed to 'the wood'. Anna saw this as important in the children's developing sense of ownership and stewardship towards the natural world.
- The children enjoyed having the opportunity to work together on mini-projects such as building dens which encouraged a cooperative approach to learning.
- The children appreciated the opportunity for physical challenge that the wooded area offered.

Alongside writing up her project for an adult audience, Anna made a book with the children based on the children's participation in the project and this is now kept in the book area so the children can look at it and recall what they had done. In this way, Anna had thought through how the findings of her project could be disseminated to the child-participants as well as for the adult audience. We will be looking at data analysis as well as writing up a research project in the final part of this book.

DRAWINGS

Children's drawings have a history of being used as a tool to assess their cognitive and/or emotional functioning (Veale, 2005). Some of you may be familiar with the 'draw-a-man' test devised by Goodenough (1926), for instance. But drawings can also be regarded as a tool that might be employed creatively in early childhood research.

Roberts-Holmes (2011) argues that drawings are a powerful means through which children represent their feelings and explore and learn. Moreover, they offer a means for children to communicate meanings about topics that have meaning for them. Veale (2005), for instance, comments on their usage in research with children in countries that have been affected by war and violence, such as Croatia and Rwanda.

Young children of varied abilities seem to enjoy painting and drawing, therefore these may be useful inclusive and participatory tools to employ in research (Roberts-Holmes, 2011). However, they are unlikely to be useful as a method in research with babies and very young children, for instance.

Drawings made by others might also be employed as a research tool. Veale (2005) discusses the use of a drawing of a happy girl and boy and a drawing of a sad girl and boy in encouraging children to discuss what the drawn figures might be thinking. She points out that the youngest children in her study tended to prefer free drawing as opposed to a drawing session (or indeed other activities) structured by adults. The youngest children in her study were 7 years old – at the top of the age range that might be considered 'early childhood'. Thus, while we would not want to make generalisations for all children based on age, we should be mindful of the ages of the child participants (and other valuable information on participants such as gender) when we examine published research.

In addition to this, we should remember that the use of children's drawings has other limitations – like any other method. One such criticism is that children need to be familiar with drawing as a medium of expression in order for it to be employed effectively (Veale, 2005). After all, we should remember that drawing is only one of the 'Hundred Languages' or means through which children represent their lives. Another charge that could be levelled at their use is that drawings might be open to multiple interpretations. However, as we have noted elsewhere in this book, this could also be said of observation and interview data, for instance. Therefore it is crucial that researchers employing drawing as a method encourage children to *talk* about their drawings. Not to do so would mean that any analysis of the drawings would be purely on the basis of the researcher's interpretation of what they may or may not signify and this is likely to be problematic. It also seems to go against the spirit of *listening* to children in the research. However, this too is not without criticism, not least the charge that it is the medium of language through which access to the children's views is elicited (Barker and Weller, 2003).

RESEARCH IN FOCUS

Angelides and Michaelidou (2009) carried out research using children's drawings as a tool to help them to understand young children's feelings of marginalisation. The use of drawings and the children's talk about them was viewed as a key strategy in 'giving voice' to children's experience of marginalisation and exclusion. The researchers define 'marginalisation' in terms of whether a child occupies a position that is marginal *academically* or *socially* (2009: 30).

(Continued)

(Continued)

The research was conducted in a class of 22 children aged 5 years in Cyprus, with the researchers visiting the school twice a week for a four-month period. After spending time getting to know the children and staff, Angelides and Michaelidou spent time with the children in small groups engaging them in drawing using a range of media. They were given a topic, 'the break', as a basis for their drawing, chosen to enable the children to express the feelings they had towards break times. The resulting drawings were discussed with the children who had drawn them. Alongside this strategy, all the children were interviewed.

When analysing the data from these phases in the research, Angelides and Michaelidou identified six children who seemed to be saying that they had experienced marginalisation. These children were then asked to draw whatever they wanted. Figures 17.1 and 17.2 are two of the drawings that came from this study plus a synopsis of what was said about them.

Figure 17.1 'It's break time and the rabbit is playing. It is playing with the games ... they do not want it to be their friend' (Angelides and Michaelidou, 2009: 39, reproduced with permission)

(Continued)

The child who drew the picture in Figure 17.1, Peter, told the researchers that he had only drawn one rabbit because no one wanted to be its friend. Angelides and Michaelidou suggest that he is expressing his own feelings of isolation at break times, projecting his own feelings of marginalisation into his drawing of a rabbit. They had noted that Peter was a quiet child in the class, who often had games taken away from him and rarely participated in activities or class discussions with his peers.

The child who drew the picture in Figure 17.2, Maria, was new to the school and seemed to have difficulties in making friends. A constant theme in her pictures was a sun playing with a girl. In this picture, we can see *two* girls. Maria told one of the researchers that the girl (who is closer to the sun in the picture) is playing with the sun. When asked whether the other girl was also playing with the sun, Maria replied 'No, she is Christiana, and she is far away in Greece. Only this girl is playing with her friend the sun' (Angelides and Michaelidou, 2009: 42). When asked further about this, Maria told the researcher that the girl is playing with the sun because she has no friends – her friends being in Greece. Maria seems to have projected her feelings of isolation onto the girl playing with the sun, far away from the friends she had known and still misses.

Angelides and Michaelidou (2009: 43) do not propose any grand theory based on their research nor do they argue that their research strategy could uncover each instance of children's marginalisation. However, they maintain that 'children's drawings and discussions with their creators revealed many hidden dimensions of children's school life', amounting to a 'deafening silence'. As inclusion is an important concept in education, it would seem that strategies that enable children to express their experiences of isolation and marginalisation are vital in helping everyone involved in early childhood education better recognise, understand and address these issues in their practice.

Figure 17.2 'The sun plays with Maria' (Angelides and Michaelidou, 2009: 42, reproduced with permission)

PLAY AS A RESEARCH STRATEGY

Malewski (2005) argues that educational research methods have tended to down-play the significance of playfulness and imagination. Edmiston is a researcher who embraces play as a strategy that children and adults can participate in *together*, as opposed to play being seen as the preserve of young children to be observed at a distance by adults. By participating in children's play, Edmiston (2005, 2008) argues that researchers can share authority with children and, in so doing, raise and explore a range of issues that are important to them both.

RESEARCH IN FOCUS

USA

Edmiston (2005) carried out research over a number of years with his son, from when he was 2 years to 7 years, in the USA. Unlike other researchers who eventually leave the field once the research has finished (see Corsaro [1985], for instance, and the discussion of 'leaving the field' in Chapter 9 on ethnography), Edmiston acknowledges that in researching play with his son he had, and indeed still has, an ongoing relationship with the research participant.

Edmiston used play and his inquiry into it to enable him to explore his different understandings about play as well as his understandings of himself as an 'adult-father-researcher' (2005: 58). The vehicle of play enabled him to disrupt commonly held perceptions of what adult–child relationships should be. For instance, he was able to take on a range of non-hierarchical and/or 'silly' roles in play and both he *and* his son were able to direct and interpret the play events.

At the age of 4, his son became fascinated by the story of Dr Jekyll and Mr Hyde, and this became a constant theme in his play with his father. The play increasingly challenged Edmiston's strongly held views as a pacifist, such as whether it is acceptable to kill someone in certain situations, as he encountered a range of perspectives on this issue through the adoption of different roles in relation to the story. Play opened up a space for Edmiston and his son to explore different ideas and possible meanings around a range of issues of importance to them. Crucially, through play, by sharing authority with his son and using the potential of play to disrupt their understandings of particular issues, they came to far deeper understandings, but Edmiston recognises that any understandings reached are temporary and not conclusive.

Edmiston was therefore able to explore a range of issues that relate to children's play. These included reflecting on questions such as 'Should adults follow children's imaginative play wherever it leads?' or 'Should children be taught during play?' or 'Is play emotionally dangerous?' (2005: 72). In exploring questions of such significance to early childhood practice, it would seem that the action of playing and being playful with children is a valuable tool for research, not least because the direction of the research is *shared* between the adult and the child rather than decided upon in advance by the adult researcher. In this way, the approach could be regarded as similar to the notion of 'play-partnering' where adults and children alike might lead or follow the direction of the other (Bruce, 1991a), but is here applied to a research context.

In reading about Edmiston's approach, you may have made links to some of the ideas about participant observation and ethnography in earlier chapters.

STORY-TELLING AND NARRATIVE APPROACHES

Drawings, photographs and play are not the only strategies that can be used to gain children's perspectives. Hyder (2002) discusses the use of Persona Dolls, which enable children to talk about their feelings in an engaging way. Persona Dolls are used to encourage children to explore issues of equality and inclusion as each doll has a personal story attached to it. Hyder also recommends puppets as another tool that can be used to encourage children to discuss their feelings. In the following Research in Focus section, you will see that puppets were used in a study which aimed to find out how children experienced their care while undergoing treatment for cancer in hospital.

RESEARCH IN FOCUS

A study was carried out by Aldiss et al. (2009) across three centres providing cancer care for children in London, England. The study aimed to find out what was important to young children whilst in hospital undergoing treatment for cancer. The children in the study were aged between 4 and 5 years. The research highlights the importance of creative strategies such as play and the use of puppets as research tools. The researchers in this study argue that the use of creative methods such as these offered a window into the children's perspectives of cancer services – a group whose perspective had rarely been sought.

ENGLAND

Clearly, the researchers had to gain ethical approval for the study (as with any study) and the sensitivity of the topic for children and their families needed to be considered carefully. Children were at different stages in their treatment and understandably their parents were also undergoing a very difficult time in their lives at the time of the research. Thus, a great deal of thought was given not only in relation to ensuring the consent of the parents (in writing) and children (verbally) both before and at the start of the actual data-collection session, but also to attending to the verbal and non-verbal cues of the children as signals that they wanted to withdraw from the research. The researchers also ensured they used language familiar to the children. The use of puppets, the researchers argue, went some way to re-addressing the power imbalance between the (adult) researchers and (child) participants as the children did not have to interact directly with the researcher but via a familiar soft toy puppet. (You may want to reflect on the degree to which young children might suspend the idea that it is the adult-researcher who controls the puppet here.) Although each child received a small gift to thank them for their

(Continued)

(Continued)

participation, they were not aware of this prior to their participation in the research as it could have been viewed as a strategy intended to coerce the children to participate.

A play specialist was utilised to gather data alongside a researcher acting as observer. Eight children were interviewed at hospital and two at home. Soft toys ('Fizz' from the 'Tweenies') were used as puppets although two of the children opted not to use these. Although the interview with puppets lasted between 15 and 30 minutes, the session began with a Lotto game, comprising use of cards with faces expressing emotions to encourage talk about feelings related to being in hospital. One or both parents were in constant attendance during the session and they were invaluable in re-wording questions for their children (if needed) – indeed the research team suggest that supporting parents to become more directly involved as co-researchers would be a useful way forward in such research. An example of one of the questions asked was: 'Fizz has been having some special medicines, have you been having some special medicines? What's it like having your medicines?'

As is usual in qualitative research, the research team analysed the data for themes. You will find out more about how to do this in Chapter 18. Here, we wish to present the themes which emerged in this study. Six main themes were identified: (1) 'lots of toys'; (2) 'getting rid of the bad guys'; (3) nurses and doctors in the background; (4) mummy and daddy are near; (5) 'not being at home'; and (6) feelings about hospital.

When thinking about the staff in the hospital, it was interesting that the children could name the play workers and play specialists they had worked with, but could not name the nurses and doctors who provided their treatment. Indeed few children talked about their actual treatment, although some could use technical terms in relation to their treatment, e.g. 'Hickman line' or 'Port', and demonstrate why these were used. All children talked about the importance of having their mum or dad nearby and that they were the most important people in hospital, with nurses and doctors playing a more peripheral role. In addition, all children talked about the importance of having things to play with while in hospital, which the researchers assert may be linked to the value of play as an outlet for expressing emotions or in coming to terms with any treatment, but also as something 'normal' and linked to the children's lives away from hospital.

You might like to think of the implications of a qualitative study like this for practice. Whilst medical research focuses on finding treatments for cancers such as through drug trials or on how to prevent cancers, research such as that conducted by Aldiss et al. (2009) and presented here *also* plays a crucial role. Ensuring children are as comfortable and happy as possible while in hospital may well be critical in ensuring positive outcomes for their health or at least may contribute towards a less stressful time during palliative care.

In addition to this, story-telling is regarded as a useful research tool for engaging young children (Hyder, 2002). Children's *own* stories can also provide a focus for research. Some of you may be familiar with the work of Paley, who has written numerous books that document the stories and enactments of them that have taken place in her kindergarten classroom (Paley, 1981, 1990). Paley uses the medium of story because she believes it enables her to gain a window into children's thinking about a wide range of enduring concerns, such as the meaning of friendship. The children's collaborations, through storying, seem to demonstrate their desire to explore the complexity of these abiding human issues. An example of this can be seen in the title *Bad Guys Don't Have Birthdays* (Paley, 1991).

Sylva (1999) argues that Paley provides an ethnographic account that emphasises authenticity but cannot make claims about the impact of the storying approach on long-term development or be generalised to all classrooms. In thinking about the children's stories, which Paley transcribes on a regular basis, Paley reflects on what they mean for classroom practice and her own role as a kindergarten teacher. If you have not read any of her work we thoroughly recommend it as thought-provoking and very readable.

THE MOSAIC APPROACH

We finish this chapter with a discussion of the Mosaic Approach to listening to young children as it encompasses a range of different tools that piece together to form a fuller picture of young children's perceptions, for instance of their early childhood setting. It is an approach devised by Clark and Moss (2011) that aims at improving the work of early childhood settings by ensuring that the views of *all* the participants in the setting are included – adults and children alike. A strong emphasis is placed on a range of documentation processes including, for example, narrative observation, children's drawings, role play, discussions with the child's family and key person, and the use of cameras and walking tours.

The use of cameras in the Mosaic Approach aims to encourage children to document the people, places and events that have particular meaning for them. Walking tours may also include the use of cameras. Walking tours may involve one child and an adult or a group of children and an adult (or adults). A tour involves the child or group of children taking an adult on a tour of a given space and taking photographs along the way of what interests them or has particular meaning for them. The adult role on the tour is to allow the child(ren) to choose where to go and what to focus on and take photographs along the way. Once finished, the child(ren) may be encouraged to make their own drawing or map and place their own photographs on it (Clark and Moss, 2011). During the process of the tour and the possible resulting representation by the child(ren), adults should be asking questions that are sensitive to the child(ren)'s concerns. In this sense, Roberts-Holmes (2011: 135) likens a walking tour to an 'interview on the move'.

The following Activity encourages you to think about a project employing the idea of the Mosaic Approach which made use of a particularly innovative research tool: the use of 'baby cams' as one of its methods of data collection.

— ACTIVITY ————————————————

Sumsion et al. (2011) undertook research in order to examine the perspectives of young infants (aged from birth to 18 months) on their childcare in Australia. Often, it is the perspectives of parents and professionals which inform understandings of issues relating to non-parental childcare; although children are very directly affected by provision, few studies have explored their perspectives. The researchers were committed to recognising the capabilities of the infants as social actors and active participants in the lives of their settings. But a key dilemma when researching the perspectives of babies and very young children is that this is a group which generally has not acquired the level of language skills needed to communicate their experiences verbally.

Sumsion et al., in the 'Infants' Lives in Childcare' project, made use of the Mosaic Approach to 'piece together fine-grained details of infants' experiences, generated from multiple sources of data and interpreted from multiple perspectives, to form what [they] hope will be a comprehensive picture of their lives in early years' settings' (Sumsion et al., 2011: 115). The study comprised a series of case studies of infants in 'family day care homes' and in four 'long day care centres'. Data were collected from infants, older children (on occasions), parents and carers using digital video footage and photography, observational field notes, time use diaries and vocabulary records.

A particularly innovative tool used was what the research team called a 'baby cam' – a micro video camera system – which comprised a video camera and sound recording equipment attached onto or indeed worn by the infant. This tool enabled children to 'speak' in ways that did not involve verbal language but enabled the researchers as well as parents and carers to view what the infant herself attended to as part of the wider research design.

Now think through the following questions:

- What technological problems can you envisage with the use of baby cams?
- What ethical issues are raised with such a tool, e.g. in relation to the infants themselves as well as those who are interacting with the infants? How might these be addressed?
- Why might it be important to involve parents, carers and researchers in the data analysis in such a project?

Elwick (2015), who writes about the same study, argues that by viewing what infants pay attention to, researchers and practitioners were prompted to (re)consider what they had felt to be the infants' concerns. For example, they found that infants spent a long time gazing at their peers, yet the field of early childhood is replete with writing which reifies *adult*-child relationships. In addition, viewing the images generated from the baby cam encouraged practitioners to review their practice as they saw themselves as seen by the infant. This in turn 'created possibilities for imagining and re-imagining infants and ECEC [early childhood education and care] practice differently' (Elwick, 2015: 335).

POSSIBILITIES AND LIMITATIONS OF CREATIVE METHODS FOR LISTENING TO CHILDREN

To conclude this chapter, one of the most important factors in developing creative methods that encourage the participation of young children is the ability of the researcher to engage the children with the process (Veale, 2005). It is possible, therefore, that personal and/or professional experience of caring for young children might be an advantage for researchers hoping to research in this way. This is because researchers with this kind of experience are likely to have a greater understanding of the types of activities children enjoy, as well as experience of interacting with children in relation to a range of child- and adult-initiated activities including play. Furthermore, early childhood practitioners may be particularly well placed to employ methods that involve leading a group, such as encouraging children to respond collectively to a group story, owing to their experience in leading similar sessions in their professional work.

However, we are mindful of what Gallacher and Gallacher (2008: 505–6) describe as the 'slippage between pedagogy and research'. Research differs from early childhood practice, not least as it is reported on beyond the setting, and negotiations of consent when research methods resemble classroom practice closely can be more difficult. One aspect of this relates to the power differentials between children and adult-educators (Waller and Bitou, 2011). This dynamic, if replicated in research activity (and there is – we contend – always a power dynamic in research), can be exacerbated when research and pedagogy are closely aligned, as children's participation may rely on their 'schooled docility' (Gallacher and Gallacher, 2008). By this, Gallacher and Gallacher are referring to the ways in which there are 'rules' of behaviour in early childhood and school settings, and how, generally, if a practitioner asks children to do something, they are expected to do it. Phelan (1997), for instance, argues that the ability to 'control' young children is a powerful discourse that operates in settings. Thus, it can be difficult for a child to withdraw their consent to a (research) activity as to do so would be to refuse to conform to the usual order of things in the classroom.

Possibly of more significance than the creative methods discussed in this chapter is having an ongoing relationship with a child or group of children as it can alert the researcher to children's persistent concerns and current interests (Albon and Rosen, 2014). Such a relationship might develop if a researcher is carrying out the research with children in his or her care or if the researcher is engaged in an ethnographic study involving extensive fieldwork. In both instances there is greater time for a relationship to develop between the researcher and the child(ren). A powerful example of this was outlined in this chapter, when we looked at Edmiston's (2005, 2008) research with his own son. Thus *time* can be a factor as it supports the development of the kinds of close relationships in which the creative methods outlined in this chapter might be employed successfully, although we would argue that negotiating relationships with children and adults is important in *any* research project and time does not necessarily lead to a 'good' relationship.

But it is important to note, in concluding this chapter, that 'hanging out' with children over time – hardly a novel method of research! – is likely to reward the researcher with greater insights into their lives as it allows the researcher to take advantage of those moments of naturally occurring talk and play as and when they happen (Lahman, 2008: 296). For Albon and Rosen (2014), this relates to the notion of *'being with'* children as opposed to presenting *'tasks to do'* with them (drawing on the work of Suissa, 2006). This point is further exemplified by Davis et al. (2008) who emphasise the use of everyday cultural practices in order to elicit children's perspectives rather than supposedly more 'innovative' practices. Perhaps what is important, then, is a commitment to finding ways of eliciting children's perspectives as a principle in research and this may or may not involve the 'creative' methods discussed in this chapter.

 KEY POINTS FROM THE CHAPTER

- There has been a growth in creative methods employed in research with young children.
- The development in creative methods for engaging children directly in research can also be allied to the idea that children are experts on their own lives and are able to act as participants in research. Thus, it is allied to the children's rights perspective.
- There are a wide variety of creative methods that might be used when researching with children. Here, we have focused on using photography, drawings, play and a range of other strategies, as well as an approach that combines methods known as the Mosaic Approach (Clark and Moss, 2011).
- Creative methods for involving young children in research may work best if employed by someone with experience of caring for young children as s/he is likely to have some knowledge of the kinds of activities that young children will find engaging as well as the ability to present them.
- As with any research, there are ethical issues that need careful reflection when employing creative methods. These include the reliance on language in some instances and also the power imbalance between children and adults, which might impact on the children's ability to withdraw their consent – especially as creative methods may resemble classroom activities.
- We should never forget that 'hanging out' with or 'being with' children over time is a useful strategy that may reward the researcher with an insight into issues of importance to those children.

FURTHER READING

Angelides, P. and Michaelidou, A. (2009) 'The deafening silence: discussing children's drawings for understanding and addressing marginalisation', *Journal of Early Childhood Research*, 7(1): 27–45. A thought-provoking article which exemplifies the use of drawings as a research tool.

Clark, A. and Moss, P. (2011) *Listening to Young Children: The Mosaic Approach*, 2nd edition. London: NCB and JRF. A significant book on the subject, not just in terms of early childhood research but of importance to practice too.

Sumsion, J., Harrison, L., Press, F., McLeod, S., Goodfellow, J. and Bradley, B. (2011) 'Researching infants' experiences of early childhood education and care', in D. Harcourt, B. Perry and T. Waller (eds) *Researching Young Children's Perspectives: Debating the Ethics and Dilemmas of Educational Research with Children*. Abingdon: Routledge. This chapter provides a fascinating account of a participatory research project with infants carried out in Australia using a range of methods. The use of 'baby cams' is especially noteworthy. The edited collection as a whole provides many other examples of participatory research with children.

PART 5

ANALYSING AND SHARING YOUR FINDINGS

So far in this book we have looked at the theory and principles which guide research and have discussed how these principles can be put into practice. You have learned about the research process and how to go about designing a research study by choosing the appropriate approaches and data-collection methods. In this final part of the book we look at how you analyse and make sense of the data that you have collected and how you disseminate your findings, focusing primarily on writing your research report.

As you conduct your research project, you may generate a mass of information in the form of observations, questionnaires, transcripts of interviews and journal entries. Chapter 18, by necessity a long chapter, discusses how to order the data so that they are ready for analysis. You will learn that quantitative data and qualitative data are analysed and presented differently, but that the overall aim is the same; that is to discover *themes* and *patterns* in the data and relate these to your overall research question, hypothesis or area of investigation. Data analysis is a dynamic and personal process, guided, as for all other aspects of the research process, by your underlying beliefs and attitudes. In the same way, writing up your research is not a neutral process.

Chapter 19, the final chapter, outlines some of the choices that have to be made to enable you to tell your research 'story' in a way that is appropriate to the research that you have undertaken. A piece of research stands or falls by the way that it is written up; after all, it is the only chance you have of persuading your 'audience' that the decisions and choices you have made throughout the research process have been based on a thorough understanding of the literature as well as research methodology and methods, and that your findings are reliable, valid and worthwhile.

18

ANALYSING AND PRESENTING DATA

---------------- **CHAPTER OBJECTIVES** ----------------

- To explore the meaning of 'analysis' in research.
- To consider how to analyse and present quantitative data.
- To consider how to analyse and present qualitative data.

When data have been collected, the next stage is to process the information so that the data can be reviewed to see if there is an answer to your research question, discover if you have proved or disproved your hypothesis, or to see what has been learnt about the research topic – depending on the type of research undertaken. Even before data have been collected, at the design stage, it is advisable to have thought ahead about how you will process and analyse the information obtained. In this chapter we will be looking at how to process and analyse data to enable you to present your findings and discuss them in relation to your original research aim(s).

We will see how the process of analysing data is dynamic; that there are decisions to be made which will reflect your underlying beliefs and feelings about the nature of research. These decisions will be informed by the underpinning paradigm which has guided your research, whether it is located within a positivist paradigm, using quantitative methodology or being guided by an interpretivist or post-structuralist paradigm, using primarily qualitative methodology. In this chapter, we will be looking at the two different approaches to analysing data: the quantitative approach, which concentrates on making sense of numerical data, and the qualitative approach that aims to come to an in-depth understanding of the topic under study. This chapter is designed to be an *introduction* to the subject as entire books are devoted to this topic, but it is necessarily a long chapter as there is a lot of basic ground to cover. When we look at how to analyse quantitative data we will be restricting the explanation to a discussion of descriptive statistics only.

WHAT DO WE MEAN BY ANALYSIS?

Once data have been collected using the methods chosen, such as interviews or observations, you may find yourself with a wealth of information. Somewhere in all of this data, organised or not according to the way you work, is to be found the answer to your research question, new insights into the area of investigation, or the proof or not of the hypothesis you are testing. Blaxter et al. (2010: 211) describe research 'as a messy business', and it is at this stage that you may feel it is at its most messy.

Data analysis is a way of summarising and describing your findings, and then seeing if you can find common patterns or themes (Roberts-Holmes, 2014). *Quantitative* approaches to research, which generate numerical data, lend themselves to statistical analysis; that is, the application of techniques that can process large amounts of numerical data and reveal trends. *Qualitative* approaches to research lend themselves to non-statistical techniques, aimed at revealing patterns in the information gathered, allowing you to understand the topic under study in greater depth.

Denscombe (2014) suggests that the aim of data analysis varies according to the objectives of the research study and identifies three possible aims: description, explanation and interpretation.

- *Description*, in terms of what, when, who and how often. Often the main focus of an ethnographic study or as a starting point for future research.
- *Explanation*, looking at how things are connected, why things happen and when they are likely to happen again. This is the aim of research which looks at cause and effect and is often used in psychology and education.
- *Interpretation*, looking at patterns which lie behind phenomena in an effort to gain a greater understanding rather than a universal truth. This is an approach taken by interpretivists who look at the data and ask such questions as: how and why things happened, who undertook the research and the effect that this may have on the findings, what was the context (social, historical, cultural, etc.) and what alternative theories exist (Denscombe, 2014: 275). Interpretivism is discussed in Chapter 5.

GETTING ORGANISED

Blaxter et al. (2010) differentiate between two different styles of working. Some students are highly organised; they have a clear action plan and timescale and they have all their notes filed and referenced, with their questionnaires filed all in one place and their observations and interviews already neatly transcribed. Other students may be more chaotic; their notes and files are in disarray, they may not be sure where they have put their completed questionnaires and they have not started transcribing their interviews or writing up their observations. Students should aim to be organised, not least because they have an ethical responsibility to ensure that the data they have obtained is stored securely. Moreover, data analysis requires that the information you have collected during your research is organised before you start. This might involve the following examples:

- Typing up information from notebooks or handwritten notes of observations, making sure that all the relevant details are included.
- Transcribing any electronic recordings of interviews and making sure relevant details are recorded on all observations.
- Checking that you have actually got all the information you require. Kumar (2014) suggests that even the most experienced researcher forgets to ask questions, record a response or write legibly. It may be that you have to go back to a particular respondent to get additional information. This is particularly the case with qualitative research, where ongoing analysis of data may indicate further avenues of research.

- Numbering each completed schedule if using a questionnaire. For example, if you have 20 questionnaires, number them 1–20. This will help with the analysis later on.
- Keeping your research journal up to date. During data collection, you will have thoughts and ideas about what the information is telling you, which will be very useful when it comes to analysing the data more systematically. This is especially important in qualitative research.

A review of these suggestions shows that you do not have to wait for *all* your findings to come in before you start organising the data. Research does not always fit into neat timelines and sensible researchers transcribe interviews and write up observations as they do them. Later in the chapter we will see that, for qualitative studies, data analysis may progress even before all the information is collected. Students are often dismayed to find out how long this aspect of research actually takes, so it makes sense to start as early as possible.

QUANTITATIVE METHODS OF DATA ANALYSIS

It is difficult to find answers to your research question or see if your research hypothesis can be accepted or rejected, with data in their raw form. There needs to be some way of summarising these data and presenting them in a way which helps you to understand the findings. There are four levels of quantitative analysis:

- descriptive statistics, which describe the data in terms of frequencies, averages and ranges
- inferential statistics, used when you are investigating to see if the difference between two groups is due to chance or not, by using tests of significance
- investigation of simple relationships between two variables such as correlations
- multivariate analysis, which looks at the effects of more than two variables (Blaxter et al., 2010: 238).

In this chapter we will be looking at how you can use *descriptive statistics* as a tool for analysing numerical data.

 — REFLECTION POINT

Review Part 4 of this book, which is concerned with *methods* of data collection. Which methods might involve the collection of *numerical* data?

At first glance, it may seem that only structured questionnaires, structured interviews and some types of observations such as time samples contain numerical data, but open questions in semi-structured questionnaires can be reduced to numerical data as well. For example, in a questionnaire about parents' satisfaction with the degree to which an early years setting communicates with them, there may be an open question at the end that asks '*What suggestions do you have that may improve the communication between the setting and parents?*' Although there will be a variety of responses, you are likely to find that the participants' responses fall into similar categories. For instance, you may find four parents who mention after-hours meetings, two may suggest communication by email and six may suggest newsletters.

One method of analysing the number of times a word appears in a document or a particular image appears on the television is content analysis.

CONTENT ANALYSIS

This approach arises primarily from the positivist position in relation to research, and tends to be quantitative in nature (Jupp and Norris, 1993). It might involve counting the number of times certain words or phrases are used in a text. For example, you could look at advertisements for baby milk and look for the number of references made to 'health' or 'good'. As Jupp and Norris (1993: 41) note, 'content analysis is typically concerned with the *manifest* content and surface meaning rather than with deeper layers of meaning' (original emphasis). Therefore, it is likely to look at *what is said* rather than *why people said it*, for instance. Importantly, the requirement in this type of research, as you will recall from Chapters 4 and 5, is that the variables are controlled in such a way that any researcher would arrive at the same results with the same set of documents (Silverman, 2013), be they newspaper headlines, minutes of meetings or sets of photographs.

 ACTIVITY

You can carry out a simple piece of content analysis by doing something like the following:

- Take a given number of books in a nursery book area – let us say 100 – and count the number of times there is an image of a child with a physical disability.
- Alternatively, you could look at a children's television channel for a given period of time (as another form of 'text') – let us say 2 hours – and, again, count the number of times you come across an image of a child with a physical disability.

(Continued)

(Continued)

In both instances, you would be controlling the number of books looked at or the period of time watched (known as the independent variables manipulated by you - the researcher; you may recall this terminology from Chapter 4). The number of images of children with a physical disability would be the dependent variable as this is what you - the researcher - are measuring. You can imagine, we are sure, how this approach to looking at documents can be applied to many different areas of focus, beyond that of images of children with a physical disability.

In doing this, consider what the data would be able to tell you and the limitations of this. As you know, there are always possibilities and limitations with any method chosen in research.

While content analysis has its uses, Silverman (2014) argues that qualitative research can offer much more than merely coding and counting data. He argues that qualitative researchers should aim for a deeper analysis of the texts that form the data set. One such approach to analysing texts is discourse analysis, which is described later in the chapter.

CODING QUANTITATIVE DATA

Transforming raw data into a numerical form, as in the example just described, is called 'coding' and is undertaken as early as possible in the research process. Sometimes coding decisions are made when the data-collecting instrument is being designed – for example, some structured questionnaires and interviews have the responses pre-coded, so findings can be input directly into the computer. You may be familiar with questionnaires containing items such as the following example. Here each response is given a code number, making analysis more straightforward.

Q1. What is your highest level of qualification or status relating to early years care and education? Please tick the appropriate box.

1. Early years practitioner (Vocational qualification)   ❒
2. Early years practitioner (Graduate qualification)   ❒
3. Early years teacher (Postgraduate qualification)   ❒

The following guidelines for coding information in quantitative analysis are suggested:

- *Codes must be mutually exclusive.* In other words, a response should only be able to be placed in one category. In the example we looked at that asked practitioners about their early childhood qualifications, it was important that they were asked to give their *highest* level of qualification, to ensure that the categories were mutually exclusive (Blaxter et al., 2010; Kumar, 2014).

- *The categories should be exhaustive.* When coding the findings from open questions, every response should be placed in a category. Previously we discussed an open question: *'What suggestions do you have that may improve the communication between the setting and parents?'* As we discussed, responses will vary, but it will be possible to group suggestions into categories, which can be coded. For example, some respondents may mention newsletters; some may suggest home/setting books; other respondents may request meetings after hours; whilst others may mention email contact. Each of these categories should be coded, with no suggestions left out (Blaxter et al., 2010; Kumar, 2014).
- *Codes must be applied consistently.* Thus, if coding a particular response in a particular way at the start of data analysis, all subsequent, similar responses should be given the same code (Blaxter et al., 2010). This is vital in terms of reliability.

In order to further exemplify how to code an open question in a semi-structured questionnaire, we will continue to use as an example the question, *'What suggestions do you have that may improve the communication between the setting and parents?'*

1. Draw up a chart similar to that in Table 18.1. You could do this straight onto a computer if you want, or use a sheet of paper.
2. Go through the responses for the question for the first respondent (R1). Write down the suggestions made in the 'suggestions' column, and indicate with a tick in the R1 column that these suggestions belong to R1.
3. Take the second questionnaire and look to see if this respondent has made similar suggestions. If yes, then indicate with a tick in the R2 column. If the respondent has suggestions not on your list, add them to the suggestion column and put a corresponding tick in the R2 column.
4. Carry on in the same way for every questionnaire.

Table 18.1 An example of how to code an open question

Q.10 What suggestions do you have that may improve the communication between the setting and parents?

Code	Suggestion	R1	R2	R3	R4	R5	R6	R7
1	Newsletters	✓	✓		✓			✓
2	Email	✓		✓		✓		
3	Meetings in evening	✓	✓		✓			✓
4	Meetings during day		✓		✓			
5	Telephone contact			✓		✓		
6	Home/setting book							✓

GROUPING THE DATA

Once all the responses have been coded, the next task is to group data together. For example, you may have wanted to find out how many babies younger than 6 months of age are in daycare settings in a particular locality. You send a questionnaire to each setting and as they are returned you record the findings:

Number of babies below 6 months of age in each setting

0 3 1 3 5 2 0 2 1 5 2 0 0 1 4 6 4 1 0 3

In this format it is difficult to discern much of a pattern, so the first thing you could do is to arrange the data into some sort of order. Denscombe (2010: 246) calls this constructing 'an array of the raw data'.

Number of babies below 6 months of age in each setting

0 0 0 0 0 1 1 1 1 2 2 2 3 3 3 4 4 5 5 6

Immediately, it is easier to see that most settings have very few infants who are below 6 months of age. Denscombe (2010: 246) suggests that a further refinement is to convert the data array into a tally of the frequency, or number of times that particular values occur.

Number of babies below 6 months of age in each setting	
Number of babies	**Frequency**
0	5
1	4
2	3
3	3
4	2
5	2
6	1

 —— REFLECTION POINT ——————————

Consider the data set that we have been using. Do you think we have all of the information we need to come to any sensible conclusion about the number of young babies in early years settings?

I expect you have concluded that just knowing *how many* very young babies there are in a setting does not tell us very much. For example, we are not given the details about the kind of setting; nursery classes in primary schools or pre-school settings probably only take children from about the age of 3, so some of the settings with no very young babies may *never* take them. Even in settings where they are set up to care for babies of this age, the number they take depends upon the size of the establishment. A small nursery may only have places for one or two young babies. It is likely that this information is to be found within the questionnaires somewhere, and should be used when grouping the information. For example, the data set could be based on the percentage of children in a setting under 6 months of age, and data from nursery classes and pre-schools could be left out. Decisions about what data to process and how to process it have a real impact on the usefulness of your findings.

LEVELS OF MEASUREMENT

One decision to be made is the type of measurement being dealt with. Different types of measurement give rise to different sorts of data. There are four main classifications: nominal, ordinal, interval and ratio (Coolican, 2014; Denscombe, 2014; Harrison, 2010). We will look at each of these in turn:

- *Nominal measurement.* This involves classification of data according to a named category, for example, male/female. In the excerpt from the structured questionnaire outlined in the previous section, practitioners were asked to tick a box to indicate their qualifications. When using nominal data, each respondent can only be assigned one category. That is why the question asked for the practitioners' highest qualification.
- *Ordinal measurement.* This level of measurement describes position, or order, in a group. In ordinal measurement it is not assumed that the interval or gap between each rank is exactly the same. For example, you could rank order a group of infants according to the ages that they began to walk. One may have started walking at 32 weeks, another at 40 weeks, the next at 53 weeks, another at 58 weeks, and so on. In this example you could assign each infant a rank, but the gap (in weeks) between each child varies. Scales which ask respondents to assign an item to a point on a scale are another instance of ordinal measurement. An example of this would be a question that asks parents to indicate their level of satisfaction with an aspect of provision according to a scale where 1 indicates a high level of dissatisfaction, 3 indicates neither satisfaction nor dissatisfaction and 5 indicates a high level of satisfaction.
- *Interval measurement.* In interval measurement, a scale is used that has an equal interval, such as the number of items recalled in a memory test or years of post-compulsory education (Harrison, 2010).
- *Ratio measurement.* Interval scales that have a zero point are known as ratio measures. Examples would be time, distance and age.

It is important to know the level of measurement you are using if you are going on to use inferential statistics, and this will also impact upon the way that you present your data. For example, you can only present your data in the form of a line graph if you are using interval measurement.

MEASURES OF CENTRAL TENDENCY

One way of describing a group of numbers, or data set, is to calculate the number that is *most* representative of that data set. You will be familiar with the most common measure of central tendency already. This is the average, or mean, in statistical terms.

 ACTIVITY

Look at any newspaper and identify how many times the term 'average' is used. What are the journalists trying to explain when they use the term 'average'?

The three most commonly used expressions of central tendency used in statistics are the mean, the median and the mode. We will look at these in turn:

- *The mean.* This is the average of a set of numbers and is achieved by finding the sum of all the numbers in a data set and dividing by the number of items in the data set. In the data set we have of the number of babies under 6 months in early years settings, the mean will be calculated as follows:

CALCULATING THE MEAN

To find the mean number of babies below 6 months of age in each setting:

- Add up 0 0 0 0 0 1 1 1 1 2 2 2 3 3 3 4 4 5 5 6
- $0 + 0 + 0 + 0 + 0 + 1 + 1 + 1 + 1 + 2 + 2 + 2 + 3 + 3 + 3 + 4 + 4 + 5 + 5 + 6 = 43$
- Divide by the number of settings (20)
- $\dfrac{43}{20} = 2.15$

The mean number of babies under 6 months in each setting is 2.15 (although this may not be a very useful way of describing data in this case!).

- *The median*. This is the middle point of a set of numbers, and for this you need to put the data in rank order and identify the middle number. If you have an uneven set of numbers in your data set, then the median is easy to identify, but with an even set of numbers the median will fall halfway between.

——————— FINDING THE MEDIAN ———————

The following is a set of marks (percentages out of 100) given to a group of 15 students:

35, 36, 42, 43, 48, 49, 50, **53**, 56, 60, 65, 66, 75, 77, 81

The median is the middle score: 53

If there were 16 students with the following marks:

35, 36, 42, 43, 48, 49, 50, 53, * 56, 60, 65, 66, 75, 77, 81, 85

the median would fall in the middle of 53 and 56. To find the median, you add 53 and 56 together and divide by 2:

53 + 56 = 109

$$\frac{109}{2} = 54.5$$

In the example we have been looking at, where nurseries have been asked the number of babies they have younger than 6 months, the median is calculated as follows:

0 0 0 0 0 1 1 1 1 2 * 2 2 3 3 3 4 4 5 5 6

The median falls between two '2s' so the median is 2.

- *The mode*. This is the most frequently occurring value in a data set.

——————— CALCULATING THE MODE ———————

Consider the data set of the number of babies aged under 6 months in early years settings:

0 0 0 0 0 1 1 1 1 2 2 2 3 3 3 4 4 5 5 6

The most frequently occurring value is 0.

It is now possible to compare the mean, median and mode for our data set on the number of babies in early years settings:

- The mean is 2.15.
- The median is 2.
- The mode is 0.

This tells us that the data within the range are not distributed evenly because most settings have few babies. With a small data set such as the one we have been using as an example, you may be forgiven for thinking that this is *obvious*, just by looking at the data set, without resorting to calculating the mean, median and mode. However, if you are dealing with hundreds of values, then calculating measures of central tendency is a good way of analysing data. You would only use such calculations if doing so would contribute to your understanding of the data you have collected. This is a very basic look at quantitative research analysis and you would also need to know about other statistical processes such as normal distribution and standard deviation. A good book on this subject is Field's (2013) *Discovering Statistics Using SPSS*.

USING PERCENTAGES

In the data set we discussed previously, consisting of students' marks, the marks were expressed in percentages. A percentage means 'out of one hundred'. For example, if we had 100 children and 10 of them were left handed we could say that 10 per cent were left handed. If you are dealing with large amounts of numbers, it sometimes helps to express them in terms of percentages because it is easier to understand what they mean. For example, if we found out that 731 early years practitioners out of 986 had a vocational award as their highest qualification, this might mean less to us than if we said that the highest qualification of 75 per cent of the workforce was a vocational award.

The choice to express raw data in terms of percentages has to be made carefully. With a small data set using percentages can be misleading. Consider this example: there are five practitioners working in a small setting – three have a vocational qualification (60 per cent) whereas two are not qualified. If one of the unqualified staff achieves a vocational qualification then that percentage would jump to 80 per cent. This means that one person can produce a 20 per cent change. Although there are no hard and fast rules about when to use percentages, we suggest that ideally you need a data set of approximately 100 before you should consider using percentages. However, each situation is different and it may be that you consider it appropriate to use percentages with far fewer participants. The Activity about the time sample later on in the chapter may be a case in point.

——————— HOW TO CALCULATE A PERCENTAGE ———————

$$\frac{\text{Given amount}}{\text{Total amount}} \times 100$$

Consider this example: 250 out of 500 children have brown eyes. Divide the given amount (250) by the total amount (500) and multiply the result by 100; that is, $\frac{250}{500} \times 100 = 50$ per cent of children have brown eyes.

Consider this example: Out of 122 parents, 31 came to a parent consultation meeting. Divide the given amount (31) by the total amount (122) and multiply the result by 100; that is, $\frac{31}{122} \times 100 = 25.4$ per cent of parents attended a parent consultation.

PRESENTING QUANTITATIVE DATA

When you are writing up your research you need to consider how you are going to present your findings. There are two main methods in quantitative research: tables and charts (Denscombe, 2014). There are no hard and fast rules as to when to use charts and tables, except that the aim should be to:

- Choose the methods that most clearly present your data. In some cases this may be a choice between a table and a chart, while in some instances it helps to have a table followed by a chart.
- Keep your presentation as simple as possible. Adding layers of complexity will not help you or the reader understand your findings. Clear communication is the key.

USING TABLES TO PRESENT YOUR FINDINGS

Presenting quantitative data in the form of a table makes it easier to see any emerging patterns, both for yourself and the people who will be reading your report. In the example we have been using about the number of very young children in early years settings, the data could easily be presented in a table (see Table 18.2).

When using a table, Green (2000: 88) suggests the following:

- All rows and columns must be clearly labelled.
- All units of measurement must be given.
- If rows and columns are totalled, this must be indicated on the table.
- Every table should have a title.

Table 18.2   Example of a frequency distribution

Frequency distribution of numbers of babies under 6 months of age in early years settings

Number of babies in the setting	Frequency
0	5
1	4
2	3
3	3
4	2
5	2
6	1
	Total: 20 settings

If you are using more than one table it should be numbered. In the table we have just used as an example (Table 18.2) the title and number tells us that:

- It is a table, not a chart.
- It is in Chapter 18.
- It is the second table in Chapter 18.
- It is an example of a frequency distribution.

 ACTIVITY

Rugina, a student on an Early Childhood degree course, has a placement in a nursery class within a primary school. Throughout the day, the children have free access to all areas of the nursery. It seems to Rugina that the boys tend to spend more time in the outside play area when compared with the girls. She decides to undertake a time sample to look at this more systematically. Every 15 minutes she will count the number of boys and girls inside and outside. She decides to start at 9.45 in the morning and continue until 11.45 when all the children have to come in for lunch.

There are 30 children altogether, who at any one time are either inside or outside. There are 15 boys and 15 girls. During the morning, if she is inside she counts the children inside, and if she is outside she counts the children outside.

(Continued)

Her data sheet looks like this:

9.45 outside 7 boys 3 girls

10.00 outside 6 girls 8 boys

10.15 inside 10 girls 6 boys

10.30 inside 3 boys 13 girls

10.45 inside 10 boys 12 girls

11.00 inside 9 girls 10 boys

11.15 outside 12 girls 10 boys

11.30 outside 6 girls 8 boys

11.45 inside 13 boys 14 girls

Assuming that the children can only be inside or outside, using these figures, draw up a table showing the number of boys and girls inside and outside at each point in time.

1. What is the mean number of girls playing outside in the morning?
2. What is the mean number of boys playing outside in the morning?
3. What is the range of the data for boys playing inside during the morning?
4. What is the range of the data for girls playing inside during the morning?
5. With equal numbers of boys and girls it is easy to make simple statements about whether boys or girls use the outdoor area predominantly. The situation is a little more complex with unequal numbers of boys and girls. What could Rugina do to get around this problem?

In thinking about this task, you might also reflect that the information gained is very *simplistic*. After all, it does not tell you anything about the resources put out indoors and outdoors or children's perceptions of the activities on offer. It also does not pick up on whether it is the *same* group of boys outdoors; that is, there may be some boys that *rarely* use the outdoor space - the time sample would not pick this up and might simplify what is a very complex issue.

In the Activity above about the number of boys and girls playing inside and outside during a morning, the mean number of girls playing outside is 4.9. The mean number of boys playing outside is 7.3. The range for the number of boys playing inside is 3–13 and the range for the number of girls playing inside is 3–14. This is a good example of when one needs to know both the range and the mean of a set of scores to make sense of the data, as the two ranges are similar, but the means for the sets of scores are quite different. If there were unequal numbers of boys and girls it may be more helpful to convert raw scores to percentages so that a true comparison can be made, even though there are relatively low numbers of children involved.

GRAPHICAL REPRESENTATIONS OF DATA

A graph is a pictorial way of showing numerical data and, as such, is a good way of showing patterns and relationships. In a graph there are usually two intersecting lines called axes:

- The X axis is the bottom horizontal line and usually represents what is being measured or counted.
- The Y axis is the left-hand vertical line that represents the frequency of what is being counted.

There are many different sorts of graphs or ways of representing quantitative data pictorially and we will be looking at line graphs, bar charts and pie charts.

Line graphs

Line graphs are used to show changes in quantities or 'progression in a sequence of data' (Denscombe, 2014: 300) and are commonly used to plot changes over time. In experimental studies, line graphs are often used to show changes in the dependent variable as a result of manipulating the independent variable.

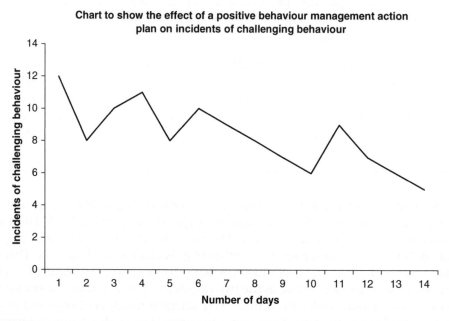

Figure 18.1 A line graph to show the number of incidents of challenging behaviour over a two-week period

The line graph in Figure 18.1 is drawn from an imagined set of results show-ing the progress made in implementing a positive behaviour management plan for a child.

Of course, in doing a study such as this, it is important to define what you mean by 'challenging behaviour' beforehand because there may be a range of practi-tioners noting these incidents and there needs to be a shared understanding of the issue.

Bar charts

Bar charts, sometimes called bar graphs, are where vertical bars are used to represent nominal data (data that are in the form of categories). In Table 18.1 we saw the suggestions that parents made for improving communication between them and the setting. This type of information is ideal for a bar chart (see Figure 18.2).

Histograms are similar to bar charts, but use interval data and the columns are set close together so that they touch each other.

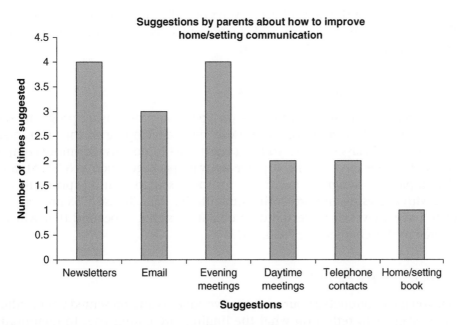

Figure 18.2 Bar chart to show the type and frequency of parents' suggestions as to how to improve communication between parents and the setting

Early childhood qualifications of staff in ten private nurseries

Figure 18.3 Pie chart to show level of qualifications of staff in ten private day nurseries

Pie charts

Pie charts are one of the most effective ways of indicating proportions. Each 'slice of the pie' represents a category and is represented as a percentage of the whole. Figure 18.3 is an example of a pie chart.

USING SPSS OR SIMILAR PROGRAMS

You can create both tables and charts on your computer, using programs such as Microsoft Excel. If your computer skills need developing in this area, many institutions hold classes where you can learn how to do this. For more complex analysis, there are specialised computer software packages such as SPSS. SPSS is a statistical package designed specifically for social scientists and is primarily concerned with analysing and presenting quantitative data. To use SPSS properly you have to have a level of understanding of statistics that is beyond that which is presented in this chapter (see Field, 2013).

WHAT DOES IT ALL MEAN?

When you have conducted your quantitative analysis and presented your findings the next stage is to reflect on what the findings are telling you. In quantitative research reports you will find a section where the findings, once analysed, are discussed. It is in this section that the researcher looks back at the original objectives of the study and the research question or hypothesis, together with the literature upon which the study is based and uses the findings to answer the research question. Some research studies use more than one data-collection method, to arrive at an all-round understanding of an issue (triangulation) and it is in the discussion section where the findings from the different data-collection methods are compared (Robson, 2011a). A classic example, where the meaning of rather confusing data was clarified by looking at findings from other data-collection methods, are the Hawthorn studies which are discussed in Chapter 1. The discussion section of a research report is looked at in more detail in Chapter 19.

QUALITATIVE METHODS OF DATA ANALYSIS

We have already seen that when analysing data there are decisions to be made about what data to include and what techniques to use to aid analysis. However, in analysing *quantitative* data the aim should be to keep the influence of the researcher to a minimum; two different researchers should be able to separately process the data and come up with similar findings. In qualitative studies the influence of the researcher, on both what is collected and recorded as data and the way that this information is analysed and understood, is profound and in some cases fundamental to the process (Coffey, 1999). Denscombe (2014) describes two ways in which researchers deal with the involvement of self. One way is for researchers to endeavour to identify how their ideas, attitudes and beliefs could affect their interpretation of findings, and to guard against this (as far as possible). The other approach is to recognise that, inevitably, a researcher's identity, beliefs and values will have an effect on the way data are interpreted and to discuss this in relation to any conclusions that are made (Guba and Lincoln, 2005). You may recall that this is linked to the notion of reflexivity. Fontana and Frey (2000) warn that often researchers are not sufficiently reflexive about interpreting their findings. They point out that in the past there has been pretence that:

- data reported tends to flow nicely
- the data are not contradictory
- no data are excluded
- improprieties never happen.

In reality, Fontana and Frey (2000: 661) suggest that researchers frequently become buried under a 'mountain of field notes' and other information. The process of imposing some sort of order is often problematic, contradictory and, by *necessity*, influenced by the researcher. Johnson and Christensen (2012) point out that although qualitative methods have been used since the early twentieth century, agreement about how to analyse the data is only slowly evolving.

PREPARING QUALITATIVE DATA FOR ANALYSIS

At the start of the chapter we discussed the importance of preparing data before analysis. In this section we will look in more detail at what this means for qualitative data. Denscombe (2007: 289) gives the following suggestions:

- Try to get all the information in a similar format (A4 paper or record cards, for example).
- When you collect data, try to do it in a way that allows comments and reflections to be recorded alongside. This may mean leaving a column for reflection at the side of observations and transcripts of interviews.
- Each item that you have collected (observation, interview and suchlike) should be given a reference number so that it is easy to identify and file in a logical way. For example, observations could be referenced by the child's initials and the date.
- Keep copies of all your original materials for the duration of the research project. This not only involves the transcripts of your interviews, for example, but also copying the actual recordings, remembering to store any data very carefully such as via password-protected files on a computer. Your original material is irreplaceable.

INTERIM DATA ANALYSIS

In quantitative research it is usual to have two distinct phases – data collection and data analysis. In qualitative studies researchers tend to enter a more cyclical process of data collection, analysis and additional data collection. As research progresses and the researcher's understanding of the material collected deepens, new themes and patterns may emerge that require additional questions to be asked. Denscombe (2014: 321) describes this as a *'data analysis spiral'*. This process continues until the point of theoretical saturation (Johnson and Christensen, 2012), when the researcher concludes that the topic being investigated is understood as fully as is possible. Practical considerations such as lack of time or resources may also bring this phase of research to an end.

It is at this stage of analysis that issues of validity and reliability need to be readdressed. You would have already thought about these concepts in the design stage (see Chapter 1), but, once the data start to be collected and the first steps towards analysis are undertaken, there are decisions to be made that may affect the reliability and/or validity of your findings. For example, you may have a preconceived idea about what you will uncover or a common theme may be emerging. If some of your data are not in keeping with your emerging theme, the temptation may be to include only the data that fit in with your ideas. Silverman (2013) suggests that far from ignoring these data, or the 'Deviant Case', the researcher should return to the participant to obtain additional information, which may facilitate a greater depth of understanding.

Silverman (2013) suggests that as the first items are analysed, you should be asking yourself if your methods of data collection and of data analysis are still appropriate. Often the research design will need to be changed at this stage. Interim analysis enables the researcher to begin to see what categories their participants are using. For example, in a qualitative study about parental involvement in their children's education, an initial perusal of interview transcripts may reveal a theme about parental guilt if they work during school hours and cannot join in with trips and outings. Future participants may be specifically asked about this theme to see if it is a common feeling.

Silverman (2013) recommends that data analysis is begun as soon as the data are collected. He also goes on to suggest that writing should not be left too late.

STAGES IN ANALYSIS

There are many different ways to approach the analysis of qualitative data, but, although they differ in approach, generally analysis proceeds in stages. Denscombe (2014) outlines the following stages:

1. *Becoming familiar with the data.* This involves reading and re-reading text data, looking at any images that are being used, and using any field notes or journal entries to help you put the information into context. As you look through the data you should look for 'implied meanings' or information that you would expect to see but is missing.
2. *Coding the data.* In the section looking at quantitative analysis we looked at how to code the responses to an open question. In the example, participants' responses were placed into similar categories, which were given a name and assigned a code number. A similar process is undertaken with qualitative data, where segments of text are identified which have specific meaning for your research study. Johnson and Christensen (2012: 520) suggest that a segment could be 'a word, a single sentence, or several sentences, or it might include a larger paragraph or even a complete document'. In qualitative analysis, codes can be a simple category label or a more complex idea. As the researcher reads through the text, identifying and coding the segments, a list of codes and their meanings is drawn up; this is known as the coding frame (Barbour, 2014). Segments that include similar ideas, attitudes, thoughts and feelings are given the same code. It is important that the coder demonstrates intra-coder reliability, meaning that the codes are applied consistently, with similar segments being assigned the same code. Coding is a highly subjective process and, in studies using more than one coder, training is usually given to achieve inter-coder reliability.
3. Barbour (2014) describes the coding of meaningful segments derived from participants' words and concepts as having its origins in Glaser and Strauss's (1967) concept of 'Grounded Theory'. This method of coding is also known as inductive coding, in contrast to a priori codes that have been developed prior to the data being collected (Johnson and Christensen, 2012).
4. *Categorising the codes.* Once you have developed a coding frame you can look to see if certain codes seem to 'fit' together.

ACTIVITY

In Chapter 1 we discussed Kerry who wanted to find out early years practitioners' views on the benefits and barriers to partnership with parents. She undertook semi-structured interviews and the following are some of the responses given and the codes that they were assigned:

Code	Response
1	I am all for partnership with parents but it is hard to find a time to talk.
1	I get stressed when several parents all want to talk to me at once.
2	There is so much I need to know about the children that only the parents can tell me.
3	We like to tell the parents what our theme is every week so they can follow up with activities at home.
2	We do home visits to get to know the children and parents before the children start.
4	It is difficult when parents send their children in when it is obvious that the children are unwell.
5	Sometimes the parents complain when their children get their clothes dirty.
6	I have a parent who comes in and tells stories to the children.
1	We had a parents' consultation afternoon but lots of parents couldn't come because they were working.
5	Some parents expect us to teach the 3-year-olds to read and write. They don't understand it is too young.
4	It is difficult when parents are late collecting the children.
3	We share our observations with parents; they often get excited about how they can do follow-up activities at home.
6	Some parents come in to help with activities like cooking.

Codes:

1 Difficulties in finding time to talk to parents.
2 Parents help practitioners get to know about the children.
3 Parents can support children's learning at home.
4 Sometimes parents don't follow 'the rules'.
5 Parents sometimes have different expectations than practitioners.
6 Parents can be very helpful in the setting.

- As we have mentioned previously, coding is very subjective. Would you have coded differently?
- Can you see any codes that seem to fit together to form a category?

5. *Identifying themes and relationships among the codes and categories.* Here the researcher looks at the codes and categories that have been generated and tries to see if broad themes can be developed that reflect the underlying meaning of the participants' responses. For example, in the practitioners' responses about parental partnership you may reflect that under the general heading of 'benefits' there are two main themes: benefits for the children and benefits for the staff. Under the general heading of barriers two main themes emerge: practical barriers, such as issues of time, and a mismatch of expectation between what parents want and what practitioners want.

   In thinking about generating themes, it is important to consider how they can be applied across the different types of data, such as observations and interviews. In addition, once codes have been identified, they need to be assigned back to the data to see if they work well (Denscombe, 2014).

6. *Developing concepts and arriving at some generalised statements.* This is the process which involves relating the themes generated back to the original research question. Do your findings allow you to make generalised conclusions about the topic being studied? You may develop suggestions that point the way towards further research. Some researchers may even be able to suggest an underpinning theory. For most students doing their undergraduate research project, this stage will involve developing a narrative explanation of the findings (Denscombe, 2014).

Silverman (2013) suggests that researchers should go back to the participants in the study with the tentative findings and ask them if the conclusions are an accurate reflection of what they perceive to be the 'truth' – sometimes known as 'respondent validity' (Silverman, 2013). He warns that participants may not have the whole picture and that their comments should be treated as an additional source of data, rather than being a true validation process.

RESEARCH IN FOCUS

In Debbie Albon's (2009) study, which looked at challenges to improving the uptake of milk in a nursery class (children aged 3-4 years), she observed 72 nursery snack times, interviewed the three practitioners who worked in the class, talked to parents and used laminated examples of the children's drink wrappers as a stimulus to elicit the children's perspectives directly. Only nine of the 39 children had school milk, despite the fact that 37 of the families were eligible for free milk.

ENGLAND

From the wealth of data generated, Albon (2009) reported on two general themes: 'A link with personal identity' and 'A link with home and the drama of family life'. Here are some examples of data that seemed to 'fit' into these themes:

(Continued)

(Continued)

Theme 1: A link with personal identity

Data obtained from talking to children with laminated drinks labels as a stimulus:

> 'I have blackcurrant drink but B [her brother] has orange. He doesn't like blackcurrant.' (child B) (p. 146)

> 'This is a mango one. My sisters – they have mango juice at their school. This is nice one – my one. This one right … is my brother's right! He loves it.' (child S1) (p. 146)

Data obtained from observation

At snack times, the children who had brought drinks from home are given their drinks first.

These drinks have the children's names on which are written as a shared activity with their parents at the beginning of the session. Milk does not have the children's names written on it – despite the use of children's written names being very affirming – and is always given out last.

There were virtually no data from 72 snack-time observations to support the idea that the milk provided by the school was linked to a sense of personal identity.

Theme 2: A link with home and the drama of family life

Data obtained from observations of snack times

> Child J says 'Mummy shouted at daddy 'cos daddy forgot to buy me some juice and mummy was cross and he had to go and get some for me.' (p. 147)

> Child M says that her brother 'cried 'cos there was only apple juice and he wanted orange. Mummy went to the shop to buy him orange.' (p. 147)

There were many observations noting that when children forgot a drink from home and had to have milk, the practitioners apologised for this and seemed to reinforce the view that drinking milk was a result of their parents' 'negligence'. One example was a practitioner saying 'your mummy didn't bring you a drink today so I *am* sorry but you'll have to have a milk today'. (p. 147).

Data from parent conversations

> 'It makes it easier to bring him in if he has something he can bring in from home.' (Child B's mother) (p. 148)

> 'She cries if I don't let her bring it [Ribena] in. I and H bring in a drink so she wants to be the same.' (Child F's mother) (p. 148)

In writing up her findings Albon (2009) weaves the different sources of data together under the two themes. She concludes by encouraging practitioners to recognise the importance of snack times and to pay attention to the minutiae of their practice in order to make healthier drink choices an attractive option for children and families.

DISCOURSE ANALYSIS

Discourse analysis is a more critical look at texts than previously discussed and is used in a range of disciplines such as psychology, sociology and literature. Rather than merely focusing on counting words that are used in texts, discourse analysis is more concerned with the social relations within which language is 'produced, reproduced and sometimes reshaped' (Jupp and Norris, 1993: 47). Very simply, discourses should be seen as narratives that shape our ideas about the world such as what we see as appropriate behaviour in given situations or the role(s) we might take in social life (Woolfitt, 2008). Discourse analysis can be applied to texts such as interview transcripts but also, more broadly, to other forms of 'texts', as we will see.

Foucauldian discourse analysis tends to focus on issues of power. Foucault is a post-structuralist theorist who is interested in exploring how power is exercised through texts as opposed to what texts tell us about their author(s) (Jupp and Norris, 1993). In doing this, he explores the way that some discourses dominate and privilege particular ways of seeing and acting in the world and, in so doing, legitimise the power of particular groups of people and the perpetuation of particular ideas. We should also note that in thinking about 'texts' Foucault interprets this widely to include 'meaningful events, processes or objects that can be interpreted' (Woolfitt, 2008: 450).

RESEARCH IN FOCUS

AUSTRALIA

Deborah Lupton (2013) wanted to find out how infants are portrayed in popular culture as a way of uncovering underlying social and cultural attitudes about infants in contemporary Australian society. She used a critical discourse analysis approach whereby she analysed a total of 82 'texts' about babies and infants which included:

- newspaper and magazine articles
- advertisements appearing in newspapers and magazines
- the online versions of newspapers and magazines
- articles and advertisements found on a website directed at mothers with infants and young children.

The critical discourse analysis was designed to ask the following questions:

How are infants' bodies portrayed using visual imagery? How are their bodies shown in relation to others' bodies? What spaces do they inhabit or are they deemed to inhabit? What rhetorical devices are used to convey meaning about the infant body? To what broader discourses concerning infant embodiment do these visual and rhetorical devices contribute? (Lupton, 2013: 2)

(Continued)

(Continued)

Qualitative analysis revealed four main themes: infants are constructed as 'precious', 'pure', 'uncivilised' and 'vulnerable'. Examples where infants were seen to be *precious* included an advert for disposable nappies that showed mothers and fathers cuddling their babies, revelling in the intimacy of these moments. Texts where infants were seen to be *pure* included an advert for a carpet where a baby (white-skinned, blond-haired and dressed in white) is lying on the carpet which is advertised as being soft and 'environmentally friendly'. The purity of the image of the baby is designed to transfer to our perceptions of the carpet. Texts which portrayed infants as *uncivilised* included an article on how air travellers disliked travelling in the same plane as crying babies. And on a letters page, where there was a debate about taking dogs into restaurants, one contributor expressed the opinion that dogs were more acceptable than babies because babies make too much noise. Texts showing babies to be *vulnerable* included an advertisement for a spray cleaner where a woman is cleaning surfaces in her home whilst a baby is seen picking up food and toys from surfaces and the floor and putting them in its mouth. The 'voiceover' talks about how we need to protect the health of our family from 'invisible germs and dirt'.

It is a fascinating article which is unusual in its exploration of *young infants* and how they are constructed in a range of media 'texts'.

USING COMPUTER PACKAGES FOR DATA ANALYSIS

Just as there are computer packages that have been developed to assist researchers with *quantitative* analysis, there are computer packages such as NVivo and ATLAS.ti that are designed to help analyse *qualitative* data. In the same way that using SPSS demands a high level of understanding of statistics, the use of computer packages for qualitative analysis should only be attempted by researchers who have a good grounding in the area. Barbour (2014: 260) advises that if researchers do not know the principles of qualitative analysis first, there is a possibility the analysis is 'driven by the properties of the package rather than the other way round'.

PRESENTING QUALITATIVE DATA

Presenting findings from a quantitative study is relatively straightforward compared with presenting qualitative data, but the aim is the same: you are presenting clearly the evidence upon which you are basing your conclusions. Bogdan and Biklen (1998: 195) suggest that 'the qualitative researcher, in effect, says to the reader, "Here is what I found and here are the details to support that view"'.

A quantitative researcher would not present raw, unprocessed data in a results section. Similarly, qualitative researchers present their analysis of the data, rather than complete transcripts of interviews or observational material. This will involve presenting their interpretations of what the data are telling them in terms of the main themes. This was seen in the Research in Focus section above, which looked at Albon's (2009) research. The interpretations should be supported by sufficient excerpts from the data to allow the reader to see that your interpretations are based on evidence. It is usual to use direct quotes from interviews, excerpts from observations and excerpts from your field notes or reflective journal to allow the reader to get close to the participants and situations you are describing (Johnson and Christensen, 2012).

Continuing with the examples of Albon's (2009: 148) research outlined in the Research in Focus section, she presents the data in the following way:

> Parents seemed to stress the link between drinks and home explicitly. Child B's mother stated:
>
> 'It makes it easier to bring him in if he has something he can bring in from home ... Does he have a milk as well?'

Without the observations and quotations as *evidence* to support the point she is making, there would be no reason to believe the claims she is making for her research.

 —— KEY POINTS FROM THE CHAPTER ——————————

- Data analysis involves looking at your data to uncover patterns and themes.
- Quantitative analysis involves the manipulation of numerical data and the use of statistics.
- Content analysis can be used to analyse texts.
- Quantitative data can be presented graphically using tables, charts and graphs.
- Qualitative data analysis uses non-statistical techniques to help us to understand the meaning of the data. In qualitative research, interim analysis can begin as soon as the first information is collected.
- A coding frame can be set up to allow categories to emerge and the identification of themes and patterns. This might be used for narrative observation and qualitative interview data.
- Discourse analysis is an approach to analysing texts more 'critically' than content analysis.
- There are a variety of ways to present findings in qualitative research, but all require that evidence in the form of excerpts from the data are presented to support your arguments.

────────────── **FURTHER READING** ──────────────

Field, A. (2013) *Discovering Statistics Using SPSS*, 4th edition. London: Sage. This text describes the statistical analysis of quantitative data, using the computer software SPSS. It is easy to read and has online resources. It goes far beyond what we have been able to cover in this chapter.

Silverman, D. (2014) *Interpreting Qualitative Data: Strategies for Analysing Talk, Text and Interaction*, 5th edition. London: Sage. This is an excellent text which gives an overview of qualitative research methods by a leading authority in the area. It is particularly useful for practical advice on how to analyse texts, naturally occurring talk and visual images.

Don't forget to visit the online resources at https://study.sagepub.com/mukherjiandalbon3e for access to free SAGE journal articles, weblinks, videos, exercises, mini quizzes and an interactive glossary.

19

WRITING UP AND SHARING YOUR FINDINGS

CHAPTER OBJECTIVES

- To develop skills in the writing up of a piece of research including how it might be structured.
- To consider how conclusions and implications for early childhood practice might be drawn from a piece of research.
- To reflect on issues of power and voice in relation to writing up research.
- To think about how a piece of research might be presented to a wider audience.

In this final chapter, we will be looking at writing up research, building on the previous chapter, which looked at analysing and presenting data. This is an area of importance because it is the stage in the research process where you will put your ideas forward in a way that is both clear and, hopefully, good to read. We will also be thinking about how you might draw tentative conclusions from your research – we say 'tentative' because it is important to be cautious about any claims you make for your research. This is something that is important for *all* researchers to consider. In addition, we will develop the idea that writing up research is not a neutral act; there are still issues of ethics to consider.

WRITING UP A RESEARCH PROJECT

We begin this chapter by looking at writing up a piece of research. For many of you, this may be the longest piece of writing you have been asked to do – on average, a BA dissertation or project is about 10,000 words in length. It may be as long as 20,000 words if you decide to do a Masters degree. While this may seem daunting, the structure of the written-up research can be helpful in making this seem more manageable. The usual structure suggested for writing up a piece of BA research is as follows:

- Introduction
- Literature review
- Methodology
- Findings and discussion (sometimes two chapters)
- Conclusion

You should note that each institution may have differences in the way they would like student projects to be presented and there can be some flexibility in this. For instance, sometimes it is useful to include a chapter that discusses the development of policy prior to the literature review chapter. Gilbert (2008b: 501) argues that it is acceptable to 'break the rules' on occasions as long as 'the message you want to convey is nevertheless communicated effectively'. The rationale for the structure of your work should be based on what helps *you* to tell the story of *your* research most effectively.

The introduction is usually preceded by an abstract that outlines the aims of the study, the way(s) in which it was carried out, the key findings and possibly the implications for early childhood practice. Although the abstract is usually about 250–300 words in length, it is an important part of the overall research project as it should entice the reader to want to read more. Although it is one of the last pieces of writing you will do in relation to your research, try not to leave it until the last minute. It can take time to write a good abstract.

—— ACTIVITY ————————————————————————

Look at an academic journal such as the *Journal of Early Childhood Research*. You will notice that at the beginning of each paper there is an abstract or short piece of writing that acts as a synopsis of the research as a whole.

  If you choose to look at a journal such as *Health Education* you will notice that the abstract is highly structured. This is sometimes the practice in science-related journals. It is interesting that each discipline seems to have a particular style of presenting research.

In thinking about the dissertation – or written-up piece of research for a student project – Hart (2005: 102) offers a useful way of conceptualising its structure. He encourages students to think of its structure as a kind of story. This works in the following way:

Beginning

- *There was once this issue or problem* … (the rationale for the topic and introduction to the dissertation).
- *Which some researchers believed was important* … (the literature review).

Middle

- *That I thought might be a suitable topic* … (aims and objectives of the research).
- *So what I did was* … (the methodology and data-collection tools).

End

- *And I found out* … (the results and findings).
- *Which means we now know this* … (the conclusions and recommendations). (Based on Hart, 2005: 102.)

Clough and Nutbrown (2007: 221) also discuss writing up research in terms of a story, arguing that, at first, you need to ask 'What is the research story I wish to tell?' then 'How can I best construct my research account?' We will now take you through the parts of a typical research project and discuss what each should usually contain.

INTRODUCTION

The introductory chapter should outline the rationale for the study. It might contain your personal interest in the topic, your professional interest in the topic (if applicable), and will give a sense of why the topic is significant. After all, you want to try and convince the reader that the area is an *important* one. We will take as an example a research project entitled '*How are children with English as an additional language (EAL) supported during literacy hour? A case study of a year one class*'.

 CASE STUDY

Priya was motivated to explore this topic as she has personal experience of being multilingual, learning English on entry to school in England. She began her introduction like this:

> This research project examines how children who are acquiring English as an additional language are supported during the literacy hour. The focus is on children in a year one classroom in a school in East London.
>
> My motivation for studying this topic comes from my personal experience of moving to England in the late 1980s with little spoken English – my first language is Punjabi. I recall the difficulties I experienced in my earliest years of schooling but also the support I received from peers and teachers. My personal experience has provided the 'initial orientation' (Jayaratne, 1993) for the research.

Typically, an introduction will usually outline some smaller aims or research objectives that fall within this topic. For Priya these were:

- To investigate the roles of the different adults who support children with EAL.
- To find out whether there are any particular resources used to support children with EAL – if so, what are these and how are these employed?
- To ascertain the perspectives of this group of year one children of their EAL support during literacy hour.

Like an essay, the introduction to a piece of written-up research should set the scene, giving the reader a sense of what is to follow. If you are looking at an issue using a particular theoretical lens, such as psychoanalytical theory, this could be flagged up in the introductory chapter. It may also be useful to introduce the reader to some information about where the study was conducted and describe the group of participants. Thus, continuing the previous example of some research into literacy hour and the way children with EAL are supported, it would be useful to briefly outline some information about the school in which the class is situated and the number of children with EAL in the school. More information about the 'case' and participants, in this example, would be provided in the methodology chapter.

LITERATURE REVIEW

We have devoted an entire chapter to conducting a literature review, so we recommend that you revisit Chapter 3. The literature review should discuss literature relevant to the research topic and helps to contextualise your own research within a wider body of research and writing that previously exists.

METHODOLOGY

In this chapter, you will need to discuss the paradigm, methodology and methods used in your research project. In doing this, try to demonstrate the following:

- An understanding of the paradigm and methodology, which underpins the study. In the example of a research project entitled *'How are children with English as an additional language (EAL) supported during literacy hour? A case study of a year one class'* and the objectives outlined earlier, it would be important to show how the research is located within (most likely) the interpretivist paradigm, using a qualitative methodological approach.
- As we have noted elsewhere in this book, the extent to which you are expected to discuss the theoretical positioning of your work depends upon the module and course that you are studying and the learning outcomes you are expected to meet. Some courses may not expect any discussion on paradigms in the assignment or indeed introduce you to this topic, whereas other courses may expect some detail in this area. This is also linked to the level at which you are studying. Clearly if you are undertaking an MA course there will be different expectations than for students at the beginning of a Foundation Degree course. This said, it is likely that any course will expect you to understand the difference between qualitative and quantitative research, so if in any doubt in this area, do revise your knowledge by looking at Chapters 4 and 5 again.
- Continuing with this example, there would need to be further discussion of research design – in this instance, a case study approach to research. Details would

need to be given about the 'case', without breaching confidentiality, and an argument presented as to why a case study approach was appropriate for this particular research project.

- The methodology chapter needs to contain anonymised details of the participants, details about how the sample was chosen for the research, as well as how the sample fits into the population as a whole. In qualitative research such as a case study, the idea that findings might be generalisable to the population as a whole is unlikely, nevertheless some detail about the participants and institutions (if relevant) in the study should be included.

 CASE STUDY

Continuing with Priya's research she presented details of the 'case' in relation to her research in the following way.

> Mulberry School (name changed) was chosen for this research as it is a school which has a linguistically diverse community and is relatively near to where I live to enable me to conduct fieldwork.
>
> Mulberry School is a two form entry primary school in East London which has an attached nursery class. The school is reflective of the linguistic and ethnic diversity of the local area; two thirds of the children come from multilingual homes. The main languages spoken in the school are Punjabi, Hindi, Gujarati, Somali, Bengali and English and the school employs a specialist teacher who supports children acquiring English as an additional language across the school. More than half of the families are in receipt of Income Support (a welfare payment).
>
> The year one class in which I conducted my study comprises 30 children aged 5-6 years. Their teacher, Moira (name changed), has worked in the school for two years and came straight from studying for a teaching qualification at university, so this is her first post. She is supported in the classroom by a teaching assistant, Sharmina, who unlike Moira, is bilingual in Bengali and English.

In examining Priya's description of her case study school here, she might have provided statistical evidence from the local authority to bolster her statement that the school community reflects the linguistic diversity of the local community. Further description of the physical setting might have been informative too, perhaps, for example, noting whether there is evidence of multilingual signage in the building. Potentially, this may also be an avenue to explore in the data analysis chapter.

- A discussion of the methods used in the research. In the hypothetical research example we have been looking at so far, the researcher might have carried out classroom observations and interviews with staff and children, as well as examining relevant documents. Again, it is important to make the argument for your choice of methods. *Why* were they appropriate? Examples of the data-collection instruments such as the interview schedule should be included in the appendices and referred to in the text.
- A discussion of ethical issues that relate to the research. It is imperative that there is a discussion of *ethics* in the methodology chapter. Try to think about the ethical issues that you had to address all the way through the research process. Here are some of the issues that it would be important to include: How did you gain access (to the setting and/or individuals)? How did you ensure people were informed about what you were doing? If involving children in the research, how was the consent of their parents obtained and how did you gain the children's consent? How did you store the data and ensure anonymity of settings and/or individuals? In what ways did you (or will you) share the findings of the study? Again, examples of consent forms sent out or letters sent to gain access to a group or setting should be included in the appendices and referred to in the text.
- Information about how you went about *analysing* the *data*. Given that the hypothetical example we have been thinking about falls under the umbrella of qualitative research, it is likely that the researcher would have used an inductive approach to analysing the data, possibly identifying themes that emerge through the data.

— 🔍 — CASE STUDY

Sometimes students are advised to write about the *approach* taken to analysing data in their data analysis or findings chapter. We would advise that the approach taken to analysis is a methodological issue and should be discussed towards the end of the methodology chapter. The actual findings themselves – drawing very directly on the data generated in the study – would go in the next chapter. In an undergraduate student project we would not expect a huge amount of detail here but we would expect students to say something about how they analysed the data. Here is how Priya discussed her analysis of classroom observations and interviews.

As is typical in qualitative research, I read and re-read the data in order to identify patterns or themes which were emerging. This is an example of inductive data analysis as the themes were generated after the data collection had taken place

(Continued)

(Continued)

(Robson, 2011). Once I was satisfied with the themes I applied them to the data to see how well they fitted. I did this through use of colour coding, highlighting text that related to a particular theme in a given colour. An example of how I did this with an observation and an interview can be found in the appendices. The themes generated related to the value of being able to speak more than one language (colour coded in green); professional training (colour coded in red); the importance of teamwork (colour coded in brown); and listening to children – an inclusive approach (colour coded in blue). The data from these themes are presented and discussed in the next chapter.

Although a fairly simple method of analysing data, it is clearly expressed for the reader and there is a sense of flow to the next chapter. She has provided some signposting for the readers as to what they will see next.

You will note that throughout the chapter we are suggesting that you are creating an argument to support the decisions made about how you went about conducting the research. In doing this, you should aim to support your arguments with reference to literature about research methodology, just as you would support points made in an essay with reference to reading. The methodology chapter should not be a hypothetical exercise about research, it should be a discussion of *what you did* and *why*, supported by relevant literature. However, different institutions may have other expectations in relation to this so it is vital to be clear about what your particular course or module requires.

FINDINGS AND DISCUSSION

In some institutions, students are encouraged to present their findings as a discrete chapter and then have an in-depth discussion of the findings separately. In other institutions students are encouraged to discuss their findings in relation to relevant literature as the data are presented; that is, as they go along. It may also depend on the type of research project undertaken. In positivist research there is a tendency to present the findings then the discussion separately. This is something to check with your supervisor. Whatever the approach suggested, there needs to be a detailed discussion of the findings somewhere.

By the time you have completed your data analysis you are likely to have generated a number of themes or generalised statements and will need to decide how to write up your findings. Chenail (1995) suggests that there are many different ways of deciding how to 'tell your story', including:

- *Natural.* The topic being studied shapes the way the findings are presented. For example, if your research is about the implementation of a new initiative, then the data will be presented in a sequential order, recreating the history of the initiative. This can be useful in writing up action research projects.
- *Most simple to most complex.* The simplest theme uncovered is presented first, with more complex themes being presented later.
- *First discovered/constructed to last discovered/constructed.* This way of presenting findings re-creates the journey made by the researcher as the analysis progresses, with the initial findings presented first.
- *Narrative logic.* Findings are presented in the way that you would tell a story, so that themes and exemplars are ordered and there is a logical flow from one concept to another.
- *Most important to least important or from major to minor.* Here the most important findings are presented first with the least important findings being presented later.
- *Dramatic presentation.* Unforeseen discoveries and 'surprises' are presented last, to give maximum dramatic effect.

Once you have decided on the order that you will present your findings in, you need to give consideration to how you will structure each section and how you will bring in the evidence from your data. Chenail (1995) suggests the following format:

- Section heading.
- Present the distinction or finding.
- Introduce the first data exemplar of this distinction.
- Display the first data exemplar of this distinction.
- Comment further on the first data exemplar of this distinction.
- Make transition to the second data exemplar of this distinction.
- Display the second data exemplar of this distinction.
- Comment further on the second data exemplar of this distinction.
- Make transition to the next data exemplar of this distinction and repeat the pattern until the closing of this section.

For some of you reading this, Chenail's (1995) format may appear too mechanistic, for others of you it may be very useful. Whatever format you use, it is likely that the findings chapter will be the longest chapter in the piece of written-up research.

Let us continue with Priya's research project entitled *'How are children with English as an additional language (EAL) supported during literacy hour? A case study of a year one class'* and consider how the findings chapter might be structured. We noted before that Priya had identified the following themes:

- the value of being able to speak more than one language
- professional training
- the importance of teamwork
- listening to children – an inclusive approach.

These themes worked well as sub-headings within the findings chapter and allowed Priya to present her findings in a clear and organised way. In writing up the findings, it is also important to include a deeper discussion of what they seem to signify, linking the findings to relevant literature. As previously noted, in qualitative research studies there will often be a discussion of the findings in relation to the literature *within* the chapter. In quantitative research within the positivist tradition, the findings and discussion may be presented *separately* – often as two chapters, but institutions may suggest such an approach for any kind of study.

CONCLUSION

The concluding chapter will remind the reader of the *story* of the research. By this we mean that it is worth re-stating the main aims of the study, how the study was carried out and the key findings of the study. There should also be a discussion about the implications of the study for our understandings of early childhood and early childhood practice. Ask yourself: What do you know now as a result of undertaking the research? There may be recommendations that you would like to put forward based on the research findings. If you do this, it is important to be tentative and try not to claim too much for your research. In Priya's research example we have looked at in this section, it would be important to note that the research was carried out in one setting and the findings may not be generalisable to all year one classes. However, there may be some issues she wishes to raise in relation to *that* setting, which is a point worth bearing in mind especially if you conduct action research which is usually highly contextual.

It is also appropriate to indicate how you might have carried out the research differently, reflect on any personal learning that has happened as a result of carrying out the research, and make suggestions, if you have any, about future research that might be conducted in the area looked at. It is not a sign of failing to reflect that the research might have worked better had you done something differently; it will demonstrate that as a new early childhood researcher, you are able to reflect on how you might make improvements to your research practice. You will need to review the validity of the study and the reliability of the methods used as is appropriate to the paradigm within which your research is located. This will stand you in good stead for any future research projects you might get involved in.

— 🔍 —— CASE STUDY ————————————————————

Nadiya looked at early years practitioners' views on the value of the outdoor area as an environment for learning for her early childhood studies research project. She carried out 12 semi-structured interviews with practitioners from four different settings.

Nadiya found that the training practitioners received seemed to have an impact on the importance they placed on the outdoor area as a learning environment, with practitioners who had attended a course on outdoor play in their local authority appearing to have positive attitudes and greater confidence in articulating why the outdoors is important. She also found that fears about children having accidents and the possible reaction of parents to this seemed to impact on the degree to which practitioners encouraged children to take risks in their physical play outdoors.

In writing up her research, Nadiya was careful to use the language 'suggests' as opposed to 'clearly demonstrates' when discussing the implications of her findings. In other words, she was *tentative* in the claims she was making. In making some recommendations for practice she stated,

> Whilst this is a small sample of practitioners and it is difficult to make generalisations based on this, the following recommendations are suggested:
>
> - There seems to be a need for high quality in-service training showing practitioners how the outdoor environment can support all areas of learning.
> - Practitioners need to reflect on how they can support children's physical risk-taking with confidence and consider the benefits such risk-taking affords.

In doing this, Nadiya was thinking about the implications of her research for early childhood practice but with the proviso that her sample size was very small. She went on to suggest that had she had more time, she could have interviewed practitioners from a range of local authorities, who possibly had different opportunities for in-service training around supporting outdoor play. She might also have broadened the types of early childhood settings the practitioners worked in and the ages of children worked with as well as the range of professional qualifications held. By doing this, Nadiya was recognising the limitations of her study.

REFERENCES

All the material referred to in the research should be included in the reference section. These should be arranged in alphabetical order by author's last name. You should be guided here by your own university or college as there are different ways of setting out references and you can lose marks if you make mistakes in this area.

APPENDICES

Appendices are useful in organising materials that would be cumbersome in the text. In a piece of written-up research, they might contain items such as:

- letter of access
- consent form (note: not each one that was signed – the pro forma)
- questionnaire (again, not each one but the exemplar)
- interview schedule
- observations.

You should note that this is not an exhaustive list.

It is important to ensure that all appendices are numbered clearly and referred to in the text. We often tell our students that we do not *weigh* research projects – all material should be *relevant* and if it is not, should not be included. Similarly, it is important to think of the reader when writing up a piece of research; if the reader has to constantly refer to appendices it can be incredibly annoying. Given that a key audience for your research is likely to be your supervisor, who is also assessing your work, this is a vital consideration.

CHECKLIST FOR USE WHEN WRITING UP YOUR RESEARCH PROJECT

Title page

Abstract

Acknowledgements (optional)

List of contents

Then you will go into the main part of the research project - often organised as separate chapters:

- Introduction
- Literature review
- Methodology
- Findings and discussion (this may be one or two chapters)
- Conclusion

References

Appendices

FINDING A 'VOICE' WHEN WRITING UP RESEARCH

One of the key things a researcher needs to do when writing up is to find their own voice. Throughout your degree programmes, you have probably been engaged in writing and have developed a personal style. This takes practice. It is important to look at any suggestions for amendments your supervisor has made for draft chapters. You might also ask friends and family to help with reviewing your work, acting as 'critical friends'. In this sense, writing up your research should be viewed as both a process and a product, because in the initial draft phases you are writing to think and then towards the end you are thinking of the writing as being more permanent; that is, a finished product (Clough and Nutbrown, 2012). This is why it is important to start writing early.

One of the things that makes reading a student project rewarding is a sense of the *person* of the student-researcher. Charmaz and Mitchell (1997: 193) state: 'Voice is the *animus* of storytelling, the manifestation of the author's will, intent, and feeling [original emphasis]. Animus is not the content of stories but the ways authors present themselves within their work'. Like the Victorian perception of children needing 'to be seen and not heard' they argue that there has been a tendency to recommend that writers are 'seen (in the credits) and not heard (in the text)' (1997: 193).

The reader of a dissertation is likely to get a sense of *you*, the researcher, in any stated interest in the subject matter in the introductory chapter; the literature you refer to (and do not refer to) and the way it is discussed; the decisions you made as to methodology and methods; the discussion you present in relation to the research findings; and any personal reflections on the research in the conclusion. In qualitative research, it is likely that a sense of the *self* of the researcher will be stronger than in quantitative research, as qualitative methodological approaches tend to embrace the way that the researcher's subjectivity impacts on the research, particularly if falling within the post-structuralist paradigm.

One way that researchers can find their voice is through the *judicious* use of the autobiographical 'I'. This may go against what some of you were taught when at school. You may have been taught to write consistently in the third person in order to ensure that your work retains objectivity – the view that it sounds more 'academic'. Letherby (2003: 141) makes an interesting point in relation to the use of 'I': 'Writing in the first person helps to make clear the author's role in constructing rather than discovering the story/knowledge'.

In using 'I', the writer is acknowledging that their knowledge is based on their own perspective on the world as, for instance, a Black, working-class woman, an early childhood practitioner or a person of a particular faith. If you are a practitioner working on an action research project, it is difficult to see how you can write up some aspects of the research without referring to yourself directly – indeed referring to yourself as 'the author' can appear strange in the text. However, as we noted in the chapter on journaling as a research tool, it can appear as overly self-indulgent and possibly relates to the research paradigm within which the research is located. It is very unlikely that positivist researchers would refer to themselves *directly* in the text. It is important to be clear about how your college or university regards the use of the personal pronoun in a research project as institutions may differ in this regard.

WRITING THE VOICES OF OTHERS

Inevitably, when writing up research, you will be referring to the voices of the research participants, be it in the views encapsulated in a completed questionnaire, an observation, or in direct quotes from an interview, for example. It is important to remember that in writing up, you are representing people's views or actions and that doing this carries an ethical responsibility. Therefore, as with all other stages of the research process, writing up is not a neutral act (Coffey, 1999; Standing, 1998). You may recall in the previous chapter we noted Silverman's (2013) discussion of 'respondent validation', in which the researcher goes back to research participants and asks them whether their analysis of the data is a 'true' representation of what took place or what was said (but review the chapter for the discussion of the limitations of this). However, some researchers go further than this in their discussion of writing up, arguing that writing up carries with it a responsibility as to *what* is represented, *who* is represented (or silenced) and the *way* that they are represented.

MacNaughton and Smith (2005: 121) ask various questions of researchers, including 'Whose voices are silenced and whose voices are privileged in your research with young children?' Similarly, Standing (1998) looks at the issue of power when writing up her research into low-income, lone motherhood. She argues that as a researcher she was in a powerful position in analysing and writing the 'private' words of her sample of women for the 'public' world of academia. Moreover, she maintains that in juxtaposing her own words, when writing with her academic voice, with the words of the women in her research – women who do not have an academic background – she was reinforcing unequal power relations between them. Standing is concerned that in writing up, researchers might reinforce stereotypical constructions of different groups, such as 'depressed lone mothers'.

It should be noted that these concerns are not expressed by all researchers. Positivist researchers believe it is possible to present their findings in a way that objectively represents the 'truth'. Indeed, it may be seen as more ethical to objectively represent research findings as 'truthfully' as possible, avoiding bias. This is an area we suggest you reflect upon further, not least whether such 'objectivity' is possible.

SHARING WHAT YOU HAVE LEARNT WITH OTHERS

In this final section we will consider the ways in which researchers might share their findings with others. You may recall that in Chapter 6, which looked at ethics, we argued that it is important to share your findings in some way with the research participants. We will be considering this as well as considering how research might be shared with a wider audience, such as through publication.

Clearly, if the research has involved human subjects then the researcher should share their findings with them in some way. This relates to the principle of 'giving something back' to those who have agreed to participate in a piece of research, although we should be careful not to assume every participant will be keen to read the finished products of our research endeavours. It is also associated with ensuring that people's experience of research is a positive one – one they might consider participating in again if asked. If undertaking content analysis of newspaper articles on early childhood issues, for instance, there are no actual people directly involved in the research. If the research has involved an institution such as a nursery or a health clinic, then the researcher could make a copy of the findings available to the setting where appropriate. Another strategy might be to provide a brief report of the main findings of the research for all the participants. This can be useful as, understandably, not everyone will have the time and/or inclination to read through a 10,000-word dissertation if this is what you have written, but may be interested in reading an A4 synopsis of the findings. This might also be an important strategy when sharing research with people who may find reading difficult in the language in which the dissertation has been written.

Alternatively, the researcher might employ a collective strategy for sharing his or her research findings. In the Froebel Blockplay Research Project (Gura, 1992), the parents, whose children attended Danebury School's nursery class (one of the settings that participated in the study), were invited to an evening event at the school. At this event, the findings of the research project were shared with the children's families and the event served as a celebration of the children's and the practitioners' learning. The video that was made to highlight the work of the project shows a snippet of this evening event. If you have the opportunity to view this snippet of the video, you will see Tina Bruce presenting the work of the research group to a packed audience of parents (Bruce, 1991b).

But so far we have only discussed sharing findings with adult participants. How, then, might findings be shared with young children? This might be especially important in research undertaken with children over time as children have got used to the researcher's presence. One such method might be to take photographs during the research process and make a book with the children or for the children, documenting what took place, the children's involvement in the study and some of its key findings.

RESEARCH IN FOCUS

In an ethnographic research project focused on identity and social interaction in a multi-ethnic classroom, Barley (2014) created an online picture library for the children based on the themes that had emerged in her conversations and activities over time with them. Using this digital resource if they wished to, children were able to create their own books celebrating their own identities. In this way, the children had some control over the way they or those sharing their cultural identity were represented.

It may well be that you decide to try to share your research findings with a wider audience; that is, beyond the actual group of participants. One way that this might be done is through presenting your research findings to the wider team, if the research has taken place in an early childhood setting. An example might be a practitioner-researcher, who has carried out a study looking at how to improve the way scientific investigations are supported in the nursery class attached to a primary school, sharing his or her ideas with the rest of the school. The findings might also be shared with other practitioners in the local authority or cluster group of settings. This, in our opinion, does not seem to happen enough or only happens when the researcher has gained some recognition, such as through publication of their work. Yet as McNiff and Whitehead (2011) observe, small-scale action research has the potential to *transform* our ideas about practice.

You may recall that we discussed this in relation to Penny Holland's (2003) research into war, weapon and superhero play in Chapter 11. As many practitioners are now undertaking further study, such as early childhood studies degrees, developing local forums where practitioners can share their research might offer a platform for new practitioner-researchers to share their ideas. Some universities encourage students who have completed their research projects to present their work orally to peers in the format of a student conference. This is another way of disseminating student research as well as learning skills which are useful for future employment.

Of course, you may decide that you would like to try and publish your work more widely, especially if you have received a very good mark for your work or if someone with experience of publishing their own work or reviewing the work of others for a publication recommends this. There are numerous journals that might be appropriate.

— —— ACTIVITY ————————————————————

Investigate the range of journals that are published in the area of early childhood. You can usually do this by carrying out an online search. Look at the range and style of the articles published in the journals.

Choose one of these journals and find out about its aims and scope as well as its instructions for authors. This is usually inside the front or back cover if you are looking at a hard copy of the journal, or a space on the journal's homepage if carrying out an online search.

It is important to note that in academic journals, any paper that is sent to the journal's editor(s) is likely to undergo a peer-review process. This means that two or sometimes more people with expertise in the area that you have written about will look carefully at your paper and decide on its suitability for publication. These people usually remain anonymous. This process can take as long as a few months. The peer reviewers will usually prepare feedback for the author of the paper and if it needs some work, the author is given some time to work on revisions. The paper may, of course, be rejected at an early or later stage in this process but this does not mean the paper cannot be submitted elsewhere.

— —— KEY POINTS FROM THE CHAPTER ————————

- Writing up research involves structuring it in a way that communicates the ideas in the study clearly. Usually, this involves a chapter format that includes an introduction, literature review, methodology, findings, discussion and conclusion.
- A well-written piece of research gives a sense of the self of the researcher, albeit unobtrusively. The extent to which this happens directly in the text is linked to the paradigm and methodological approach within which the researcher is working.
- Writing up research is an act of representation that carries with it ethical responsibilities; that is, it can reinforce particular views of particular groups of people.
- Research findings can be shared with a wider audience. Researchers should think about how to share their research findings with participants, including children. In addition, findings can be shared with a wider audience, such as disseminating findings to practitioners in a local authority or through publication.

———— FURTHER READING ————

Clough, P. and Nutbrown, C. (2012) *A Student's Guide to Methodology*, 3rd edition. London: Sage. Chapter 8 is very useful when thinking about writing up research.

Standing, K. (1998) 'Writing the voices of the less powerful: research on lone mothers', in J. Ribbens and R. Edwards (eds) *Feminist Dilemmas in Qualitative Research: Public Knowledge and Private Lives*. London: Sage. This thought-provoking chapter looks at the issue of representing the voices of research participants. It is an issue that is picked up elsewhere in this edited volume.

Don't forget to visit the online resources at
https://study.sagepub.com/mukherjiandalbon3e for access to free SAGE journal articles, weblinks, videos, exercises, mini quizzes and an interactive glossary.

CONCLUSION

We hope that in reading this book you have learnt more about early childhood research and will feel inspired to carry out your *own* research. It is something that we think is both personally rewarding and important in terms of developing a greater understanding of issues relating to young children and their families. Crucially, research is significant in further developing early childhood practice. We hope, too, that as you carry out research, you try to share what you have learnt in order to develop the understanding and practice of others in the field. But most of all, we hope that in carrying out early childhood research you are drawn to studying with and about young children 'through some intuitive sense of desiring to see the world through children's lives, attempting to improve children's lives, and simply experiencing joy when with young children' (Lahman, 2008: 296).

GLOSSARY

Abstract: a paragraph placed at the beginning of a research report or article which outlines the reasons for the research, the research question, brief details of how the study was conducted, and a summary of the findings.

Action research: research which is concerned with changing and improving practice in some way. It is collaborative, being initiated and implemented by practitioners working in a setting. Action research operates in a series of cycles each involving reflections of practice.

Analytical surveys: surveys used to test a hypothesis or to answer specific research questions.

Appendix (appendices pl.): supplementary material placed at the end of a research report which is referred to in the text but is too bulky to be placed in the main account.

Bar chart: a graphical way of presenting nominal data where vertical bars are used.

Before and after study design: also known as test–retest; used to assess the effect of an intervention on a group of participants. Participants are 'tested' against a variable, an intervention aimed at modifying the variable is applied following which the group is retested to see if the intervention has had an effect.

Case study: an in-depth investigation of an individual, group, situation or event.

Child study: a case study based on observations of a single child, sometimes with the aim of recommending a course of action for the child, or with the aim of finding out more about child development in general.

Clinical interview: an observational method which involves the use of interview and child observation. An example would be researchers investigating Piaget's three-mountain experiment.

Closed question: a question where the respondent has to choose from a number of answers that the researcher has chosen beforehand.

Coding: an analytical process whereby quantitative data (such as from questionnaires) and qualitative data (such as from interviews) are transformed into meaningful categories.

Collective case study: a collective case study, or multiple case design, is one that contains more than one case.

Confirmatory stage of scientific research: where a researcher starts with a theory about why a particular phenomenon is occurring and develops a hypothesis (a prediction) based on the theory. The next stage of this approach is when the researcher conducts an empirical investigation to test the hypothesis. If the data uphold the hypothesis then this supports the underlying theory. This approach is sometimes known as the deductive method.

Confounding variables: variables which have not been controlled by the researcher which may affect the findings of the research, making them unreliable.

Content analysis: a quantitative, numerical technique for systematically describing written, spoken or visual communication.

Correlation: a statistic used to demonstrate the relationship between two sets of paired measurements. One might say that there is a correlation between obesity and diabetes.

Critical analysis: a process used in writing a literature review where the 'literature' is not merely described but subject to a process of interrogation in order to assess the relevance, authenticity and reliability of the literature together with the summarising of common thematic areas of discussion.

Cross-sectional study: a type of research design where participants are investigated at one point of time or over a brief time period.

Data: information that is collected during the research process. Quantitative data are recorded numerically. Qualitative data are recorded in the form of words, concepts and ideas.

Data analysis: the process of extracting meaning from raw data. In quantitative studies this often involves the application of statistical tests. In qualitative studies it involves the identification of common themes which occur in the collected data.

Deductive reasoning: the process of drawing conclusions about something on the basis of prior knowledge known to be true. For example, one may agree that the following statement (premise) is true: 'Newborn babies cannot talk'. Then, given another statement, 'Baby John can say "DaDa"', it is possible to deduce that John cannot be a newborn baby. Deductive reasoning is only successful if the first premise is true.

Dependent variable: the variable to which measured changes are attributed to the manipulation of the independent variable by the researcher.

Descriptive statistics: a process of describing quantitative data by calculating the frequency, average and range of a set of numbers.

Descriptive survey: one that sets out to discover what people from a particular target population think and do.

Discourse analysis: the study of social life, understood through analysis of language in its widest sense, including face-to-face talk, non-verbal interaction, images, symbols and documents (Potter and Wetherell, 1987).

Discussion (conclusion): the section of a research report which interprets the findings of the research and positions the findings in the light of what is already known. The discussion may be followed by an overall conclusion, or, alternatively, the discussion section and conclusion may be conflated and referred to as 'the conclusion'.

Empiricism: the idea that knowledge comes from experience and is derived via the senses.

Epistemology: 'ways of researching and enquiring into the nature of reality and the nature of things' (Cohen et al., 2011: 3).

Ethics: moral 'rules' or principles which underpin research.

Ethics committee: a group of people, commonly working in universities and hospitals, who come together to scrutinise research proposals with the aim of protecting the well-being of all those whose well-being could be affected by the research.

Ethnography: a qualitative approach to research that aims to provide rich and detailed data about people in particular sociocultural contexts.

Event sample: an observation where a pre-determined behaviour or event is recorded whenever it happens.

Experimental design: a quantitative research design where the researcher manipulates the independent variable(s) to see the effect this has on the dependent variable. An experimental design involves the strict control of external factors which may influence the findings, this includes the random assignment of participants to groups.

Exploratory scientific approach: starts with the researcher making observations and searching for a pattern. If a pattern is found then the researcher puts forward a theory or idea about why this pattern occurs. This approach is sometimes known as the inductive method.

Field experiments: experiments carried out in 'naturalistic' situations, rather than in a laboratory.

Focus groups: group interviews, where a group leader or moderator leads a group discussion.

Gatekeeper: in research, a gatekeeper is someone or an organisation/body, who has to give permission before research can proceed.

Generalisability: the extension of research findings or conclusions from a sample to the wider population from which the sample is drawn.

Hypothesis: a prediction based on theory.

Independent sample design: an experimental design where there are two different groups being tested under similar conditions.

Independent variable: the variable that is being manipulated by the researcher to find out its effect on the dependent variable.

Inductive reasoning: is when one draws conclusions about something on the balance of probability that a statement is true, based on what has previously occurred. However, when using inductive reasoning it is always possible that the exception to the rule may come along, which will disprove the theory.

Inferential statistics: used when you are investigating to see if the difference between two groups is due to chance or not, by using tests of significance.

Instrumental case study: a case study where the 'case' is an instrument or tool used to help the researcher understand more about a general phenomenon.

Interpretivism: a paradigm, developed as a response to positivism, which focuses on the meanings people attribute to phenomena and actions.

Interval data: data derived from the measurement of a variable using a scale such as height or weight.

Interval measurement: in interval measurement, a scale is used which has an equal interval. Interval measurement gives rise to interval data.

Interview: a research method where one person asks questions of an individual or group of people with the expectation of getting answers to a particular question or an elaboration of their views on a particular topic.

Intrinsic case studies: single case designs where the aim of the research is to obtain a deep understanding of the case, such as an in-depth child study.

Laboratory experiments: experiments conducted in a scientific laboratory where it is easier to control variables than experiments undertaken in a natural environment.

Laboratory observations: observations undertaken under laboratory conditions in an effort to reduce the effect of confounding variables.

Line graph: a graphical way of presenting data that is used to show changes in quantities and is commonly used to plot changes over time.

Literature review: an evaluative overview of what is known about a topic, based on published research and theoretical accounts, which serves as a basis for future research or policy decisions.

Longitudinal prospective study/survey: a term commonly used to describe studies that follow a cohort of children until adulthood and beyond such as the Millennium Cohort Study.

Longitudinal study: a research design where a situation or participants are investigated over a period of time.

Matched pair design: an experimental design where two groups of participants are used, but each participant in one group is matched as far as possible with someone from the other group, according to relevant variables.

Mean: the average of a set of numbers.

Measures of central tendency: ways of describing a group of numbers, or data set, that calculate the number that is *most* representative of that data set. Measures of central tendency include the mean, median and the mode.

Median: the middle point of a set of numbers.

Method: the data-collection technique used in research, the choice of which is guided by the methodological approach of the study.

Methodology: ideas about how to approach research based on an underlying paradigm.

Mode: the most frequently occurring value in a data set.

Multivariate analysis: a statistical technique that allows for the effect of two or more variables to be analysed at the same time.

Narrative observations: observations where everything a participant says or does is written down. Also known as 'naturalistic' observations, descriptive narratives, running records or written observations.

Natural experiments: the exploitation of a naturally occurring event for research purposes. For example, a nursery may introduce a key person approach and it may be possible to compare the time taken for new children to settle before and after the change.

'Naturalistic' observations: observations undertaken in the natural environment of the person being observed. The term is also commonly used to describe narrative observations.

Nominal measurement: the classification of data according to a named category, for example, male/female.

Non-experimental designs: quantitative research designs that are descriptive and do not depend upon the manipulation of independent variables. Large-scale surveys and correlational studies are examples of non-experimental designs.

Non-participant observation: observations conducted by a researcher who is not part of the group/environment being observed and who endeavours to remain unnoticed and anonymous.

Non-probability sampling: a method of sampling used in qualitative research where there is no requirement for the sample to be representative of a whole population. It does not involve random selection.

Null hypothesis: a statement that the independent variable will have no effect on the dependent variable.

Observer bias: occurs when factors, personal to the researcher, affect the way that an observation is recorded and analysed. Ethnicity, culture, religion, gender and social class and past experience are among factors that may lead to bias.

Ontology: 'assumptions about the nature of reality and the nature of things' (Cohen et al., 2011: 3).

Open question: one that encourages the respondent to answer the question in any way they want, using the language that they want.

Opportunity/convenience sampling: a sampling method which relies on choosing anyone who is available to take part in research.

Ordinal measurement: the level of measurement which describes position, or order, in a group.

Paradigm: a theoretical framework which underpins how one sees the world.

Participant observation: observations where the observer is part of the observation or environment being observed. The degree of participation can vary from complete participation, participant as observer and observer as participant.

Photo elicitation: where photographs are used in interviews to elicit responses from participants.

Pie chart: a graphical way of presenting data used to indicate proportions. Each 'slice of the pie' represents a category and is represented as a percentage of the whole.

Population: the large group to which the researcher wants the findings to apply.

Positivism: a paradigm which assumes that scientific methodology is the most appropriate way of studying the world and that strict application of scientific methodology will reveal universal truths.

Probability sampling: methods of sampling that are designed to choose samples which are representative of the whole population, such as random sampling.

Prospective study design: one that is designed to wait until the future to find out the outcome of an event/intervention on a variable.

Purposive sampling: also known as theoretical sampling or criterion-based sampling. This method of sampling is often used in qualitative research where participants are chosen as the research evolves according to an understanding of the theoretical strands which emerge.

Qualitative methodology: the methodological approach which uses methods concerned with describing experiences, emphasising meaning and exploring the nature of an issue in some detail. It is less concerned with being able to make generalisations about the world than quantitative research.

Quantitative methodology: the methodological approach which emphasises the collection of data in the form of numbers and often, but not always, involves the formulation of a hypothesis. Quantitative methodology is used to measure or quantify the extent of a phenomenon.

Questionnaire: a list of questions, with space for people to respond. Questionnaires may be paper or computer based.

Random sampling: a method of sampling where every individual in the sampling frame has an equal chance of being selected for inclusion in the study.

Ratio measurement: interval scales which have a zero point. Examples would be time, distance and age.

Reference list: the list of works, placed at the end of a piece of academic writing such as a research report or dissertation, which contains the sources for all the citations in the text.

Reliability: relates to how well the research has been carried out. In quantitative research, findings are said to be reliable if other researchers can replicate the findings of a study by using the same methods. In qualitative research, reliability may be assessed by the degree to which researchers are consistent in the way they have identified themes and interpreted the data.

Repeated measures design: an experimental design where the same group is tested under different conditions.

Research design: the strategy or plan that is used to investigate a research question or hypothesis. Experimental design is one example of this.

Research journal: an ongoing record of your research which documents the research process as it unfolds. In qualitative studies the research journal is used to record reflections, ideas and feelings about the research.

Research proposal: a 'written document summarising prior literature and describing the procedure to be used to answer the research question' (Johnson and Christensen, 2012: 87).

Research supervisor: usually a member of the academic team in an institution such as a university, who has the responsibility of overseeing your project.

Retrospective study design: a design that investigates issues which have happened in the past, using data available at the time, or relying on the memory of the participants.

Sample: the individuals chosen for a research study from a sampling frame, drawn from the population to which the findings of the study are designed to apply.

Sampling frame: the elements (individuals) in the population for your research, who could be included in the sample.

Scientific method: a way of finding answers to questions by using a process of observation, the formulation of a hypothesis and the rigorous, systematic collection of data to confirm or refute the hypothesis.

Self-selected sampling: a sample consisting of people who volunteer to participate in the research.

Snowball sampling: a method of sampling where each individual recruited onto a study is asked to identify other individuals who may be appropriate and willing to be participants.

Stratified sampling: a method of sampling where the population is divided into groups (or strata) according to criteria relevant to the research, from which a random sample is drawn.

Structured interview: one where the questions are decided beforehand and are 'closed', where only limited responses can be given.

Structured observations: observations that have a pre-determined aim. Often quantitative in nature. Structured observations include: time samples, event samples, checklists.

Structured questionnaire: one where only closed questions are used or the respondent has to choose from a limited set of options.

Survey: a quantitative research approach where standardised questions are asked of a large sample of participants chosen to be representative of a larger population. The questions can be administered in the form of a printed questionnaire, online questionnaire, face-to-face structured interviews or interviews via the telephone.

Systematic sampling: a method of sampling where participants are drawn from a list at fixed intervals.

Target child observation: a form of observation where a pre-prepared template is devised to record children's behaviour, using a pre-decided set of abbreviations. Commonly employed when more than one observer is being used in an effort to standardise recording.

Thematic analysis: a method of data analysis used in qualitative research, where themes and patterns in data are identified.

Theoretical sampling: another name for purposive or criterion-based selection.

Time sample: a structured observation, where a participant (adult or child), a group of participants or an area of a nursery is observed at regular intervals during the day.

Triangulation: the use of a variety of methods, researchers' perspectives, theories and methodological approaches to answer research questions, in order to corroborate results and increase reliability. Triangulation is primarily used in qualitative research.

Unstructured interview: these are designed to investigate a topic in depth. Although there is an overall aim there is no preconceived idea beforehand about what issues may be discussed, with the researcher being free to follow paths of inquiry as they emerge.

Unstructured questionnaire: one which contains open questions, designed to elicit the thoughts and ideas of the respondent.

Validity: the validity of a piece of research relates to how sound it is considered to be and whether the data collected truly represents what the researcher claims s/he is measuring. There may be differences between qualitative and quantitative research traditions in how validity is demonstrated.

Variables: variables are factors which may affect the findings of a research study. For example if one is looking at the effects of exercise on individuals, variables could include the age of the individual, gender and weight.

Triangulation: the use of a variety of methods, researchers, perspectives, theories and methodological approaches to answer research questions in order to corroborate results and increase reliability. Triangulation is primarily used in qualitative research.

Unstructured interview: these are designed to investigate a topic in depth. Although there is an overall aim there is no preconceived idea beforehand about what issue may be discussed, with the researcher being free to follow paths of inquiry as they emerge.

Unstructured questionnaire: one which contains open questions, designed to elicit the thoughts and ideas of the respondent.

Validity: the validity of a piece of research relates to how sound it is considered to be and whether the data collected truly represents what the research claims. There is inevitably... There may be differences between qualitative and quantitative research traditions in how validity is demonstrated.

Variables: factors which may affect the findings of a research study. For example if one is looking at the effects of exercise on individuals, variables could include the age of the individual, gender and weight.

REFERENCES

Acheson, D. (1998) *Independent Inquiry into Inequalities in Health Report*. London: The Stationery Office.

Adamson, P. (2013) *Child Well-being in Rich Countries: A Comparative Overview*, Innocenti Report Cardno. 11. Florence: UNICEF Innocenti Research Centre. www.unicef-irc.org/publications/683 (accessed 17 July 2017).

Ailwood, J. (2008) 'Learning or earning in the "smart state": changing tactics for governing early childhood', *Childhood*, 15(4): 535–51.

Ainsworth, M. and Bell, S. (1970) 'Attachment, exploration and separation: illustrated by the behaviour of one-year-olds in a strange situation', *Child Development*, 41: 49–65.

Ainsworth, S., Blehar, M., Walters, E. and Wall, S. (1978) *Patterns of Infant Attachment: A Psychological Study of the Strange Situation*. Hillsdale, NJ: Erlbaum.

Alanen, L. (2001) 'Explorations in generational analysis', in L. Alanen and B. Mayall (eds) *Conceptualizing Adult–Child Relations*. London: Routledge.

Albon, D. (2005) 'Approaches to the study of children, food and sweet eating: a review of the literature', *Early Child Development and Care*, 175(5): 407–18.

Albon, D. (2007) 'Exploring food and eating patterns using food-maps', *Nutrition and Food Science*, 37(4): 254–9.

Albon, D. (2009) 'Challenges to improving the uptake of milk in a nursery class: a case study', *Health Education*, 109(2): 140–54.

Albon, D. (2011) 'Post-modern and post-structuralist perspectives on early childhood education', in L. Miller and L. Pound (eds) *Theories and Approaches to Learning in the Early Years*. London: Sage.

Albon, D. and Rosen, R. (2014) *Negotiating Adult–Child Relationships in Early Childhood Research*. London: Routledge.

Alderson, P. (2000) 'Children as researchers: the effect of participation rights on research methodology', in P. Christensen and A. James (eds) *Research with Children: Perspectives and Practices*. London: Falmer Press.

Alderson, P. (2005) 'Designing ethical research with children', in A. Farrell (ed.) *Ethical Research with Children*. Maidenhead: Open University Press.

Aldiss, S., Horstman, M., O'Leary, C., Richardson, A. and Gibson, F. (2009) 'What is important to young children who have cancer while in hospital?', *Children and Society*, 23: 85–98.

Alldred, P. (1998) 'Ethnography and discourse analysis: dilemmas in representing the voices of children', in J. Ribbens and R. Edwards (eds) *Feminist Dilemmas in Qualitative Research: Public Knowledge and Private Lives*. London: Sage.

Allen, G. (2005) 'Research ethics in a culture of risk', in A. Farrell (ed.) *Ethical Research with Children*. Maidenhead: Open University Press.

Anderson, G. (1998) *Fundamentals of Educational Research*, 2nd edition. London: Taylor and Francis.

Angelides, P. and Michaelidou, A. (2009) 'The deafening silence: discussing children's drawings for understanding and addressing marginalisation', *Journal of Early Childhood Research*, 7(1): 27–45.

Angrosino, M. (2005) 'Recontextualising observation: ethnography, pedagogy, and the prospects for a progressive political agenda', in N.K. Denzin and Y.S. Lincoln (eds) *Handbook of Qualitative Research*, 3rd edition. London: Sage.

Angrosino, M. and Perez, K.A.M. (2000) 'Rethinking observation: from method to context', in N.K. Denzin and Y.S. Lincoln (eds) *Handbook of Qualitative Research*, 2nd edition. London: Sage.

Anning, A., Cottrell, D., Frost, N., Green, J. and Robinson, M. (2006) *Developing Multi-professional Teamwork for Integrated Children's Services*. Maidenhead: Open University Press.

Arnold, C. (2003) *Observing Harry: Child Development and Learning 0–5*. Maidenhead: Open University Press.

Athey, C. (2007) *Extending Thought in Young Children*, 2nd edition. London: Sage.

Atkinson, R.L., Atkinson, R.C., Smith, E., Bem, D. and Nolen-Hoeksema, S. (1996) *Hilgard's Introduction to Psychology*. Fort Worth, TX: Harcourt Brace.

Aubrey, C., David, T., Godfrey, R. and Thompson, L. (2000) *Early Childhood Educational Research: Issues in Methodology and Ethics*. London: Routledge Falmer Press.

Avon Longitudinal Study of Parents and Their Children (ALSPAC). www.bristol.ac.uk/alspac/about (accessed 16 February 2017).

Axline, V. (1971) *Dibs in Search of Self*. Harmondsworth: Penguin.

Backstrom, C.H. and Hursh-César, G. (1981) *Survey Research*, 2nd edition. New York: Macmillan.

Bandura, A., Ross, D. and Ross, S. (1963) 'Imitation of film-mediated aggressive models', *Journal of Abnormal and Social Psychology*, 66(1): 3–11.

Barbour, R. (2008) *Introducing Qualitative Research: A Student Guide to the Craft of Doing Qualitative Research*. London: Sage.

Barbour, R. (2014) *Introducing Qualitative Research: A Student Guide to the Craft of Doing Qualitative Research*, 2nd edition. London: Sage.

Barker, J. and Weller, S. (2003) '"Is it fun?" Developing children centred research methods', *International Journal of Sociology and Social Policy*, 23(1–2): 33–58.

Barley, R. (2014) *Identity and Social Interaction in a Multi-Ethnic Classroom*. London: Tufnell Press.

Bath, C. (2013) 'Conceptualising listening to children as an ethic of care in early childhood education and care', *Children and Society*, 27: 361–71.

Bell, J. (2010) *Doing Your Research Project: A Guide for First-Time Researchers in Education, Health and Social Science*, 5th edition. Maidenhead: Open University Press.

Bell, J. with Walters, S. (2014) *Doing Your Research Project: A Guide for First Time Researchers*, 6th edition. Maidenhead: Open University Press.

Bell, L. (1998) 'Public and private meanings in diaries: researching family and childcare', in J. Ribbens and R. Edwards (eds) *Feminist Dilemmas in Qualitative Research: Public Knowledge and Private Lives*. London: Sage.

Ben-Ari, E. (1997) *Body Projects in Japanese Childcare: Culture, Organisation and Emotions in a Pre-School*. Richmond: Curzon Press.

Bertram, T. and Pascal, C. (2001) *Effective Early Learning: Case Studies in Improvement*. London: Sage.

Björk, M., Nordström, B. and Hallström, I. (2006) 'Needs of young children with cancer during their initial hospitalization: an observational study', *Journal of Pediatric Oncology Nursing*, 23(4): 210–19.

Black, K. (2010) *Business Statistics: Contemporary Decision Making*, 6th edition. London: John Wiley and Sons.

Blaxter, L., Hughes, C. and Tight, M. (2010) *How to Research*, 4th edition. Maidenhead: Open University Press.

Bogdan, R. and Biklen, S. (1998) *Qualitative Research Education: An Introduction to Theory and Methods*. Boston, MA: Allyn and Bacon.

Bolton, G. (2001) *Reflective Practice: Writing and Professional Development*. London: Sage.

Bolton, G. (2005) *Reflective Practice: Writing and Professional Development*, 2nd edition. London: Sage.

Booth, C., Kostadintcheva, K., Knox, A. and Bram, A. (2013) *Parents' Views and Experiences of Childcare: Research Report*. London: Ipsos MORI and Department for Education. www.gov.uk/government/uploads/system/uploads/attachment_data/file/212589/DFE-RR266.pdf (accessed 2 August 2013).

Bordo, S. (2003) *Unbearable Weight: Feminism, Western Culture and the Body*. Berkeley, CA: University of California Press.

Bowlby, J. (1969) *Attachment and Loss. Vol. 1: Attachment*. London: Hogarth.

Bowlby, J., Robertson, J. and Rosenbluth, D. (1952) 'A two-year old goes to hospital', *The Psychoanalytic Study of the Child*, 7: 82–94.

Braun, V. and Clarke, V. (2006) 'Using thematic analysis in psychology', *Qualitative Research in Psychology*, 3(2): 77–101.

Brice-Heath, S. (1983) *Ways with Words: Language, Life and Work in Communities and Classrooms*. Cambridge: Cambridge University Press.

British Educational Research Association (BERA). www.bera.ac.uk (accessed 2 March 2009).

British Educational Research Association (BERA) (2011) *Ethical Guidelines for Educational Research*. www.bera.ac.uk/researchers-resources/publications/ethical-guidelines-for-educational-research-2011 (accessed 14 May 2014).

British Psychological Society. www.bps.org.uk/system/files/Public%20files/inf180_web.pdf (accessed 14 July 2017).

British Sociological Association. www.britsoc.co.uk/ethics (accessed 2 March 2009).

Bromley, D. (1986) *The Case Study Method in Psychology and Related Disciplines*. Chichester: Wiley.

Brooker, L. (2011) 'Taking children seriously: an alternative agenda for research?', *Journal of Early Childhood Research*, 9: 137–49.

Brown, T. and Jones, L. (2001) *Action Research and Postmodernism: Congruence and Critique*. Buckingham: Open University Press.

Bruce, T. (1987) *Early Childhood Education*. London: Hodder and Stoughton.

Bruce, T. (1991a) *Time to Play in Early Childhood Education*. London: Hodder and Stoughton.

Bruce, T. (1991b) *Building a Future: Blockplay and Young Children*, video and booklet, Froebel Blockplay Research Project.

Bruner, J.S. (2006) *In Search of Pedagogy. Vol. 1: The Selected Works of Jerome S. Bruner*. Abingdon: Routledge.

Buchbinder, M., Longhofer, J., Barrett, T., Lawson, P. and Floersch, J. (2006) 'Ethnographic approaches to child care research', *Journal of Early Childhood Research*, 4(1): 45–63.

Bunting, G. and Freeman, R. (1999) 'The influence of socio-demographic factors upon children's breaktime food consumption in North and West Belfast', *Health Education Journal*, 58(4): 401–9.

Buzan, T. (2011) *Buzan's Study Skills*. London: Pearson Education.

Campbell, A., McNamara, O. and Gilroy, P. (2004) *Practitioner Research and Professional Development in Education*. London: Paul Chapman Publishing.

Cannold, L. (2001) 'Interviewing adults', in G. MacNaughton, S. Rolfe and I. Siraj-Blatchford (eds) *Doing Early Childhood Research: International Perspectives on Theory and Practice*. Buckingham: Open University Press.

Cardwell, M., Clark, L. and Meldrum, C. (2000) *Psychology for A Level*, 2nd edition. London: Collins Educational.

Carr, C. and Worth, A. (2001) 'The use of the telephone for research', *Nursing Times Research*, 6(1): 511–24.

Central Advisory Council for Education (1967) *Children and Their Primary Schools*. The Plowden Report. London: HMSO.

Central Statistics Office (Ireland). www.cso.ie/en/census/index.html (accessed 28 July 2013).

Centre for Longitudinal Studies (CLS) (2007) *National Child Development Study*. www.cls.ioe.ac.uk/page.aspx?&sitesectionid=724&sitesectiontitle=Welcome+to+the+National+Child+Development+Study (accessed 14 May 2014).

Chang-Kredl, S. (2010) 'Cinematic representations of childhood: privileging the adult viewer', in G.S. Cannella and L.D. Soto (eds) *Childhoods: A Handbook*. New York: Peter Lang.

Charmaz, K. and Mitchell, R.G. (1997) 'The myth of silent authorship: self, substance, and style in ethnographic writing', in R. Hertz (ed.) *Reflexivity and Voice*. London: Sage.

Chenail, R. (1995) 'Presenting qualitative data', *The Qualitative Report*, 2(3), December. www.nova.edu/ssss/QR/QR2–3/presenting.html (accessed 8 March 2009).

Christensen, P. and Prout, A. (2002) 'Working with ethical symmetry in social research with children', *Childhood*, 9(4): 477–97.

Christians, C.G. (2005) 'Ethics and politics in qualitative research', in N. Denzin and Y. Lincoln (eds) *The Sage Handbook of Qualitative Research*, 3rd edition. London: Sage.

Clark, A. (2005) 'Ways of seeing: using the Mosaic Approach to listen to young children's perspectives', in A. Clark, A.T. Kjorholt and P. Moss (eds) *Beyond Listening: Children's Perspectives on Early Childhood Services*. Bristol: Policy Press.

Clark, A. and Moss, P. (2011) *Listening to Young Children: The Mosaic Approach*, 2nd edition. London: NCB and JRF.

Clark, A., Kjorholt, A.T. and Moss, P. (eds) (2005) *Beyond Listening: Children's Perspectives on Early Childhood Services*. Bristol: Policy Press.

Clough, P. and Nutbrown, C. (2007) *A Student's Guide to Methodology*, 2nd edition. London: Sage.

Clough, P. and Nutbrown, C. (2012) *A Student's Guide to Methodology*, 3rd edition. London: Sage.

Coady, M.M. (2010) 'Ethics in early childhood research', in G. MacNaughton, S.A. Rolfe and I. Siraj-Blatchford (eds) *Doing Early Childhood Research: International Perspectives on Theory and Practice*, 2nd edition. Maidenhead: Open University Press.

Cocks, A.J. (2006) 'The ethical maze: finding an inclusive path towards gaining children's agreement to research participation', *Childhood*, 13(2): 247–66.

Coffey, A. (1999) *The Ethnographic Self: Fieldwork and the Representation of Identity*. London: Sage.

Cohen, L., Manion, L. and Morrison, K. (2000) *Research Methods in Education*, 4th edition. London: Routledge.

Cohen, L., Manion, L. and Morrison, K. (2011) *Research Methods in Education*, 7th edition. London: Taylor and Francis.

Connolly, P. (2008) 'Race, gender and critical reflexivity in research with young children', in P. Christensen and A. James (eds) *Research with Children: Perspectives and Practices*, 2nd edition. London: Routledge.

Cook, T. and Hess, E. (2007) 'What the camera sees and from whose perspective: fun methodologies for engaging children in enlightening adults', *Childhood*, 14(1): 29–45.

Coolican, H. (2009) *Research Methods and Statistics in Psychology*, 5th edition. Abingdon: Routledge.

Coolican, H. (2014) *Research Methods and Statistics in Psychology*, 6th edition. Abingdon: Routledge.

Corsaro, W. (1985) *Friendship and Peer Culture in the Early Years*. Norwood, NJ: Ablex.

Corsaro, W. (1996) 'Transitions in early childhood: the promise of comparative longitudinal ethnography', in A. Colby, R. Jessor and R.A. Schweder (eds) *Ethnography and Human Development: Context and Meaning in Social Inquiry*. Chicago, IL: University of Chicago Press.

Corsaro, W. and Molinari, L. (2008) 'Entering and observing in children's worlds: a reflection on a longitudinal ethnography of early education in Italy', in A. Christensen and A. James (eds) *Research with Children: Perspectives and Practices*, 2nd edition. Abingdon: Routledge.

Crawford, C., Dearden, L., Micklewright, J. and Vignoles, A. (2016) *Family Background and University Success: Differences in Higher Education Access and Outcomes in England*. Oxford: Oxford University Press.

Crotty, M. (1998) *The Foundations of Social Research: Meaning and Perspective in the Research Process*. London: Sage.

Darte, P. (2007) *Children's National Medical Center Scientists Discover Fundamental Protein Instrumental to Brain Development and Repair*. www.eurekalert.org/pub_releases/2007-07/cnmc-csd070607.php (accessed 25 July 2017).

Darwin, C.R. (1877) 'A biographical sketch of an infant', *Mind: A Quarterly Review of Psychology and Philosophy*, 2(7): 285–94. http://darwin-online.org.uk (accessed 31 January 2014).

David, T., Tonkin, J., Powell, S. and Anderson, C. (2005) 'Ethical aspects of power in research with children', in A. Farrell (ed.) *Ethical Research with Children*. Maidenhead: Open University Press.

Davies, C. and Robinson, K. (2010) 'Hatching babies and stork deliveries: risk and regulation in the construction of children's sexual knowledge', *Contemporary Issues in Early Childhood*, 11(3): 249–62.

Davis, J., Watson, N. and Cunningham-Burley, S. (2008) 'Disabled children, ethnography and unspoken understandings: the collaborative construction of diverse identities', in P. Christensen and A. James (eds) *Research with Children: Perspectives and Practices*. Abingdon: Routledge.

Dawson, C. (2009) *Introduction to Research Methods*. Oxford: How To Books.

Deegan, M.J. (2007) 'The Chicago School of ethnography', in P. Atkinson, A. Coffey, S. Delamont, J. Lofland and L. Lofland (eds) *Handbook of Ethnography*. London: Sage.

Deming, W. (1960) *Sample Design in Business Research*. New York: John Wiley and Sons.

Denscombe, M. (2007) *The Good Research Guide for Small-Scale Research Projects*, 3rd edition. Maidenhead: Open University Press.

Denscombe, M. (2010) *The Good Research Guide for Small-Scale Research Projects*, 4th edition. Maidenhead: Open University Press.

Denscombe, M. (2012) *Research Proposals: A Practical Guide*. Maidenhead: Open University Press.

Denscombe, M. (2014) *The Good Research Guide for Small Scale Research Projects*, 5th edition. Maidenhead: Open University Press.

Denzin, N. and Lincoln, Y. (2011) 'Introduction', in N. Denzin and Y. Lincoln (eds) *The Sage Handbook of Qualitative Research*, 4th edition. London: Sage.

Department for Children, Schools and Families (DCSF) (2007) *Confident, Capable and Creative: Supporting Boys' Achievements. Guidance for Practitioners in the Early Years Foundation Stage*. Norwich: DCSF.

De Souza, N., Sardessai, V., Joshi, K., Joshi, V. and Hughes, M. (2006) 'The determinants of compliance with an early intervention programme for high-risk babies in India', *Child: Care, Health and Development*, 32(1): 63–72. http://onlinelibrary.wiley.com/doi/10.1111/j.1365-2214.2006.00576.x/full (accessed 2 August 2013).

DeVault, M.L. (1997) 'Personal writing in social research: issues of production and interpretation', in R. Hertz (ed.) *Reflexivity and Voice*. London: Sage.

De Vaus, D. (2013) *Surveys in Social Research*, 6th edition. London: Routledge.

Diamond, K. and Hestenes, L. (1996) 'Preschool children's conceptions of disabilities', *Topics in Early Childhood Special Education*, 16(4): 458–75.

Dockett, S. and Perry, B. (2007) 'Trusting children's accounts in research', *Journal of Early Childhood Research*, 5: 47–63.

DoH (Department of Health) (2014) *National Child Measurement Programme*. www.gov.uk/government/collections/national-child-measurement-programme (accessed 14 May 2014).

Donaldson, M. (1979) *Children's Minds*. London: Fontana.

Douglas, M. and Nicod, M. (1974) 'Taking the biscuit: the structure of British meals', *New Society*, 30(637): 744–7.

Driskell, D. (2002) *Creating Better Cities with Children and Youth*. London: Earthscan/UNESCO.

Duffy, B. (2010) 'The analysis of documents', in J. Bell (ed.) *Doing Your Research Project: A Guide for First-time Researchers in Education, Health and Social Science*, 5th edition. Maidenhead: Open University Press.

Dunn, J. (2005) 'Naturalistic observations of children and their families', in S. Greene and D. Hogan (eds) *Researching Children's Experience: Approaches and Methods*. London: Sage.

Edmiston, B. (2005) 'Coming home to research', in D.S. Soto and B.B. Swadener (eds) *Power and Voice in Research with Children*. New York: Peter Lang.

Edmiston, B. (2008) *Forming Ethical Identities in Early Childhood Play*. Abingdon: Routledge.

Edmond, R. (2005) 'Ethnographic research methods with children and young people', in S. Greene and D. Hogan (eds) *Researching Children's Experience: Approaches and Methods*. London: Sage.

Edwards, A. (2001) 'Qualitative designs and analysis', in G. MacNaughton, S. Rolfe and I. Siraj-Blatchford (eds) *Doing Early Childhood Research: International Theories on Theory and Practice*. Maidenhead: Open University Press.

Edwards, A. (2010) 'Qualitative research designs and analysis', in G. MacNaughton, S. Rolfe and I. Siraj-Blatchford (eds) *Doing Early Childhood Research: International Perspectives on Theory and Practice*, 2nd edition. Maidenhead: Open University Press.

Elfer, P., Goldschmeid, E. and Selleck, D. (2012) *Key Person Relationships in the Nursery*, 2nd edition. London: Sage.

Eliot and Associates (2005) *Guidelines for Conducting a Focus Group*. http://datainnovationproject.org/wp-content/uploads/2017/04/4/_How_to_Conduct_a_Focus_Group-2-1.pdf (accessed 10 November 2017).

Elliott, J. (1991) *Action Research for Educational Change*. Buckingham: Open University Press.

Elwick, S. (2015) '"Baby-cam" and researching with infants: viewer, image and (not) knowing', *Contemporary Issues in Early Childhood*, 16(4): 322–38.

Emerson, R.W. (2015) 'Convenience sampling, random sampling, and snowball sampling: how does sampling affect the validity of research?', *Journal of Visual Impairment and Blindness*, 109(2): 164–8.

Emerson, R.M., Fretz, R.I. and Shaw, L.L. (2007) 'Participant observation and fieldnotes', in P. Atkinson, A. Coffey, S. Delamont, J. Lofland and L. Lofland (eds) *Handbook of Ethnography*. London: Sage.

Etherington, K. (2004) *Becoming a Reflexive Researcher: Using Ourselves in Research*. London: Jessica Kingsley.

Evangelou, M., Sylva, K., Kyriacou, M., Wild, M. and Glenny, G. (2009) *Early Years Learning and Development Literature Review*. London: Department for Children, Schools and Families.

Eysenck, M. (2004) *Psychology: An International Perspective*. London: Psychology Press.

Farrant, B. and Zubrick, S. (2013) 'Parent–child book reading across early childhood and child vocabulary in the early school years: findings from the Longitudinal Study of Australian Children', *First Language*, 3(3): 280–93.

Farrell, A. (2005) 'Ethics and research with children', in A. Farrell (ed.) *Ethical Research with Children*. Maidenhead: Open University Press.

Farrell, A., Tayler, C., Tennent, L. and Gahan, D. (2002) 'Listening to children: a study of child and family services', *Early Years*, 22(1): 27–38.

Fawcett, M. (2009) *Learning through Child Observation*, 2nd edition. London: Jessica Kingsley.

Fawcett, M. and Watson, D. (2016) *Learning through Child Observation*, 3rd edition. London. Jessica Kingsley.

Field, A. (2013) *Discovering Statistics Using SPSS*, 4th edition. London: Sage.

Fielding, N. (2008) 'Ethnography', in N. Gilbert (ed.) *Researching Social Life*, 3rd edition. London: Sage.

Fielding, N. and Thomas, H. (2008) 'Qualitative interviewing', in N. Gilbert (ed.) *Researching Social Life*, 3rd edition. London: Sage.

Fielding, N. and Thomas, H. (2015) 'Qualitative interviewing', in N. Gilbert (ed.) *Researching Social Life*, 4th edition. London: Sage.

Fielding, S. (2000) 'Walk on the left! Children's geographies and the primary school', in S.L. Holloway and G. Valentine (eds) *Children's Geographies: Playing, Living and Learning*. London: Routledge.

Fine, M., Weis, L., Weseen, S. and Wong, L. (2000) 'For whom? Qualitative research, representations and social responsibilities', in N.K. Denzin and Y.S. Lincoln (eds) *Handbook of Qualitative Research*, 2nd edition. London: Sage.

Flewitt, R. (2005) 'Conducting research with young children: some ethical considerations', *Early Child Development and Care*, 175(6): 553–65.

Fontana, A. and Frey, J.H. (2000) 'The interview: from structured questions to negotiated text', in N.K. Denzin and Y.S. Lincoln (eds) *Handbook of Qualitative Research*, 2nd edition. London: Sage.

Fontana, A. and Frey, J. (2005) 'The interview: from neutral stance to political involvement', in N. Denzin and Y. Lincoln (eds) *The Sage Handbook of Qualitative Research*, 3rd edition. London: Sage.

Fraser, S. and Robinson, C. (2004) 'Paradigms and philosophy', in S. Fraser, V. Lewis, S. Ding, M. Kellett and C. Robinson (eds) *Doing Research with Children and Young People*. London: Sage.

Gallacher, L.A. and Gallacher, M. (2008) 'Methodological immaturity in childhood research? Thinking through "participatory methods"', *Childhood*, 15(4): 499–516.

Gallagher, K. and Fusco, C. (2006) 'I.D.ology and the technologies of public (school) space: an ethnographic inquiry into the neo-liberal tactics of social (re)production', *Ethnography and Education*, 1(3): 301–18.

Geertz, C. (1973) 'Thick description: toward an interpretive theory of culture', in C. Geertz (ed.) *The Interpretation of Cultures: Selected Essays*. New York: Basic Books.

Gilbert, N. (2008a) 'Research, theory and method', in N. Gilbert (ed.) *Researching Social Life*, 3rd edition. London: Sage.

Gilbert, N. (2008b) 'Writing about social research', in N. Gilbert (ed.) *Researching Social Life*, 3rd edition. London: Sage.

Gillborn, D. (2006) 'Critical race theory and education: racism and anti-racism in educational theory and praxis', *Discourse: Studies in the Cultural Politics of Education*, 27(1): 11–32.

Glaser, B. and Strauss, A.L. (1967) *The Discovery of Grounded Theory: Strategies for Qualitative Research*. Chicago: Aldine Publishing Company.

Glass, N. (1999) 'Sure Start: the development of an early intervention programme for young people in the United Kingdom', *Children and Society*, 13(4): 257–64.

Golding, J., Pembrey, M., Jones, R. and the ALSPAC Study Team (2001) 'ALSPAC – The Avon Longitudinal Study of Parents and Children', *Paediatric and Perinatal Epidemiology*, 15, Supplement 1 (January): 74–87.

Goodenough, F. (1926) *Measurement of Intelligence by Drawings*. New York: Harcourt, Brace and World.

Government of India: census website. www.censusindia.gov.in (accessed 28 July 2013).

Green, N. (2008) 'Formulating and refining a research question', in N. Gilbert (ed.) *Researching Social Life*, 3rd edition. London: Sage.

Green, S. (2000) *Research Methods in Health, Social and Early Years Care*. Cheltenham: Nelson Thornes.

Greene, S. and Hill, M. (2005) 'Researching children's experience: methods and methodological issues', in S. Greene and D. Hogan (eds) *Researching Children's Experience: Approaches and Methods*. London: Sage.

Greenwood, D.J. and Levin, M. (2000) 'Reconstructing the relationships between universities and society through action research', in N.K. Denzin and Y.S. Lincoln (eds) *Handbook of Qualitative Research*, 2nd edition. London: Sage.

Gregory, E. and Ruby, M. (2011) 'The "insider/outsider" dilemma of ethnography: working with young children and their families in cross-cultural contexts', *Journal of Early Childhood Research*, 9(2): 162–74.

Greig, A., Taylor, J. and Mackay, T. (2007) *Doing Research with Children*, 2nd edition. London: Sage.

Greig, A., Taylor, J. and Mackay, T (2013) *Doing Research with Children*, 3rd edition. London: Sage.

Grieshaber, S. and McArdle, F. (2010) *The Trouble with Play*. Maidenhead: Open University Press.

Guba, E.G. and Lincoln, Y.S. (2005) 'Paradigmatic controversies, contradictions, and emerging confluences', in N. Denzin and Y. Lincoln (eds) *The Sage Handbook of Qualitative Research*, 3rd edition. London: Sage.

Gura, P. (1992) *Exploring Learning: Young Children and Blockplay*. London: Paul Chapman Publishing.

Halsan, A. (2014) 'Girls have better motor skills than boys do.' *ScienceNordic*, September 8. http://sciencenordic.com/girls-have-better-motor-skills-boys-do (accessed 17 December 2016).

Hammersley, M. (2007) *Methodological Paradigms in Educational Research*. London: TLRP. www.tlrp.org/capacity/rm/wt/hammersley (accessed 2 November 2008).

Harper, D. (2002) 'Talking about pictures: a case for photo elicitation', *Visual Studies*, 17(1): 13–26.

Harrison, L. (2010) 'Quantitative designs and statistical analysis', in G. MacNaughton, S. Rolfe and I. Siraj-Blatchford (eds) *Doing Early Childhood Research: International Perspectives on Theory and Practice*, 2nd edition. Buckingham: Open University Press.

Hart, C. (2005) *Doing Your Masters Dissertation*. London: Sage.

Hart, R. (1992) *Children's Participation: From Tokenism to Citizenship*. Florence: UNICEF Innocenti Research Centre.

Harvard University Information Technology, *Surveys*. http://huit.harvard.edu/services/survey-tool (accessed 16 February 2017).

Hatch, J.A. (1995) 'Studying childhood as a cultural invention: a rationale and framework', in J.A. Hatch (ed.) *Qualitative Research in Early Childhood Settings*. Westport, CT: Praeger.

Hayes, A. (2010) 'Design issues', in G. MacNaughton, S. Rolfe and I. Siraj-Blatchford (eds) *Doing Early Childhood Research: International Perspectives on Theory and Practice*, 2nd edition. Maidenhead: Open University Press.

Heath, M. and Tynan, C. (2010) 'Crafting a research proposal', *The Marketing Review*, 10(2): 147–68. www.nottingham.ac.uk/business/nexus/Documents/MaMSc/Dissertation/PereiraTynan-CraftingaResearchProposalTMR_2010.pdf (accessed 26 December 2016).

Heise, D. (1970) 'The semantic differential and attitude research', in G. Summers (ed.) *Attitude Measurement*. Chicago, IL: Rand McNally. www.indiana.edu/~socpsy/papers/AttMeasure/attitude.htm (accessed 14 May 2014).

Hodder, I. (2000) 'The interpretation of documents and material culture', in N.K. Denzin and Y.S. Lincoln (eds) *Handbook of Qualitative Research*, 2nd edition. London: Sage.

Holland, P. (2003) *We Don't Play with Guns Here: War, Weapon and Super Hero Play in the Early Years*. Buckingham: Open University Press.

Holland, P. (2004) *Picturing Childhood: The Myth of the Child in Popular Imagery*. London: Tauris.

Hollingsworth, L. and Buysse, B. (2009) 'Establishing friendships in early childhood inclusive settings: what roles do parents and teachers play?', *Journal of Early Intervention*, 31(4): 287–307.

Holmes, J. (1993) *John Bowlby and Attachment Theory*. London: Routledge.

Holstein, J.A. and Gubrium, J.F. (1995) *The Active Interview*. Thousand Oaks, CA: Sage.

hooks, b. (1990) *Yearning*. Boston: South End Press.

Hughes, P. (2001) 'From nostalgia to metatheory: researching children's relationships with the media', *Contemporary Issues in Early Childhood*, 2(3): 354–67.

Hughes, P. (2010) 'Paradigms, methods and knowledge', in G. MacNaughton, S. Rolfe and I. Siraj-Blatchford (eds) *Doing Early Childhood Research: International Perspectives on Theory and Practice*, 2nd edition. Maidenhead: Open University Press.

Hutton, P. (1990) *Survey Research for Managers: How to Use Surveys in Management Decision Making*, 2nd edition. Basingstoke: Macmillan.

Hyder, T. (2002) 'Making it happen: young children's rights in action – the work of Save the Children's Centre for Young Children's Rights', in B. Franklin (ed.) *The New Handbook of Children's Rights: Comparative Policy and Practice*. London: Routledge.

Isong, A., Luff, D., Perrin, J., Winickoff, P. and Ng, M. (2012) 'Parental perspectives of early childhood caries', *Clinical Pediatrics*, 51(1): 77–85. http://cpj.sagepub.com/content/51/1/77.full.pdf+html (accessed 18 December 2016).

James, A. (2007) 'Ethnography in the study of children and childhood', in P. Atkinson, A. Coffey, S. Delamont, J. Lofland and L. Lofland (eds) *Handbook of Ethnography*. London: Sage.

James, A. and Prout, A. (eds) (1990) *Constructing and Reconstructing Childhood: Contemporary Issues in the Sociological Study of Childhood*. Cambridge: Polity Press.

James, A., Jenks, C. and Prout, A. (1998) *Theorising Childhood*. Cambridge: Polity Press.

Jarvis, M., Russell, J., Flanagan, C., Gorman, P. and Dolan, L. (2004) *Angles on Psychology*, 2nd edition. Cheltenham: Nelson Thornes.

Jenks, C. (2000) 'Zeitgeist research on childhood', in P. Christensen and A. James (eds) *Research with Children: Perspectives and Practices*. London: Falmer Press.

Johnson, B. and Christensen, L. (2012) *Educational Research*, 4th edition. Thousand Oaks, CA: Sage.

Johnson, B. and Christensen, L. (2017) *Educational Research: Quantitative, Qualitative, and Mixed Approaches*, 6th edition. Thousand Oaks, CA: Sage.

Jones, S.H. (2005) 'Autoethnography: making the personal political', in N. Denzin and Y. Lincoln (eds) *Sage Handbook of Qualitative Research*, 3rd edition. London: Sage.

Jupp, V. and Norris, C. (1993) 'Traditions in documentary analysis', in M. Hammersley (ed.) *Social Research: Philosophy, Politics and Practice*. London: Sage.

Kamler, B. and Thompson, P. (2014) *Helping Doctoral Students Write: Pedagogies for Supervision*, 2nd edition. Abingdon: Routledge.

Kasunic, M. (2005) *Designing an Effective Survey*. Pittsburgh, PA: Carnegie Mellon University. http://resources.sei.cmu.edu/library/asset-view.cfm?assetID=7277 (accessed 30 July 2014).

Kavanagh, K., Zixin, L., Nicklas, J., Habibi, M. and Murphy, L. (2012) 'Breastfeeding knowledge, attitudes, prior exposure, and intent among undergraduate students', *Journal of Human Lactation*, 28(4): 556–64.

Keesing, R. (2008) *A Brief History of Isaac Newton's Apple Tree*. University of York Department of Physics. www.york.ac.uk/physics/about/newtonsappletree (accessed 14 May 2014).

Kellett, M. (2005) *How to Develop Children as Researchers: A Step-by-Step Guide to the Teaching Process*. London: Sage.

Kemmis, S. (2008) 'Critical theory and participatory action research', in P. Reason and H. Bradbury (eds) *The Sage Handbook of Action Research*, 2nd edition. London: Sage.

Kemmis, S. and McTaggart, R. (2005) 'Participatory action research: communicative action and the public sphere', in N.K. Denzin and Y.S. Lincoln (eds) *The Sage Handbook of Qualitative Research*, 3rd edition. London: Sage.

Kincheloe, J.L. (1991) *Teachers as Researchers: Qualitative Inquiry as a Path to Empowerment*. London: Falmer.

King, N. and Horrocks, C. (2010) *Interviews in Qualitative Research*. London. Sage.

Komulainen, S. (2007) 'The ambiguity of the child's "voice" in social research', *Childhood*, 14(1): 11–28.

Kumar, R. (2014) *Research Methodology: A Step-by-Step Guide for Beginners*, 4th edition. London: Sage.

Kurban, F. and Tobin, J. (2009) '"They don't like us": reflections of Turkish children in a German preschool', *Contemporary Issues in Early Childhood*, 10(1): 24–34.

Laevers, F. (ed.) (2005) *Well-being and Involvement in Care Settings. A Process-oriented Self-evaluation Instrument*. Leuven: Research Centre for Experiential Education, Leuven University.

Lahman, M. (2008) 'Always Othered: ethical research with children', *Journal of Early Childhood Research*, 6(3): 281–300.

Lancaster, P. and Broadbent, V. (2003) *Listening to Young People*. Maidenhead: Open University Press.

Langston, A., Abbott, L., Lewis, V. and Kellett, M. (2004) 'Early childhood', in S. Fraser, V. Lewis, S. Ding, M. Kellett and C. Robinson (eds) *Doing Research with Children and Young People*. London: Sage.

Lee, D. (2008) *Science Timeline*. www.sciencetimeline.net (accessed 2 November 2008).

Lee, N. (2001) *Childhood and Society: Growing Up in an Age of Uncertainty*. Buckingham: Open University Press.

Lee, T. (2011) 'The wisdom of Vivian Gussin Paley', in L. Miller and L. Pound (eds) *Theories and Approaches to Learning in the Early Years*. London: Sage.

Lefèvre, A., Lundqvist, P., Drevenhorn, E. and Hallström, I. (2015) 'Managing parental groups during early childhood: new challenges faced by Swedish child health-care nurses', *Journal of Child Health Care*, 19(3): 381–91. http://chc.sagepub.com/content/early/2013/11/28/1367493513509421 (accessed 17 July 2017).

Letherby, G. (2003) *Feminist Research in Theory and Practice*. Buckingham: Open University Press.

Lincoln, Y.S. and Guba, E.G. (2000) 'Paradigmatic controversies, contradictions and emerging confluences', in N.K. Denzin and Y.S. Lincoln (eds) *Handbook of Qualitative Research*, 2nd edition. London: Sage.

Löfdahl, A. and Hägglund, S. (2007) 'Spaces of participation in pre-school: arenas for establishing power orders?', *Children and Society*, 21: 328–38.

Lupton, D. (2013) 'Precious, pure, uncivilised, vulnerable: infant embodiment in Australian popular media', *Children and Society* (online first). DOI:10.1111/chso.12004.

Macdonald, K. (2008) 'Using documents', in N. Gilbert (ed.) *Researching Social Life*, 3rd edition. London: Sage.

Macdonald, K. and Tipton, C. (1993) 'Using documents', in N. Gilbert (ed.) *Researching Social Life*. London: Sage.

Mackenzie, N. and Knipe, S. (2006) 'Research dilemmas: paradigms, methods and methodology', *Issues in Educational Research*, 16: 193–205.

MacNaughton, G. (2001) 'Action research', in G. MacNaughton, S.A. Rolfe and I. Siraj-Blatchford (eds) *Doing Early Childhood Research: International Perspectives on Theory and Practice*. Maidenhead: Open University Press.

MacNaughton, G. and Hughes, P. (2003) 'Curriculum contexts: parents and communities', in G. MacNaughton (ed.) *Shaping Early Childhood: Learners, Curriculum and Contexts*. Maidenhead: Open University Press.

MacNaughton, G. and Rolfe, S.A. (2010) 'The research process', in G. MacNaughton, S.A. Rolfe and I. Siraj-Blatchford (eds) *Doing Early Childhood Research: International Perspectives on Theory and Practice*, 2nd edition. Maidenhead: Open University Press.

MacNaughton, G. and Smith, K. (2005) 'Transforming research ethics: the choices and challenges of researching with children', in A. Farrell (ed.) *Ethical Research with Children*. Maidenhead: Open University Press.

Malewski, E. (2005) 'Epilogue: when children and youth talk back', in D.S. Soto and B.B. Swadener (eds) *Power and Voice in Research with Children*. New York: Peter Lang.

Mandell, N. (1988) 'The least-adult role in studying children', *Journal of Contemporary Ethnography*, 16(4): 433–67.

Manning-Morton, J. (2006) 'The personal is professional: professionalism and the birth to threes practitioner', *Contemporary Issues in Early Childhood*, 7(1): 42–52.

Manning-Morton, J. and Thorp, M. (2003) *Key Times for Play: The First Three Years*. Maidenhead: Open University Press.

Marsh, J. (2012) 'Children as knowledge brokers of playground games and rhymes in the new media age', *Childhood*, 19(4): 508–22.

Mayall, B. (1996) *Children, Health and the Social Order*. Buckingham: Open University Press.

Mayall, B. (1999) 'Children and childhood', in S. Hood, B. Mayall and S. Oliver (eds) *Critical Issues in Social Research: Power and Prejudice*. Buckingham: Open University Press.

Mayall, B. (2008) 'Conversations with children: working with generational issues', in P. Christensen and A. James (eds) *Research with Children: Perspectives and Practices*, 2nd edition. Abingdon: Routledge.

McAndrew, F., Thompson, J., Fellows, L., Large, A., Speed, M. and Renfrew, M. (2012) *Infant Feeding Survey 2010*. Health and Social Care Information Centre. http://content.digital.nhs.uk/catalogue/PUB08694/Infant-Feeding-Survey-2010-Consolidated-Report.pdf (accessed 16 February 2017).

McCoyd, J. and Kerson, T. (2006) 'Conducting intensive interviews using email: a serendipitous comparative opportunity', *Qualitative Social Work*, 5(3): 389–406.

McNiff, J. and Whitehead, J. (2011) *All You Need to Know about Action Research*, 2nd edition. London: Sage.

Mertens, D. (2015) *Research and Evaluation in Education and Psychology*, 4th edition. Los Angeles, CA: Sage.

Mies, M. (1993) 'Towards a methodology for feminist research', in M. Hammersley (ed.) *Social Research: Philosophy, Politics and Practice*. London: Sage.

Miller, K. (2015) 'Dear critics: addressing concerns and justifying the benefits of photography as a research method,' Forum *Qualitative Sozialforschung/Forum:*

Qualitative Social Research, 16(3): art. 27. www.qualitative-research.net/index. php/fqs/article/view/2434/3874 (accessed: 15 March 2017).

Miller, K. (2016) 'Learning about children's school preparation through photographs: the use of photo elicitation interviews with low-income families', *Journal of Early Childhood Research*, 14(3): 261–79.

Moon, J. (2006) *Learning Journals: A Handbook for Reflective Practice and Professional Development*, 2nd edition. Abingdon: Routledge.

Moss, P., Clark, A. and Kjorholt, A.T. (2005) 'Introduction', in A. Clark, A.T. Kjorholt and P. Moss (eds) *Beyond Listening: Children's Perspectives of Early Childhood Services*. Bristol: Policy Press.

Mukherji, P. (2001) *Understanding Children's Challenging Behaviour*. Cheltenham: Nelson Thornes.

Mykhalovsky, E. (1997) 'Reconsidering "table talk": critical thoughts on the relationship between sociology, autobiography, and self-indulgence', in R. Hertz (ed.) *Reflexivity and Voice*. London: Sage.

NHS (National Health Service) (2016) *The Personal Child Health Record*. South Shields: Harlow Printing.

NICHD Study of Early Child Care and Youth Development (SECCYD). www. nichd.nih.gov/research/supported/seccyd/Pages/overview.aspx (accessed 16 February 2017).

Nolen-Hoeksema, S., Fredrickson, B., Loftus, G. and Wagenaar, W. (2009) *Atkinson and Hilgard's Introduction to Psychology*, 15th edition. Andover: Cengage Learning EMEA.

Nolen-Hoeksema, S., Fredrickson, B., Loftus, G. and Lutz, C. (2014) *Atkinson and Hilgard's Introduction to Psychology*, 16th edition. Andover: Cengage Learning EMEA.

Northedge, A. (1990) *The Good Study Guide*. Milton Keynes: Open University Press.

Oakley, A. (1981) 'Interviewing women: a contradiction in terms', in H. Roberts (ed.) *Doing Feminist Research*. London: Routledge and Kegan Paul.

O'Connell, R. (2013) 'The use of visual methods with children in a mixed methods study of family food practices', *International Journal of Social Research Methodology*, 16(1): 31–46.

Office for National Statistics. www.ons.gov.uk/ons/guide-method/census/2011/ index.html (accessed 28 July 2013).

O'Kane, C. (2008) 'The development of participatory techniques: facilitating children's views about decisions which affect them', in P. Christensen and A. James (eds) *Research with Children: Perspectives and Practices*, 2nd edition. London: Falmer Press.

Oller, D. (2010) 'All-day recordings to investigate vocabulary development: a case study of a trilingual toddler', *Communication Disorders Quarterly*, 31(4): 213–22.

Olsen, R. and Clarke, H. (2003) *Parenting and Disability*. Bristol: Policy Press.

Osgood, J. (2010) *Narratives from the Nursery: Negotiating Professional Identities in Early Childhood*. London: Routledge.

Paley, V.G. (1981) *Wally's Stories: Conversations in the Kindergarten*. Cambridge, MA: Harvard University Press.

Paley, V.G. (1990) *The Boy Who Would Be a Helicopter: The Uses of Storytelling in the Classroom*. Cambridge, MA: Harvard University Press.

Paley, V.G. (1991) *Bad Guys Don't Have Birthdays*. Chicago, IL: University of Chicago Press.

Papen, U. (2008) 'Pregnancy starts with a literacy event: pregnancy and antenatal care as textually mediated experiences', *Ethnography*, 9(3): 377–402.

Patton, M. (1987) *How to Use Qualitative Methodology in Evaluation*. Newbury Park, CA: Sage.

Phelan, A.M. (1997) 'Classroom management and the erasure of teacher desire', in J. Tobin (ed.) *Making a Place for Pleasure in Early Childhood Education*. New Haven and London: Yale University Press.

Plowman, L. and Stephen, C. (2003) 'Developing a policy on ICT in pre-school settings: the role of research', paper presented at the British Educational Research Association Annual Conference, Heriot-Watt University, Edinburgh, 11–13 September. www.leeds.ac.uk/educol/documents/00003362.htm (accessed 14 May 2014).

Pole, C. and Morrison, M. (2003) *Ethnography for Education*. Maidenhead: Open University Press.

Potter, J. and Wetherell, M. (1987) *Discourse and Social Psychology: Beyond Attitudes and Behaviour*. London: Sage.

Qvortrup, J. (1994) 'Childhood matters: an introduction', in J. Qvortrup, M. Bardy, G. Sgritta and H. Wintersberger (eds) *Childhood Matters: Social Theory, Practice and Politics*. Aldershot: Avebury.

Reinharz, S. (1997) 'Who Am I? The need for a variety of selves in the field', in R. Hertz (ed.) *Reflexivity and Voice*. London: Sage.

Richardson, L. and Adams St Pierre, E. (2005) 'Writing: a method of inquiry', in N. Denzin and Y. Lincoln (eds) *The Sage Handbook of Qualitative Research*, 3rd edition. London: Sage.

Ringrose, J., Gill, R., Livingstone, S. and Harvey, L. (2012) *A Qualitative Study of Children, Young People and 'Sexting'*. London: NSPCC. www.nspcc.org.uk/Inform/resourcesforprofessionals/sexualabuse/sexting-research-report_wdf89269.pdf (accessed 30 July 2014).

Roberts-Holmes, G. (2011) *Doing Your Early Years Research Project: A Step-by-Step Guide*, 2nd edition. London: Sage.

Roberts-Holmes, G. (2014) *Doing Your Early Years Research Project: A Step-by-Step Guide*, 3rd edition. London: Sage.

Robertson, M. and Sundstrom, E. (1990) 'Questionnaire design, return rates, and response favourableness in an employee attitude questionnaire', *Journal of Applied Psychology*, 75: 354–7.

Robinson, C. and Kellett, M. (2004) 'Power', in S. Fraser, V. Lewis, S. Ding, M. Kellett and C. Robinson (eds) *Doing Research with Children and Young People*.London: Sage.

Robson, C. (2011a) *Real World Research*, 3rd edition. Chichester: John Wiley.

Robson, C. and McCarten, K. (2015) *Real World Research*, 4th edition. Chichester: John Wiley.

Robson, S. (2011b) 'Producing and using video data with young children: a case study of ethical questions and practical consequences', in D. Harcourt, B. Perry and T. Waller (eds) *Researching Young Children's Perspectives: Debating the Ethics and Dilemmas of Educational Research with Children*. Abingdon: Routledge.

Robson, S. (2012) *Developing Thinking and Understanding in Young Children: An Introduction for Students*, 2nd edition. Abingdon: Routledge.

Rogers, S. (2011) 'Play and pedagogy: a conflict of interests?', in S. Rogers (ed.) *Rethinking Play and Pedagogy in Early Childhood Education*. London: Routledge.

Rolfe, S. and Emmett, S. (2010) 'Direct observation', in G. MacNaughton, S. Rolfe and I. Siraj-Blatchford (eds) *Doing Early Childhood Research: International Perspectives on Theory and Practice*, 2nd edition. Maidenhead: Open University Press.

Rosen, R. (2010) '"We got our heads together and came up with a plan": young children's perceptions of curriculum development in one Canadian preschool', *Journal of Early Childhood Research*, 8(1): 89–108.

Sachs, J. (1999) 'Using teacher research as a basis for professional renewal', *Journal of In-Service Education*, 25(1): 39–53.

Saldivar, M. (2012) *A Primer on Survey Response Rate*. Tallahassee, FL: Learning Systems Institute, Florida State University. http://mgsaldivar.weebly.com/uploads/8/5/1/8/8518205/saldivar_primer_on_survey_response.pdf (accessed 10 November 2017).

Scheurich, J.J. (1997) *Research Method in the Postmodern*. London: Falmer Press.

Schmuck, R.A. (2006) *Practical Action Research for Change*, 2nd edition. London: Sage.

Schön, D. (1983) *The Reflective Practitioner*. San Francisco, CA: Jossey-Bass.

Schum, T., Kolb, T., McAuliffe, T., Simms, M., Underhill, R. and Lewis, M. (2002) 'Sequential acquisition of toilet training skills: a descriptive study of gender and age differences in normal children', *Pediatrics*, 109(3): e48. http://pediatrics.aappublications.org (accessed 22 March 2008).

Schwandt, T. and Gates, E. (2017) 'Case study', in N.K. Denzin and Y. Lincoln (eds) *The Sage Handbook of Qualitative Research*, 5th edition. London: Sage.

Schwartz, D. (1989) 'Visual ethnography: using photography in qualitative research', *Qualitative Sociology*, 12(2): 119–54.

Scotland, J. (2012) 'Exploring the philosophical underpinnings of research: relating ontology and epistemology to the methodology and methods of the scientific, interpretive, and critical research paradigms', *English Language Teaching*, 5(9): 9–16.

Scott, K. (2002) '"You want to be a girl and not my friend": African-American/Black girls' play activities with and without boys', *Childhood*, 9(4): 397–414.

Sharma, A. and Cockerill, W. (2014) *Mary Sheridan's From Birth to Five Years: Children's Developmental Progress*, 4th edition. Abingdon: Routledge.

Setia, M.S. (2016) 'Methodology series module 5: sampling strategies', *Indian Journal of Dermatology*, 61(5): 505–9.

Silverman, D. (2013) *Doing Qualitative Research*, 4th edition. London: Sage.

Silverman, D. (2014) *Interpreting Qualitative Data: Strategies for Analysing Talk, Text and Interaction*, 5th edition. London: Sage.

Simmons, R. (2008) 'Questionnaires', in N. Gilbert (ed.) *Researching Social Life*, 3rd edition. London: Sage.

Siraj-Blatchford, I. (2010) 'Learning in the home and at school: how working class children "succeed against the odds"', *British Educational Research Journal*, 36(3): 463–82.

Siraj-Blatchford, I. and Siraj-Blatchford, J. (2001) 'Surveys and questionnaires: an evaluative case study', in G. MacNaughton, S. Rolfe and I. Siraj-Blatchford (eds) *Doing Early Childhood Research: International Perspectives on Theory and Practice*. Buckingham: Open University Press.

Skånfors, L. (2009) 'Ethics in child research: children's agency and researchers' "ethical radar"', *Childhoods Today*, 3(1): 1–22.

Skea, Z.C., Entwhistle, V.A., Watt, I. and Russell, E. (2008) '"Avoiding harm to others": considerations in relation to parental measles, mumps and rubella (MMR) vaccination discussions – an analysis of an online chat forum', *Social Science and Medicine*, 67: 1382–90.

Smith, A.B. (2011) 'Respecting children's rights and agency: theoretical insights into ethical research procedures', in D. Harcourt, B. Perry and T. Waller (eds) *Researching Young Children's Perspectives*. Abingdon: Routledge.

Soto, L.D. and Swadener, B.B. (eds) (2005) *Power and Voice in Research with Children*. New York: Peter Lang.

Stake, R.E. (1995) *The Art of Case Study Research*. Thousand Oaks, CA: Sage.

Stake, R.E. (2000) 'Case studies', in N.K. Denzin and Y.S. Lincoln (eds) *Handbook of Qualitative Research*, 2nd edition. London: Sage.

Stake, R.E. (2003) 'Case studies', in N.K. Denzin and Y.S.Lincoln (eds) *Strategies of Qualitative Enquiry*, 2nd edition. London: Sage.

Standing, K. (1998) 'Writing the voices of the less powerful: research on lone mothers', in J. Ribbens and R. Edwards (eds) *Feminist Dilemmas in Qualitative Research: Public Knowledge and Private Lives*. London: Sage.

Statistics New Zealand. www.stats.govt.nz/Census.aspx (accessed 28 July 2013).

Stewart, D., Shamdasani, P. and Rook, D. (2008) 'Group depth interviews: focus group research', in L. Bickman and D. Rog (eds) *The Sage Handbook of Applied Research Methods*, 2nd edition. Thousand Oaks, CA: Sage.

Suissa, J. (2006) 'Untangling the mother knot: some thoughts on parents, children and philosophers of education', *Ethics and Education*, 1(1): 65–77.

Sumsion, J., Harrison, L., Press, F., McLeod, S., Goodfellow, J. and Bradley, B. (2011) 'Researching infants' experiences of early childhood education and care', in D. Harcourt, B. Perry and T. Waller (eds) *Researching Young Children's Perspectives: Debating the Ethics and Dilemmas of Educational Research with Children*. Abingdon: Routledge.

Survey Monkey. www.surveymonkey.com (accessed 17 March 2017).

Swantz, M.L. (2008) 'Participatory action research as practice', in P. Reason and H. Bradbury (eds) *The Sage Handbook of Action Research*, 2nd edition. London: Sage.

Sylva, K. (1999) 'The role of research in explaining the past and shaping the future', in L. Abbott and H. Moylett (eds) *Early Education Transformed*. London: Falmer Press.

Sylva, K., Roy, C. and Painter, M. (1980) *Childwatching at Playgroup and Nursery School*. London: Grant McIntyre.

Sylva, K., Melhuish, E., Sammons, P., Siraj-Blatchford, I. and Taggart, B. (2004) *The Effective Provision of Pre-School Education (EPPE) Project: Findings from the Pre-school to End of Key Stage One*. London: Institute of Education. www.ioe.ac.uk/RB_pre-school_to_end_of_KS1%281%29.pdf (accessed 14 May 2014).

Tay-Lim, J. and Gan, L. (2013) 'Peer rejection in preschool: foregrounding children's voices', *Journal of Early Childhood Research*, 11(1): 45–62.

Taylor, A.S. (2000) 'The UN Convention on the Rights of the Child: giving children a voice', in A. Lewis and G. Lindsay (eds) *Researching Children's Perspectives*. Buckingham: Open University Press.

Taylor, L. (2010) 'Action research', in G. MacNaughton, S. Rolfe and I. Siraj-Blatchford (eds) *Doing Early Childhood Research: International Perspectives on Theory and Practice*, 2nd edition. Maidenhead: Open University Press.

The Christchurch Health and Development Study. www.otago.ac.nz/christchurch/research/healthdevelopment (accessed 16 February 2017).

The Effective Pre-School, Primary and Secondary Education Project (EPPSE). www.ucl.ac.uk/ioe/research/featured-research/effective-pre-school-primary-secondary-education-project (accessed 16 February 2017).

The Fragile Families and Wellbeing Study. www.fragilefamilies.princeton.edu/about (accessed 16 February 2017).

Tickell, C. (2011) *The Early Years: Foundations for Life, Health and Learning – An Independent Report on the Early Years Foundation Stage to Her Majesty's Government*. London: Department for Education.

Tobin, J., Wu, D. and Davidson, D. (1989) *Preschool in Three Cultures: Japan, China and the United States*. New Haven, CT: Yale University Press.

Tobin, J., Hsueh, Y. and Karasawa, M. (2009) *Preschool in Three Cultures Revisited: China, Japan, and the United States*. Chicago: University of Chicago Press.

Towers, J. (1997) 'The neglect of playtime: a review of the literature', *Early Child Development and Care*, 131: 31–43.

Townsend, E. and Pitchford, N. (2012) 'Baby knows best? The impact of weaning style on food preferences and body mass index in early childhood in a case controlled sample', *BMJ Open*, 2(1): 1–6. http://bmjopen.bmj.com/content/2/1/e000298.full.pdf+html (accessed 18 December 2016).

Townsend, P. (1979) *Poverty in the United Kingdom*. Harmondsworth: Penguin.

Tripp, D. (1993) *Critical Incidents in Teaching: Developing Professional Judgement*. Abingdon: Routledge.

University of Exeter (2012) *Cascade Briefing Paper: Creating and Using Online Surveys*. https://as.exeter.ac.uk/media/universityofexeter/academicservices/educationenhancement/cascade/Creating_and_using_online_surveys.pdf (accessed 16 February 2017).

Vanson, S. (2014) *What on Earth are Ontology and Epistemology?* https://theperformancesolution.com/earth-ontology-epistemology/ (accessed 15 March 2017).

Veale, A. (2005) 'Creative methodologies in participatory research with children', in S. Greene and D. Hogan (eds) *Researching Children's Experience: Approaches and Methods*. London: Sage.

Viruru, R. (2001) *Early Childhood Education: Postcolonial Perspectives from India*. New Delhi: Sage.

Wadsworth, B. (1996) *Piaget's Theory of Cognitive and Affective Development: Foundations of Constructivism*, 5th edition. London: Longman.

Walker, S., Chang, S., Vera-Hernández, M. and Grantham-McGregor, S. (2011) 'Early childhood stimulation benefits adult competence and reduces violent behaviour', *Pediatrics*, 127(5): 849–57. http://pediatrics.aappublications.org/content/127/5/849.full.pdf+html (accessed 18 December 2016).

Wallbank, J.A. (2001) *Challenging Motherhood(s)*. Harlow: Pearson.

Waller, T. and Bitou, A. (2011) 'Research with children: three challenges for participatory research in early childhood', *European Early Childhood Research Journal*, 19(1): 5–20.

Walliman, N. (2001) *Your Research Project: A Step-by-Step Guide for the First-Time Researcher*. London: Sage.

Warming, H. (2005) 'Participant observation: a way to learn about children's perspectives', in A. Clark, A.T. Kjorholt and P. Moss (eds) *Beyond Listening: Children's Perspectives on Early Childhood Services*. Bristol: Policy Press.

Warnock Committee (1978) *Special Educational Needs: The Warnock Report*. London: DES.

Wasserfall, R.R. (1997) 'Reflexivity, feminism, and difference', in R. Hertz (ed.) *Reflexivity and Voice*. London: Sage.

Westcott, H. and Littleton, K. (2005) 'Exploring meaning in interviews with children', in S. Greene and D. Hogan (eds) *Researching Children's Experience: Approaches and Methods*. London: Sage.

Wicks, P.G., Reason, P. and Bradbury, H. (2008) 'Living inquiry: personal, political and philosophical groundings for action research practice', in P. Reason and H. Bradbury (eds) *The Sage Handbook of Action Research*, 2nd edition. London: Sage.

Winter, K. (2010) 'Ascertaining the perspectives of young children in care: case studies in the use of reality boxes', *Children and Society*, 26: 368–80.

Woodhead, M. and Faulkner, D. (2008) 'Subjects, objects or participants? Dilemmas of psychological research with children', in P. Christensen and A. James (eds) *Research with Children: Perspectives and Practices*, 2nd edition. Abingdon: Routledge.

Woolfitt, R. (2008) 'Conversation analysis and discourse analysis', in N. Gilbert (ed.) *Researching Social Life*, 3rd edition. London: Sage.

INDEX